studies in jazz

Institute of Jazz Studies
Rutgers—The State University of New Jersey
General Editors: Dan Morgenstern and Edward Berger

1. BENNY CARTER: A Life in American Music, *by Morroe Berger, Edward Berger, and James Patrick, 2 vols., 1982*
2. ART TATUM: A Guide to His Recorded Music, *by Arnold Laubich and Ray Spencer, 1982*
3. ERROLL GARNER: The Most Happy Piano, *by James M. Doran, 1985*
4. JAMES P. JOHNSON: A Case of Mistaken Identity, *by Scott E. Brown;* Discography 1917–1950, *by Robert Hilbert, 1986*
5. PEE WEE ERWIN: This Horn for Hire, *as told to Warren W. Vaché Sr., 1987*
6. BENNY GOODMAN: Listen to His Legacy, *by D. Russell Connor, 1988*
7. ELLINGTONIA: The Recorded Music of Duke Ellington and His Sidemen, *by W. E. Timner, 1988; 4th ed., 1996*
8. THE GLENN MILLER ARMY AIR FORCE BAND: Sustineo Alas / I Sustain the Wings, *by Edward F. Polic; Foreword by George T. Simon, 1989*
9. SWING LEGACY, *by Chip Deffaa, 1989*
10. REMINISCING IN TEMPO: The Life and Times of a Jazz Hustler, *by Teddy Reig, with Edward Berger, 1990*
11. IN THE MAINSTREAM: 18 Portraits in Jazz, *by Chip Deffaa, 1992*
12. BUDDY DeFRANCO: A Biographical Portrait and Discography, *by John Kuehn and Arne Astrup, 1993*
13. PEE WEE SPEAKS: A Discography of Pee Wee Russell, *by Robert Hilbert, with David Niven, 1992*
14. SYLVESTER AHOLA: The Gloucester Gabriel, *by Dick Hill, 1993*
15. THE POLICE CARD DISCORD, *by Maxwell T. Cohen, 1993*
16. TRADITIONALISTS AND REVIVALISTS IN JAZZ, *by Chip Deffaa, 1993*
17. BASSICALLY SPEAKING: An Oral History of George Duvivier, *by Edward Berger; Musical Analysis by David Chevan, 1993*
18. TRAM: The Frank Trumbauer Story, *by Philip R. Evans and Larry F. Kiner, with William Trumbauer, 1994*
19. TOMMY DORSEY: On the Side, *by Robert L. Stockdale, 1995*
20. JOHN COLTRANE: A Discography and Musical Biography, *by Yasuhiro Fujioka, with Lewis Porter and Yoh-ichi Hamada, 1995*
21. RED HEAD: A Chronological Survey of "Red" Nichols and His Five Pennies, *by Stephen M. Stroff, 1996*
22. THE RED NICHOLS STORY: After Intermission 1942–1965, *by Philip R. Evans, Stanley Hester, Stephen Hester, and Linda Evans, 1997*
23. BENNY GOODMAN: Wrappin' It Up, *by D. Russell Connor, 1996*
24. CHARLIE PA[...] [...]N, *by Henry Martin,* 1996

Florence Mills

Harlem Jazz Queen

Bill Egan

Studies in Jazz, No. 48

THE SCARECROW PRESS, INC.
Lanham, Maryland • Toronto • Oxford
2004

SCARECROW PRESS, INC.

Published in the United States of America
by Scarecrow Press, Inc.
A wholly owned subsidary of
The Rowman & Littlefield Publishing Group, Inc.
4501 Forbes Boulevard, Suite 200, Lanham, Maryland 20706
www.scarecrowpress.com

PO Box 317
Oxford
OX2 9RU, UK

British Library Cataloguing in Publication Information Available

Library of Congress Cataloging-in-Publication Data

Egan, Bill, 1937–
  Florence Mills : Harlem jazz queen / Bill Egan.
    p. cm. — (Studies in jazz ; no. 48)
  Includes bibliographical references (p.) and index.
  ISBN 0-8108-5007-9 (pbk. : alk. paper)
  1. Mills, Florence, 1896–1927. 2. African American singers—Biography. I. Title. II.
Series.
ML420.M5132E43 2004
782.42165'092—dc22

                                                        2004005586

To:
Duke Ellington, who inspired it
Kid Thompson, who wanted it
Delilah Jackson, who helped it happen
Jean Egan, whose support made it possible

~

Contents

Acknowledgments

It is inevitable in a book like this that I have had to rely on assistance, advice, material, and encouragement from an army of people and organizations. I will try to mention all of them, but if some have been inadvertently omitted, I can only plead the enormity of the task and apologize for the omission.

Two major contributors were Delilah Jackson and Dr. Helen Armstead Johnson. Delilah contributed from her own immense personal knowledge of African American entertainers and by allowing me to acquire her treasured collection of U. S. "Kid" Thompson interviews, collected over a number of years during the later stages of Kid Thompson's long life. Delilah was also a valued friend and mentor during my many visits to New York. Her devotion to Florence Mills's memory was inspirational.

Dr. Johnson's contribution came through the immense collection of research materials she donated to the Schomburg Institute, in particular the Florence Mills scrapbooks and related U. S. Thompson materials. These offered a treasure trove of information and insights into Florence and Kid's life. I am deeply indebted to the staff of the Schomburg for all the assistance I received there on my many visits and in particular to Mr. Howard Dodson (chief of the Center), Ms. Diana Lachatanere (curator, Manuscripts, Archives and Rare Books Division), and Ms. Mary Yearwood (curator, Photographs and Prints Division) for facilitating my early access to the Florence Mills materials while cataloging of the Armstead Johnson Collection was still in progress.

Hyacinth Curtis's and the late Maude Russell's gracious sharing of their memories of Florence Mills with me gave me a sense of personal contact that was inspiring as well as highly informative. Other contemporaries of Florence whose contributions were valued included Leonard Reed, Louis Simms, the Nicholas Brothers, and the late Doc Cheatham and Peg Leg Bates.

Stephen Bourne graciously allowed me access to his prize-winning (the Commission for Racial Equality's "Race in the Media award for Best Radio Entertainment") interview with Elisabeth Welch, his interview with Adelaide Hall, and numerous other useful and interesting items, as well as the hospitality of his home in London.

Janet and Eric Glass, literary agents for the Beverley Nichols estate, gave permission for use of material from Mr. Nichols's interview with Florence Mills, "Florence Mills, or a Lonely Blackbird," from *Are They the Same at Home?* (London: Jonathan Cape, 1927).

There are many others whose friendship, support, and hospitality lightened my way. These include Terry Waldo (world's greatest ragtime piano player) and Janice Lee; Bill Coleman (a valued mentor) and Joyce Mordecai; Morris and Jo Hodara of The Duke Ellington Society (TDES), New York; Marvin Keenze (Philadelphia); Neil Gladd (D.C.); Don and Sandy Rouse (D.C.); and Judith Still (Flagstaff). I would like to thank all the members of the Ellington Internet list Duke-LYM for their support and information. They are too numerous to mention individually, but David Palmquist, who researched Vancouver and Seattle newspapers for me, Annie Kuebler, who recommended Scarecrow, and Marcello Piras, who offered valuable musicological information, deserve special mention.

Some people who offered valued encouragement include Dr. Sam Floyd, Center for Black Music Research (CBMR); Charles Blockson, curator, Blockson Collection, Temple University; the late Henry Whitehead; and the late Richard Newman (DuBois Institute, Harvard). Pamela Johnson was a valuable mentor on matters of writing style and presentation. Deborah Williams graciously put the Johnny Nit Collection at my disposal, Jacqueline Still Scott-Burton provided Aida Ward material, and Jim Lyons supplied the photo of Bricktop and Florence. My friend the late Brendan Guilfoyle was my very early mentor in jazz.

A veritable army of researchers, writers, and others assisted in many ways, including, in alphabetical order: Professor Robert Asher, John Cowley, Frank Cullen (*Vaudeville Times* magazine), Claudia Depkin, Tim Gracyk, Jeffrey Green, John P. Gunnison, Bill Haesler, Melba Huber, Patricia Prattis Jennings, Professor Robin Kelley, Wolfram Knauer, Ross Laird, Sally Maxwell, Mike Meddings, Tom Morgan, Valantyne Napier, Hans Pehl, Dr. Michelle

Potter, the late Frank Powers, Howard Rye, Marika Sherwood, the late Mark Tucker, Libby Tudiver, Anne Turbe, and Iain Cameron Williams (Adelaide Hall biographer).

There was also an army of librarians and archivists in many institutions whose devotion to their work was very helpful. Some of these institutions are Moorland-Spingarn Research Center (Ms. Joellen El Bashir and staff), New York Public Library, Center for Black Music Research (Chicago), the Historic New Orleans Collection (Ms. Siva Blake), the Philadelphia Free Library (Mrs. Geraldine Duclow), Mander and Mitchenson Theater Collection (Richard Mangan), Columbia University (Butler Library), Chicago Historical Society, Chicago Jazz Archive (Debbie Gillaspie), The British Library (Colindale), Royal Albert Hall (Jackie Cowdrey), Atlanta University Center (Cathy Lynn Mundale), and Woodlawn Cemetery (Susan Olsen, historian).

Finally, many of my personal friends and family became ensnared in the web, including Neil and Judy McKinnon in Calgary; Bearnard O'Riain and Justin O'Riain in South Africa; Jean (Jamie) Jamieson-Black in England; Fred von Reibnitz in Canberra for translation services; my son Liam, who re-engineered the U. S. Thompson tapes; my sister, Pat Tandy, who located numerous database articles for me; and, finally, my sternest critic and staunchest supporter, my wife Jean.

Editor's Foreword

Way back in the days when I was becoming more and more serious about jazz, I would devour discographies, absorbing the fascinating personnels and intriguing titles. Among the latter were a number that had reference to Florence Mills, clearly occasioned by her untimely death.

Who, I wondered, might this lady have been to cause such an outpouring of public grief. A singer, perhaps? If so, not one that was listed in jazz sources. Maybe a dancer or an actress? As you will learn from this great work, she was all of these.

My curiosity peaked when I learned that Florence Mills had been the inspiration for one of my favorite early Duke Ellington records (Duke was the first artist I collected), "Black Beauty," and as you will discover, this splendid piece of music would also become the launching pad for Bill Egan's fascination with Florence.

A great star in her homeland and abroad, adored by all who came within her aura, her brilliant career came to a sudden and tragic end when she was only in her thirty-second year of life. Because she made no recordings and did not appear in films (which had yet to acquire sound), she has been almost forgotten.

Until now, some 75 years after her passing, with the publication of this remarkable book, which should restore Florence Mills to her rightful place in the pantheon of not just African-American but 20th-century performing artists.

Through dedicated and meticulous research, Bill Egan has managed to almost bring his subject back to life. She emerges from these pages, not as a relic from the past but as a surprisingly contemporary and fully fledged human being, a woman not only of great beauty, charm, and talent, but also of remarkable intelligence and humanity. That old cliché, "labor of love," truly applies here.

It is not only Florence who comes to life in these pages, but also a whole vanished world of entertainment. Call it "show business" if you must, but it was much more than what that tag implies—an international and integrated world in which Florence Mills found surprising fulfillment (surprising to those who view anything pertaining to the history of black Americans through today's prismatics).

This is a fascinating, multi-faceted biography, and we are proud indeed to add this distinguished title to Studies in Jazz series, where it belongs, though Florence Mills was a Jazz Queen in the usage of her time.

Dan Morgenstern
Director, Institute of Jazz Studies
Rutgers University

~

Preface

During the ten years I have spent researching and writing the life of Florence Mills, many people have expressed surprise, puzzlement, even amusement that an Irish-born Australian should be so obsessed with the story of an obscure African American entertainer who died ten years before his birth. The rationale lies in my lifetime love of jazz music and its associated African American culture.

I discovered jazz during my teen years, and my life has been enriched by it ever since. Reading about the lives of the great figures of jazz inevitably stimulated curiosity about the wider black culture from which it developed. This path led me to discover literary figures like Langston Hughes, Richard Wright, and James Weldon Johnson and historic figures like Booker T. Washington, Frederick Douglass, and many more.

In particular, I was deeply impressed by the music of Duke Ellington. Initially this fascination was directed toward the great bands of the 1940s and later. Retirement allowed more time to explore the Ellington of the 1920s and 1930s. The first time I heard his 1928 recording of "Black Beauty" was a moment of revelation. Here was the most inspiring piece of music I had ever heard, combining jaunty vitality with a haunting strain of melancholy.

"Black Beauty" so enthralled me that I set about collecting every version I could find, whether by Ellington or by the many others who have recorded it. In the process I found that the sleeve notes to many LPs (long-playing phonograph records) or CDs referred to it as Duke's tribute to a long-dead singer named Florence Mills. When he gave his first Carnegie Hall concert, in 1943, he explicitly renamed "Black Beauty" as "A Portrait of Florence Mills." He included it in his portraits of the three people he considered the all-time greatest black entertainers, the other two being comedian Bert Williams and tap dancer Bill "Bojangles" Robinson.

Anyone who inspired such a tribute from Ellington must have been remarkable. I searched for anything I could find about her. Biographies of Ethel Waters, Alberta Hunter, Lena Horne, and Paul Robeson revealed that they all considered Florence Mills one of their greatest peers. Nevertheless, no one had ever written her biography. The mystery deepened further when I found this reputedly great singer had never been recorded!

I was thoroughly hooked. I had just completed a graduate diploma in professional writing and embarked on my first project (to do with chess). I now decided it was more important to unravel the story of this enigmatic, forgotten star of the 1920s and write her first biography. I had no idea then that this lightly made decision would absorb ten years of my life and take me to eighteen cities in seven countries.

As I began to discover something of the reality of Florence Mills's life, I realized that this was no mere story of a great but forgotten entertainer. It was also the story of a truly remarkable human being who had been a shining beacon of humanity and a tireless worker for justice for people of color. The near idolatry with which African Americans regarded her during her lifetime clashes with the virtual absence of her memory among them today. Reading the views of her contemporaries, I saw clearly that she had been a remarkable and innovative jazz performer. I felt that by seeking to restore Florence Mills in the memory of her people, I could in some small way repay the great joy that jazz has brought to my life.

A revival of the memory of Florence Mills does more than present an inspiring story. It provides a valuable role model today for younger African Americans struggling to understand their history and define their sense of identity. In an earlier era, many African Americans held an optimism that reason and logic would in time prevail over the injustices of racial persecution and discrimination. Today, in many communities the hopes fueled by the victories of the civil rights struggle have turned sour. Anger and frustration have replaced optimism. Many turn to confrontation and feel alienated from the wider society. Florence Mills never wavered from her belief that persuasion and leading by example could overcome prejudice. Her life and its remarkable achievements are a shining testimony to this truth.

She is a particularly important role model for black American women. In the words of Maya Angelou:

Image making is very important for every human being. It is especially important for black American women in that we are, by being black, a minority in the United States, and by being female, the less powerful of the genders. . . . We need to see our mothers, aunts, our sisters, and grandmothers. We need to see Frances Harper, Sojourner Truth, Fannie Lou Hamer, women of our heritage. We need to have these women preserved. We need them all.

—From *Black Women Writers at Work*,
edited by Claudia Tate (New York: Continuum, 1983, 1–11).

Florence Mills is an outstanding example of such a heritage figure.

It may seem strange that no other biography of Florence Mills has been written. The truth is that many plans and ventures for a biography existed, but none came to fruition. In 1927, immediately after Florence's death, Raymond Pace Alexander, later a prominent African American lawyer and judge, wrote to Florence's husband, U. S. "Slow Kid" Thompson, offering himself as a possible biographer. The offer was presumably refused because in early 1928 U. S. Thompson asked James Weldon Johnson to undertake the task. Around this time Florence's manager, Lew Leslie, also claimed to be planning a biography. Nothing came of these ventures.

The issue cropped up several times again over the years. In 1940 the *Baltimore Afro-American* carried a report of plans for a full-length all-black cast film titled *The Little Blackbird*, based on the life of Florence Mills. Details of the cast, including Madame Sul-Te-Wan, and the names of the writers and composers were provided. The production company was an African American company called Duo-Art Pictures. Nothing appears to have eventuated.

Sometime in 1943 a report circulated that Metro-Goldwyn-Mayer had a screen treatment based on a forthcoming book about Florence Mills, to be called *Dixie Nightingale*, by an Edward Thompson. Lew Leslie's former stage manager, Walter Herzbrun, had approached U. S. Thompson to allow Edward Thompson access to Florence Mills's scrapbooks and papers for the purpose of the book and film. A contract was actually signed, but U. S. Thompson withdrew when he came to believe that the production would not be grandiose enough to do justice to the lavish scale of Florence's shows. "We ain't goin' to have no half-assed stuff," he said.

The same concern surfaced again in 1965, when author and playwright Loften Mitchell wrote in the *Amsterdam News*, "[Florence Mills] deserves a play and I am going to write one about her." His plan was for a one-act musical play called *Ballad of a Blackbird*. U. S. Thompson objected on behalf of "the Florence Mills estate," fearing again that the production would not be lavish enough to do justice to Florence's shows. Mitchell went ahead anyway, with a thinly disguised leading character loosely based on Florence's life. A planned Broadway production in 1967 did not happen. The play had only limited exposure and was not published. The script is preserved today at the Manuscripts and Rare Books Division of the Schomburg Institute. *Storyville* 134 (June 1988) reported that Richard Newman (then of the New York Public Library, now deceased) at that time had a biography of Florence Mills that was "well advanced" and was seeking assistance from England.

Toward the end of his life, Florence's husband was depressed about the topic, telling his friend, social historian Delilah Jackson, "I don't want to be bothered with it no more." He gave his collection of Florence Mills material to the noted historian and collector Dr. Helen Armstead Johnson, believing she was best equipped to preserve Florence's memory. Today, through Dr. Johnson's generosity, these papers are available in the Schomburg Institute for research and public access.

The passage of time and the deaths of most of the leading figures have greatly complicated the task of accurately documenting Florence Mills's life. It is unfortunate that so little was done over the years to capture the personal memories of her contemporaries, such as Eubie Blake, Maude Mills, Lew Leslie, Johnny Hudgins, and Edith Wilson, to name but a few. We must be grateful for the valiant efforts of those like Delilah Jackson and Dr. Johnson, who captured so much of U. S. Thompson's reminiscences. In particular, I am grateful that Delilah allowed me to acquire her treasured collection of U. S. Thompson interviews, believing that I had the persistence to see the task through. I hope the result justifies her faith.

In addition to those invaluable resources, I was also fortunate, with Delilah's assistance, to be able to talk to Florence's contemporaries Maude Russell and Hyacinth Curtis, who generously shared their memories. Through Stephen Bourne's generosity I was also able to have access to valuable reminiscences by Elisabeth Welch and Adelaide Hall.

For the rest I have had to rely mainly on access to original sources in newspapers, documents, and periodicals of the time, as well as the very helpful (although not always reliable) written memoirs and biographies of numerous contemporaries of Florence. To collect this material I have traveled to New York, Washington, Chicago, Philadelphia, Los Angeles, San Francisco, Flagstaff, Calgary, London, Paris, Versailles, Brussels, Ostend, Berlin, Darmstadt, and Baden-Baden.

I am intensely conscious that the end product is much less complete and satisfying than could have been produced by an author who started twenty or twenty-five years before I did. However, I believe the story is almost as good as it could be under the prevailing circumstances. I also believe it is vitally important to have even a flawed and limited biography of Florence Mills rather than none at all.

My purpose has been to produce a straightforward chronological biographical narrative of Florence Mills's life. Apart from some personal opinions in the "Reappraisal" chapter, particularly related to her significance in jazz, I have not attempted any form of deconstructionist, interpretive analysis of her social, racial, or professional status or significance. I hope that the information I provide will stimulate others to undertake such analysis.

Finally, I also believe there is still much scope for further research on the facts of Florence Mills's life and that there may well be important new evidence still to be discovered. I will continue my own research in that direction and will be happy to assist others similarly engaged. In the meantime I offer the present text as my humble tribute to a truly great human being.

~

Introduction

Wherever possible, the facts presented in this narrative have been verified from more than one source. Where independent verification was not possible, such as in anecdotes about Florence's early life, I have accepted them at face value for want of better. In all cases the original source is documented.

On issues of interpretation, for example, Florence's emotions and thoughts, I have allowed myself occasional authorial privilege. I have also occasionally drawn inferences about events or circumstances when the facts seemed to point clearly in a particular direction, but again, sources are always identified.

Wherever unattributed quotations from Ulysses "Slow Kid" Thompson appear, they have been taken from the series of tapes, recorded by Delilah Jackson, of many meetings she had with Kid Thompson during the 1970s and 1980s; the same tapes are now in the Bill Egan Collection. Quotations from Hyacinth Curtis and Maude Russell come from interviews I taped with these two ladies during the 1990s. Finally, quotations from Elisabeth Welch come from Stephen Bourne's interview with her in London on August 15, 1993.

~

Abbreviations

For frequently quoted sources, the following abbreviations have been used in endnotes:

AMST: *Amsterdam News* (New York)
BAA: *Baltimore Afro-American*
ChDef: *Chicago Defender*
HAJC: Helen Armstead Johnson Collection, Schomburg Institute
LT: *London Times*
NYA: *New York Age*
NYT: *New York Times*
PhTr: *Philadelphia Tribune*
PiCou: *Pittsburgh Courier*
SCRAP: Florence Mills Scrapbooks, Schomburg Institute
TC FLP: Theatre Collection, Free Library of Philadelphia
VAR: *Variety*

CHAPTER ONE

~

Young Florence

Baby Florence Takes the Stage

October 1899—a three-year-old girl with dark copper skin and bright eyes stands on the stage of the Bijou Theatre in Washington, D.C. Dressed in a nightgown, she holds a candle in her hand. She is waiting to sing a beddy-bye song, "Don't Cry My Little Pickaninny." Sam Adams, a white tramp comedian, stands beside Baby Florence Mills. He had taught her the song when her father, a friend of the manager, brought her to the Bijou. Later, when Adams stands on stage at the end of his act and his audience demands more, he spies Florence standing in the wings and plants her on the stage to do her piece. Baby Flo, having started well, catches a glimpse of another performer, breaks down in tears, and is led offstage. Black faces are familiar to her, but blackface, a white face smeared with burned cork, is alarming; her debut comes to a tearful end. A year or so later, however, she is back on stage, launching a stellar career that will make her one of the greatest entertainers the world has ever known.[1]

Born on January 25, 1896, Florence Winfrey was the third surviving daughter of Nellie and John Winfrey. At the time of her birth, the family lived at 610 K Street NW, a middle-class area of Washington, D.C. They had recently moved there from Lynchburg, Virginia. The family's fortunes soon took a downward turn, and they moved to a rough-and-tumble area of town known as Goat Alley.

Jules Bledsoe, a famous African American actor who introduced the role of Joe in the timeless musical *Show Boat*, paints a picture of the Winfreys's lot. "I never saw Florence's original home but I know how the colored folk lived down there then. One big room with a stove in the center on a barren floor. Bunks lining the walls. Windows sometimes. In such a room a whole family of colored people lived."[2] Some years later an American author, Ernest Howard Culbertson, used it as the setting for a play called *Goat Alley*, "to present the horrible surroundings of the Negro, with a view of improving civic conditions for them."

At the 1900 census, record takers found nine people living in Florence's home at 23 Goat Alley. Six were members of her family. The census taker noted "B" for black in the "Color or Race" column. Florence reportedly had one white grandfather, presumably on her father's side as her maternal grandfather was a freed slave.[3] Her skin tone was a dark copper, and her features unmistakably African American. In later life, as a staunch race woman, she would proclaim herself "coal black and proud of it."[4]

Florence was the seventh of eight children born to Nellie Winfrey. Only four were still alive by the time of the 1900 census. The Winfrey girls were Olivia, 16; Maude, 11; Florence, 4; and Mary, 2. Mary's name is never mentioned after, so presumably she also died very young, and Florence became the baby of the family. At the turn of the century, the rate of infant mortality for nonwhite children was high, with roughly one in four dying before the fourth birthday.

The family's circumstances were precarious. For her father, finding steady work as a day laborer was difficult enough even before he became ill with tuberculosis. He died when Florence was still quite young. Florence's mother had to compete as a laundress with many other struggling women in the community. She took laundry work where she could find it, even when it led her into the red-light district. Many years later, Florence's husband, U. S. "Slow Kid" Thompson, said:

> Florence's mother used to take in washing for the whores in Washington, D.C.—sportin' women. In those days you didn't have a cab or nothin' like that to bring the washing in. If you were a little close to the sportin' house, you put the bundle on your head, and you went in with the washing on your head. So Florence used to go with her mother to take the clothes to these sportin' women in Washington, D.C. They found out Florence could sing, so the mother used to make Florence sing these songs, and they'd all give Florence dollars, fifty cents. Well that was more than she got for washing the clothes, see, so she soon found out that she had a jewel.[5]

The engaging little toddler charmed the ladies of the bordellos with renditions of sentimental Irish ballads such as "Mother Machree" and "Little

Grey Home in the West," taught to her by her sisters. Although the family was struggling to stay above the poverty line, it was close knit, with music an important part of the home life. It was her mother, Florence once said, who filled her heart with music:

> In the old days my mother would sing Negro spirituals. She sang them during times of storm and thunder and lightning, and I can still see her, rocking backwards and forwards crooning to herself, while I hid, frightened to death, behind the door, waiting for the storm to be past. She sang those songs not because she thought that she was frightening away evil spirits, or anything like that, but simply because they seemed the right thing to sing when the whole world was in the grip of the storm.[6]

If her mother gave her the gift of song, it was her father, before his untimely death, who gave her the gift of theater. Through his friendship with the manager of the Bijou Theatre, she discovered the stage, which, she later wrote, "instead of the street, was my playground."[7] Florence's aptitude for dancing matched, even excelled, her singing ability. Describing her early love of dance, a relative recalled, "Florence loved to dance, to spread joy and happiness. Why, her eyes would light like ship flares when she heard music. . . . She would throw out her little limbs, and her arms would go waving, swaying, flying. It didn't seem to us children as if she touched the sidewalk. We would all stop play to watch Florence when she broke into a dance."[8]

Florence was growing up in the 1890s, the era when the cakewalk dance swept America, to wild enthusiasm. The dance's history stretched back to plantation days, when enslaved African Americans dressed up and parodied the high-flown ways of their white mistresses and masters. The cakewalk would play an important role in Florence's early development as an entertainer. Brilliant black performers like Bert Williams, George Walker, and his beautiful and talented wife, Aida Overton Walker, featured the dance in their highly successful shows, including *The Sons of Ham* (1900) and *In Dahomey* (1903). Lovely, stylish Aida was much in demand giving cakewalk lessons to wealthy white New York society members. Classically trained African American soprano Sissieretta Jones, known as Black Patti, was another leading exponent of the cakewalk and other black dances like buck-and-wing dancing, a forerunner of tap dance.

One of Florence's early opportunities to see top-class black entertainment came when Sissieretta Jones presented her Black Patti Troubadours at the Academy Theater, near Florence's home. The *Washington Star* for May 12, 1900, trumpeted the arrival—in the racially insensitive terms of the times—of "The

World Famous Black Patti Troubadours, in a repertoire of coon comedy, darkey fun, Cakewalks, Buck Dances and sweet melodies." For young black children, entry to the Academy was not cheap, even for matinees. To get money for herself and her pals to see the show, Florence used her newly developed theatrical skills, singing for pennies on the street. Her song was the popular "Oh Promise Me" from Reginald de Koven's recently successful opera *Robin Hood*.[9]

There was a special cakewalk contest on three successive nights of the Black Patti show, "for the championship of the District of Columbia and the Black Patti Gold Medal." Florence entered contests early and often and probably tested the bunch in the Black Patti competition, but the results were never published. What we do know is that by the time she was five years old, she was winning medals for the cakewalk and the buck dance. In Kid Thompson's words, "They had an amateur night there, and Florence, she got in the amateur night, and of course she made good, and after that a lot of people saw her, and from that [time] on she never looked back." She was known as Florence Mills, rather than Florence Winfrey, from the beginning. Her birth certificate lists the officiating doctor at the event as R. N. Mills, MD. In tribute to him, her family chose Mills as her stage name when she began her career as a child performer. When her older sisters joined her onstage later, they too adopted the name Mills.

While young Florence earned money for her family by entertaining the ladies of the night, she was also a familiar figure in the drawing rooms of the society matrons. Her reputation as a dancer resulted in invitations from Washington's diplomatic set. A striking memento of this time is a picture of Florence as a tiny girl with medals for championship cakewalking and buck dancing pinned to her chest. She also proudly shows off, on an outstretched arm, a bracelet. The British ambassador's wife, Lady Pauncefote, had presented it to her for entertaining the elite of Washington in her drawing room.

Baby Flo was so delighted with her gift that she insisted on wearing it whenever she appeared in public. On the day of the photograph, the photographer asked for a shot without it. She replied, "No bracelet, no picture."[10] Like a budding diva, Florence was learning to enjoy the spotlight. Years later, recalling her early childhood ambition, she wrote, "[My wish] was that I should see my name shining on the signs of a big theatre as brightly as the glorious moneymoon."[11]

For an aspiring singer and dancer, the principal female role models of the day were Black Patti and Aida Overton Walker. There was also the sensational dancer Ida Forsyne, who went to Europe for five years beginning in 1906, becoming "the cakewalking toast of Russia." On her return to America, she introduced Russian Cossack-style dancing to the world of tap and jazz. This style featured bent knees and wild kicking, starting a craze that lasted for many years and later became part of Florence Mills's repertoire.

The late 1890s and the early years of the twentieth century were a time of great change for black music and entertainment. The minstrelsy era of black-face performers making stereotypical fun of black people was coming to a close. Ragtime, with great classical ragtime composers like Scott Joplin and the more-jazz-tinged Tony Jackson and Jelly Roll Morton, was turning American popular music on its ear. Jazz stepped out of the cloak of Negro marching bands, Buddy Bolden in New Orleans leading the charge. Blues and spirituals (sometimes called "sorrow" songs) remained an intrinsic part of black musical heritage, even while it was beginning to evolve into something new.

The result of all these dazzling musical talents was a new golden era of black musical theater. From Bob Cole's *Trip to Coontown* in 1898 right through the first decade of the new century, a steady stream of productions delighted Broadway and regional audiences, black and white alike. Highlights included Will Marion Cook's *Clorindy, the Origin of the Cakewalk* and Cole and Johnson's *The Shoo-fly Regiment*. Although the subject matter of many of these shows still had stereotypical elements, the gross caricatures of minstrelsy were gone, and blacks were portrayed in a less-demeaning manner.[12]

Florence was ready to say yes to it all. But despite her early success and her passion for her budding career, she was, in other ways, an ordinary kid. She had to show up for school like the rest of the neighborhood kids. The local school was the combined Garnet School, built in 1880, and Patterson School, built in 1893, at 10th and U Streets, NW.[13] A contemporary pupil, a year or two ahead of her, was Jean Toomer, author of the novel *Cane*. The young Edward Kennedy "Duke" Ellington followed a few years later. Though no school records of Florence's time there survive, contemporaries suggested she was not academically remarkable[14]—hardly surprising in view of the amount of time and effort she devoted to her performance activities.

During these early school days, she had her first brush with racial discrimination. When she was scheduled to perform before the diplomatic elite at a fashionable "whites only" theater, a group of playmates came along, keen to see her perform. At the door of the theater, her entourage was refused entry. Indignant, she turned away from the theater to go home with them. According to a newspaper account, "The management rushed after [Florence] and it was not until Mabel, her chum, and her two brothers were admitted that the fiery little miss consented to do her act."[15]

In April 1903, the road-show version of Williams and Walker's *The Sons of Ham* played an extended season at the Empire Theatre in Washington, a return engagement after a successful week's run the previous December. Comedians

Charles Hart and Dan Avery were the leading company members, playing the roles Williams and Walker had originated. Hart had been Bert Williams's understudy in the original production and bore a striking resemblance to the comedic genius. In the convention of the times, both were performing in blackface. By now Florence was older and wiser about the curious phenomenon, whether the actors underneath the cork were black or white.

The Sons of Ham was a major event for the theater-going public in D.C., black and white alike. The Empire catered predominantly to whites, with occasional restricted access for blacks. However, the Washington Star commented that "noting the great demand for seats by colored people whenever any African [sic] entertainers appeared on the bill [the management] resolved to lift the ban which has customarily been placed on Afro-American patronage." The revenue from many blacks keen to see a leading production by members of their own race was too much to resist. A large newspaper advertisement for the second week of the season announced a "Grand Prize Cake Walk" on Tuesday night and a "Prize Buck Dancing Contest" on Thursday night.

Florence Mills already had a strong local reputation as a tiny performer with great firepower, and The Sons of Ham production was to be a milestone event for her. Her magical singing and dancing led to an invitation for her to make a guest appearance with the visiting company, her first true professional engagement. The Washington Star made a big deal of it: "The peerless child artist who has appeared before the most exclusive set in Washington, delighting them with her songs and dances, is appearing this week at the Empire Theatre with The Sons of Ham Company No. 2. An extra attraction is Baby Florence Mills singing "Hannah from Savannah." Baby Florence made a big hit and was encored for dancing."[16]

"Hannah from Savannah," one of the hit tunes from the show, had strong associations with its original performer, the lovely Aida Overton Walker.[17] There is a charming but untrue story that Aida herself coached Florence for this occasion. At the time, Aida was actually in England with Williams and Walker's latest hit show, In Dahomey. (Its success was crowned with a command performance at Buckingham Palace as a birthday surprise for the young Prince of Wales and marked the beginning of his lifelong fascination with black entertainment and jazz.) Without Aida's tutelage, Florence nevertheless experienced her first exposure to the world of professional show business and carried it off in triumph.

After her Sons of Ham appearance, Florence was ready for her next triumph. Her precocious talents made her a natural for a role as a "pick," or pickaninny, a term, by turns affectionate and offensive, born during slavery.

Originally it referred to little black children who picked cotton in the fields. Picks performed alongside some of vaudeville's top stars, including the inestimable Sophie Tucker, giving their acts extra punch. Only black children between six and twelve years of age and possessing exceptional singing and dancing skills need apply. The kids would be nattily dressed in silk and tuxedo jackets, their natural talents enhanced by the seasoned professionals who hired them.

Young Florence Mills was an obvious candidate to fit this bill. Her appearances had not escaped the notice of talent scouts from the many shows passing through Washington. One of these was a popular white burlesque star known as Bonita. Bonita's real name was Pauline Hall, but a contemporary opera singer of that name was already well known. Bonita was one of the earliest performers to feature picks in her act. While performing with her sister Artie for a short time, Bonita developed a blackface style using a brown pigment instead of burnt cork. The pigment gave her a mulatto appearance. She would bill herself as Cuban except for those parts of the show when she switched from blackface to whiteface. Later, she added two African American boys, billed as her African, or sometimes Cuban, midgets. This innovation earned her the reputation of being one of the first to use picks. Bonita's original boy picks came from near Bonita's family's plantation home in Georgia, where they lived close to their parents during the off-season.[18]

Bonita had played the New Bijou Theatre in D.C. in March 1901 as a solo act in a production called *Wine, Woman and Song*. In August and September of that year she appeared at Kiernan's Lyceum Theatre, this time as Bonita and Her Company, "favorably and well known for their fine ability in the creation of coon songs and dances." From early 1903 through mid-1906, Bonita was performing regularly with her "Cuban and African midgets" and her "Pickaninny Trio" in New York, Boston, D.C., Philadelphia, Toledo, and smaller cities, always to highly favorable notices. In October 1905 she played the Walnut Theatre, Philadelphia, with the *Wine, Woman and Song* company, sharing the bill with a troupe of "six international lady wrestlers" and, of course, her "Cuban and African Midgets."

Sometime during this period Florence became one of Bonita's picks. How long this role lasted is difficult to establish. However, it was long enough that when, years later at the height of her fame, Florence met Bonita again, she paid her a great compliment. "I owe it all to you, Miss Bonita," she said. "You taught me how to put over a song."[19] Florence's steady work as a pick meant good income for her family, but her newfound career proved short lived. The Gerry Society at that time was the nemesis of underage theater performers. "Gerry" referred to the founder, lawyer Elbridge Gerry, and had become the nickname by which the New York Society for the Prevention of Cruelty to Children (NYSPCC) was known.

Since it was founded in 1875, the Gerry Society had made protection of child performers a high priority in New York and other East Coast cities. Its concerns centered on possible moral danger as well as neglect of education.[20] Lillian Gish, Buster Keaton, Milton Berle, and Al Jolson were among the child actors who either came into the custody of the Gerry Society or narrowly escaped its clutches. Little Al Jolson, who later went on to blackface fame singing the sentimental "Mammy," was taken by the Gerry Society in Baltimore. It placed him in Saint Mary's Catholic Home, much to the consternation of his Jewish family. Florence's successful career with Bonita came to a tearful end in similar fashion.

The Society took her into custody and placed her in an institution for a time, reportedly with Catholic nuns, to the great distress of her family. So once again Florence's entry into the world of entertainment ended in tears. Nevertheless, the dream of stardom that started on the stage of the Empire Theatre was not dimmed. She had entertained the low and high of Washington society, from the bordellos to the drawing rooms. She had shared the stage with one of the leading white figures of the burlesque theater. Possessing an extraordinary talent and surprising confidence for one so young, especially one born black and into such difficult circumstances, she endured a setback that could only be temporary.

The Mills Sisters—On the Road

How long Florence's separation from her family lasted after the Gerry Society took her into custody is unknown. Sometime around this period, the family moved to New York, probably around 1906. The move came during the time the great African American migration to Harlem was beginning to change from a trickle to a flood. Like many other black families, the Winfreys didn't immediately go to Harlem. They may have settled initially in mid-Manhattan somewhere around the area known today as Greenwich Village. In due course they too would join the general exodus to Harlem.[21]

Florence vanishes from the public gaze for the next few years, presumably into normal childhood and school attendance. She continued to perform and develop her skills as an entertainer while growing up. Someone who had experienced being a pick in white vaudeville would not lack opportunities to strut her stuff in early-twentieth-century Harlem. For the family, show business was now a useful source of income, and the two older sisters, Olivia and Maude, were no slouches when it came to singing a ballad or tripping the light fantastic. After Florence's enforced retirement, it was Olivia who picked up the family's show business baton.

By early 1909 Olivia's talent had earned her a niche in an established troupe called the Kentucky Minstrels, which included Evon Robinson, wife of songwriter-producer J. Leubrie Hill. A short time later she joined a plantation show run by Benjamin J. (Ben) Butler, who promoted regular summer shows at Rockaway Beach and Coney Island. Butler had been a successful showbiz entrepreneur for nearly thirty years. He was a tall, distinguished-looking man who dressed immaculately, with top hat and cane. Romance soon blossomed between him and Olivia, and they were married sometime in 1909 or 1910. The 1910 census shows twenty-six-year-old Olivia married to the fifty-one-year-old Bernard Butler, both living at West 68th Street. When the summer trade declined, Olivia and Ben Butler's Colored Troubadours toured the South during the autumn.

While Olivia was establishing herself in the entertainment world, Florence reportedly worked for a while as a helper at a pawnshop and secondhand store. However, Olivia was soon joined by her two sisters, and the three Mills Sisters made their debut singing at an Opportunity Night talent contest to raise money for treatment for their sick father. Unfortunately, the treatment proved unsuccessful, and tuberculosis carried him off soon afterwards.[22] By 1910 Nellie Winfrey was a widow. The census, held in April and May of that year, showed her as the head of household at 310 East Eightieth Street in Manhattan, some distance below Harlem. She was working on her own account as a laundress. The other members of the household were listed as daughter Florence, described as an actress seventeen years of age, and granddaughter Nellie Jackson, six. The "seventeen" was obviously part of Nellie Winfrey's attempt to keep the Gerry Society off fourteen-year-old Florence's trail. The ruse had a long-term effect: For the rest of her life, Florence's birth date was moved back by at least a year; it is even recorded inaccurately on her tombstone. It is apparent from the 1910 census that the two older sisters were now living on their own.

Some mystery surrounds the status of Florence's niece Nellie Jackson, later known as Nellie Henry. She doesn't appear to have been the child of either of Florence's two sisters. She may have been the child of a relative of Florence's mother. In any case, Nellie Jackson and Florence were close friends. She said many years later, "I was but a baby. Florence would tuck me safe in a door and when a roving hurdy-gurdy came along it just seemed that she became an elf. I remember that in my baby days and that impression has remained with me all my life." She traveled with the performing sisters. "I was with them but not as part of the act. I just went along because Florence loved me so and insisted on toting me about."[23]

The Eightieth Street address was on the Upper East Side a few blocks from Central Park and, for a healthy young person, within easy walking distance of Harlem. Today's Lexington Avenue subway didn't exist then, but the regular rail system from Grand Central Station ran northwards, parallel to Central Park. Although the family was now in some sense a "show business" family, due mainly to Florence's early achievements, it was also a strongly religious family. In Harlem, Nellie Winfrey became a staunch member of the local AME (African Methodist Episcopal) Church, then located on 136th Street. From an early age, Florence was an enthusiastic attendee at Sunday school. When she was five, her mother, with whom she was always very close, gave her a gift of her own Bible, which she carried with her in later years.[24]

The black show-business world to which Florence returned was different from that of the opening years of the century. By 1910 fickle white American audiences had lost their enthusiasm for black musical theater and was on a craze for Viennese light operas such as Franz Lehar's *The Merry Widow*. By 1911 Ernest Hogan, George Walker, and Bob Cole had all died (within a space of three years), and Bert Williams had accepted Florenz Ziegfeld's offer to become the first black man to star in the *Ziegfeld Follies*.

The main outlet for hopeful young black talent at the end of the first decade was in Harlem, mainly at the Lincoln Theatre, also known as the Nickellette. It was a movie house, with live acts sandwiched between the movies. Established in 1909 and owned by Maria C. Downs, the Lincoln presented black acts for a black clientele. Its notoriously raucous audiences showed their appreciation or disapproval vigorously. Ribald audience participation was the norm. The regulars who delivered a running commentary were known as sharpshooters, and their heckling was often funnier than the jokes onstage. This was the setting in which Florence made her comeback to professional show business sometime in the latter half of 1909. As veteran journalist Alvin White expressed it many years later, "It was right there [in the Lincoln] she had made her pro debut with her sisters, a scared, skinny, big-eyed teenager."[25] Jules Bledsoe also remembered seeing the teenage Florence:

> I wandered one night, many years ago, into a small burlesque theatre in Harlem. It was a dark, dingy, poorly lighted place. The air was heavy with tobacco smoke and fouled by lack of ventilation. The audience that night was unappreciative, listless and noisy. The shuffling of feet on the rough wooden floor was distracting. On the stage, so barren and unattractive, a dozen girls were dancing, working hard to captivate attention—I eyed them casually. My

eyes stopped on the girl, third from the left in the front row, an undersized thin, dynamic little creature, dancing with abandon and fury and grace. She stood out among them—to my eyes at least, and if I never saw her again I would never have forgotten her. The raucous chatter, the occasional hoots, the lack of attention and interest must have stung her. But she gave no sign; she danced on, more wildly, more gaily, than ever. In later years I grew to know this girl as a close friend. Her name was Florence Mills.[26]

Bledsoe's account rings true to the general picture given of the Lincoln then.

Another who remembered the Mills Sisters's appearances at the Nickellette was James P. Johnson, an originator of the New York stride-piano style of jazz. Years later he remembered Florence singing there while he was playing piano for the silent movies.[27] Florence was earning $9.00 a week, and she was now part of a team with her sisters. Before long they were on the road together, billed as the Mills Sisters or sometimes the Mills Trio. Only fourteen years old in 1910, Florence was still potentially within the Gerry Society's reach. However, her mother's subterfuge of adding a year to her age may have helped, and the Gerry Society was also facing some strong organized opposition from the theatrical profession between 1910 and 1912.[28]

After the southern tour, Ben Butler's shows closed down for the winter and Olivia resumed her role with the Mills Sisters. The "Theatrical Jottings" of the New York Age noted on January 6, 1910, "The Mills Sisters, with Edna Dabney, are having success in Vaudeville." The Mills Sisters show up in the Age's "Jottings" over the next four months as they played several theater circuits around the New York region, including the Loew's circuit. They went as far afield as the other side of New York state, to Oswego and Watertown on the shores of Lake Ontario. With the return of summer, Olivia rejoined Ben Butler's summer season show at the Surf Avenue Opera House and the Orpheum Music Hall. This time she brought her sisters with her under the Mills Sisters title. They picked up extra money by entering and winning local cakewalk competitions. During much of 1911, the New York Age referred to "Olivia Butler of the Mills Sisters." However, the marriage to Ben Butler doesn't seem to have been a long-lived one, and by 1913 she had reverted to Olivia Mills.

To a fourteen-year-old city girl, Coney Island in 1910, with its glittering sideshows, amusement arcades, wild animal shows, freaks, and novelty rides, must have been like heaven to Florence. Coney Island was in its heyday then, with extravagant new feature parks, including Luna Park, which opened in 1903, and Dreamland, which opened the following year. Exhibits she could have seen at Dreamland included "wild" people from Africa and

Asia. Coney Island was readily accessible from downtown Manhattan by elevated railway in 1910 and less conveniently so from further uptown. With evening performances, the sisters had to board locally for at least some of their time in Coney Island, presumably at premises belonging to Ben Butler. Apart from being interesting and profitable, the Coney Island season did a lot to raise their profile in black show business. Their engagements appeared in the *Age* alongside many leading acts, including S. H. Dudley and the Smart Set Company, Belle Davis, and Florence's former *Sons of Ham* costars Avery and Hart.

Following the Coney Island engagements, the Mills Sisters were soon back playing Harlem. This time they played the more respectable Crescent Theatre as well as the Nickellette. The Crescent catered to a black middle-class audience. Established in 1909, slightly later than the Lincoln, it was Harlem's first true black theater. While the Lincoln was a glorified movie house, the Crescent presented full-blown shows, staged by comedian Eddie Hunter. On this occasion the Mills Sisters, listed as "one of the principal attractions," shared the bill with Jerry Mills (no relative). He was a veteran comedian, composer, and stage manager in creole, minstrel, and jubilee singing troupes and would soon be stage manager of the Black Patti company.[29]

Up to now the sisters had mostly been performing within commuting distance of home, but 1911 saw them spreading their wings more widely. They were now a respected act on black vaudeville circuits. Between May and July they played black theaters in Philadelphia. The Philadelphia season nearly ended in tragedy when they narrowly escaped a fire at their lodgings. Following their Philadelphia season, they played in Washington, D.C., at the Ford Dabney Theatre, run by Dabney himself. Ford Dabney was a skilled musician who had been official court musician to the president of Haiti. He later had a leading dance band associated with Vernon and Irene Castle in New York. He is known today as the composer of the jazz standard "That's Why They Call Me Shine."

Toward the end of 1911, Olivia was ill for a time. When she recovered, the sisters performed close to home for a while. In October, the *Age* noted that "Baby Florence is the hit of the act." Although now approaching sixteen, she was still tiny, appealing to audiences with her nymphlike figure and appearance. Young though she might appear, Florence already had a professional, and perfectionist, approach to her art. "Even as a child [she] would practice her steps by the hour. When she wanted to learn a new number, she would keep after it constantly until she had mastered it,"[30] her niece recalled.

Her dedication to her art soon began to earn her attention in influential circles, specifically from a leading figure of black music at the time, R. C.

McPherson, also known as Cecil Mack. Cecil Mack had contributed lyrics to many of the songs for the Williams and Walker shows, including Florence's featured piece with *The Sons of Ham*, "Miss Hannah from Savannah," as well as being the lyricist for the already mentioned "That's Why They Call Me Shine." In later years he would achieve even greater fame as author of the lyrics for "The Charleston." He had been a cofounder, along with Will Marion Cook, of one of the first black-owned music publishing companies, the Gotham-Attucks Company. By late 1911 the publishing company had been sold, and Cecil Mack was looking around for new ventures to suit his talents. The result was a show called *School-Days in Darktown*, which included the Mills Sisters, with Florence having a featured role.

The leading figure in the production was Andrew Tribble, famed for his ability as a female impersonator, in which capacity he had starred in two of the most famous black shows, Cole and Johnson's *Red Moon* and *The Shoo-fly Regiment*. In this instance he played a male comedy role as a schoolteacher, with Florence as a precocious schoolgirl. The show opened in Brooklyn at the Olympic Theatre to an enthusiastic review by the dean of New York black drama critics, Lester Walton. Florence's performance particularly caught his attention, inspiring the prophetic words, "Florence Mills, of the Mills Sisters, is a clever little girl who can sing, dance and speak lines in an artistic manner, and her name should be in big type some day."[31]

To celebrate the success of the show, the entire company, as well as Florence's mother, was entertained at the Harlem home of Lulu Mathews in December. Lulu Mathews was the daughter of Mae Grant Hicks, who had recently achieved the notable feat of being a black member of a white vaudeville show, Lew Fields's *The Hen-Pecks*. Apart from featuring the great Lew Fields himself and Blossom Seeley (dancing the "Texas Tommy," a black dance), this was the show that gave Vernon Castle his first Broadway break and led to his teaming up with Irene Castle. At the time, although black and white acts frequently featured on the same Broadway bill, they were strictly segregated and the union, Equity's forerunner, known as the White Rats, barred black membership. However, about 1909 Lew Fields adopted the practice of including black actors for bit parts in his troupe and was sufficiently well established to get away with it. Sadly, in January 1912, Lulu Mathews died of heart trouble. Lew Fields, Blossom Seeley, and other members of the *Hen-Pecks* cast sent beautiful floral tributes to her funeral, as did the members of the still running *School-Days in Darktown* act. Florence sang a solo at the funeral.[32]

After the *School-Days* run, the sisters were back on the road again. Although traveling widely from home, Florence was not lacking supervision. Her mother usually traveled with her and prepared all meals. As Florence said many years later, "I can boil water. I wish I could cook. I never had to."[33] Nevertheless, despite her mother's closeness, Florence still found time for social activities. Although always clean living, she had a teenager's natural appetite for life. As Florence's lifelong friend and fellow performer Ada "Bricktop" Smith once said to Delilah Jackson, "Florence wasn't no angel, she had lots of boyfriends."[34]

Sometime during 1912 Florence contracted a brief marriage with a man named James Randolph. Little is known of him other than his profession: taxi driver.[35] The marriage was very short, as were similar relationships entered into by Josephine Baker and Alberta Hunter early in their lives. It must have been either a common-law marriage or a marriage that was terminated quickly. At any rate it presented no obstacle to Florence's marriage in later years. Nevertheless, it may help to explain the low profile of the Mills Sisters in the media during the latter part of 1912. By 1913 they were on the road again, traveling widely over the newly set up black circuit owned by Sherman H. Dudley, a veteran of black vaudeville.

Dudley was popularly known as "Mule" because for many years his act included Patrick, a live mule dressed in pants. Onstage, Patrick seemed more intelligent than his master. Dudley was a shrewd businessman, even if his mule could run rings around him. He retired from performing to set up the first black theater circuit in 1913. Performers referred to bookings on his circuit as being "on the Dudley time." Initially his circuit consisted of seven theaters on the East Coast. Within a year it had grown to twenty-three and stretched from Baltimore south to Atlanta. Dudley's circuit was the forerunner of the Theatre Owners' Booking Association (TOBA, often referred to as Tough on Black Asses), which earned some notoriety in the 1920s for its harsh conditions and treatment of black acts, but Dudley himself always retained the respect of black entertainers.[36]

Because he was one of them himself, Dudley understood the needs of black performers. He was able to provide them with reliable bookings in reputable theaters that could be depended on to pay the agreed sums. This was no small benefit in a world where whites controlled most theaters and race prejudice abounded. A few black acts, such as Bill "Bojangles" Robinson, played fancy white venues such as the Keith circuit. For most black acts, however, it was either the Dudley circuit or a tour in the South, a prospect not relished by most.

This was the world in which the sisters resumed their show business careers. They would share the bill with a mixture of vaudeville acts—singers, dancers, and specialty turns, including acrobats, jugglers, magicians, or animals. Any act could be terminated by the manager on a whim or if the audience didn't respond. Previously they had played close to home or in the major centers of Philadelphia and their old hometown, Washington. They now traveled much farther afield, even venturing into southern centers. Their world consisted of continuous travel, critical audiences, demanding managers, rundown theaters, cheap accommodations, and uncertain pay. Their starting point was Norfolk, Virginia, during the week of April 7, 1913. They were playing the Globe Theater, "on the Dudley time." The *Indianapolis Freeman* announced the bill of fare as "Baby Jim, The Mills Sisters, Princess Sotanka." Two weeks later they opened at the Dixie Theater in Richmond, Virginia, where they shared the bill with the Peewees, a singing, dancing, and juggling act. By May they were in Washington, D.C., at the Fairyland Theater, where a local critic noted, "The young miss was a scream, being above the average child performer."[37]

Florence's youthful appearance belied her seventeen years. The pattern of the sisters' act was lively dancing interspersed with sentimental ballads. For some numbers Olivia dressed up in male formal wear, following Aida Overton Walker's "That's Why They Call Me Shine" routine. On this occasion, their repertoire included "Goodbye, Rose," a song from *Captain Jasper*, a full-length musical show by the Black Patti Troubadours and originally sung by Black Patti herself. The sisters' run at the Fairyland must have been successful as they were held over for another week. The *Freeman* noted, "The bill opened with the Mills Sisters, going good as usual. . . . Good pictures at this house." The "pictures" referred to the increasingly common practice of having a mixed bill of vaudeville acts and movies.

Following the D.C. engagements, the sisters started a circle on the "Southern time," beginning at the Auditorium Theatre, Philadelphia. They shared the bill with Perry "Mule" Bradford. Bradford was just another struggling vaudeville "wannabe" then, playing piano in a double act with his partner, Jeanette. Born in Atlanta, he was a year or two older than Florence. He was touring the black circuits while based in Chicago. Talking about their experiences backstage, Florence advised him to go to New York as "the place for an actor to get started in show business."[38] Bradford did go to New York and became a successful jazz composer and entrepreneur, responsible for the first recordings featuring a Negro blues singer, Mamie Smith. Smith's 1920 recording of Bradford's composition "Crazy Blues" sparked the craze for black women blues singers that saw the rise of Bessie Smith, Ida Cox, and many others. Bradford credits Florence with being the one who, by her advice to go to New York, started his rise.

Following the Philadelphia engagement, the sisters spent four weeks at the Pekin Theatre, Savannah, Georgia, and then went to Atlanta. They were not to remain a trio for long. Maude teamed up with a popular comedian,

Hamtree Harrington, and they toured the vaudeville circuit as Harrington and Mills. Olivia and Florence continued as the Mills Sisters. The *Chicago Defender* of May 16, 1914, notes, "The Mills Sisters in character songs and dances went fairly well" at the Old Monogram in Chicago. The Old Monogram was typical of the conditions that prevailed. Ethel Waters, touring the same circuit then as one of the Hill Sisters, paints a graphic picture:

> Of all those rinky-dink dumps I played, nothing was worse than the Monogram Theatre in Chicago. It was close to the El, and the walls were so thin that you stopped singing or telling a joke every time a train passed. Then, when the noise died down, you continued right where you left off. In the Monogram you dressed away downstairs with the stoker. The ceiling down there was so low I had to bend over to get my stage clothes on. Then you came up to the stage on a ladder that looked like those on the old-time slave ships. Ever since I worked at the Monogram, any old kind of dressing room has looked pretty good to me so long as it had a door that could be closed.[39]

The Defender was more enthusiastic in its praise of the sisters' performance at the New Monogram in June. "The Mills Sisters are a clever team and did well. In fact they set a pace that Larrivee and La Page, a bum white act that followed them, couldn't keep." The *Indianapolis Freeman* had been even more enthusiastic about their season at the New Crown Garden Theatre in May:

> The Mills Sisters, Florence and Olivia, are new faces to this house. They are a graceful, classy pair, doing refined singing and dancing steps. Olivia does male impersonations with a delightful, rompish freedom thus making scenes with her partner. She is a comedienne, showing this especially when she does her "Green Grass All Around" stunt. Her steps here are eccentric and amusing. Florence sings prettily, and in a pathetic way, "I Love You Most of All." She is nicely received. They do a neat running song, "If I Had Someone at Home Like You, I Wouldn't Want to Go Out." Both are seen here to advantage, including their neat dance movements. The act is pleasing all the way through. The sisters are of pleasing personality off the stage. They are also of good appearance when performing.[40]

The songs they were performing were current popular hits. "The Green Grass Grew All Around" was a popular 1912 song by the ragtime composer Harry Von Tilzer, who is considered the founder of Tin Pan Alley. It was a sardonic tale of a marriage blighted by bad home cooking and was a vaudeville hit for Eddie Foy. "If I Had Someone at Home," written by James V. Monaco, best known as the composer of "You Made Me Love You," was a big hit in 1914 for popular singer Elida Morris.

Olivia and Florence continued together for most of 1914. *The Freeman*, in its "Annual Review of the Stage," included them among the better acts seen in Indianapolis during the year, noting, "The Mills Sisters will be remembered for their fine and graceful steps. Olivia succeeds nicely in her male impersonation," which followed the tradition of Aida Overton Walker in her "That's Why They Call Me Shine" routine. Toward the end of that year, Aida Overton Walker herself died, only thirty-six years of age. After George Walker's death, she had made a successful career on her own, but ill health overtook her. Did Florence Mills ever see her? They were traveling the same circuits over the final years of Aida's life, one a big-name star, the other a struggling beginner. In later years people debated whether Florence Mills was the new Aida Overton Walker or whether there could ever be another. The most notable characteristic they shared was a remarkable versatility. There is no reliable record of their paths having crossed, but it is likely, at least, that Florence saw Aida perform.

Somewhere toward the end of 1914, Olivia decided to drop out of the act and settle down to private life. She was thirty years old by then. Florence soon teamed up with a new partner, Ethel Caldwell, professionally known as Kinky. Ethel Waters suggests there was a period when Caldwell was a member of the Mills Sisters with Olivia and Florence, in the same way Ethel herself had been a (nonsister) member of a group called the Hill Sisters. "Sister" acts that weren't real sisters were not uncommon. That may have been the intent for Florence and Kinky Caldwell. Their billing, however, usually dubbed them either Mills and Caldwell or Mills and Kinky. Ethel "Kinky" Caldwell was a seasoned vaudevillian, having been performing since at least 1909. At that time she was the singer with the Buddy Gilmore Trio, with Buddy as drummer and his wife, Mattie, as pianist. Buddy had been the sensational drummer of the Memphis Students, the band that gave the first documented concert of syncopated music, in 1905. He was famous later in Paris as a showman drummer.

Florence was now out in the wide world on her own, with neither mother nor elder sisters to supervise her. She was already a fairly seasoned performer. For the first time she was no longer the junior member of an act. The new partnership worked well, with Florence and Kinky forming a strong friendship. In May 1915 they played over the Dudley circuit, starting at the Howard in D.C., billed as Mills and Caldwell, with the Flying Kellers and the McKarvers, and then appearing at the Palace as Mills and Kinky. Next stop was Philadelphia at Gibson's New Standard, where they were described as "singing the blues to perfection." A week later they were back playing the Palace in D.C., followed by a week at the Dudley Theatre; the *Indianapolis*

Freeman urged theater bookers to take note that "Kinky and Mills, a new formed sister act, is kicking them out here . . . [these girls] have got the goods."[41]

By 1916, Florence was once again on her own, however. The team broke up in Chicago when Ethel Caldwell left to marry Joseph Clark Jr., a fellow entertainer, with whom she formed a double act. Florence decided to survey the Chicago scene while taking stock of where her career was headed.

Notes

1. Florence named Sam Adams as the comedian in an undated interview (probably 1925–1926) with P. L. Prattis. Notes from this conversation are in the Claude Barnett Collection, Chicago Historical Society. She also described these events in the article "Magic Moon That Brought Me Money," undated clipping, circa 1926, SCRAP, HAJC. The blackface performer is identified as singer Carl Anderson in "Burlesque and Vaudeville at the Bijou," *Washington Post*, Oct. 10, 1899, which also lists Sam Adams as a performer.

2. *New York Journal*, Nov. 5, 1927.

3. H. Swaffer, *London Daily Express* interview, reproduced in AMST, Aug. 10, 1927. There is no reason to doubt Swaffer's report that Florence told him one grandfather was white and the other a freed slave although I have been unable to verify this from any other source.

4. H. Swaffer, "London as It Looks," VAR, Dec. 29, 1926.

5. From this point forward, where Ulysses "Kid" Thompson is quoted without attribution, it is from the Delilah Jackson–Kid Thompson Interview Tapes (DJKT) in the Bill Egan Collection.

6. Beverley Nichols, *Sketch* magazine, London, Feb. 16, 1927.

7. Florence Mills, "Magic Moon That Brought Me Money," undated clipping, SCRAP, HAJC, 1926.

8. Robert Campbell, "Florence Mills' Life Story," PhTr, Nov. 17, 1927.

9. Virginia Wright, undated clipping, SCRAP, HAJC, c. 1943.

10. Dressing Room Club Programme, Moorland-Spingarn Collection, Howard University, Washington, D.C.

11. Mills, "Magic Moon That Brought Me Money."

12. For a description of the music of that era, see Thomas L. Riis, *Just before Jazz: Black Musical Theater in New York, 1890 to 1915* (Washington, D.C.: Smithsonian Institute Press, 1989).

13. Still functioning and known today as the Garnet-Patterson Junior High School. James W. Patterson was a U.S. senator who authored the law creating a system of public schools for black children in D.C. Henry Highland Garnet was a prominent abolitionist and ambassador to Liberia. (Courtesy Charles Sumner School Archives.)

14. *Washington Post*, Nov. 2, 1927.

15. ChDef, Dec. 19, 1925, 6.

16. Dressing Room Club Program. I have not been able to trace this *Washington Star* item for myself, but Florence's appearance in *The Sons of Ham* is well authenticated from numerous sources, including her own words.

17. Born Ada, she adopted the form Aida during her performing career. I have followed her version throughout.

18. *Toledo Blade*, Mar. 12, 1906.

19. Although Florence's link with Bonita is well documented, I have been unable either to find a contemporary report that names her as part of Bonita's act or to pin down a precise date. At some point Bonita married and teamed with Lew Hearn, another successful burlesque performer. Some reports, written long after, link Florence with Bonita and Hearn, but my research suggests that when Bonita was with Hearn, she no longer used picks in her act. The movements of Bonita and her picks can be traced through the columns of the *New York Clipper* for much of 1904 and 1905. The report of Florence's later-life meeting with Bonita is in an undated clipping (c. 1924?) from TC FLP.

20. For a good overview of the Gerry Society and its activities, see Benjamin McArthur, "Forbid Them Not: Child Actor Labor Laws and Political Activism in the Theatre," *Theatre Survey* 36:2, 63–80 (Nov. 1995).

21. Jervis Anderson, *Harlem: The Great Black Way 1900–1950* (London: Orbis Publishing, 1982), 49–56, documents the black "invasion" of Harlem and points to 1905 as a significant date.

22. Wright, HAJC. The article refers to the "Lyric Theater" but probably means the Lincoln.

23. Campbell, "Florence Mills' Life Story," *New York Evening Graphic*, Nov. 3, 1927.

24. Campbell, "Florence Mills' Life Story," PhTr, Dec. 15, 1927.

25. Alvin White, *Sepia*, Nov. 1977.

26. Jules Bledsoe, *New York Journal*, Nov. 5, 1927.

27. Tom Davin, "Conversations with James P. Johnson," in *Ragtime: Its History, Composers and Music*, ed. John Edward Hasse, 173 (New York: Schirmer Books, 1985).

28. McArthur, "Forbid Them Not."

29. NYA, June 30, 1910.

30. Campbell, "Florence Mills' Life Story," PhTr, Dec. 22, 1927.

31. Lester Walton, NYA, Nov. 23, 1911.

32. I am indebted to Frank Cullen (*Vaudeville Times*) and Armond Fields, great-nephew of Lew Fields, for information about *The Hen-Pecks* and Fields's hiring policies.

33. Notes from P. L. Prattis interview. Claude Barnett Collection, Chicago Historical Society.

34. Delilah Jackson; related to author from private conversation with Bricktop.

35. Richard Newman, "Florence Mills," in *Notable Black American Women*, ed. Jessie Carney Smith, 752–756 (Detroit: Gale Research, 1992); and HAJC, Notes to U. S. Thompson interviews by Dr. H. A. Johnson.

36. Ted Vincent, *Keep Cool, The Black Activists Who Built the Jazz Age* (London: Pluto Press, 1995), 57–62, has an excellent account of Dudley's career as a theatrical entrepreneur. See also Athelia Knight, "In Retrospect: Sherman H. Dudley," *Black Perspective in Music* 15: 2 (fall 1987), 152–181.

37. *Indianapolis Freeman*, May 17, 1913.

38. Perry Bradford, *Born with the Blues* (New York: Oak Publications, 1965), 170. Bradford suggests an earlier date. Their paths may have crossed in Philadelphia more than once, but there is clear evidence they shared the bill on this occasion. It's likely, writing many years later, his memory was at fault about the precise date.

39. Ethel Waters with Charles Samuels, *His Eye Is on the Sparrow* (New York: Doubleday, 1951), 77.

40. *Indianapolis Freeman*, May 30, 1914.

41. Their movements can be traced through the entertainment columns of the *Indianapolis Freeman*, ChDef, and PhTr during mid-1915.

~

CHAPTER TWO

Out in the World

Chicago Days and the Panama Club

Chicago in 1916 is just the right place for Florence to try a change of direction. She is no longer the child star or the juvenile of a group. Although only twenty, and even younger in appearance, she has already racked up more show business experience than many a veteran twice her age. She has honed her skills in the tough arena of Harlem's Lincoln Theatre and the black vaudeville circuits. Her early ability as a singer and dancer is now amplified and rounded by a mischievous talent for mimicry and pantomime. This versatility enables her to fit into any entertainment setting. Onstage she projects a lively extrovert image, but offstage she is unassertive and quiet in manner, although friendly. She is happy with her own company and enjoys reading. She prefers socializing with a few close friends rather than at public occasions. But those who get to know her find a quiet charm and friendly warmth. Performing is still second nature to her, but right now she is tired of the endless travel and poor pay in black vaudeville. Chicago offers a chance to try her luck in cabaret. The money might be better, and at least she will get to stay in one place for a time.

A thriving center for ragtime entertainers, Chicago was one of the throbbing focal points of the new jazz spreading northward rapidly from New Orleans. The conventional picture is that Chicago didn't become a major jazz center until 1918. In that year the U.S. Navy closed down New Orleans's Storyville red-light district, causing a mass exodus of newly unemployed musicians to Chicago, New York, and other northern cities. However, they merely swelled the flow of a migration that had been under way for some time. As jazz historian Rex Harris says, "The occasional movement northwards early in the twentieth century, in the general direction of Chicago, by some New Orleans jazz musicians became a flood in 1918, when the cabarets and sporting houses of the Delta City closed down."[1] Many New Orleans musicians already had a taste for moving north as a result of their experiences playing on the riverboats. The young Louis Armstrong would soon follow them.

New Orleans holds a special place as the birthplace of traditional jazz in its purest form. However, black music all over America had been evolving in a broadly similar direction for a long time. St. Louis, close neighbor of Chicago, holds a similar status in the pantheon of ragtime. Much of this music spilled over into Chicago in the early years of the century. In the words of ragtime historian Terry Waldo:

> Of all the musical centers in the Midwest, Chicago was probably the most active and diverse. . . . As the industrial focal point of the Midwest, Chicago attracted a great deal of talent and consequently produced a large volume of published music. Among the numerous musicians who did significant work in the city are Tony Jackson and Jelly Roll Morton from New Orleans; Louis Chauvin, Scott Joplin, and Arthur Marshall, from St. Louis; and New York's big ragtime star, Ben Harney.[2]

When Florence decided to try her luck in the Chicago scene, the South Side already had a reputation as a rip-roaring center of cross-racial fraternization and wide-open entertainment. Plentiful liquor and brilliant entertainment promoted easy sexual liaisons. A distinctive feature of the South Side was the jazz cabarets and cafes. During the first decade of the century, Tony Jackson and Jelly Roll Morton were featured acts in places like Dago & Russell's Café and The Elite No. 1 and No. 2.

In 1912 world heavyweight boxing champion Jack Johnson, hero to blacks and bête noire (literally and metaphorically) for many whites, established his Café de Champion on the South Side. It followed a definite "black and tan" policy, welcoming customers of all races. Johnson himself did not last long. By 1913 he had been forced to flee a trumped-up vice charge. By then, however, he had started a trend that other cafes and cabarets soon followed. The report of a commission investigating racial relations around 1917 paints a lewd picture of the practice:

> Lawless liquor, sensuous shimmy, solicitous sirens, wrangling waiters, all the tints of the racial rainbow, Black and tan and White, dancing, drinking,

singing, early Sunday morning at the Pekin cafe. . . . At one o'clock the place was crowded. Meanwhile a syncopating colored man had been vamping cotton field blues on the piano. A brown girl sang. . . . Black men with White girls, White men with yellow girls, old, young, all filled with the abandon brought about by illicit whiskey and liquor music.[3]

Florence's introduction to this wild and colorful world came at a similar venue, known as the Panama Café. Cabarets like the Panama and the Pekin were fashioned after European cafes and saloons. They had rich furniture and polished bars, lavish foods, and continuous entertainment. The upstairs café of the Panama had borders of green latticework mingled with pale and red autumn leaves descending from the ceiling. There was an awning-covered dancing area in the center, and inside windows, also shaded with awnings. Lighting of the latest contemporary design illuminated tables seating four, and stylish, silver-backed chairs. The show lasted from 8 p.m. till midnight. Entertainers moved around the tables, encouraging customers to spend big in return for their attentions. The Panama's customers were mostly white and generally good tippers.

How Florence got started at the Panama was a typical show business story of being in the right place at the right time. When she and Kinky broke up their act, Florence was staying at Thirty-first and State streets, a rooming house run by Gertie Jordan and popular among traveling black theatrical folk. Several of the Panama's performers, Ada "Bricktop" Smith, Cora Green, and Mattie Hite, were also staying there. Bricktop took an instant liking to the "eager, pleasant, young girl." When Florence asked whether Bricktop could help her get a cabaret job, Bricktop was keen to help.

The owner-manager of the Panama was a white man, Isadore Levine, known as Izzy. Despite his gruff personality, he had a high regard for Bricktop. However, she had trouble persuading him to take Florence on. He considered Florence too skinny, too small-voiced, and unskilled in the cabaret style of entertainment. Bricktop persisted, pointing to Florence's dancing skills, and he relented on condition that Bricktop coach Florence in singing and dancing from table to table. Always a quick learner, Florence mastered the art of playing to the clientele of the cabaret-style establishments as effectively as she had previously charmed the tough audience of Harlem's Nickellette theater.[4]

By the time Florence started there, the Panama was already coming in for its share of unfavorable publicity. In August 1916 Sylvester Russell had written in the *Freeman*, "The Panama buffet, cafe and cabaret was open again in full bloom, and the usual large number of waiters, musicians and entertainers were again assured a means of livelihood the same as others."[5] The reference to being "open again" referred to the Panama's closure after being "mentioned frequently in [State's Attorney] Hoyne's expose of vice and gambling in the 'black belt.'" At one point Izzy Levine was arrested, accused of paying a $1,000 bribe to have a closure revoked. Another closure occurred on March 6, 1916, because of a knifing incident, and the license was restored after five days. It was revoked again on July 11 on account of "immoral conditions" and restored on August 10.[6]

A possible clue to how the performers coped with the closures can be found in *Billboard*'s vaudeville listings for November and December 1915, which show engagements on the Pantages theater circuit at Winnipeg and Calgary for the Panama Girls. Examination of the local press for those centers at the time suggests that they didn't actually play these particular dates, but they may have played others around that time.[7]

The downstairs area of the Panama, where Florence got her start, featured a "quiet, reserved type of entertainment," in contrast with the raunchier upstairs. Fellow downstairs entertainers included Bricktop, Cora Green, Mattie Hite, and Nettie Compton, talented singers and dancers who had already established strong reputations in the region. Among the upstairs entertainers was Alberta Hunter. She had arrived in Chicago from Memphis about the time Jack Johnson started his club. At fifteen, passing for eighteen, she got her first job at Dago Frank's, a hangout for prostitutes and pimps. She worked her way up through cafes, cabarets, and clubs until she found a niche at the Panama Café. There she introduced W. C. Handy's "St. Louis Blues" in 1914.

Alberta related, "I was makin' seventeen-fifty a week—and that was money!" She went on to say, "The Panama had an upstairs and a downstairs— five girls and a piano player downstairs, and another five girls and a piano player upstairs." The musicians included piano player Glover Compton, Nettie's husband. "Everybody knew Glover Compton. He was doing the stuff that Willie 'The Lion' Smith did later on, you know, the big fat cigar hangin' out of the corner of his mouth and sittin' sideways at the piano talking to the people."[8] The trap drummer was Ollie Powers, noted also for his skills as a lyric tenor. Powers would later (1922) have his own band, which briefly included Louis Armstrong, at Dreamland. Louis loved Powers's singing and was a featured performer in the church at his funeral.

Jazz musician Milton "Mezz" Mezzrow recalled Florence at the Panama for her "grace and dignified, relaxed attitude." Petite and demure, she "just stood at easy and sang like a [hummingbird]."[9] The engagement at the Panama not only brought Florence a steady, well-paid job free from endless travel. It also brought a close friendship with Bricktop that was to last the rest of life. Bricktop's real name was Ada Beatrice Queen Victoria Louise Virginia Smith. All the neighbors had wanted to name her, and her mother, so as not to offend them, accepted all their suggestions. The future headliner was small, freckle-faced, and far from conventionally pretty. Her bright red hair was the inspiration for her nickname. Chicago born and bred, she had done her share of traveling the vaudeville circuits before returning to Chicago and getting a steady engagement at the Panama.

Summarizing her own assets at age sixteen, Bricktop commented, "Besides youth I had flaming red hair, a happy freckled face, and a pair of beautiful legs and feet. I could sing well enough to get by and there weren't many people who didn't agree that Ada Smith was a terrific natural dancer."[10] She left out her single biggest asset, an engaging, good-natured personality that would earn her friends all over the world and eventually make her the toast of European aristocracy at her famous club in Paris during the 1920s and 1930s. She had a personality that made people trust her judgment. Time and again she was able to persuade managers and promoters to help her deserving friends. Florence was one of the earliest beneficiaries. Later ones would include the young Duke Ellington.

Florence was serving a long, hard apprenticeship that would stand her in good stead in later years. Before long, she, Bricktop, and Cora Green formed the Panama Trio. Initially it was a quartet, with Mattie Hite, but Hite soon dropped out to seek more money in New York, where she and Cora Green had worked at Barron Wilkins's club in 1914. The new trio worked well together. "We were singing harmony and dancing together long before the Boswell Sisters became big stars," said Bricktop. "When the three of us were out on the floor we really kept the audience applauding and asking for more."[11] Alberta Hunter described their individual styles. "Cora Green was 'nice' and had an 'in-between voice,' between sweet and jazz. . . . Brick couldn't sing. She talked most of her songs. But, boy, could she dance awhile. . . . Florence Mills was a smash hit whether she was singing sweet as a nightingale or impersonating men onstage."[12]

The Panama Trio quickly became a popular act on the local scene, so popular, in fact, that one astute businessman recognized their commercial advertising potential. Claude A. Barnett, one of the most enterprising and interesting black men of his era, selected the girls as ideal models for his Kashmir cosmetics line. Barnett was a graduate of Booker T. Washington's Tuskegee Institute. Frustrated with the limited opportunities for an educated black man, he teamed with some entrepreneurial friends to set up the Kashmir Chemical Company. They marketed high-quality cosmetics and hair preparations specially developed for black women.

Barnett had noted that established products in the field, such as Madame C. J. Walker's hair straightener, showed ugly hair to promote their benefits. He chose the opposite approach, associating Kashmir products with "beautifully

turned out Negro women and elegant males in exquisitely proper surroundings." The name Kashmir was intended to evoke images of elegant dark-
skinned women from the mystic East. To promote the product, Barnett
searched far and wide for beautiful black women to feature in advertisements
and brochures. His keen eye soon fell on the popular Panama Trio. He featured
them in several brochures, describing them as "Chicago's favorite cabaret entertainers."[13] Years later Barnett was proud that he had used as models the three
popular local entertainers, who each went on to become famous in her own
right.

The Panama was a popular drop-in spot for entertainers passing through
on the vaudeville circuits. One who used to look in was Bill Robinson. He
took a liking to the three girls. By late 1916 he had established himself on
the prestigious, mostly white Keith circuit as the great Bojangles. Bojangles
was a complex mixture of charm and arrogance. To the people and causes he
espoused he could be extraordinarily generous while to those who displeased
him he could be most unpleasant, physically as well as verbally. He was
known to carry a gun, which added menace to his image.

Florence and her partners were definitely among those he favored. One
night Bojangles complimented the girls on their act and told them he would
send someone to see them. They were delighted with such a compliment
from one of the greatest names in black show business. They wondered who
he might send. As evenings went by and they heard nothing, the memory
faded. A couple came in late in the show one evening. Business was otherwise slow, and the trio went through the motions in a desultory fashion. Later
it turned out the man had been the head of the Keith circuit, and the woman
was Eva Tanguay, vaudeville's famous "I Don't Care" girl. The next day an
irate Bojangles gave the Panama Trio a tongue-lashing for their unprofes-
sionalism. Bricktop decided that forever after, "I don't care if there is just one
person out in the room or at the bar, you go out and do your best. You never
know."[14]

The incident did not lessen Bojangles's affection for Florence. They were
close friends for the rest of her life. During this time they worked intensely
together to perfect Florence's tap dancing skills. Using the rooftop of Gertie
Jordan's boardinghouse as their impromptu stage, they practiced routines before and after breakfast. In her later years of fame, Florence would give Bojangles credit for developing her skills. Years later he would cite "teaching
the young and unknown Florence Mills dance steps on the roof of 3028 S.
State Street, Chicago" as one of the highlights of his life.[15]

Despite the hard work, the time at the Panama was relatively happy for
Florence. She had a steady job in partnership with two likable companions,

and their act was popular. Their friendship is illustrated by an incident that occurred one hot night when they were taking a break between sets. Cora Green thought she heard a noise in a nearby garbage can. On examination they found a newborn baby in a shoebox. Cora rocked it while Bricktop raised the alarm. The police arrived and collected the baby. For the rest of that evening, the three girls discussed trying to get the baby for themselves. After all, if nobody wanted it, why shouldn't they look after it with nice baby clothes and a crib to put it in? Eventually they realized that they didn't know anything about looking after a baby, and it would probably be better off where it was going. "But," Bricktop concluded, "it gave each of us a warm and tender feeling to think about taking care of a little breath of new life that someone had discarded along with the rest of the day's trash."[16]

There was a darker side to life at the Panama. The racial openness of the South Side lent itself to incidents that could be exploited by politicians looking for excuses to crack down on the area. Much of the trouble came from southern whites' "slumming." Around mid-November 1916, Sylvester Russell's *Freeman* column noted the need "for the police department to keep an eye on low southern white men who come to Chicago to inhabit the [colored] district of the South Side. They do a lot of harm for both white and colored when they assert themselves."

Another problem the performers had to deal with was grenades. This was the slang name for a note reading something like, "Call me at such and such a number." White women with a fascination for black men would ask waiters or performers to pass the note to their preferred target. The South Side cabarets and cafes offered the only favorable scene for such liaisons. While some of the Panama performers were willing to pass grenades, Bricktop refused to join in. She described an incident when a white woman's white male escort found a grenade passed by another Panama entertainer that had fallen from his companion's bag. The unpleasant incident resulted in the entertainer's losing her job.

Florence would have run a mile before getting involved in such activities, and not just because of her innate shyness. Throughout her life she evinced a strong preference for mixing with her own people. The kind of liaisons across the racial line that were popular at the Panama held no attraction for her. Not that she shunned socializing with white people; her early childhood experiences had given her an easy familiarity with whites that many African Americans of her generation would never know. In fact, one of the Panama Trio's favorite pastimes was to meet with three white male singers performing nearby for impromptu harmonizing sessions. These informal practices were very much a matter of shared professional interest and love of music, however.

When the cabarets closed at 1 a.m., the sextet would spend the night wandering around the after-hours "buffet flats" that were a feature of the Chicago scene. These were private apartments where watered-down illicit drinks were available at extortionate prices in return for space to socialize. In Bricktop's words, "There was no hanky panky. . . . We really paid for a place to get together where we could sit around and harmonize."[17] The three boys were the team of Benny Fields, a blues singer; Benny Davis, later a well-known songwriter ("Margie," "Carolina Moon"); and Jack Salisbury. The male trio would soon give Shelton Brooks's hit tune "Darktown Strutters' Ball" its first performance in vaudeville, which led to its sensational recording by the Original Dixieland Jazz Band in 1917.[18]

Inevitably, given its lawless image, serious trouble eventually came to the Panama Café. In late December 1916, Sylvester Russell reported the threesome still playing there. "The cabarets have a merry program for the holidays. The bill at the Panama includes Ada (Brick) Smith, Cora Green, Corinne Bowen, Florence Mills, and "Snow" Glads Fisher, downstairs. Upstairs has Goldie Crosby, Twinkle Davis, Mamie Carter, Nellie Carr, and Alberta Hunter." However, by early 1917 the police had closed the Panama. A local character known as "Curley" got into a fight with another man at the bar, and a man was stabbed to death. Both men were employees of the Café, but the local authorities had been looking for an excuse to close the Panama. Now they had found it. The *Defender* commented cryptically, "The killing last Friday was given as the cause but those familiar with the situation knew different." On January 30, Police Chief Schuettler revoked the Panama's license for the final time.[19]

Once again Florence was out of a job, but at least she was unemployed in good company. For her and Cora Green, the answer was simple—back to good old vaudeville. Bricktop, less enthusiastic, went along with the idea for a while. They got a booking quickly at the Grand Theatre on Thirty-first and State streets, right on the site of the house Bricktop had grown up in. Her mother came to see her and proudly show off her daughter to the neighbors.

While the Trio was playing the Grand, it was also the venue for a two-week season by the well-known black theatrical group the Smart Set. It performed a musical comedy called *How Newtown Prepared*, with a cast of forty. (The Smart Set was the same troupe that Aida Overton Walker had been performing with at the time of her death a few years earlier.) It was billed as "America's greatest colored show" and led by veterans Salem Tutt Whitney and J. Homer Tutt, and the *Defender* hailed its visit as "of a classy order." The Panama Trio alternated with the Smart Set for part of the week. In the same review the *Chicago Defender* noted, "The Panama Trio, a clever cabaret of-

fering, created a great impression. The three girls are well known and popular locally, and as a consequence they can be said to be greatly responsible for
the crowded houses of the half. They were billed as Cora, Brick and Florence
and made good."

By now, however, Bricktop had realized that her true niche was in the intimate setting of cabarets and saloons. She was finding the theater alien, with
its dark rows of anonymous faces. She left the trio and by May of 1917 was
in Los Angeles seeking new horizons.

By this time Florence's multifaceted talent had attracted attention from
managers and promoters around the black circuits. She was recruited to join
a highly successful group called the Tennessee Ten, a major turning point in
her career.

Florence, Kid, and the Tennessee Ten

Florence joined the Tennessee Ten sometime early in 1917. The invitation
to join came through one of the group's founding members, Jesse A. Shipp.
A father figure of black entertainment, Shipp had been a coauthor of several
Williams and Walker shows and had traveled to England with In Dahomey in
1903. His many show business activities included having at times "owned"
several vaudeville acts, among them the Mills Sisters. Although he may have
been a performer when it started, Shipp had retired from active participation
in the Tennessee Ten by the time Florence joined.

The Tennessee Ten was one of a stable of acts owned and managed by
Ralph Dunbar of Chicago and promoted through a leading agent, Harry
Webber. Dunbar's other acts included the Salon Singers, Maryland Singers,
Bell Ringers, and Ding-Dong Five. The Ten comprised eight men and two
women. They played the better-class burlesque theaters on the Keith circuit.
The ten people included a full jazz band, described by Marshall and Jean
Stearns as "in part from Johnson's Creole Band."[20] The Creole Band, with
trumpeter Freddie Keppard, was one of the most famous early jazz bands.
Robert Johnson, the Ten's guitar player, was the brother of Bill Johnson, the
founder-manager of the Creole Band. Both had been members in 1908 of a
predecessor group, the Big Four String Band of Biloxi.[21]

The personnel of the Tennessee Ten varied over time. In 1917 it had Florence Mills (prima donna), Lulu Walton (soubrette), H. Qualli Clark (manager and cornetist), Kid Thompson (dancing director), Earl Walton (violin),
Blaine Gatten (clarinet), John Moberley (trombone), John Turner (banjo),
Young Killaire (drums), and Edward "Ed" Garland (bass). By February 1921
it had Kid Thompson (cornet), Florence Mills (prima donna), Hilaria Friend

(soubrette), John Moberley (trombone and manager), Thomas Morris (cornet), John Warren (bass), Robert Johnson (guitar), J. A. O'Bryant (clarinet), Freddie Johnson (drums), and Hugh Turner (saxophone).

Several of these names will be familiar to devotees of jazz. Thomas Morris made many records in the 1920s under his own name (Morris's Hot Babies and Morris's Past Jazz Masters) as well as with famous names like Fats Waller and Clarence Williams. J. A. "Jimmy" O'Bryant is perhaps best known for his accompaniments on Ida Cox's records. New Orleans–born Ed Garland played and recorded with many of the big names in jazz, including Freddy Keppard, King Oliver, Kid Ory, and Bunk Johnson. H. Qualli Clark was the composer of the jazz standard "Shake It and Break It." Other notable jazz musicians who passed through the group's ranks at one time or another included drummer Curtis Mosby, trumpeter Gus Aiken, and saxophonist Horace Eubanks. The presence of musicians like Morris, Garland, Eubanks, O'Bryant, Mosby, Aiken, and Clark shows that the jazz band tag was no idle boast. Quite a few capable early jazz bands that worked within the theater environment were never recorded and hence are largely unacknowledged in jazz history.

The Tennessee Ten's routine, originally written by Jesse Shipp, opened with the traditional plantation scene. Florence, as the prima donna, sang "Darling Nellie Gray," followed by the entire company doing a cakewalk to "Waiting for the Robert E. Lee." Then the jazz band marched onstage. The leader of the jazz band was the handsome, talented Ulysses "Slow Kid" Thompson. Although nominally a musician, he was really a dancing, clowning conductor billed as "The Black Sousa." The band, conducted by Thompson, "blundered into a comedy rehearsal. 'Getting the band to tune up was the problem.' After a lot of fussing conductor Thompson brought down his baton. 'The band would hit a horrible chord,' says Thompson, 'and I would do a front somersault as if I was surprised out of my skin.'"[22]

For Florence the Tennessee Ten was a whole new world. They were playing the prestigious Keith circuit in more fancy theaters than she had previously experienced. She was also now a member of a large team, a small community in its own right. As the prima donna she had a major featured role that challenged her singing and dancing skills. Most important of all, though, was the presence of the dancing conductor, Kid Thompson. Here was someone who could match her own skills at acrobatic dancing and even teach her a thing or two, as well as grip an audience's attention with his humorous antics. It was love at first sight, professionally and personally. Florence had found her ideal partner.

Ulysses S. "Slow Kid" Thompson was born in Prescott, Arkansas, on August 28, 1888, to George Washington Thompson and Hannah Pandora Driver. He was christened simply Ulysses. An aunt who was also his schoolteacher added the "S" later because the other children couldn't manage Ulysses, and in this way he became U. S. Thompson.[23] His mother died of typhoid when he was seven years of age. At age fourteen he left home to fend for himself. He had already developed entertainer skills while dancing on the street for nickels and dimes. He worked in various manual jobs: in a sawmill, a brickyard, a steelyard, and a rock quarry and as a grocery delivery boy.

His dancing skills got him a job helping a "high-pitch" doctor whose "pitch" was selling patent medicines on the streets. Kid Thompson's job was to dance, sing, and tell jokes to attract a crowd so the doctor could make his pitch and sell his brew. Medicine shows, common then, were a good source of work for black entertainers, giving them the opportunity to develop professional skills. Thompson claimed the medicines were mostly alcohol. Jazz historians Marshall and Jean Stearns recount that Jelly Roll Morton was run out of town for selling a mixture of salt and Coca-Cola as a cure for consumption. They quote comedian Pigmeat Markham, later famous as "The Judge" in television's *Laugh In*, as saying "It wasn't nothing but Epsom Salts and coloring."[24]

In 1904, at age sixteen, U. S. Thompson discovered the world of carnivals and circuses. For several years he followed the big top to earn his living. Carnivals and circuses usually had a "plantation" that featured fast-paced black entertainment, an ideal setting for someone with his experience. Among the circuses he worked with were Mighty Hagg, Sells-Floto, Hagenback & Wallace, and Ringling Brothers. He also worked in a host of other stock shows, medicine shows, and animal shows.

Besides his brilliant natural talent for dance, he could play music reasonably on several instruments. He would also clown in a style he described as hokum, fooling around and telling a few jokes. Following the circuses in summer, he had gravitated by 1912 to vaudeville during the winter season. There he earned the nickname "Slow Kid" by a remarkable slow-motion dance he performed (although he could also do fast tap and acrobatic routines). A contemporary description of his act in 1912 ran, "Unlike his name, he is not slow. The fact is, he is the fastest slow man you ever saw. He tells a few jokes that are old and new, but the way he tells them he gets the laughs. He finishes his act with a song and a dance—and what I mean, he dances. Unlike other dancers his dance is of a comedy nature that brings plenty of laughs and applause from the audience." The medicine wagon and sideshow experience are obviously reflected in this description: Grab your audience's attention quickly or lose it.[25]

The attraction between Florence and Kid Thompson was mutual. He may even have had a hand in recruiting her for the Tennessee Ten. He was familiar with her work as their paths had crossed previously. As early as 1913, when the Mills Sisters were playing the Dudley circuit, he had been playing similar bills around Chicago and Indianapolis. In June 1914 they played the New Monogram in Chicago within a week or two of each other.

The path of new love was not destined to run smoothly for Florence. Although living singly, Kid Thompson was in fact legally married. In August 1913 the *Indianapolis Freeman* had carried a brief item: "U. S. Thompson (Slow Kid) pulled off a surprise. He married the pretty Letepha Rogers a few days ago. The former Miss Rogers is well known to the stage patrons at the Crown Gardens. Indianapolis will remember her as the lady who danced with a lighted lamp on her head."

The marriage had been in trouble from the start. Letepha Rogers was a light skinned black girl born and raised in Indianapolis. She had "passed" for white, doing a Spanish dance, while married to a white man who was, in Thompson's words, a "liquor head" and who had died not long after the marriage.[26] By the time she married Kid Thompson, she was on the black vaudeville circuit. He had assumed they would travel together in the same shows. However, "She and I got married in Indianapolis on a Monday, and we didn't see each other no more until November; she went with the show she was with, I went with the show I was with."

By then Kid Thompson was building a strong reputation in the Chicago and Indianapolis vaudeville scenes. In December 1913 the *Freeman's* theatrical pages carried a write-up on him with a photo. "Slow Kid has seen all kinds of comedian service. In the summer he is a showman comedian, following the white tops to wherever they light. In the winter he hikes to the vaudeville field, where he continues to make them laugh. Thompson is coming up in his work which is that of the all round comedian. His droll style of monologue gets 'em. His eccentric dancing is his strongest card."

By early 1915, it was clear all was not well with the Thompson-Rogers marriage. Following another favorable write-up of Kid Thompson's appearances, the *Freeman's* "Annual Review of the Stage" for 1914 adds, "His pretty wife is generally in a different show, a thing he does not like very much." Even after their reunion in November, Kid's expectation that they would follow the circuit together was not to be realized. He and Letepha set up housekeeping together in a flat on Wabash Avenue in Chicago. They brought her mother from Indianapolis to live with them. Letepha's mother became ill and died shortly after. Kid's stage career continued to prosper, but his wife, in his words, "went to pieces," meaning she lost her nerve for performing. He persuaded her to enroll in a hairdressing and manicure course, but she became ill and never completed it.

In 1916 Kid Thompson joined the Tennessee Ten and was never again out of work. His already rocky marriage deteriorated even further with his absences on the road. It was well and truly on the rocks when Florence joined the act. By then he had learned his lesson about partners who could not share an itinerant show business lifestyle, but his still-legal marriage was sure to cast a shadow over any new relationship he formed. Although the Tennessee Ten was highly successful, the touring life was no bed of roses for the performers. "They kept it working all the time," Kid recalled. "Didn't pay big salaries in those days, but it worked all the time. Of course, we had to break some time in the summer to let us off for a while, go home and rest." Jazz was still very much a novelty for white audiences between 1916 and 1920, and that fact probably helped to increase the group's success.

Veteran comedian Billy King described the rivalry between the two theater-based jazz bands, the Tennessee Ten and the Creole Band, as "The first jazz invasion in America."[27] At one of their 1917 appearances, at Chicago's Majestic theater, the wildly enthusiastic audience compelled the members of the Ten to walk individually across the stage as each received a rousing standing ovation. Such a demonstration of appreciation was unprecedented for a black act in that theater and at that time.

Their highest-profile engagement came in May 1917 when they were engaged as part of a colored supporting troupe for the legendary vaudeville star Nora Bayes. Bayes had been the star of the *Ziegfeld Follies* in 1909 and by 1917 was one of the biggest names in the business. Cocomposer with husband Jack Norworth of "Shine on Harvest Moon," she had tremendous talent for dramatizing a song and pleasing an audience. She was also shrewd enough to know the value of lively black singing and dancing to showcase her own efforts. "I have surrounded myself with aides who won't interfere with my holding the centre of the stage as long as the audience will let me," she said, announcing her planned appearance in *The Songs You Love* at the Thirty Ninth Street Theatre. The show opened with a plantation scene, and the first half closed with the cakewalk, obvious opportunities for Florence to strut her stuff. There were also Wild West, oriental, and Hawaiian scenes. The advertisements proudly trumpeted the presence of a jazz band. This was one of the early uses of the word *jazz* in public media, especially with "zz" rather than the early usage "*jass.*"

The show started the day after the United States entered the First World War and ran for three weeks. The New York *Age* reported that "[Miss Bayes] has a company of forty people, three quarters of which are colored. Ralph Dunbar's Tennessee Ten, the best colored act that has appeared on the vaudeville stage in a score of years is now part of the Bayes Company. The

Tennessee Ten dance and sing and have a jazz band that is the best of its kind that has ever appeared on the stage."[28] Lester A. Walton, experienced ob-server of the black entertainment scene, also waxed lyrical over the show in its entirety and wrote in highly complimentary terms about the Ten. "The Tennessee Ten has been making a big hit in vaudeville and Miss Bayes has played a trump card in corralling this energetic and clever bunch. They can sing, dance, create merriment and, what's more, carry a jazz band that is some more jazz band. I'll wager it can out-jazz any jazz band in these parts, and pro-duce a "director" who can outdance any director when it comes to eccentric stuff."[29]

Walton concluded, "There is also a little girl who sings in the first scene of Part I, who must remind even Miss Bayes that she is not the only warbler at large." The dancing director was Kid Thompson, but it is not difficult, with the gift of hindsight, to realize that "the little warbler" was none other than Florence Mills. She would continue to attract similar anonymous at-tention for some years before eventually achieving fame under her own name. Whether Walton realized this was the same Florence Mills whose name he had once predicted would be "in big type" is not clear.

By the time the Nora Bayes show finished, Florence was beginning to find new status back home in Harlem. Her new higher profile brought her a side engagement from the Tennessee Ten in June 1917 when she was listed on the bill of fare at Mrs. Downs's Lincoln (Nickellette) Theatre as "Florence Mills, Harlem's dainty, sweet singer." She was a support feature for a musical com-edy show. Florence had returned to her home turf in Harlem, billed for the first time as a single under her own name.[30]

The favorable attention from the Nora Bayes show ensured the Ten would not be short of bookings. In July and August the group played an ex-tended engagement at one of Chicago's leading cabarets before continuing on the Keith circuit to good reviews. Sometimes the ten would supplement their earnings with engagements in addition to their regular vaudeville bookings. Kid Thompson recalled, "When we first hit New York, we were such a hit. We were then at Reisenweber's, the big night club down on Fifty-ninth Street." One of their support musicians for these occasional stints was the great jazz piano player and composer Luckey Roberts, composer of "Moonlight Cocktail" and "Spanish Venus." He was considered the founder of the Harlem "stride" piano style.[31] When Kid Thompson mentioned their early collaboration to Delilah Jackson, she said, "I didn't know you played with Luckey Roberts." Kid corrected her with great dignity: "Luckey worked with me." Luckey Roberts became a loyal, lifelong friend to Florence and her family.

Even with a successful group, it was still a stressful life. In those days, black performers on the road kept in contact with friends and family through the Mail Wagon service offered by the *Chicago Defender*. Mail for performers was sent care of the *Defender* and stored at the famous Roll Top Desk that entertainment columnist Tony Langton proclaimed as his headquarters, until it was collected or could be forwarded. Florence's name featured frequently during 1918 as one of a long list of such mail recipients. A February report noting the members of the Ten being entertained by a local citizen during a Denver engagement also commented, "The work of Florence Mills and the Slow Kid [is] a real riot." This was the first time the names of Florence and Kid were linked in print. The *Defender* had scented the blossoming romance. However, there were still obstacles in its path. Kid was still legally married to Letepha and was sending some of his earnings to support their joint household in Chicago.

There was worse to come. The United States had entered the First World War on April 6, 1917. By 1918 many young men were receiving draft notices to serve Uncle Sam in foreign climes. One of those to receive the call was Kid Thompson. A week after the report publicly linking Kid and Florence, he was noted as "soon to join his battalion." Kid had no desire to interrupt his newfound success in the Tennessee Ten, or to leave his new romance, by joining the army. His best chance of exemption was his marital status. However Letepha, who had previously refused to join him in New York, and who now also had a lover of her own, a dining-car waiter, refused to sign any papers for this purpose. She had picked up on the rumors about Florence and was jealous. Bluffing, Kid told her he would rather go to jail than be shot by the Germans. She was unmoved. Finally, he told her to send him half the money he had sent her while on the road. She responded, "Oh no, the money you sent home is my money. You spent yours on the road."[32] So he found himself, to Florence's distress, with no choice but to accept his call-up gracefully.

America in 1917–1918 was a hotbed of racial tension. Apart from occasional serious race riots, a continuous pattern of lynchings and other brutal atrocities intimidated the African American population. America's entry into the war created a dilemma for both sides of the racial debate. For the government and the military, the able-bodied African American population was an important source of manpower. Whether it should be managed in a segregated or an integrated fashion presented thorny issues. African Americans were equally perplexed over whether to fight for their oppressors and, if they did, whether they would reap a reward of gratitude and better treatment.

In the African American community, Reverend Adam Clayton Powell, father of the later famous member of Congress, urged that they not cooperate with the war effort overseas unless some firm guarantees of protection of their lives and rights were forthcoming. Even stronger in opposition were socialists like A. Philip Randolph, editor of the *Messenger*. W. E. B. DuBois expressed the more common view in an editorial in *Crisis* called "Close Ranks," which urged them to "forget all special grievances." Many African American people shared the mood of patriotism sweeping America and were optimistic that participation in the war would be effective in convincing whites of their essential humanity and right to fair treatment.

The attitude of the government and the military to their African American troops was, at best, distinctly ambivalent. Opportunities for black officers to advance beyond junior ranks were very limited. Most of the troops went into labor and stevedoring battalions, which offered much hard work and little opportunity for whatever imagined glory war might offer. In addition, they were often under the command of southern white officers who, as a common expression put it, "knew how to deal with Negroes." Despite such tensions, something like 400,000 African Americans served in the U.S. armed forces during the war. Of these about 200,000 went overseas, and about 50,000 saw combat duty. The combat troops, in the 369th, 370th, 371st, and 372nd regiments, were very highly regarded by the French troops they fought alongside. They earned many individual and group honors, as well as the first two Croix de Guerre awarded to American soldiers by the French.[33]

The 369th Regiment, fondly dubbed the "Harlem Hellfighters," has another claim to fame. Its orchestra leader was the great James Reese Europe, and its drum major was Sergeant Noble Sissle. This regimental orchestra was the first band to introduce jazz to European ears. It caused great puzzlement among French military musicians, who thought the strange sounds produced by the black musicians were due to some peculiarity of their instruments. When the French borrowed the instruments, they found they could not produce the same sounds.

Whatever the tensions of the time, Kid Thompson took the call-up in stride, viewing it as a new adventure. He and Florence continued performing with the Tennessee Ten while waiting for his directions to present himself at a training camp.

In January the whole troupe was greeted with dinners, luncheons, sightseeing parties, and buffet breakfasts when they played Los Angeles. This engagement gave Florence and Kid a chance to meet up again with West Coast–based Chicago friends, including Cora Green and Bricktop from the Panama Café and Carolyn Williams, who had performed nearby at the Elite

No. 1 along with Tony Jackson and Jelly Roll Morton. This is also one of several candidate opportunities for the reported occasion when Jelly Roll Morton played with the Panama girls.

By late February the Ten were playing Des Moines, Iowa, and Lulu Walton reported that she and Florence were busy knitting for the black troops heading off to war and had already finished scarves, wristlets, and socks. She declared their readiness to go to Europe to support the troops. She quoted Florence, no doubt mindful of her own man's imminent departure, as "willing to go if it was just to hold their hands."[34]

The act revisited Chicago, playing the Majestic Theatre in late March, and the *Defender* ran an article with a photo about Kid and his career. It wasn't till late April that he finally had to present himself at Camp Grant, Illinois. He assured journalist Langton at the *Defender's* "Roll Top Desk" that "He was happy at the prospects which the future holds out to him and that he will make it hot for the notorious 'Beast of Berlin' when he gets 'Over There.' If he doesn't get a chance to operate on the Kaiser with his 'Gatt' he will put on some make-up and make the Mad Dog of Europe laugh himself to death."

While Kid joined the 15th Company of the 161st Infantry, the Tennessee Ten continued touring with a new comedian, Phillip Gyles. By early August Kid Thompson was in France. He had written to the *Defender* advising his address care of the 366th Infantry Regiment. The Mail Wagon on that same day noted a letter waiting for Florence Mills, obviously from him. With Florence touring and Kid's army movements unpredictable, the Mail Wagon was their main link while he was away. His occasional letters to Langton were short and to the point, consisting of assurances of good health, best wishes, and an appeal for feedback.

Although not in a combat regiment, Kid escaped the more mundane life of a laboring, stevedoring regiment by virtue of his talents as a musician and entertainer. "I was a clown drummer," he said; "I used to do all the stuff, throw sticks up and catch 'em in time, you know. They had an army band. They gave a concert for the soldiers. They had a big circle, and I used to get in the circle and dance and bounce around and all that stuff. I got three other boys and went in the hospital and entertained—didn't have no USO shows in those days." Although the war ended in November 1918, many troops had to wait a long time before they could return to the United States and be demobilized.

When Kid went off to France, the Tennessee Ten lost its appeal for Florence. Soon the idea of re-forming the Panama Trio was raised. Bricktop was still intent on following her own star and preferred to stay on the West Coast, working in San Francisco and Vancouver. Bricktop's replacement was a girl named Carolyn Williams, also known as Carolyn Lillison and Carolyn Boyd. Carolyn was no stranger to the other two girls, having been a regular feature just a few blocks up State Street at Teenan Jones's Elite No. 1 and 2 cafes, which also featured Tony Jackson and Jelly Roll Morton.[35] Exactly when the new Panama Trio formed is not clear. Details of their whereabouts for the middle part of 1918 (April to October) are hard to pin down. Shep Allen, who had worked in a managerial capacity at the Panama Café, suggests that they regrouped in Los Angeles, with Allen as their manager. He described them playing at the Cadillac Café, on Los Angeles's famed Central Avenue, with Jelly Roll Morton as their solo accompanist.[36]

By November the Panama Trio was back in Chicago, working the vaudeville circuits. At first, rather than working as an act on their own, they joined a group known as the Bob Russell Stock Company. Bob Russell was a veteran producer whose stock company was in its third incarnation, having previously been part of the "Russell-Owens-Brooks Stock Company" (1903–1910), then the "Russell-Owens Stock Company" (1911–1918). It was originally based in the Pekin Theatre, in Savannah, touring widely from there.

The show had a first half presenting a comedy drama with music and a second half featuring a straight cabaret with the Panama Trio. The trio spent a large part of 1918 touring the South with the Russell Stock Company in a show called *The Charming Widow*. There is a report that Florence played the lead for some of the time although the popular "Smart Set" veteran Blanche Thompson normally played that role.[37] By November 1918 the company was back in Chicago and featured at the Grand Theatre. The drama portion that week was a "military comedy drama," *The Colored Volunteer*, followed the second week by *The Charming Widow*. Tony Langston's review in the *Defender* was favorable to the drama and lavish in its praise of the Panama girls' last-half cabaret presentation. It was "A cabaret offering extraordinary" and "a classy and fast-working piece of entertainment."[38]

The most interesting feature of the occasion was their billing as the Panama Four. The legendary Tony Jackson made up the fourth as their accompanist. One of the few existing photographs of Tony Jackson, a faded shot with Tony at the piano and the remarkably young-looking trio sitting on top of it, their hair neatly tied with long bows, comes from this period. Tony Jackson was one of the era's greatest composers and players. He was also one of the very few musicians Jelly Roll Morton acknowledged as a superior.[39]

Tony Jackson is remembered today only as the composer of "Pretty Baby," the big song hit of the previous season, and a handful of ragtime pieces. He steadfastly refused to sell his music for less than he considered its worth.

Asked once why none of his ragtime pieces were published, he replied that he would rather burn them than sell them for five dollars apiece. His peers in his hometown of New Orleans recognized him as the doyen of piano players. By the time he settled in Chicago (where he spent the rest of his life), he had established a reputation as possibly "the world's greatest single-handed entertainer." An always dapper little man, he had mastered all forms of music, so he could cope with any request. The Panama Trio could hardly have wished for a better accompanist.[40] From the picture it looks as if they enjoyed playing alongside Tony.

By early 1919 they were back on the traditional vaudeville circuit. Described as "the best singing girls in the business," they were playing the Empress Theatre in Omaha, Nebraska. They had contracts for the next eight months. May and June 1919 saw them back in Chicago again at McVicker's and the Grand Theatre. The *Defender* headline proclaimed, "Panama Three Makes Hit at Grand," describing them as "the best 'girl' act in vaudeville." It was about this time that Kid Thompson arrived back in the United States, a civilian again. The African American troops came home proudly from the war. The Fighting 369th returned to a magnificent parade up Fifth Avenue in New York. However, the optimism with which many had enlisted soon evaporated. It became obvious that nothing much had changed on the race-relations front. The year 1919 was a bad one for race riots. Lynchings were the highest, at eighty-three, since 1904. Some riots turned into virtual race wars as returned servicemen asserted their new sense of independence.

On his return Kid Thompson went first to Hot Springs, Arkansas, to visit relatives for a few weeks but was soon in the *Defender* office predicting an early return to vaudeville. Within a month he was back on the circuit with a new partner, Jimmy Marshall, playing Chicago and Detroit.[41] Florence still had obligations to her present partners, so she and Kid could not immediately get together. Kid's overseas absence had an important side effect. On his return he found Letepha had "got mixed up with some man," presumably the same Pullman porter, and "she had broken up housekeeping." This development made Kid feel he was on the way to being a free man at last.

Although the race-relations scene was depressing for blacks in 1919, those involved in show business saw a brighter side: The postwar euphoria led to a big demand for black entertainment. The so-called Jazz Age was beginning to emerge, and the Harlem Renaissance was in gestation. On May 13, 1919, the *New York Age* wrote, "Since the return of colored bands from France to these shores the country simply has gone wild about jazz music. It is as much the rage in all sections as the spring styles and there is every reason to believe that its popularity will increase rather than diminish in the near future." There was a feeling of optimism among black entertainers that something like the golden age of Williams and Walker and Cole and Johnson might be about to arrive again.

The week after the Panama Trio returned to the Grand in Chicago, Kid Thompson and his partner Jimmy Marshall, billed as the Jazzerinos, also played there to good reviews.[42] The closeness of the two engagements enabled Florence and Kid to get together again briefly. However, Marshall and Thompson soon left for New York, so the togetherness did not last long. On June 14 the *Defender* reported the Panama Trio would soon be a featured act on the prestigious Pantages circuit, a major white vaudeville circuit owned by Greek entrepreneur Alexander Pantages. Pantages had bought his first theater, in Seattle, Washington, in 1902 with the proceeds of gold mining in the Klondike. He eventually built up a chain of sixty theaters or movie palaces up and down the West Coast, featuring hit movies and the best musical comedy acts. Alexander Pantages was liberal in his approach to hiring black acts. He had launched the vaudeville career of the Creole Band when he saw them providing entertainment between bouts at a heavyweight prizefight in Los Angeles in 1914. He reputedly had a soft spot for Florence Mills. As we saw previously, the Panama Girls may have previously played occasional short engagements on his circuit locally in the Midwest. The proposed six-month tour on his circuit would see the three girls traveling with a road show on a trip to the Coast and back.

Notes

1. Rex Harris, *Jazz* (London: Penguin Books, 1952), 95.
2. Terry Waldo, *This Is Ragtime* (New York: Da Capo Press, 1991), 124–127.
3. "Report of Commission on Race Relations," in Ted Vincent, *Keep Cool* (London: Pluto Press, 1995), 73.
4. Bricktop, with James Haskins, *Bricktop* (New York: Athenaeum, 1983), 54.
5. Sylvester Russell's "Chicago Review" column in the *Indianapolis Freeman*, Aug. 19, 1916.
6. *Chicago Daily News*, Jan. 30, 1917.
7. *Billboard*, Nov. 20 & Dec. 4, 1915.
8. Alberta's account is drawn from Nat Shapiro and Nat Hentoff, *Hear Me Talkin' to Ya* (New York: Dover Publications, 1955), 87 and 100.
9. Milton "Mezz" Mezzrow and Bernard Wolfe, *Really the Blues* (London: Corgi, 1961), 35.
10. Bricktop and Haskins, 25.
11. Bricktop and Haskins, 55.

12. Frank C. Taylor, with Gerald Cook, *Alberta Hunter* (New York: McGraw Hill Book Company, 1987), 32.

13. Publicity brochure *Beauty, Health, Success: The Kashmir Way* and Claude A. Barnett, *Fly Out of Darkness* (unpublished autobiographical material), both in Claude A. Barnett Collection, Chicago Historical Society.

14. Bricktop and Haskins, 55.

15. For Florence on Bojangles, see ChDef, Nov. 5, 1927. For Bojangles on Florence, see BAA, June 20, 1931.

16. Bricktop and Haskins, 60.

17. Bricktop and Haskins, 57.

18. David Jasen, *Tin Pan Alley* (New York: Omnibus Press, 1988), 87.

19. ChDef, Feb. 3, 1917; *Chicago Daily News*, January 30, 1917; and George W. Kay, "The Shep Allen Story," *Jazz Journal*, Feb. 1963.

20. Marshall and Jean Stearns, *Jazz Dance* (New York: Macmillan, 1970), 178.

21. The early history of the Creole Band, including the Big Four String Band, has been well documented in Lawrence Gushee, "How the Creole Band Came to Be," *Black Music Research Journal* 8:1 (1988).

22. Stearns and Stearns, 178.

23. The birthplace of Prescott, Arkansas, is generally accepted, although his Social Security application gives it as Cairo, Illinois. According to that document, his middle initial stood for Sampson.

24. Stearns and Stearns, 63–64.

25. *Indianapolis Freeman*, Dec. 7, 1912. By 1912 he was already being billed as "Slow Kid" Thompson, although he was sometimes also referred to as U. S. Thompson. He was generally known to his friends and associates as Kid for the rest of his life, and so he is called here, except in direct quotations.

26. "Passing" was the term used for light-skinned black people's crossing over into the white population to avoid the disadvantages of segregation.

27. Billy King memoirs, Leigh Whipper Collection, Moorland Spingarn Research Centre, Howard University.

28. NYA, May 10, 1917.

29. Lester A. Walton, NYA, May 17, 1917.

30. NYA, June 21, 1917.

31. Luckey is used throughout because it occurs more commonly than the full form, Luckeyth.

32. HAJC.

33. For this brief summary of African American troops in the war, I have drawn on material from Langston Hughes and Milton Melzer, *A Pictorial History of the Negro in America* (New York: Crown Publishers, 1968); Leslie H. Fisher and Benjamin Quarles, *The Negro American: A Documentary History* (Illinois: Scott Foresman, 1967); John P. Davis, Ed., *The American Negro Reference Book* (New Jersey: Prentice Hall, 1966); and Carole Marks, *Farewell We're Good and Gone* (Bloomington: Indiana University Press, 1989).

34. Lulu Walton letter, ChDef, Mar. 2, 1918.

35. ChDef, Sylvester Russell column, Dec. 16 (or 23?), 1916.

36. Kay, "The Shep Allen Story," and "Interviews with Musicians about Jelly Roll Morton," *Bill Russell Papers: MSS 506*, in the Historic New Orleans Collection at the Williams Research Center, New Orleans. Shep Allen worked at the Panama Café during the Panama Trio's time and was for many years the manager of the Howard Theatre in D.C., starting in 1931. The exact timing and circumstances of the rebirth of the Panama Trio are obscure. I have drawn here on interviews with Allen by George Kay (1962) and Bill Russell (1970). Allen was a respected figure, but his memory for the events of 1917–1919, recalled forty-five years and more afterwards, are vague and conflicting on dates. He was consistent in his claim that the Panama Trio, including Florence Mills, played with Jelly Roll Morton at the Cadillac in Los Angeles but conflicting in his accounts of when and related details. Comparison of my Florence Mills chronology and that of Morton in Lawrence Gushee's "A Preliminary Chronology of the Early Career of Ferd 'Jelly Roll' Morton," *American Music* (winter 1985), shows sufficient uncertainty about the movements of both during much of 1918 that there is ample room for a meeting.

37. Bernard L. Peterson Jr., *The African American Theatre Directory, 1816–1960* (Westport, Conn.: Greenwood Press, 1997), 178.

38. Tony Langton, ChDef, Nov. 9, 1918.

39. Alan Lomax, *Mister Jelly Roll* (London: Pan Books, 1959), 116.

40. Waldo, *This Is Ragtime*, and Rudi Blesh and Harriet Janis, *They All Played Ragtime* (New York: Oak Publications, 1966). Chapter 2 of Terry Waldo's book has a good account of Tony Jackson's career. Blesh and Janis have specific material on Jackson in chapter 8.

41. ChDef, May 17, 1919.

42. ChDef, May 24, 1919.

CHAPTER THREE

~

The Rocky Road to Fame

The Great Panama Pantages Odyssey

It may seem grandiose to equate the Panama Trio's tour to the Midwest, Canada, and the West Coast with the travels of the great Grecian hero Ulysses. However, it takes a considerable act of imagination today to realize what it must have been like for three black women still in their early twenties to spend five months touring the far West with an otherwise all-white vaudeville bill during the second decade of the last century. Florence had already covered some of the same terrain with the Tennessee Ten, but that was in a large, predominantly male group with Kid Thompson as her personal protector.

Even in the 1940s and 1950s, accommodation and access to facilities were problematic for black entertainers on the road with mixed troupes. Admittedly their schedule did not include the Deep South. They therefore escaped some of the problems associated with that region's racial biases. Black acts traveling the circuits kept each other well informed of available options. The Rucker and Winfred act preceded the Panama Trio on the Pantages circuit by a few months. A message in the *Defender* from them recommended the home of Mrs. Willis Foster, Vancouver. "The nicest stopping place in town . . . just a minute's walk from all the theaters." Traveling performers routinely exchanged information like this.[1]

The schedule for the tour started on June 30, 1919, in Minnesota. It finished in late November. It wound its way through twenty-five cities and towns in eleven states or provinces. The route initially crossed middle and western Canada, through Manitoba, Saskatchewan, and Alberta. It then dipped down through the Rocky Mountains to Montana and Washington state and back to Canada via British Columbia. The final stage ran down the U.S. West Coast via Oregon and California, finishing in Utah and Colorado. Sophie Tucker, "The Last of the Red Hot Mommas," had followed the same route some years earlier. She remembered it as "like the series of quick flashes the movie directors use to give you the feeling that a lot of events are happening very fast."[2]

The venues for the circuit included some of the finest theaters in the United States and Canada. Alexander Pantages demonstrated his faith in vaudeville by commissioning specialist theatrical architect B. Marcus Priteca to build a series of magnificent classically styled theaters in some of Pantages's major locations. Priteca was a devotee of the old-style theater interior—graceful curving balconies, sloping floors, and good sight lines. Many of his Pantages buildings still exist today, and some are still operational theaters. The 1929 Hollywood Priteca theater was for many years home to the Academy Awards, and the Tacoma theater is now the Broadway Center for the Performing Arts.

The primary method of travel on the circuit was rail. Pantages paid the acts an agreed rate plus rail fares. Acts traveling the remoter vaudeville routes had to organize their own travel. With a package like the Pantages bill, some coordination may have occurred. The Panama Trio certainly faced segregated travel arrangements for the U.S. portions of the tour.[3] For Florence, the odyssey was without her own Ulysses Kid Thompson. However, this was not as great a separation as first appears.

The three young women were sharing a typical vaudeville bill of its time, with music, comedy, and several specialist acts. Their billing described them as The Panama Trio (Maids of Syncopation), "Three colored girls with exceptionally good voices, capable of great harmony in unison numbers."[4] The package stayed much the same throughout the tour. This was a credit to the quality of the acts Pantages had put together. Local vaudeville managers were notorious for arbitrarily sacking acts that didn't appeal to them. As well as the live acts, the bill at each stopover usually featured a movie newsreel and a Pathe comedy or documentary feature. Besides the Panama Trio, the bill that summer featured:

- *The Kremlin at Moscow* (the main featured attraction), with "Russian melodies, Balalaika orchestra and whirlwind dancers"
- *Marie Fitzgibbon*, "a monologist of rare talent and personality"

- *The Le Grohs*, "a trio of comedy contortionists"
- *Chisholm and Breen*, "A boy and girl team presenting a novelty satire on modern ideas of love and marriage"
- *Dorsch and Russell*, "who appear as a railroad employee and a tramp, and proceed to get plenty of melody out of the various articles around a railway yard"

The Panama Trio's act included six songs, performed in trio, duet, and a solo by Florence. The songs were a mixture of traditional ballads and current popular numbers described as, "old southern melodies and jazz selections." Florence's featured solo was a ballad with a World War I theme called "Don't Cry, Frenchy, Don't Cry." The music, by Walter Donaldson, carried lyrics by Sam M. Lewis and Joe Young: "They met while clouds were hanging over Flanders, a soldier's glance, a war romance." Florence would have been amazed if told then that lyricists Lewis and Young would be part of her personal songwriting team a few years down the track. There was also a Hawaiian melody. This may well have been another Joe Young song, "Yaaka Hula Hicky Dula," popularized by Al Jolson in 1916. Songs with a Hawaiian theme had a big vogue on Broadway in the second decade of the century. Nora Bayes had featured a Hawaiian scene when the Tennessee Ten supported her.

The opening engagement of the tour was at the Pantages theater in Minneapolis on Monday, June 30, 1919. Many local citizens might have envied the Panama girls setting off to Canada on that particular day. It was the final day before the start of Prohibition. As the *Minneapolis Tribune* expressed it, "John Barleycorn dies at midnight tonight." Put less poetically, it was the day the terms of the Eighteenth Amendment to the U.S. Constitution, denying Americans the right to drink intoxicating liquor, came into practical effect. The daily papers reported a noisy night of crime, booze-related disturbances, and injuries in Minneapolis. However, the lack of alcohol in the following days probably encouraged thirsty drinkers to forget their problems by attending the theater.

Within a week the tour had rolled on to Canada. Winnipeg, Manitoba, was a more sedate venue. The most sensational news of the day in the local press was Jack Dempsey's dethroning of heavyweight champion Jess Willard in Toledo, Ohio. Willard had taken the title in dubious circumstances in 1915 from the first black heavyweight champion, showman Jack Johnson, whose career in Chicago has already been noted. Coincident with the troupe's arrival, the *Manitoba Free Press* reported the addition of forty-five theaters to the Pantages circuit. The Winnipeg Pantages was one of the most distinctive theaters of its kind in North America. It still functions today as the Playhouse Theatre.

The Pantages show got a warm review from the *Free Press*. It was "a programme unequalled in many weeks." Generally the local papers of the time were kind to traveling shows, damning with faint praise rather than outright criticism. The show's success could be gauged from the warmth of the review rather than the absence of negative comment. Florence and company passed this test with flying colors. "The Panama Trio—three colored young women of the south—can sing, dance and cut up, just in the way the audience wanted them to. Nothing was out of place but besides the darky ditties there was a pretty Hawaii melody that pleased immensely. To a tremendous encore the girls came out and danced and sang again, almost carrying the audience with them—off their feet."[5]

After Winnipeg the show was due to share a week between the smaller centers of Regina and Saskatoon. As it was annual show week there, Saskatoon preempted the Pantages bill for the full week at Regina's expense. The next stage was the Rocky Mountains cities of Edmonton and Calgary. The reviewer for the *Edmonton Journal* called the girls "decided favorites." He said they were "good looking, sprightly and sing with all kinds of animation" and singled Florence out: "She can give most performers a good many pointers as to how to put a song over in vaudeville."[6]

Calgary was still warming up for its famous Stampede when the troupe arrived there for the week of July 28. The Stampede traditionally occurs in early July nowadays. The 1919 Stampede, first of the modern era after an abortive start in 1912, occurred in August that year. The Pantages show drew capacity crowds. The Panama girls were noted for "some very good jazz time stuff and a little 'way down south' dancing." From Calgary the schedule was a hectic series of one- or two-day stints in cowboy and mining towns in Montana. These included Great Falls, Butte, Helena, Anaconda, and Missoula, ending in Spokane, Washington. This itinerary involved skirting the edge of the Rocky Mountains down to Helena, then crossing over the mountains to Spokane—the country of the Lewis and Clark Expedition of 1805, rich in the traditions and culture of Native Americans.

This section epitomized the description in Sobel's *History of Vaudeville*: "The lives of touring variety actors were far from easy. They often were obliged to travel at odd hours to meet split week engagements. . . . At each new theater, whether it was a one-night stand or a week, they had to adapt themselves anew to the peculiarity of the conductor, the orchestra, the stagehands and the all-powerful manager. They had to put up with all sorts of dressing-rooms and hotels, with unheated wings and indifferent lunch-counter cooks, with cindery train trips and jolting street car rides."[7] On the other hand, the inhabitants of the remote Montana mining towns appreciated the opportunity to enjoy high-quality city entertainment. The Montana copper mining industry, in decline today, was thriving in those days. The towns were full of hardworking, hard-drinking miners eager for entertainment—not a genteel audience. For Florence, who had served her apprenticeship at the Lincoln in Harlem, they were a pushover.

While the Pantages troupe was wending its way across the Rocky Mountains, dramatic developments, in more than one sense, were occurring back East. For many years stage performers had been at the mercy of powerful theater owners, promoters, and managers. In 1913 Actors' Equity was formed to seek better conditions. Equity purported to cover the full spectrum of performers, although initially it focused strongly on East Coast legitimate theater and Broadway. Its membership was mainly white but was never segregated. Following six years of fruitless negotiations with the owners, Equity affiliated with the American Federation of Labor. Together they agreed to take on the owners and the promotional syndicates. On August 7, 1919, at the union's bidding, the cast of a Broadway play called (appropriately) *Lightnin'* walked out and the great theatrical strike was on.

The strike lasted thirty days, spread to eight cities, closed thirty-seven plays, prevented sixteen others from opening, and cost millions of dollars. *Variety* noted that nearly all the acts playing on the Pantages circuit in the West received wires asking their attitude in the event of vaudeville trouble. Some Pantages bills received a lengthy message sent to one act for the information of all. No answers to the wires were reported. Whether the wire to Pantages vaudeville performers ever reached the intrepid band of Pantages performers somewhere in the Rocky Mountains is unknown. If it went to only one act on the Pantages bill, the act would certainly not have been the sole black act.[8]

In general, the strike had no impact on the Pantages theaters, or any of their rivals, in the West. The mining towns welcomed them enthusiastically. The *Helena Daily Independent* noted the Panama girls' "harmony was wonderful." It also commented on the "particularly pleasing mezzo-soprano voice" of Florence.[9] The strike was still in progress while the troupe was in Spokane and Seattle. The *Seattle Post Intelligencer* reported its progress in some depth but treated it as purely a New York matter. It concluded that if it did spread to Seattle, it would affect only legitimate drama theater rather than vaudeville. In fact, the Orpheum and Palace theaters were both running full vaudeville bills in competition with Pantages. The Orpheum, part of a chain owned by one of the strikers' most dedicated enemies, E. F. Albee, was featuring a Spanish dancing act we shall meet again, Elisa and Eduardo Cansino.

The strike ended on September 5 after almost a month. The managers backed down and conceded Equity's demands, ushering in a whole new era for theatrical performers. By then the Pantages troupe was back in Vancouver, Canada. The *Vancouver Daily World* applauded the Panama Trio, described as "colored girl warblers." It hailed them as "well versed in the intricacies of syncopation, who sing six songs, dance a little and stop the show every time." The *Vancouver Daily Sun* was equally complimentary, calling the act "a pleasingly jazzy and syncopated offering." The *Daily Province*, reporting packed houses, noted that on Monday, "Continuous performances were run from the first show in the afternoon until late at night to accommodate holiday patrons." Florence's solo on "Don't Cry, Frenchy" was "well received, the singer possessing a rich, sweet voice."[10]

There was a reason Florence's performance may have had more than its usual zest and style in Vancouver. The Orpheum circuit closely paralleled the route followed by the Pantages circuit. The Orpheum was featuring a "Special added attraction" on its vaudeville bill, none other than Ralph Dunbar's Tennessee Ten, with their dancing director, U. S. Thompson. Ulysses had finally joined the Odyssey. After Florence set off on the Pantages route, Kid Thompson had continued with partner Jimmy Marshall until Marshall got homesick for Harlem. By early August, Kid had rejoined the Tennessee Ten on the Keith circuit at a point conveniently coinciding with the Panama Trio's schedule.[11]

However, the happy reunion for Florence and Kid was to have interruptions as the two troupes followed a more or less parallel schedule down the West Coast. The Pantages troupe had its next stop in the beautiful garden city of Victoria on Vancouver Island. Victoria's *Daily Colonist* considered the Le Grohs's contortionist extravaganza the hit of the Pantages performance but saw the Panama Trio as a close second. "The youngest of the trio possesses a clear sweet voice and adds to her singing talent that of a clever mimic." Although now twenty-three years old, Florence was invariably still mistaken for a teenager.[12]

From Victoria the troupe made its way down the West Coast via Tacoma and Portland. In Portland it was held over for an extra week. This success was frustrating for Florence as Kid Thompson and the Tennessee Ten had by now worked their way down to San Francisco. However, they also had an extra week's holdover in San Francisco, so the routes converged again. *Variety's* San Francisco reporter described the girls as "very good jazz singers" and went on to note that Florence's solo rendition of "Don't Cry, Frenchy" stopped the show. For about a month the Panama Trio played around major California centers: San Francisco, Oakland, Los Angeles, San Diego, and Long Beach. Florence and Kid were able to spend time together while they were playing San Francisco and Los Angeles. This may also have been the time when Shep Allen described the Panama Trio playing at the Cadillac with Jelly Roll Morton as their accompanist.[13]

It was noticeable that in the United States the Trio's racial origin was often the subject of coy euphemisms, although the reviews continued to be enthusiastic. Billed in the publicity as "maids of syncopation," they were variously described in Los Angeles as "Black-face maids with charming voices," "Three dusky brunettes from the isthmus [of Panama]," and "three brunette maidens." This preoccupation with circumlocution presumably reflected the unease some of the American population felt at being entertained by the descendants of former slaves. Better to pretend they were from Panama, Egypt, or some other exotic locale. By contrast, the three girls were generally referred to in Canada and the more northerly states simply as "colored," sometimes as "dusky maidens," and occasionally without any comment on their racial background.

The San Diego date produced enthusiastic reviews, for instance: "For real pep it would be hard to equal the amount instilled in their work by these young women."[14] The California segment of the circuit ended in early November with a week in Long Beach. Sometime during this period, Carolyn Williams decided to stay in Los Angeles to marry her boyfriend. She played out the remaining California dates and then dropped out of the act.

As the Panama Trio approached the end of its epic tour, the name Florence Mills was also featuring prominently back on Broadway. One of the most cherished American musicals, *Irene*, with its hit tune "Alice Blue Gown," had its debut at the Vanderbilt Theatre. A Cinderella story, *Irene* set records for a Broadway run. A white singer-actress named Florence Mills played the role of Irene's mother-in-law, Mrs. Marshall and later played the lead in a road version. Although she had a successful burlesque career stretching from 1909 to 1926, she was eventually overshadowed by her black namesake and is forgotten today.[15]

Following Carolyn Williams's departure, Florence and Cora Green continued the act. They were listed in Salt Lake City as the Panama Duo. The Tennessee Ten and Kid Thompson were following the same route, and both shows were lapped up by Salt Lake City audiences. The *Salt Lake Tribune* declared that the "two dusky-haired maids" could "sing and dance jazz with good effect, with the proper emphasis and expression." At the

Orpheum, "U. S. Thompson dances his way through the directing of several snappy tunes played by the jazz band."[16]

The Pantages troupe doesn't seem to have completed the remaining scheduled engagements, Ogden (Utah) and Denver (Colorado). After the troupe dispersed, the two girls agreed to go their separate ways, although their careers would intertwine over the coming years. Alberta Hunter suggests that Florence actually finished out the schedule as a single. "Florence was such a success by herself that no one mourned the passing of the trio."[17] Cora Green stayed on in the West and worked as a single act at Purchell's Café in San Francisco. Florence's immediate priority was to take a break and enjoy a reunion with family and friends back home in Harlem. The path was then clear—back to the good old Tennessee Ten and Kid Thompson.

Early in 1920 the Tennessee Ten took a few weeks' break in Chicago. The purpose was to revamp the act before going on the road again with the Orpheum circuit. Part of the revamp was to fit Florence back into the act, which happened very smoothly. Even the changes in personnel since her previous engagement had not been too dramatic. Lulu Walton's replacement, as "soubrette" to Florence's "prima donna," was Hilaria Friend. Hilaria had been the cashier at the Crescent Theatre in Harlem when the Mills Sisters played there in 1911.

The new Tennessee Ten started off with a two-week engagement in Chicago. Florence was billed as "The Spirit of Dreamland," a reference to the famous jazz café. During the Chicago stay, band member Robert Johnson was royally entertained by his brother Bill and the other members of the Creole Band, then playing at the Royal Gardens Café.[18] The occasion was a wonderful opportunity for the members of the Creole Band and the Tennessee Ten's jazz band to jam together. This was also around the time that the great King Oliver was playing with Johnson's Creole Band.

For Florence, back safely in the Tennessee Ten, reunited with Kid Thompson, the engagement in the familiar environment of Chicago was a favorable start to the next major phase in her career. The triumphant exploits of the three Panama girls on their Pantages tour went down in the legends of black entertainment and added to her growing reputation.

From *Folly Town* to *Shuffle Along*

Florence and Kid were now clearly romantically linked in the eyes of their showbiz peers. The next big step in their linked careers came in 1920, when James E. Cooper produced a burlesque show called *Folly Town*. *Folly Town* was one of the first racially integrated productions on the New York stage. It was also part of the new "clean" burlesque, which was trying to live down the image of raunchy strip shows. Apart from the Tennessee Ten, the cast had a strong lineup of white stars, including rising comedians Bert Lahr and Jack Haley, later famous as the Cowardly Lion and the Tin Man in the Judy Garland movie *The Wizard of Oz*. *Folly Town* was an important early career step for both. The budget for *Folly Town* was somewhere between $20,000 and $25,000, an unprecedented sum for that time. It made its debut in May at the Columbia Theatre, New York, home base of burlesque on the East Coast.

Folly Town represented a switch for Florence and the Ten from vaudeville to burlesque. The change was not great. Many performers crossed over between the two formats, their individual acts remaining much the same. In vaudeville the playbill featured a collection of individual variety acts. In burlesque the entire show was an integrated package with a theme. The burlesque format was loosely adapted from the old minstrel show three-part format: introductory jokes and comedy followed by the olio, which was essentially a sequence of variety acts, then a riotous finale involving the whole company.

The *New York Times* was enthusiastic over the opening performance of *Folly Town*:

> Ten colored performers in a riot of jazz, a perfect blend of male voices in a California trio, four cyclonic oriental acrobats and a host of comedians, vaudevillians, singers, dancers and show girls provided the entertainment last night at The Columbia theater in *Folly Town*, one of the most ambitious productions ever attempted on the New York stage. . . . The comedians Bert Lahr, Frank Hunter and Johnny Walker, were capably supported by a large cast. . . . The colored group that brought down the house was billed as Ralph Dunbar's Tennessee Ten.[19]

Billboard was even more enthusiastic, devoting more than a full page to its review. Under the heading "For better burlesque," the writer emphasized that *Folly Town* was an important victory for those who had been working to rescue burlesque theater from its lewd image.[20]

Folly Town had two acts and sixteen scenes. The Ten had their main appearance in scenes six and seven, which took a satiric look at the New York subway and its varied ethnic groupings at different points along the ride. Their reward was a "prolonged applauded session that stopped the show." Florence wasn't mentioned by name, but *Billboard* noted that "the agile and able dancing of one of the feminine members was remarkable." Another enthusiastic reviewer declared, "Several of the men are sensational eccentric dancers. All are fine singers, and one little girl displays a soprano that many an opera singer might envy. 'Nellie Gray,' 'Down on the Swanee River,' 'Hear Dem Bells,' and other typically southern songs were sung by the little bird-like soprano [clearly Florence] and a very musical tenor in a way that revived memories among the old-timers, memories of famous minstrels of the past."

Variety was more subdued in its assessment, noting that the Tennessee Ten was the only showstopper and their part should be enlarged. It also gave Bert Lahr a big tick and noted the clean image, commenting, "Burlesque needs publicity of the kind it has been receiving in the New York papers since *Folly Town* opened at the Columbia."[21] In his father's biography, Bert Lahr's son John noted that playing in *Folly Town* was "an honour for the performers, a chance for them to be seen by the big-time theatrical managers and producers." In Bert Lahr's case it paid off well: His immediate success won him promotion to the top comic role shortly after the opening, and he soon moved on to major vaudeville and Broadway roles.[22]

James Cooper lost no time cashing in on the favorable reaction. In the largest advertising splurge burlesque had ever seen, he spent $3,000 reproducing the rave reviews in the New York dailies. The gamble paid off: The Columbia took in nearly $11,000 at the box office that week. As a sign that the Tennessee Ten were widely regarded as stars of the show, they featured in the annual benefit of the Burlesque Club in June at the Columbia Theatre. Florence got to meet Sam Lewis and Joe Young, the lyricists for her popular hit with the Panama Trio, "Don't Cry, Frenchy," who had provided special lyrics and music for the benefit. Lewis was a member of the board of governors of the Burlesque Club.

Apart from the favorable notices, a big advantage of playing in *Folly Town* was just getting to stay in one place for two months. In New York, Florence was close to home and family and friends. Around this time the Ten shared a bill at Shea's Theatre with Mae West, a review noting, "Florence Mills gave a corking act." The attention was doing her reputation and career no harm. Not surprisingly, the Lincoln Theatre beckoned again. On July 17 *New York Age* reported: "The Florence Mills Trio, direct from *Folly Town* . . . was featured at the Lincoln during the first half of the week." The other members of the trio were Kid Thompson and Freddie Johnson, the drummer from the Tennessee Ten. Freddie Johnson was a dancer and sometime piano player as well as a drummer. He has occasionally been confused with a Freddy Johnson who played piano with Sam Wooding's orchestra and was well known in Europe during the 1930s.[23] Kid Thompson stated Johnson played drums on this occasion, so this may also have been one of the times he mentioned when Luckey Roberts worked with him and Florence.

At any rate, this period at the Lincoln proved to be one of Florence's tougher engagements. The self-appointed "sharpshooters" in the gallery decided to give her a hard time. Her partners had to fill in with some fancy dancing to win back the audience. The owner, Mrs. Downs, commented, "As a rule both management and patrons accepted the verdict of the 'sharpshooters' . . . but this was one of the few occasions when we went to the gallery to express a difference with them, and quiet their racket, under threat of expulsion."[24]

Folly Town's long engagement in New York gave Florence and Kid opportunity for social contact that the grind of touring on the road would not normally allow. They liked to congregate with other Harlem show folk in the many clubs and speakeasies that white tourists in search of the exotic had not yet discovered. A favorite spot was Leroy Wilkins's club in Harlem. Leroy's elder brother, Barron Wilkins, ran the Exclusive Club, which catered mainly to wealthy whites. Leroy catered to a black clientele. Drinking was tightly controlled. Entertainment consisted of just a pianist and some excellent singers.

One of the regular singers was Florence's former partner at the Panama, Mattie Hite. The great Willie "The Lion" Smith held down the piano chair. This was the era when stride piano was evolving. The Lion recalled Florence and Kid as regulars when they were with the Tennessee Ten. This was the first time he had seen Florence since her early Nickellette days. He also recalled elder sister Maude sometimes joining them to make up a party. The Lion liked to tease Maude about her one-legged dancing, calling out "Dance with the other leg." Other regulars at Leroy's were Bojangles, Bert Williams, and comedians Miller and Lyles.[25] Another popular haunt for Florence and Kid was Edmond's Cellar in Harlem, where old vaudeville fellow-traveler Ethel Waters was providing the entertainment. Ethel recalled that Florence "was at the ringside every night with her husband."[26]

After its successful New York run, *Folly Town* played the provinces, Philadelphia, Baltimore, and other major centers, into early 1921. By this time Kid knew that Florence had talent of an exceptional order. He knew she was destined for more than the Tennessee Ten could offer. He became her self-appointed manager as well as her husband-to-be, effectively abandoning any independent career of his own. Strangely, despite Kid's great talent, he and Florence were never a performing duo in any real sense. He was always more of an individual act or performed with male partners, giving more scope for his humorous "hokum" approach. By early 1921 he sensed that the time was right for Florence and him to settle in New York and seek new directions for her career. Major developments were occurring in black show business, spearheaded by the sensationally successful new show *Shuffle Along*. New York was the action hotspot for an aspiring entertainer. Florence had served a long apprenticeship that began in her early childhood. Kid Thompson believed now was the time for her to try to break into the big time.

Florence, however, wanted a more secure status before taking on this new arrangement. "Kid," she said, "we ought to get married but first you've got to get rid of that wife of yours." He agreed to go to Chicago to seek a divorce. While he set off on this mission, Florence stayed in New York. Her old pal Bricktop was at Barron Wilkins's club. Florence asked if Bricktop could find her a job to help her keep afloat while she was on her own for a while. Bricktop, delighted to see Florence again, had no trouble convincing Barron Wilkins to take her on. The skills she had learned at the Panama Cafe in singing from table to table paid off well. Florence was a big hit at the club.[27]

Meanwhile, Kid Thompson was not faring as well with his side of the deal. On arrival in Chicago he found himself straightaway in hot water. "They locked me up," he said, "put me in jail for nonsupport. My first wife, I hadn't sent her no money since I came out of the army because I didn't know where she was." After the initial shock, he managed to sort the matter out. He got his divorce and went back to Florence. The couple went downtown to City Hall for a simple marriage ceremony. They could not afford a fancy honeymoon. As they rode home to Harlem, on top of a downtown-to-uptown double-decker bus, Kid said to Florence, "This is our honeymoon now, just on the bus." They both knew times could be lean until the opportunity they were hoping for came along.[28]

The launching pad that was soon to catapult Florence Mills to the attention of the world was *Shuffle Along*. This dynamic show changed the history of black entertainment. In many important respects it also changed American popular culture. *Shuffle Along* was no freak event. A major cultural phenomenon never occurs in a vacuum. Invariably it is the result of a long gestation. In the widest sense, the nurturing medium for *Shuffle Along* was the whole panorama of black music and dance that had grown out of slavery and the African diaspora. In a more specific sense, its roots were in that golden era of black entertainment that produced the Williams and Walker, Cole and Johnson shows and all the other talented people who shared that world.[29]

Many of the brightest of that era had died or had forsaken show business when it became obvious white audiences had found other interests. Some persisted, believing a bright future still lay ahead. Among these were Will Marion Cook, a composer, Will Vodery, a brilliant orchestrator and arranger who was the genius behind most of the music for the *Ziegfeld Follies*, and James Reese (Jim) Europe, brilliant conductor and bandleader. Among the outstanding young new talent rising in their footsteps were two partnerships, singer-composer duo Noble Sissle and Eubie Blake and playwright-comedians Flournoy Miller and Aubrey Lyles.

To observers of the black vaudeville scene in 1920, Sissle and Blake and Miller and Lyles were significant emerging talents. The two sets of partners met when they played an NAACP (National Association for the Advancement of Colored People) benefit in Philadelphia in 1920. They discussed putting their two acts together, and the eventual result was *Shuffle Along*. They used an old sketch of Miller's, *The Mayor of Dixie*, as a basis for the plot. Sissle and Blake provided the music and lyrics, Miller and Lyles the book.

Shuffle Along was described as a musical melange. Its plot, based loosely on *The Mayor of Dixie*, involved a mayoralty contest in the imaginary township of Jimtown. Steve Jenkins (played by Miller) and Sam Peck (played by Lyles) were the shady candidates whose antics provided the humor of the show. Blake and Sissle's music included the beautiful "Love Will Find a Way," the sensuous "I'm Craving for That Kind of Love," the infectious "I'm Just Wild about Harry," and a host of jazz-flavored numbers such as "Oriental Blues," "Baltimore Buzz," and "Bandana Days." The financial backing they were able to raise initially was enough to run only a shoestring production that used costumes left over from a failed show. After struggling through the traditional pre-Broadway tryout on the road, they arrived in New York, heavily in debt, for the opening at Daly's Sixty-third Street Music Hall on Monday, May 23, 1921.

The female leads in the talented cast were Lottie Gee and Gertrude Saunders, both experienced and polished vaudeville performers. Lottie performed the softer ballad-style numbers ("Love Will Find a Way" and "I'm Just Wild about Harry") while Gertrude Saunders had the hot, jazzy numbers ("Simply Full of Jazz," "I'm Craving for That Kind of Love," and "Daddy"). In Sissle's words, Gertrude's flamboyant performance was "the sensation of our show— stopped it cold every night."[30]

On the New York opening night, the audience loved the show. Influential critics like Alan Dale, George Jean Nathan, and Heywood Broun were highly enthusiastic. Gradually *Shuffle Along* built up a cult status. So big were the crowds that the police had trouble controlling the traffic. Eventually they had to make Sixty-third a one-way street. A black show was back on Broadway, even if Sixty-third Street, a long way uptown, was barely Broadway! In Eubie Blake's words, "It wasn't Broadway but we made it Broadway."

Shuffle Along was the magnet that had drawn Kid Thompson to New York. As Florence's new manager and promoter, he was confident her talents would assure her a niche in the new blossoming of black entertainment that was expected to follow *Shuffle Along*. While waiting for fortune to smile, the two still had to keep themselves afloat in the show business world. Florence continued performing at Barron Wilkins's Exclusive Club, which catered predominantly to whites because of its high prices but was a good place for a black entertainer to be seen to advantage in the Harlem scene. They both knew they couldn't just sit around waiting for the big opportunity. Singing table-to-table at Barron Wilkins's was all right as a stopgap measure but not something Florence wanted to keep doing. Kid approached the doyen of vaudeville material writing, James Madison, to prepare an act for them. Madison was the publisher of a monthly vaudeville trade publication known as *Madison's Budget*. It carried gags, monologues, and routines for partner acts. He had written special material for many stars. Kid Thompson paid him $300 to prepare an act for them. According to well-known African American entertainer Tom Fletcher, in his book *100 Years of the Negro in Show Business*, it was "considered a classic."[31] However, they never got to launch the new act. In August, *New York Age* reported that Gertrude Saunders had closed her engagement with the *Shuffle Along* company. This was the break they had been waiting and hoping for. However, Florence still had to stake her claim to the highly prized role.

Notes

1. ChDef, June 14, 1919.
2. Sophie Tucker, *Some of These Days* (New York: Garden City Publishing, 1946), 102.
3. The detailed schedule, from June 30 to November 24 was Minneapolis (Minn.), Winnipeg (MB), Regina (SK), Saskatoon (SK), Edmonton (AB), Calgary (AB), Great Falls (Mont.), Helena (Mont.), Butte (Mont.), Anaconda (Mont.), Missoula (Mont.), Spokane (Wash.), Seattle (Wash.), Vancouver (BC), Victoria (BC), Tacoma (Oreg.), Portland (Oreg.), San Francisco (Calif.), Oakland (Calif.), Los Angeles (Calif.), San Diego (Calif.), Long Beach (Calif.), Salt Lake (Utah), Ogden (Utah), Denver (Colo.).
4. *Manitoba Free Press*, July 5, 1919.
5. *Manitoba Free Press*, July 8, 1919.
6. *Edmonton Journal*, July 22, 1919.
7. Bernard Sobel, *A Pictorial History of Vaudeville* (New York: Citadel Press, 1961), 54.
8. A 1985 issue of *Playbill* (Vol. 3, No. 5) carried the article "Remembering Florence Mills," which claimed that "She was the first Black member of Actors' Equity, joining the union in 1919." No evidence was provided, and Actors' Equity was unable to confirm the membership. If Actors' Equity's records did show such an entry for 1919, it probably referred to the white Florence Mills, who was performing on

Broadway that year. Probably the first black member of Equity was Bert Williams, invited to join during the strike, at the instigation of his costar W. C. Fields.

9. *Helena Daily Independent*, Aug. 6, 7, and 8, 1919.

10. *Daily Province*, Vancouver, Sept. 2, 1919.

11. ChDef, Aug. 9, 1919.

12. *Daily Colonist*, Victoria, BC, Sept. 9, 1919.

13. Shep Allen interviews by George Kay (1962) and Bill Russell (1970), held in the *Bill Russell Papers* in the Historic New Orleans Collection at the Williams Research Center, New Orleans. As noted before, Allen's chronology is confused, but he was consistent about Florence's playing with Jelly Roll Morton.

14. *San Diego Union and Bee*, Oct. 28, 1919.

15. For *Irene* see Gerald Bordman, *American Musical Theatre: A Chronicle* (New York: Oxford University Press, 1978), 345; and Gerald Bordman, *American Musical Comedy: From Adonis to Dreamgirls* (New York: Oxford University Press, 1982), 108–109. Bordman wrongly gives the name as "Florence Hills." For details of white Florence Mills's career, see clippings in Billy Rose Theatre Collection at Lincoln Center Library for the Performing Arts under "Florence Mills (White)."

16. *Salt Lake Tribune*, Nov. 12 and 13, 1919.

17. Frank C. Taylor, with Gerald Cook, *Alberta Hunter* (New York: McGraw Hill, 1987), 34.

18. *Chicago Whip*, Feb. 14, 1920.

19. "'Folly Town' at Columbia," NYT, May 18, 1920.

20. "For Better Burlesque," *Billboard*, June 5, 1920.

21. *Folly Town* review, VAR, May 21, 1920.

22. John Lahr, *Notes on a Cowardly Lion* (New York: Alfred A. Knopf, 1969), 57.

23. This confusion is the likely source of an entry in John Chilton's *Who's Who of Jazz*, 4th ed., 171, which says the piano player Freddy Johnson was Florence Mills's accompanist in 1922. The Tennessee Ten's Freddie Johnson had some success later (mid-1920s) collaborating with Glover Compton on a series of black shows (*Aces and Queens, Lucky Sambo, An Oil Well Scandal*).

24. J. A. Jackson's Page, *Billboard*, Dec. 13, 1924.

25. Willie "The Lion" Smith, *Music on My Mind* (New York: Da Capo, 1978), 94–95.

26. Ethel Waters with Charles Samuels, *His Eye Is on the Sparrow* (New York: Doubleday, 1951), 135.

27. Bricktop, with James Haskins, *Bricktop* (New York: Athenaeum, 1983), 78–79.

28. The exact timing of the wedding is difficult to pin down. The year 1922 is mentioned in the HAJC collection, but 1921 seems more consistent with other events. Florence was generally considered to be already married by the time she started in *Shuffle Along*. By 1922 they would have been relatively well off. The New York City Municipal Archives could not trace a record for either year.

29. The most informative and entertaining description of *Shuffle Along* is in Robert Kimball and William Bolcom, *Reminiscing with Sissle & Blake* (New York: Viking,

1973), 84–135. Shorter but useful and interesting accounts are in Allen Woll, *Black Musical Theatre* (Baton Rouge: Louisiana State University Press, 1989), 58–75; Al Rose, *Eubie Blake* (New York: Schirmer Books, 1979), 69–83; Marshall and Jean Stearns, *Jazz Dance*, 132–139.

30. Kimball and Bolcom, 118.

31. Tom Fletcher, *The Tom Fletcher Story: 100 Years of the Negro in Show Business* (New York: Burdge, 1954), 196.

CHAPTER FOUR

~

Shufflin' to the Top

At this point in her career the newly married Florence is twenty-five years old and has more than twenty years' experience in show business behind her. She has served a long apprenticeship in shabby theaters, nightclubs, and grinding circuit engagements. She has never known a life other than show business and has always lived in cities. Her only knowledge of the countryside is from traveling between engagements. She has a natural talent for singing, most effectively with sweet ballads, but she can handle hot and blues numbers very capably, and with dramatic flair, whenever necessary. Her dancing is perhaps her most outstanding asset. The precocious natural talent that won her medals for cakewalking and buck dancing as a tot has blossomed through association with the great Bojangles, from whom she has learned tap skills, and from partner U. S. Thompson, who is a skilled eccentric dancer as well as a tapper.

Florence is tiny, never weighing much above a hundred pounds. Her thin frame is extremely lithe, enabling her to perform the most extraordinary acrobatic feats. She is also a consummate improviser in all her work, producing surprising little twists to delight and amaze an audience. Finally, she also has a natural genius for mimicry and pantomime: a capacity to communicate emotions through movement, gesture, and expression.

Privately, she is still shy, reserved, and quiet in manner although friendly to all she comes in contact with. She dresses unostentatiously, and her appeal comes more from an inner radiance, big expressive eyes, and a mobile face than from any conventional beauty. This then is the performer who is ready to rocket to the heights of stardom.

Gertrude Saunders was a smash hit performer with a no-stops style. Even before *Shuffle Along* reached New York, the Okeh Company had recorded her singing her hit numbers from it. *Billboard* enthused, "She is one of the very few sopranos with a voice of such timbre as to qualify for the successful production of records. This is in itself an unusual distinction." Today Gertrude is mainly remembered as a rival for the affections of Bessie Smith's husband, Jack Gee, a situation that caused a violent reaction from the ever-volatile Bessie. In 1921, however, Gertrude was one of the hottest properties in show business. Hurtig and Seamon, leading promoters of vaudeville entertainment, noted Gertrude's success in *Shuffle Along* with interest. They offered to increase her salary of $125 per week to $175 if she would star in a burlesque show at Reisenweber's Cabaret. It was enough to tempt her away from *Shuffle Along*, and it created an opening for a new star in the show that was still drawing huge crowds.

The principals of *Shuffle Along* saw Gertrude's departure as a major setback. They despaired of finding someone with her dynamic presence. Florence and Kid used to dine at the same place in Harlem's fancy Striver's Row as Noble Sissle and his wife, Harriet. Kid proposed Florence for the part, but Sissle thought she was too demure to carry it off with the same fire that Gertrude had brought to it.

Bricktop used her friendship with Harriet Sissle to press Florence's claims. Noble Sissle was still not convinced. "She's a ballad singer. Gertrude's part calls for dancing and singing blues." Harriet persisted, eventually persuading him to at least go and see Florence at Barron Wilkins's. Florence and Kid were ready for just such a chance. She had developed her own version of Gertrude's big number, "I'm Craving for That Kind of Love." Her interpretation totally won over the reluctant Sissle. Florence, he declared, was "Dresden china, and she turns into a stick of dynamite." He went back to his partners to tell them they had found their new star. In Bricktop's version of the story, Florence still had to undergo many auditions before the part was finally hers.[1] Whatever the truth, a new chapter in Florence's life, and in American show business, was about to dawn. Later, referring to the years before, Florence said, "I don't like to think of that part of my life; it was too horrible. I like to think I started with *Shuffle Along*."[2]

Florence's contract with *Shuffle Along* was dated August 4, 1921. It stipulated that the first performance was to be on August 1 "or not later than fourteen days thereafter." The salary was listed as "One Hundred Dollars," but a marginal note, countersigned N. Sissle, specified "One Twenty Five," beginning September 5. The deal also involved finding a role for Kid Thompson. A new part was written for a dancing porter in the Jimtown Mayor's office.

Exactly what day Florence first trod the boards in *Shuffle Along* is not clear. *Variety's* issue of August 12 reported her as having recently joined the show, along with the Four Harmony Kings.

Getting the part and the contract was only the beginning. Florence had to fill Gertrude Saunders's shoes convincingly. There were plenty willing to predict disaster for the unassuming, shy little singer-dancer who was about to join the cast of one of the highest-profile shows on Broadway. One of the cast, Bee Freeman (later featured in black movies, billed as the "Sepia Mae West"), recalled, "The first time I saw Florence Mills she was walking on-stage, . . . wearing a black, rusty looking dress. It seemed like she had no glamour at all. She looked like one of those little girls you would see working in a store. . . . We thought 'How dare they inflict this thing on us.'"[3] Florence knew she had to make good on the opening night. The crucial moment would come with her big number, "I'm Craving for That Kind of Love." Before that she was sharing the stage with other members of the cast. This would be her big test, the limelight fully on her. Kid Thompson, nervous about her prospects, had taken out his own insurance policy.

> The first night I had about twenty fellows in the show, in the theatre, what they call a clique. I don't think anybody in the country ever heard tell about that, in this part of the world. Of course it was very popular in Europe. I had three or four fellows on this side, three or four fellows on that. I bought tickets for them, put them in, see. So when she came on by herself, that's when I had the clique all rehearsed. So Florence was singing "Kiss Me, Kiss Me, Kiss Me with Your Tempting Lips" [from "I'm Craving for That Kind of Love"], and she could flaunt, you know, a lot of things, and make her eyes look so good. When she got through and finished, . . . I gave [the clique] the signal.

Well-intentioned as Kid's orchestrated applause was, Florence needed no help. When the moment came, she began the number midstage. As she slowly built the song toward its climax, she kept inching closer to the audience, building up tension. By the end of the song, she was right down at the footlights, with the audience screaming and hollering. Bricktop recounts that she had seventeen encores. Eubie Blake claimed that her performance spoiled the sheet music sales. "She killed the song," he said. At the music store, the fans would ask for "Kiss Me," a phrase repeated often in the lyric. The title line was the very last line in the song and was invariably drowned out by the clamoring audience.[4]

Florence's success was instantaneous and complete. She fully eclipsed Gertrude Saunders's performance. For the jaded palates of Broadway, a new kind of star had appeared—a black female singer and dancer who could de-liver everything that black entertainment was renowned for, but with an added gamine delicacy that was uniquely her own. Those who feared that she couldn't handle the hot numbers like Gertrude Saunders did had failed to un-derstand she was never going to imitate someone else's style. The essence of her art was to combine pathos and humor in a blend that was uniquely her own. As black critic Theophilus Lewis said later, of another of her songs, "I never imagined such a tempestuous blend of passion and humour could be poured into the singing of a song."[5]

Maude Russell, herself a leading performer throughout the period, was in no doubt about Florence's ability to handle the hot numbers. Talking about *Shuffle Along* to the author in 1998, she said, "Lottie Gee was more like the prima donna and Florence Mills was more like the jazz singer." Asked whether she would describe Florence as a jazz singer, she replied, "Florence Mills was an all-round singer; she could sing a sweet song would make you cry, and then she could sing a jazz song and jazz it." The critics, black and white, responded enthusiastically. Gilbert Seldes, art critic for *Vanity Fair*, wrote, "The most skilful [sic] individual player has been Florence Mills. Merely to watch her walk out upon the stage, with her long free stride and her superb, shameless swing, is an aesthetic pleasure: she is a school and ex-emplar of carriage and deportment."[6]

Claude McKay, a noted black journalist with the *Liberator*, an avant-garde African American periodical, wrote: "Never had I seen a colored actress whose artistry was as fetching as Florence Mills's. [She] ran away with the show, mimicking and kicking her marvelous way right over the heads of all the cast and sheer up to the dizzying heights until she was transformed into a glorious star."[7] While Florence was an overnight star, Kid Thompson's dancing also got good critical notices. However, up till then Florence had been "U.S. Thompson's wife." From now on, for the rest of their lives to-gether, he would be "Florence Mills's husband." This never bothered him, as he saw himself as Florence's protector and promoter. Although Florence quickly became the latest novelty for white audiences seeking new sensations on Broadway, there were many in the black entertainment world, like Bo-jangles Robinson and Salem Tutt Whitney, who had watched her career de-veloping for years and were not surprised.

The world Florence and Kid entered, in joining the *Shuffle Along* cast, was more than just a successful theatrical engagement. It was a community of friends and companions of huge ability. Apart from the talented cast, many of whom, such as Fredi Washington and Eva Taylor, would become close friends of Florence's, the orchestra included some of the most brilliant musical minds in America. Will Vodery had provided the orchestrations for the music. Vodery was one of the most revered names in black music, closely associated with Bert Williams in the earlier black Broadway era and in later years with Duke Ellington, George Gershwin, and Jerome Kern. Playing the oboe in the pit orchestra was the young William Grant Still, who would become the acknowledged dean of African American classical composers. His friend Hall Johnson, later famous as the leader of the Hall Johnson choir, was also there, playing the viola. Several of the musicians, especially Vodery and Still, were to be important figures in Florence's later career. Still also became a close friend.

Florence loved playing in *Shuffle Along*. It offered the type of audience rapport she reveled in. At the same time, she was only one of a large cast, unlike the star carrying responsibility for the entire show on her shoulders. One of her biggest triumphs came on October 17, when the cast of *Shuffle Along* went to the Lafayette Theatre, on her home turf in Harlem, for a Midnight Benefit Performance for the NAACP. The event was advertised widely to ensure maximum revenue for the organization. Jessie Fauset, novelist, and Dr. Gertrude Curtis, New York's first African American female dentist and also wife of Charleston composer Cecil Mack, were among those lending their organizing talents to the publicity campaign. Jessie Fauset was an usher that night. The event was a huge sellout, with the cream of black society attending. The crush of disappointed patrons smashed a pane of glass in the lobby door. Billed as "Miss Florence Mills and the Jazz Girls and Boys," Florence was one of the major hits of the evening and was encored enthusiastically.[8]

In late October, J. A. Jackson noted in *Billboard* that *Shuffle Along* had "reached its 150th performance, thereby establishing the high mark for a colored attraction in any house." By December 1921, it was still breaking box office records on Broadway, and Florence Mills was unquestionably its leading attraction. There were many patrons who came back again and again, often primarily to see Florence. One such was the budding poet Langston Hughes. Langston's father, detesting the race prejudice in America, wanted him to study in Switzerland. Langston recalled, "*Shuffle Along* had just burst into being, and I wanted to hear Florence Mills sing. So I told my father I'd rather go to Columbia [a New York university] than to Switzerland." Langston got his way, and in his own words, "sat up in the gallery night after night at *Shuffle Along*, adored Florence Mills."[9]

For Noel Coward also, *Shuffle Along* was Florence Mills; "[Throughout it all] there darted the swift vivid genius of Florence Mills, at one moment moving like a streak of quicksilver, the next still against some gaudily painted backdrop. Nothing animated about her at all, except her wide smile and the little pulse in her throat, throbbing like a bird while she sang 'Love Will Find a Way.'"[10] Another English visitor around this time, impresario C. B. Cochran, was so impressed that he offered $5,000 a week plus all expenses to take *Shuffle Along* to England. The producers were not interested in a move at that time. They would later regret the lost opportunity.

Shortly after Florence joined *Shuffle Along*, two white men, Sam Salvin and Lew Leslie, prospecting for ideas to liven up a cabaret owned by Salvin, came to see the show. Leslie described the occasion: "We really went to hear a girl named Gertrude Saunders, but this night . . . an understudy did her songs. The understudy rolled a pair of flashing black eyes. She sang 'Gypsy Blues' and 'Love Will Find a Way' and 'Baltimore Buzz.' . . . Her name was Florence Mills."[11]

Lew Leslie and Florence Mills were to be of immense importance in each other's lives for as long as each would live. Leslie was one of the more colorful and interesting show business personalities of the 1920s and 1930s. Of Russian-Jewish background, he was born in America in 1886. He had started performing as an impressionist, then added songs and patter to his act when he teamed up with future star Belle Baker. He promoted her career, and she became his wife. They had split up amicably by the time of *Shuffle Along* although they remained friends for the rest of their lives. By the time they split, Leslie had concluded his strength lay in discovering and promoting new talent rather than in performing.[12]

Leslie was a good-natured man but also a shrewd, sometimes ruthless businessman. He had a keen appreciation of the commercial potential of black entertainment. His first venture in that direction was a presentation of *George White's Scandals of 1921*. It featured a white actress, Tess Gardella, in blackface as "Aunt Jemima," singing ragtime and plantation songs. However, from the time he saw Florence Mills, Leslie had found his mission in life, the discovery and promotion of black female talent. From that moment he was driven by a consuming vision: to glorify the black American showgirl the way Ziegfeld was doing for white girls. In Noble Sissle's words, "[Lew Leslie] was the pioneer of the Negro nightclub revue, the first to glamorize Negro girls and the one who set the pattern for such clubs as the Cotton Club, the Alabam and others."[13]

In January 1922, Florence and Lew Leslie signed a contract that was much simpler than the legal pro forma she had signed with *Shuffle Along*. It was actually a typed version of an earlier, handwritten one. The terms gave Florence a five-week engagement at $200 per week, with seven performances a week, starting not earlier than mid-night.[14] Leslie's concept didn't initially require Florence to leave *Shuffle Along*. His idea was to present a sophisticated after-theater entertainment for the smart set, with supper and a floor-show. For this purpose he convinced Sam Salvin to lavishly renovate his for-mer Folies Bergère cabaret premises over the Winter Garden Theater on Broadway. It was redesigned as a mythical Southern plantation scene some-where on the Mississippi, renamed the "Plantation Room," and described as "A Dancing Room of American Charm." It was commonly referred to there-after as the Plantation and would provide Florence with a home base for sev-eral years.

The Winter Garden Theater belonged to the powerful Shubert brothers and was for many years the home of *The Passing Show*, a rival revue series to the *Ziegfeld* and *Greenwich Village Follies* and the *George White Scandals*. The Plantation cabaret offered theater patrons the opportunity of following their theatrical evening with sophisticated dining and entertainment in the roof garden setting of the Plantation Room. In April, shortly after the opening, they would have the opportunity of seeing Eddie Cantor in the main theater in his hit *Make it Snappy*, followed by Florence Mills in the garden theater.

The show, called *Plantation Revue*, subtitled "Night Time Frolics in Dix-ieland," opened on February 15. To keep it exclusive, a cover of $2, later ap-parently raised to $3, was charged. A gala opening was held, with a special charge of $10, at which formal dress was required. Leslie's ex-wife, white vaudeville star Belle Baker, was in attendance. Kid Thompson recalled hear-ing a columnist complaining, "Who ever heard of evening dress to go in and see a lot of niggers." The show ran for forty-five minutes, and the bill of fare, in line with the entertainment, featured waffles and other southern dishes.

Apart from Florence, and Kid Thompson with his partner Lew Keane, the all–black revue included blues singer Edith Wilson; Chappelle and Stinette, a stylish dancing partnership; Arthur 'Strut' Payne's vocal quartet; well-known jazz cornetist Johnny Dunn; and a female chorus line. Juanita Stinette was described as "wearing one of the costliest gowns ever worn by a colored actress, consisting of twelve Birds of Paradise, costing $2,500." This descrip-tion presumably referred only to the bird's feathers.[15]

J. Russel Robinson wrote the music for the revue. Robinson was a histor-ically significant ragtime piano player and also sometime member of the Original Dixieland Jazz Band. He was known as "the White man with Col-ored fingers." His hits had included "Margie" (words by Benny Davis, who had harmonized with the Panama girls in Chicago), "Singing the Blues," "A Portrait of Jennie," and "Palesteena." Lyrics for his tunes for *Plantation Revue* were by Roy Turk, best known for his later collaboration with Fred Ahlert on tunes like "I'll Get By," "Mean to Me," "Walkin' My Baby Back Home," and "Where the Blue of the Night Meets the Gold of the Day."[16]

Both Johnny Dunn and Edith Wilson were to have a long association with Florence Mills. Dunn was one of the best-known jazz cornetists of the 1920s. He was for a time even more famous than Louis Armstrong. He started out with W. C. Handy about 1917 and was one of the first to record blues records, with Mamie Smith in August 1920. His backup group for that recording session was christened the Jazz Hounds. Mamie Smith's record from that session, "Crazy Blues," started the mania for blues and race records[17] that ultimately led to the rise of Bessie Smith, Alberta Hunter, and a host of other black female vocalists.

"Crazy Blues" had been written by the same Perry Bradford whom, back in Philadelphia in 1912, Florence had advised to go to New York. He had followed her advice and by early 1921 was reveling in the success of his songwriting ventures, fueled by the blues craze. Along with his songwriting and performing, Bradford was also operating a booking agency for black acts. Lew Leslie saw Edith Wilson, backed up by Johnny Dunn and the Jazz Hounds, performing in one of Bradford's shows. He approached Bradford with a proposition to book Edith and the Jazz Hounds for the new *Plantation Revue*.

Bradford was initially skeptical. While they were discussing it, his phone rang. On the other end was Florence Mills, his former vaudeville associate. She told him she had signed a contract with Leslie and urged him to sign up Edith and the Jazz Hounds. Once again he followed her advice. Thus it was that Mamie Smith's and Edith Wilson's Jazz Hounds, of recording fame, became Florence Mills's Plantation Orchestra. Bradford claimed that a disagreement between Johnny Dunn and another musician over the leadership led to the name change and the appointment of Will Vodery as leader. A more likely explanation is that Leslie wanted the name of the orchestra to reflect his show and also wanted Vodery for his skills as a musical director in the widest sense, rather than as just a bandleader.[18] For the first few weeks, another well-known black musician, Tim Brymn, led the orchestra, and then Vodery took over in mid-March.[19] Johnny Dunn continued to make records with the orchestra, billed as "Johnny Dunn's Original Jazz Hounds."

Getting Will Vodery as orchestra leader and musical director was a masterstroke on Leslie's part. This was the man Noble Sissle credited with having "solved the problem of getting theater orchestras to play with African American rhythmic inflections," calling him the "rhythm life of legitimate Broadway."[20] Leslie had also hit the jackpot with his novel approach to presenting sophisticated revue. Under the headline "Now The Plantation Room," J. A. Jackson wrote in *Billboard*, "Bohemian and aristocratic New York has taken on another colored attraction and placed the stamp of sophisticated approval upon it. The new object of enthusiastic ravings is the entertainment provided the selected clientele of the Plantation Room, a new nightclub in the Winter Garden Theater Building."[21]

The tone of this report illustrates the excitement among black entertainers at the newfound acceptance of their talents, epitomized by the success of Florence Mills. *Shuffle Along* had been hailed with genuine joy across the industry, without any hint of jealousy or rivalry, as the long-awaited breakthrough. Black entertainers had known for a long time that they had something special to offer. They just wanted the predominantly white Broadway audiences to give them a chance to prove it. *Shuffle Along* was that chance.

It is ironic that as Florence Mills began blazing that new trail, the doyen of black performers, Bert Williams, collapsed on stage and died on March 4, 1922, of pneumonia. His name had been synonymous with black entertainment for two decades. His notable achievements included starring in the Ziegfeld Follies and performing in private for the British royal family. With his death, one era ended just as another was beginning. Bert Williams lived long enough to see and appreciate the one who would inherit his mantle as the greatest black entertainer. A member of Florence's family recalled Bert favorably comparing the diminutive Florence to himself. He said, "This is once where the pint is better than the quart."[22] Florence was there to honor him at the end, along with the other members of the *Shuffle Along* company, who presented a floral tribute at his memorial service at Saint Philip's Church.

Leslie's new direction was the next step after *Shuffle Along* in the evolution of black entertainment, although in one way it was a backward step. The Plantation Room's decor was a throwback to the earlier image associated with black entertainment, the ubiquitous plantation that Kid Thompson had described from his carnival days. Leslie's vision was commercial rather than cultural. He had a very accurate sense of what white audiences would pay to see and a keen eye for talent. He would come in for criticism from some black intellectual quarters for his philistine approach to matters artistic and aesthetic. Nevertheless, to the entertainers, he was opening up new avenues of opportunity.

Above the dance floor, the Plantation Room had a replica of a huge sliced watermelon as the ceiling. There was a backdrop depicting the Suwannee River, and a papier-mâché steamboat plied a hesitating course directly behind Will Vodery's jazz orchestra. A bandanna-coifed black woman flipped flapjacks in a log cabin on the left. The watermelon's "seeds" were electric lights. A well with a windlass for pulling up water, plus images of sundry animals, completed the scene. The woman cooking pancakes was the same Aunt Jemima figure as in Leslie's production of *George*

White's Scandals of 1921, but at least this time it was Edith Wilson, not a white actress in blackface.[23]

In March, *Variety*, reporting on plans for *Shuffle Along* to go on the road, noted that Florence was not planning to go along and intended to give notice. The success of the Plantation Room had encouraged Lew Leslie and Sam Salvin to expand the floor show and seek to contract Florence full time, which had been Leslie's expectation all along. The initial version was merely a tryout before he committed himself fully. The significance of this new development is easy to underestimate today. That a black woman entertainer would have a sophisticated show built around her, right in the heart of Broadway, was revolutionary in its implications at the time.

The managers of *Shuffle Along* did not give up its star without a fight. They sought an injunction to prevent her appearing at the Plantation, on grounds of breach of her *Shuffle Along* contract. However, when their attorneys showed that her contract included a two-week cancellation clause, the *Shuffle Along* management backed down.[24]

Kid Thompson recalled Aubrey Lyles's amazement that Kid would encourage Florence to leave such a successful show:

> And Lyles didn't want me to take it. Lyles raised hell. He said "What damn, what kind of [man] is you?" 'cause Lyles was kind of coarse, "What kind of [man] is you? You got a girl here, she's a jewel," and they was paying her $125, see, 'cause she went in the show to take Gertrude Saunders's place, and I said, "Well, it's a gamble, so the man's going to give her $300." He said, "But goddammit, you're workin' in a damned restaurant, so I don't give a damn if you're makin' high C with a pork chop in your mouth."

Florence gave her two weeks' notice and was free to go with her new show. By April she was full-time with the Plantation. In a demonstration of "If you can't beat 'em, join 'em," Al Mayer, promoter and manager of *Shuffle Along*, set up a rival all-black revue, called *Bandanaland*, with songs by Sissle and Blake. It opened at Reisenweber's, the same establishment that had lured Gertrude Saunders away from *Shuffle Along*, with a $2 cover charge. J. A. Jackson reported in early April that the new contract Florence had signed with Lew Leslie was for three years, and no fewer than thirty-five weeks a year, at $500 per week. This was "the best ever given to a colored woman, both as to terms and as to salary."[25] The deal also provided that the show would employ Kid Thompson at $125 a week. (He had been getting $65 a week in *Shuffle Along*.)

Apart from the commercial considerations, the switch to full-time at the Plantation was very welcome to Florence. Performing in *Shuffle Along* had been a demanding schedule: two performances a day, the perennial rehearsals, and the additional late-night show at the Plantation Room, plus frequent special-benefit performances and occasional extra, paid engagements. In a four-week period in March and April, in addition to her two regular engagements, she played at least two special engagements. One was a contract by Claude McKay to sing three songs at the New Star Casino for the Liberator Publishing Company.[26] The other was a Gala Performance for the Speedwell Society for Abandoned and Convalescent Children. This latter was not too onerous as she was part of a large bill that included, among others, Nora Bayes, Irene Bordoni, Frank Crummit, Ruth Draper, Basil Rathbone, and Paul Whiteman.[27]

That Lew Leslie had come up with a winner in *Plantation Revue* was dramatically demonstrated by the imitations that soon began to spring up in all sorts of places, following the precise plantation model he had established. In June, *Variety* reported that Jenny Dolly, of the Dolly Sisters, had converted the Acacia Gardens in Paris to a duplicate of the New York Plantation. She was appearing there with Clifton Webb as her partner throughout the summer. One week later, *Variety* reported the establishment of a new Chicago venture patterned on the Plantation. It was "presenting an all-colored show entitled *Plantation Days* at Green Mill Gardens, Chicago, . . . including Harper and Blanks, Marjorie Sipp, Dave and Tressie and the Plantation Four." Harper and Blanks's *Plantation Days* show would also play a later role in Florence's career.

Variety was amazed at the remarkable success of the Plantation Room:

> The Plantation wave that has given Broadway cabaret capacity business nightly with a $2 coveur [sic] charge per person to see an all-colored revue running 50 minutes must have made Broadway theater owners and producers think what caused it. Plantation seats 225. The revue has been running there for some weeks. *Shuffle Along* gave an entire evening's performance of all colored for $2.50. Other $2.50 and $3 shows have been doing hardly more in gross than the total of Plantation's coveurs.[28]

The writer speculated that this anomaly must be due to some very expert public relations work. It didn't occur to him that it might have something to do with the revue's star. *Billboard*'s J. A. Jackson had no doubts on that score. Under the headline "Florence Mills in Lights," he reported that she had her name in lights on Broadway on the front of the Winter Garden building. He had even counted the light bulbs himself, "an even hundred of them." He concluded that this, plus highbrow attention in *Vogue* and *Vanity Fair*, meant that Florence "has arrived."[29]

The inhabitants of Harlem eagerly watched the success of *Plantation Revue* and its illustrious star. Not many of Florence's neighbors could afford to attend the swanky, up-market, uptown Plantation Room. It was not formally segregated, as the Cotton Club would be in later years. However, a combination of practical economics and prejudice discouraged all but the wealthiest Harlemites from frequenting fancy uptown venues. The opportunity to see Florence and her show on their own home ground came in early July when the Lafayette Theatre staged an adapted version of *Plantation Revue*.

It was always Florence's desire to perform for black audiences, especially her Harlem friends and neighbors. J. A. Jackson credited Will Vodery with persuading Lew Leslie to allow the special, two-week engagement. It involved complex logistics with scenery and equipment, not to mention the cast's taking taxis back for the midnight performance at their regular venue. The following week the *Age* reported:

> The biggest attraction ever presented in Harlem, Florence Mills and the *Plantation Revue*, with a supporting cast of several of the best vaudeville acts in the country, is the attraction at the Lafayette Theatre this and next week. No show in the past year has proved so popular with theatergoers in Harlem. Every performance has been given before a capacity house. . . . "Hawaiian Night in Dixieland" by Florence Mills and the Six Dixie Vamps put the house in an uproar, and it was several minutes before the applause subsided. Miss Mills was showered with flowers and was called back a half dozen times.[30]

How sweet this triumphant return to Harlem was for the girl who had started out there as "a scared, skinny, big-eyed teenager" facing the raucous patrons of the Lincoln Theatre. Many of those same patrons were among the throng welcoming her back now at the Lafayette. *Billboard* counted more than 300 performers and musicians in the audience, paying tribute to one of their own. Many were the same people Florence and Kid were socializing with at Leroy Wilkins's only a year or two before.

Lew Leslie was always generous about allowing his players to perform at other venues, but a secondary motive was also at work in this case. The short (forty-five-minute) *Plantation Revue* was expanded to provide a full theatrical evening at the Lafayette; hence the *Age* reviewer's reference to a supporting cast of vaudeville acts. One of the acts, comedian Shelton Brooks, was in fact to continue as part of the extended *Plantation Revue*, which would soon start a mainstream theater run at the Forty-eighth Street Theatre. The Lafayette run was effectively a tryout for the Forty-eighth Street engagement. Having broken into the Broadway world as a headline act in her own right, via the after-hours Plantation Room, Florence was now to be the star of a full-blown Broadway theatrical production. She was no longer just "working in a restaurant," as Lyles had complained.

Adding Shelton Brooks was a brilliant coup by Leslie. Apart from being an outstanding comedian, Brooks was also a very talented composer and singer. Born in Canada in 1886, he came to the United States as a teenager and started earning his living as a ragtime piano player. His specialty as a comedian was imitating Bert Williams, who reportedly commented, on seeing Brooks, "If I'm as funny as he is, I got nothin' to worry about." Today Brooks is best known as the composer (tune and lyrics) of "Some of These Days," which became Sophie Tucker's theme song, and "The Darktown Strutters Ball." The revamped *Plantation Revue* had Brooks as a Bert Williams–style comedian. He was also a master of ceremonies in the very popular style of the quaint Russian Nikita Balieff, known to New Yorkers from the delightful Russian folk entertainment *Chauve Souris*. Advance publicity even announced *Plantation Revue* as a "colored *Chauve Souris*." The show opened at the Forty-eighth Street Theatre on July 17. The reviewers this time were from the hard-bitten white press, rather than the sympathetic black press, which had greeted the Lafayette performances with delight.

In the main, the reviews were sympathetic, in many cases highly enthusiastic, but there were exceptions. Shelton Brooks was universally acclaimed and Florence was generally highly praised, although the *Herald's* critic achieved the distinction of being probably the only person ever to express an active dislike of her voice: "Her jazzing voice is the nearest thing to a squealing gate on the stage today." The main complaints focused on slowness and some rough humor in the first half, which was the extra material added to the *Plantation Revue* proper. Respected critic Alan Dale, in the *New York American*, was highly enthusiastic, describing Shelton Brooks as a "Prince of entertainers." Florence he described as "an artist; she has the mannerisms of the artistes who do duty at the Parisian shows—at the Scala, The Folies Marigny, and the Folies Bergère. Florence is chic and febrile. She has a thousand facial expressions, a sinuous body, and a perfect lack of self-consciousness. Moreover, she can sing. Her voice is sweet and pure, cultivated and not aggressive."

There was praise also for the songs and lyrics by Robinson and Turk. With his ragtime and jazz background J. Russel Robinson tended to write music that emphasized Florence's skill with the hot numbers, as in *Shuffle Along's* "I'm Craving for That Kind of Love." New material for the expanded show included a specialty number for her, "I've Got What It Takes but It Breaks My Heart to Give It Away." Its performance caused the critic for the *Mail* to comment, "[Florence Mills] presented just about the most suggestive song ever heard on a Broadway stage." He went on to say, "Miss Mills displayed real aptitude for 'putting over' jazz songs, and was especially good in the 'patter' passages. Last night she had no difficulty keeping the audience with her so long as she adorned the stage." Florence also performed Irving Berlin's popular hit of early 1922, "Some Sunny Day," as well as "I'm Just Wild about Harry" and "Gypsy Blues" from *Shuffle Along*. Edith Wilson performed the number that was to be associated with her evermore, "He May Be Your Man, but He Comes to See Me Sometimes."

The lengthy *Variety* review made some unfavorable comparisons between the slow first part of the expanded *Plantation Revue* and *Shuffle Along*. It also noted the rawness of some of the lyrics and the vigor of the dancing by the Six Dixie Vamps in support of Florence in the Hawaiian number. "The gals may have gone a bit further in their wiggling than usual. That and the slapping of the loins was the thing the house liked. And those dusky vamps did look good in the costumes of black net and silver—with the lighting just right for the bare, browned thighs."[31]

Whatever varied views the critics expressed, the fact was Florence had triumphed in her first starring role in a full-scale Broadway theater. She was now the undisputed leading black entertainer. Under the caption "dainty Florence Mills," the *Age* published her photograph, labeling her "the highest salaried colored actress on the American stage." Florence took it all in her stride. Although she was delighted with the success of the production, the fame didn't go to her head. She continued to be approachable and friendly to all her friends and associates. The *Age* had noted that "Florence Mills on Broadway retains her modest charms." Her lack of affectation were to be among the things that most endeared Florence to her friends and admirers and the general public and would be a perennial theme in published descriptions of her.

Among those who sent Florence congratulatory telegrams on opening night was Joe Jordan[32] the ragtime composer for Williams and Walker shows and for the *Ziegfeld Follies*, for which his work included Fannie Brice's big hit, "Lovie Joe." The veterans of black entertainment like Jordan understood fully what Florence's breakthrough meant to them. This was aptly summed up in an article in Jackson's Page titled "It's getting darker on Broadway." The article referred to a song performed by Gilda Gray in the 1922 *Ziegfeld Follies*, which declared, "The great white way is white no more, It's just like a street on the Swanee shore."[33]

Although black entertainment was in demand, most promoters trod a conservative line, constrained to give white audiences what they expected without venturing too far from the approved model and its stereotypes. Lew Leslie's revue format fitted the bill very nicely in this regard, but, at least with Florence Mills, it was forging a new image of the black performer as a sophisticated figure of dignity. Florence might be surrounded by the trappings of a plantation when she performed, but no one was fooled for one minute that she was an unsophisticated figure of the Old South. The words of the drama critic for the *New York Sunday Graphic* sum up her image. "In that season not to have seen and heard Florence Mills was to be quite out of the know on Broadway. She established a tremendous vogue and the resort was crowded nightly by the connoisseurs of the town who welcomed a talent so new, so rich, so provocative in its tropical appeal, so saturated with emotion, and yet fastidious in its refinement."[34]

Like many of the great black performers, including Fats Waller and Billie Holiday, Florence had the ability to take banal material and transcend it by the sheer magnetism of her personality and the genius of her talent. In another sense also, she and Lew Leslie were revolutionizing black theater. Since the days of Williams and Walker, practically all black shows had been built round two male comedians. They had also been plot-based, or "book," shows, hanging songs and jokes on a flimsy libretto story. *Plantation Revue* broke the mold by discarding any pretence of a story. Instead it presented a fast-moving, plotless revue built round a female star.

Following the run at the Forty-eighth Street Theatre, the Plantation reopened for the 1922–1923 season on October 4. The enthusiastic first-night audience included Charlie Chaplin, Irving Berlin, and Irene Bordoni. The audience gave Florence an ovation, "with Charlie Chaplin vying with the enthusiasts in the matter of applause."[35] Respected critic S. J. Kaufman, astonished at Florence's dynamic performance in the 3:00 a.m. second show, described her as "competitor-less." He also declared, "Society has a new toy and this latest fad of the town is The Plantation."[36]

One of Florence's most popular new songs for the revised edition by Turk and Robinson was the tune "Aggravatin' Pappa." It was also one of radio's most popular songs of the period 1923–1930. Sophie Tucker, always a true admirer of black entertainers, recorded it soon after Florence's show opened. Tucker was just one example of a trend that quickly became obvious: As Florence introduced new tunes and made them popular, female singers would rush to record them. In late 1922 and early 1923, twelve versions of "Aggravatin' Pappa" were released by female vocalists. In addition to Sophie Tucker, they included Bessie Smith, Alberta Hunter, and Lucille Hegamin. Lucille, one of Florence's old Chicago associates, had also recorded "I've Got What It Takes" in 1922.[37]

Notes

1. Robert Kimball and William Bolcom, *Reminiscing with Sissle & Blake* (New York: Viking, 1973), 118–120; and Bricktop, with James Haskins, *Bricktop* (New York: Athenaeum, 1983), 79.

2. Undated publicity release, "Florence Mills Interviewed between Dances," in Florence Mills file TC FLP.

3. Jim Haskins and N. R. Mitgang, *Mr. Bojangles: The Biography of Bill Robinson* (New York: William Morrow, 1988), 112–113.

4. From notes by "Eubie Blake and His Girls" to the record titled *Eubie Blake Song Hits*. Eubie may well have been correct because today sheet music for that particular song is the rarest of all the *Shuffle Along* numbers.

5. Theophilus Lewis, *Messenger*, VII (Jan. 1925), 62.

6. Gilbert Seldes, *The 7 Lively Arts* (New York: Sagamore Press, 1957), 149.

7. Claude McKay, *A Long Way from Home* (London: Pluto Press, 1985), 141.

8. Playbill, NAACP Collection, Administrative files Part 1, C216, Library of Congress, and "Shuffle Along Co. in Midnight Revue," NYA, Oct. 22, 1921.

9. Langston Hughes, *The Big Sea* (New York: Hill and Wang, 1963), 62–63, 85.

10. Noel Coward, *Autobiography* (London: Methuen, 1986), 100.

11. Robert Sylvester, *No Cover Charge: A Backward Look at the Night Clubs*, uncorrected proof edition (London: Peter Davies, 1957), 36.

12. Allen Woll, *Black Musical Theatre* (New York: Da Capo, 1989), 98, and Bernard Sobel, *A Pictorial History of Vaudeville* (New York: Citadel Press, 1961), 120, 124, 145.

13. "Lew Leslie dies: An Era Ends," obituary at time of Leslie's death on March 10, 1963 (publication unknown).

14. HAJC.

15. "They Startled Broadway," clipping, probably from *Inter-State Tattler*, in Gumby Scrapbook Collection, Columbia University.

16. See John Edward Hasse, "J. Russel Robinson: The White Man with Colored Fingers," *Resound* 2:2 (Apr. 1985).

17. Race records refer to the products of small niche labels targeting the black population. When these recordings proved popular, some major recording companies created their own subsidiary labels to cash in on the craze.

18. Perry Bradford, *Born with the Blues* (New York: Oak Publications, 1965), 134–135. Like much of Bradford's book, the chronology of this section is confused, with references to the 1928 *Keep Shufflin'*, but the actual events depicted seem reasonably accurate and consistent.

19. VAR, Mar. 17, and BAA, Feb. 17 and Mar. 24, 1922.

20. Noble Sissle, NYA article, quoted in Mark Tucker, "In Search of Will Vodery," *Black Music Research Journal* 16:1 (spring 1996).

21. J. A. Jackson's Page, *Billboard*, Mar. 4, 1922.

22. Robert Campbell, "Florence Mills' Life Story," PhTr, Nov. 24, 1927.

23. Daphne Duval Harrison, *Black Pearls* (New Brunswick: Rutgers University Press, 1988), 193. Edith Wilson continued as Aunt Jemima in Quaker Oats commercials right up to the 1960s, when they were abandoned due to civil rights groups' pressure.

24. VAR, Mar. 17, 1922, 28, and Apr. 21, 1922, 8.

25. BAA, Apr. 7, 1922.

26. Contract document, HAJC.

27. Playbill, HAJC.

28. VAR, June 2, 1922 ("Inside Stuff Legit" section).

29. *Billboard*, May 13, 1922.

30. NYA, July 1, 1922.

31. VAR, July 21, 1922, "On Broadway."

32. SCRAP, HAJC.

33. "It's Getting Dark on Old Broadway," by Louis A. Hirsch, Gene Buck, and Dave Stamper, 1922.

34. *New York Sunday Graphic*, quoted in AMST, June 24, 1925.

35. SCRAP, HAJC.

36. SCRAP HAJC, and *Plantation Revue* playbill.

37. William Randle Jr., "Black Entertainers on Radio 1920–1930," *Black Perspective in Music* (spring 1977). The Turk, Robinson song "I've Got What It Takes," recorded by Lucille Hegamin in 1922, is not the similarly named "I Got What It Takes" recorded by Bessie Smith in 1929, which is by Clarence Williams.

CHAPTER FIVE

~

Transatlantic Star

Rival Plantations

1923 started off quietly for Florence. She was still a star attraction in a re-vamped edition of *Plantation Revue*. For the new edition, Leslie engaged a new songwriting team of Joe Young, Sam Lewis, George Meyer, and Harry Akst to prepare a whole set of new material for Florence. All were veterans of the Tin Pan Alley scene. Young and Lewis, as previously noted, wrote the words to the Walter Donaldson song "Don't Cry, Frenchy," Florence's big hit on the Panama Trio's Pantages tour. Now they were to be part of her personal songwriting team. George Meyer had already written his best-known song, "For Me and My Gal." Akst had worked with Irving Berlin and Walter Don-aldson during the war. He would go on to write "Dinah" with Lewis and Young.

Songwriters in those days tailored their songs to the personality and style of the star performer. Robinson and Turk had chosen to play up the jazzy side of Florence's performance with songs like "I've Got What It Takes" and "Aggra-vatin' Papa." The new team highlighted her outstanding skill with gentle bal-lads. The wistfully dreamy "Down among the Sleepy Hills of Ten-Ten-Tennessee" was the first significant result of this collaboration. It was an instant success. As soon as Florence popularized it in the new *Plantation Revue*, Blos-som Seeley and the Brox Sisters recorded it.[1] Various orchestras, jazz groups, and male vocalists recorded at least another eight versions within a few months. It also made a big impression on the young Paul Robeson. Recently married, he was struggling to complete his law degree and trying to come to grips with his future. Should he be a lawyer, an actor, a singer, or a professional sports star? He had gained a temporary spot in *Shuffle Along* shortly after Florence had left. With the help of his close friend and fellow gridiron hero Fritz Pollard, he now found another temporary niche, in *Plantation Revue*.[2]

Pollard was the first black All-American football player, in 1916, and later the first black professional coach. He and Robeson had confronted racial opposition together to claim their place in college football. Pollard brought Robeson into the Plantation one day and introduced him to Florence, hoping to help promote Robeson's singing future. "Miss Mills was just as nice as she could be," said Pollard.[3] Already knowing of Robeson's sporting prowess and his *Shuffle Along* role, and always a sucker for someone needing a hand, Florence was happy to help. After she consulted with Lew Leslie and musical director Will Vodery, they slotted Paul into the show singing a specialty piece, "Li'l Gal." This was a charming dialect poem by Paul Laurence Dunbar, originally set to music by J. Rosamund Johnson for the Cole and Johnson show *The Shoo-fly Regiment*.

Robeson said, "I donned some overalls and a straw hat and warbled 'Li'l Gal' to a chorine. How thrilling it was to listen to Florence Mills sing nightly 'Down among the Sleepy Hills of Tennessee.'"[4] Big, genial Paul was initially in awe of tiny Florence because of her fame. Like many others, he found that fame made no difference to her friendly nature and approachability. It surprised him to find she traveled home after the show on the same subway train as he did. "How proud I was when she gave me a nod and a smile of recognition."[5] The temporary engagement helped Robeson through a difficult period in his career before he went on to achieve international fame.

The new version of *Plantation Revue* involved more than just freshening it up for the new season. It had a major role to play in plans to launch Florence on an international career. English theatrical impresario Charles B. Cochran had seen her in *Shuffle Along*, and her performance had made a deep impression on him. He already held the contract for an English production of *Shuffle Along*, but with Florence no longer in the show, it had lost its appeal for him. Toward the end of 1922, he visited New York searching for ready-made new attractions to present in London's sophisticated West End. Cochran was one of the world's leading theatrical impresarios. His passion in life was to present the world's greatest theatrical performers and entertainers to the English theatergoing public, regardless of cost. His breadth of interest took in every corner of show business—circus, boxing, wrestling, and Wild West shows, as well as straight drama, opera, and ballet. He had presented some of the greatest figures of the theater, including Sarah Bernhardt, Eleonora Duse, and Diaghilev. Some of his greatest successes were in revue, where he originated the style called intimate revue.

Cochran believed the speed and vigor of a typical all–black show would
enthrall London audiences. From earlier years spent in America he had a
wide knowledge of and respect for black entertainment. He had seen Isham's
Octoroons in Montreal in the 1890s, Johnson and Dean in Budapest, and
Williams and Walker in London.[6] Seeing Florence in *Shuffle Along* had already convinced him she was one of the world's greatest performers. As soon
as he saw her in her own show, he was certain *Plantation Revue* would be a
bigger draw than *Shuffle Along* without her. In one of his autobiographies, he
said, "Florence Mills was one of the greatest artists that ever walked on to a
stage. But for her colour she would have been internationally accepted as one
of the half dozen leading theatrical personalities of this century, and worth
all the money in the world."[7]

Cochran decided to present an adapted version of *Plantation Revue* as part
of his new season. Under the overall title *Dover Street to Dixie*, it would be
the second, or the *Dixie*, half of a two-part show. A separate white English
cast would provide the *Dover Street* part. In January, on his return from New
York, he announced his plan of producing six shows: *Anna Christie, Partners
Again, Dover Street to Dixie, Little Nelly Kelly, The Music Box Revue,* and *So
This Is London.* Competitors like Andre Charlot ridiculed the program, saying it was impossible for one man to mount six productions simultaneously.
They were wrong! Within six months, he had all these shows running in
London's West End and, in addition, presented a season of plays by avant-
garde French playwright Sacha Guitry with a series of matinees starring
Eleonora Duse.[8]

The prospect of an overseas engagement was exciting for Florence but also
a bit intimidating. She knew how to handle an American audience but had
no idea how English ones would react. Cochran's enthusiasm was reassuring.
However, before London could get a chance to decide if he was right, a rival
black show tried to jump the gun. Cochran had powerful competitors in the
English promotional arena. Apart from the already mentioned Andre Charlot, whose *Charlot's Revue* was popular in America, Sir Alfred Butt, a member of Parliament, was a keen rival. Hearing of Cochran's plan to stage a
black show, Butt told his manager, Albert De Courville, to find a counterattraction. He found the Chicago-based Harper and Blanks's *Plantation Days,*
the direct copy of Leslie's *Plantation Revue. Plantation Days* leader Leonard
Harper was an outstanding dancer. Osceola Blanks, his partner, was a sister
of Birleanna Blanks, one of Florence's colleagues at the Panama Club in
1916. On the musical side, *Plantation Days* had some names that rank high

in the jazz pantheon, including James P. Johnson, Darnell Howard, and Wellman Braud. There was also a first-rate dance troupe, the Crackerjacks, headed by the outstandingly acrobatic Archie Ware.

The *Plantation Days* visit to England fared badly from the outset. An injunction from the *Shuffle Along* company seeking to block the use of material from that show delayed the departure. Racial opposition fomented problems getting British work permits. Arriving in London in March 1923, the company was to appear as part of a larger revue called *The Rainbow* at the Empire Theatre, Leicester Square. The *Plantation Days* part was to follow acts with white performers, some of whom were also American imports. The intention was that the black troupe would also perform at a cabaret and restaurant before and after the evening stage performances, set up in the foyer and decorated with plantation-style cabins, verandas, and scenery of cotton fields. There, after the show, the audience could stay on to see the black performers in a cabaret while enjoying southern-style refreshments like waffles.[9]

Sir Alfred Butt encountered two problems in getting his show before the public. The less serious one was an injunction sought by Cochran and his coplaintiff, Sam Salvin, owner of the original New York Plantation Restaurant. They sought to restrain Butt "from producing . . . a cabaret entertainment under the name of *The Plantation* or any other name that was similar." They claimed that calling his revue *The Plantation* was misrepresenting it as the original Florence Mills show. Among the witnesses supporting Cochran's case was famous Hollywood film star Tallulah Bankhead. The judge refused to make any order, leaving Butt free to continue.[10] The more serious problem came from Butt's proposal to have the foyer of the Empire Theatre decorated as a plantation, with dancing and cabaret. This revived an old theatrical controversy. In the 1890s, and up to 1916, the Empire promenade had been a notorious center for high-class prostitutes. It was closed down in 1916 as a threat to the health of troops on leave. Butt now had to defend himself against accusations of wishing to revive it.

The publicity created by the controversy sparked off a new round of an earlier debate involving racist opposition to imported black musicians and entertainers. The previous October, *John Bull*, a right-wing scandal sheet, had run a campaign against a touring black theatrical troupe, Will Garland's Colored Society, claiming they would be a cause of scandal and immorality. The home office found nothing to support the allegations. The troupe gained a limited approval for six weeks as "a specialty turn for which Britons could not be substituted." When it became general knowledge that Butt and Cochran were planning to bring other black shows to London, the controversy over black performers became very public and nasty. Concerns were voiced over "a cabaret where black artistes would actually mix with white folk at the tables."[11]

The leading complainant, stirring up mischief with spiteful glee, was prominent journalist Hannen Swaffer. Swaffer used his columns in the *Sunday Times* and the *Daily Graphic* to promote his populist prejudices. In an article headlined "The Scandal of Negro Revues," Swaffer took swipes at both Cochran and Butt, asserting that "while the actors and actresses of England are concerned about their bread and butter . . . Sir Alfred Butt and C. B. Cochran are quarrelling apparently about which niggers they have got." He printed a lengthy list of out-of-work performers, finishing with the question, "If good revue artistes are wanted, why is Nelson Keys not working now? And why is Daphne Pollard not in a show?"

Cochran denied claims by Butt that Florence's *Plantation Revue* was just one of many equally good black shows on offer. He wrote:

> The facts are that I saw Florence Mills and considered her a truly great artiste, a phrase I rarely use. I saw her several times. She can be mentioned in the same breath as Yvette Guilbert or Marie Lloyd. . . . I was offered several Negro shows described by agents as equal to Salvin's *Plantation Revue*. A Duse, an Edith Evans and a Nelly Farren are not duplicated and I saw only one Florence Mills. I shall be very proud to present her in London. She is unique.[12]

Swaffer continued to pen offensive articles with headings like "Nigger Problem brought to London." Sometime later he reported that Daphne Pollard, whose unemployment he had complained about, had gained a part in the white segment of *The Rainbow* on her terms. Pollard's name would crop up again later in Florence's story. *The Rainbow* finally opened several days late. The *Plantation Days* part of the main stage show occurred as planned, but the cabaret never opened. Noisy hecklers interrupted the opening night performance of *The Rainbow* with boos and whistles. There were further problems at the end of the night, when Jack Edge, "a low comedian," addressed the audience to complain that his part was too small. *Variety* reported, "The curtain was hastily dropped and a hand through the centre opening seized Edge by the neck and yanked him out of sight. The curtain was raised again and the audience had a glimpse of a stage hand carrying out the struggling Edge."[13] His outburst triggered some cries of "Send the niggers back." Among those witnessing the scene with some alarm were Fred and Adele Astaire. They were in London for the first time, launching their own London debut in a show called *Stop Flirting*. Their agent had to assure them that this was not normal for a London first night and that they had no cause for alarm.[14]

The critics received *The Rainbow* poorly, complaining of lack of humor. They were not much kinder to the *Plantation Days* segment of it, with some exceptions. The *Plantation Days* part was soon reduced to about twenty minutes and later fourteen minutes. The other white American imports were also cut back. The Plantation troupe had its payment reduced, causing *Variety* to suggest the management was trying to make them walk out on their contracts. By May 12 their work permits had expired, and *The Rainbow* continued without them. As a final insult, the employers took advantage of the absence of a clause stipulating the class of their return fares and refused to pay better than steerage class. Just as their venture was ending, Florence and the *Plantation Revue* troupe were stepping off the liner *Albania* and straight into the line of fire.

The Real Plantation

While the *Plantation Days* London venture was beset with difficulties from the start, the opposite proved true for Florence and her group. Before the troupe left, Harlemites were greeting Florence's engagement to perform overseas as a compliment to the race. A big send-off was arranged. She played the Lafayette in Harlem again as part of a farewell season. The response was so enthusiastic that the farewell engagement ran a second week to full houses.

While Florence and her overseas-bound troupe played the Lafayette, her former Panama Trio companion Cora Green took over as the replacement lead at the Plantation. She was aided by Leslie's new recruits Maude Russell, fresh from her triumph in *Liza*, and a young Hyacinth Curtis, both of whom would reappear in Florence's story. On Sundays during the following summer, the replacement Plantation cast was supported by the Elmer Snowden band, which included the young Duke Ellington on piano. In due course, the Snowden band would become the nucleus of the Duke Ellington orchestra.[15]

The entire cast of the currently successful black show *Liza* attended the final Friday midnight performance at the Lafayette to give Florence their personal big bon voyage. She performed as a single, helped by a couple of girls from her show, and supported by a program of vaudeville acts. Her seventeen-minute act included four numbers, with solo accompaniment by her pianist, George Rickson. She performed against a backdrop of a beautiful blue and gold "eye," with piano cover to match. Wearing a simple silk dress, Florence came down the center of the stage singing "Homesick Blues" as her first number. She then changed to a white feather costume for her "Indian Habits" number. Next she donned a white-beaded Georgette evening gown and sang the currently popular "You Gotta See Mamma Every Night" and a new Henry Creamer song, "Fidgety Fidge." Responding to the enthusiastic audience's demand for an encore, she did "Aggravatin' Papa," her newest hit. On some evenings, in response to audience demand, she performed her old *Shuffle Along* hit, "Kiss Me (I'm Craving for That Kind of Love)."[16]

Salem Tutt Whitney, veteran vaudevillian who had trouped with both Black Patti and Aida Overton Walker, was singularly impressed. "It was one of the largest, jolliest and most appreciative nocturnal gatherings ever assembled in Harlem to do honor to any colored theatrical celebrity." He went on to say:

> Florence Mills is the most deservedly popular colored star since the heyday of the late lamented Aida Overton Walker. And let it be known that Miss Mills is not a made-overnight star. She has successfully travelled the rough road that the gods of destiny have decreed one must travel before writing one's name with indelible letters of gold upon the walls of the Hall of Fame. A becoming modesty and sweet personality endear her to all fortunate enough to know her. If you have known Florence in the days of her struggles, don't hesitate to renew your acquaintance; success has not given obesity to either her head or her figure.[17]

Following the Lafayette engagement, Florence played one of the season's biggest concerts of its kind, a Big Farewell Concert at the New Star Casino. The full cast of the *Plantation Revue* was there, including the dancing team of Thompson and Covan. Willie Covan was Kid Thompson's new partner. The pair had known each other since Kid's Tennessee Ten days. Covan had also auditioned unsuccessfully for the dancing conductor job.[18] Kid persuaded Leslie to find a spot for Covan in *Plantation Revue* when Covan found himself out of work. Kid recalled, "Willie was a better dancer than I was. Willie danced straight and I'd do a lot of muggin' and clownin'. I've always been a kind of a comedian. When Willie and I were together, Willie was a good dancer, and I'd do my bit and always get some laughs, and that made our act something different from the other acts, and we had a nice appearance which, you know, was absolutely necessary."

The concert at the New Star Casino was a sellout, the attendance surpassing 5,000. Enthusiastic fans forced their way in well beyond the building's capacity. At one point the alarmed owners climbed out on the fire escape, checking to see how much the walls were bulging. A few days later, Florence and an entourage from the Plantation, including her sister Maude, Edith Wilson, Kid Thompson, and Willie Covan, were entertained by friends at the Club Cabaret into the small hours. The original planned departure date was Sunday, April 15, but they didn't embark on the Cunard liner *Albania* until two weeks later. An accident in England injuring the lead comedian delayed the show's opening.[19]

Although leaving in a spirit of enthusiasm, Florence was aware of the hazards of racial opposition she would have to face. Everyone in show business back home, especially in Harlem, had followed the experiences of the *Plantation Days* troupe in London with interest—and anger. *Variety* reported the bad treatment; "Theatrical, artistic and social London is becoming incensed over the treatment of the imported American artists by the Empire management."[20] Black militant Marcus Garvey, after quoting one of Swaffer's more venomous columns, called it further proof of the hopelessness of blacks' seeking justice in a white country. "We may not hope to make good in the future in the music halls of London, or the theatres or opera houses of Paris, but we may look forward by our own effort to the day when we will entertain ourselves in our own theatres, music halls and opera houses in our Homeland Africa."[21]

There was little time to think about the danger in the tumult of the big send-off at the docks by a throng of well-wishers. They were on the way to a great adventure. For most, it was their first time overseas. Viewing the animated farewells, a *New York Times* correspondent commented, "Orchids and jewellery aplenty were noticed on the dusky actresses." However, once the *Albania* was on the ocean, Florence and her entourage got their first taste of what might be in store. The *Albania* was a single-class ship with one dining room. Some bigots among the 141 white passengers took offense at the idea of sharing the dining salon with thirty-four black passengers. Perhaps some were upset that the *New York Times* listed "The Plantation Revue a colored troupe," at the top of the notable passengers list.[22]

Eager to appease the troublemakers, the ship's authorities made a rapid rearrangement of the dining salon layout. They assigned the black passengers to "a removed section," an obvious euphemism for segregated.[23] Although the performers were angry and upset, they took it in their stride; after all, Jim Crow was no stranger to them in the United States. However, the unpleasant incident was an ominous foreboding of what might await them in England. The rest of the voyage was uneventful. The *Albania* docked in London on May 10, 1923, just two days before *Plantation Days* played its last date at The Rainbow. By May 13 the two troupes were together. Whatever rivalry and ill will existed between their managers and promoters, no such rancor existed among the performers. They greeted one another like long-lost friends, as indeed they were. James P. Johnson's association with Florence went back to the Nickellette in 1913. Osceola Blanks's sister had been one of Florence's fellow performers in the Panama Café in 1916.

The occasion that brought the two troupes together was a social gathering organized in their honor by a group known as the Coterie of Friends. The Coterie was founded in 1919. It was the brainchild of a brilliant young black classical musician, clarinetist, and composer, Edmund Thornton Jenkins. Although Jenkins is remembered today as a brilliant classical composer, he was no stranger to jazz. He had played with the Southern Syncopated Orchestra and made records in 1921 that, in the words of scholars, "reveal a jazz quality that . . . was rare among performers of the day."[24] He was the son of the Reverend Daniel Joseph Jenkins, founder of the Jenkins Orphanage in Charleston, South Carolina. The Jenkins Orphanage was famed for its brass band, a remarkable nursery for musical talent, especially in jazz. Duke Ellington employed several former Jenkins musicians, and his trumpet player Freddy Jenkins was a relative of Rev. Jenkins and Edmund.[25]

The Coterie's stated purpose was "to further social intercourse amongst young men of colour, resident or temporarily resident in Great Britain; to provide its members with a library containing books and papers relating to people of colour." The members included West Indians and Africans as well as English-born blacks.[26] The gathering on Sunday, May 13, was at the Adelphi Hotel, in the Paddington–Hyde Park area of London. The organizers were Edmund Jenkins and Dr. Felix H. Leekham. Leonard Harper acted as master of ceremonies, and James P. Johnson's Orchestra had "kindly taken charge of the Musical Programme." The program listed "Guests of Honor, Miss Florence Mills, Mr. Will Vodery, Mr. Shelton Brooks, Mr. James P. Johnson, and the members of the West Indian Cricket Team," which included the later famous Learie Constantine. The program noted the evening began at 8 p.m. and finished with carriages at 1 a.m.[27]

Although the event was essentially a private one for the Coterie and its honored guests, some outsiders attended. Swaffer caught wind of the event and ridiculed it in his usual fashion, referring to it as "the Negroes Jubilee." He reported that the callboard at the Empire stage door had carried a notice of the event: "By Invitation Only, Price of invitation 5 shillings." It had been more widely publicized, and among "the score of White people" attending were Nora Bayes, Paul Whiteman, and Daphne Pollard. Swaffer described them as "going to see but not to take part."[28]

In Pollard's case he was right. However, Swaffer didn't know that Nora Bayes's association with Florence and Kid Thompson went back to 1917, when she had chosen them and the Tennessee Ten to be her support team. She had then been still at her peak, and they were rising hopefuls. She was now in London, playing at the Coliseum, in an attempt to revive her flagging career. Her entourage on arrival—two adopted children, pianist, four servants, and eleven trunks—suggests she was not yet down to her last dollar.[29] Nora was delighted to see her former Tennessee Ten protegé arriving in London as a star. Paul Whiteman also was no mere spectator. He was well aware of Florence's success. His high regard for black jazz musicians made an opportunity to meet with James P. Johnson and Will Vodery a welcome event. The evening offered a sparkling smorgasbord of jazz, with the musicians from both shows seeking to outdo one another in a traditional cutting contest.

The function was also an opportunity for Florence and Kid to catch up with gossip on the local scene, especially the race issues. They discussed this with their friends from *Plantation Days*, Leonard Harper and Osceola Blanks. Harper was philosophical, noting that the white Americans in the show had also been the target of complaints but that the race issue made it harder for the blacks. He was angry, however, that the English management had reneged on the understanding that they would pay for second-class tickets for the boat trip back to America. The troupe was faced instead with steerage. Never one to leave a friend in difficulties, Florence generously offered them a loan to cover the difference, and they happily accepted.

Cochran's show, titled *Dover Street to Dixie*, had two parts. The entertainers in the first half, *Dover Street*, were all white, and in the second half, *Dixie*, all black. *Dixie* was essentially the *Plantation Revue*. *Dover Street* was a loose series of sketches built around the idea of John Gay, author of *The Beggars Opera*, waking in modern (1923) London after a sleep of several centuries. The stars of *Dover Street* were the popular comedians Stanley Lupino, a cockney, and Odette Myrtil. Choreography was by Eddy Dolly and his sister Jenny Dolly, one of the famous Dolly Sisters, who had staged their own Plantation imitation in Paris. The planned start date for the show had been early in the second half of May. However, Lupino's accident that had delayed the original planned departure was still causing problems. He could not do any falls or dance or change his clothes between scenes, and the opening of *Dover Street to Dixie* was therefore delayed. The Pavilion's alternative entertainment during the lull was a film, *Hunting Big Game in Africa*.

Dover Street to Dixie

Florence has butterflies in her stomach in the days before the opening of her new show in London. Although she is an established star and confident performer, she is still at heart the little girl from Goat Alley. The challenge of facing her first performance in a new country and continent is daunting. She is intensely aware of her role as a representative of her people. English audiences are notoriously less demon-

strative than American ones. Winning them over is a formidable challenge. In her own words, "When I am faced with a stolid audience, I know that I must make them my friends, and [I] am on my mettle." She sees also that C. B. Cochran is worried about the possibility of racial demonstrations.

Florence's worries about the race issue soon faded as hectic rehearsals and preparations for an unfamiliar theater consumed her time. Lew Leslie was a genial, easygoing man away from the stage, but when it came to business, he was a workaholic and a relentless rehearser. Florence shared this outlook. Her apparently spontaneous performances were not as effortless as they appeared. They required thorough awareness of the performance space available in a new theater and of the roles of her fellow performers. She rehearsed relentlessly, saying, "All my life I have worked and practiced hard. The little glance or movement that looks so easy on the stage often takes hours of rehearsal to get it just right."[30]

Dover Street to Dixie finally opened on the evening of Thursday, May 31, 1923. It was a typical London West End first-night audience, dressed in the latest glittering fashion. One fashion correspondent rhapsodized over the extravagant gowns and jewelry, noting "gardenia buttonholes were almost as much favored by the men as orchid clusters by the women." The glittering display of fashionable opulence distracted attention from the controversy surrounding the imported black performers making their debut that night. Nevertheless, the tension was palpable. All society was aware of the controversy. Many expected some form of demonstration. There was also a high level of curiosity about the mysterious black star on whose behalf Cochran had made such extravagant claims. Could she really be in the same class as great white performers like Eleonora Duse and Edith Evans?

Charles Cochran had called off his feud with the critics for the occasion. He had relaxed his embargo against their attending his first nights, and he allocated them free tickets for the occasion. His pacific overtures did not extend to Swaffer, however. Swaffer's articles, filled with racist insults, heavily infused with the insulting N-word, had offended Cochran deeply. Swaffer's public sneering at his claims about Florence's talent particularly annoyed him. Never daunted, Swaffer had managed to arrange an invitation to the performance from a lady friend. She was a regular first nighter and paid for his ticket. Cochran soon recognized Swaffer's familiar face and grating voice. Discarding his cigar, he limped down the center aisle and confronted the unwelcome critic. He dragged him out of his seat, and with one hand at his neck, the other on the seat of his trousers, he bodily propelled Swaffer out of the theater. Swaffer's version of the event confirms Cochran's account while presenting himself as a sweet and reasonable victim who bore no malice over the incident. At the box office Swaffer politely requested a refund.[31]

With the unwelcome critic out of the way, Cochran could concentrate on the audience's reaction to his show. The opening *Dover Street* part, performed by the local white cast, was on first. It did not get a good audience reaction. Experienced comedian Stanley Lupino failed to amuse the audience. They were feeling dull and listless by the interval. The opening scene of the *Dixie* second half, *Plantation Revue*, started with spirited music from the Plantation Orchestra; then the chorus entered dancing frantically, followed by statuesque blues singer Edith Wilson singing the upbeat "Yankee Doodle Blues." To that point any planned demonstration had little chance of being heard above the lively din.

Backstage, as she waited nervously for her cue, Florence knew a jazzy din would not protect her entry. Her opening number was the soft, dreamy music of "Down among the Sleepy Hills of Ten-Ten-Tennessee." She would occupy the stage alone, dressed in her ragged costume of a pathetic plantation boy carrying a hobo's bundle. This would be the ideal moment for any noisy outburst or ribald heckling. Tense as she stepped out on the historic London Pavilion stage for her first performance on foreign soil, Florence immediately felt the energy that always surged as soon as she was in front of an audience.

There was a hush as the audience got its first glimpse of the tiny Black figure that had attracted so much attention. Florence's sweet, high tones spread through the theater as she sang of "a little nest beyond the fields of golden grain," . . . "down among the sleepy hills of Ten-Ten-Tennessee." The people in the audience sat forward on the edge of their seat, and Cochran sat back with relief. He knew she had won them over. Leaning over to choreographer Eddy Dolly, he said, "She owns the house—no audience in the world can resist that." He would recall that "she controlled the emotions of the audience as only a true artist can."

There was a throb in her bird-like voice that brought a lump to the throat, then her eyes would flash. Her thin, lithe arms and legs became animated with a dancing delirium. It was all natural art, there was not a false note in any part of her performance. And the audience applauded as any audience applauds an artist in whom it detects genius. That night, [and every night] Florence Mills received an ovation each time she came on the stage—before every song she sang. That is a tribute which in my experience I have never known to be offered to any other artist.[32]

In the words of one critic, "All our prejudices against these *café-au-lait* entertainers melt when Florence Mills begins to sing. Her liquid voice made

'The Sleepy Hills of Tennessee' a haunting gem of exquisite pathos."[33] She had conquered the audience and defused any planned protest with a gentle, dreamy song. Florence could now be sure of a warm response for her more lively later numbers. These included "Homesick" from Irving Berlin's *Music Box Revue*, one of the many shows Cochran was staging in London at the time. Irving Berlin himself had come to London at his own expense to supervise the staging of *Music Box Revue*. Listening to Florence performing his song, he said to Cochran, "If I could find a white woman to put over a song the way she does, I would be inspired to write a hit a week."[34] Her other song, "You Got to See Sweety," was an adapted version of the Billy Rose–Con Conrad song "You've Got to See Mama Every Night." The American slang expression *Mama*, referring to a lover, had to be changed to "Sweety" so that English audiences would grasp the meaning.

As the finale and last encores finished, the audience applauded enthusiastically. Scattered boos and catcalls could just be heard above the din. Swaffer, who wasn't there, later claimed it was cries of "Send the niggers home." Respected critic Herbert Farjeon differed. "There were a few boos at the end of the show. . . . I cannot believe that they were intended for Florence Mills, who is the most beautiful half-caste [sic] I have ever seen, and who, besides singing well, tingles with such vitality that one wonders whether motion does not come more easily to her than rest."[35]

There was no question the general reaction was strongly positive. Florence knew she had scored a personal triumph in her first performance in Europe. The reaction was equally enthusiastic for the rest of the cast. The extraordinarily energetic dancing and singing erased the memory of the weak first half of the show. However, it was still too early to break out the champagne. The real test would come when the staid and cynical critics of the London dailies had their say. There would be no sleep until the early editions were delivered to Cochran at the crack of dawn. When they came, the critics' judgments were pretty much as Cochran had anticipated from the audience reaction. They highly praised the black part of the show and panned the white part. Even the staid London *Times*, while dismissing the first half as "a trifle dreary," was enthusiastic about the *Dixie* half. "Miss Mills, in particular, is endowed with a great deal of personality, but all the members of the company work as though each was its principal and this, perhaps, is the secret of their success."[36]

The reviewers for the periodical journals were even more enthusiastic. The *Era* noted, "Above all, there is Florence Mills, a lithe, slender girl, with eyes full of expression, a sweet voice, now strident, as when she reproaches a lover tending to slack off, now pathetic, and a way of dancing that makes a fool of perpetual motion!" The *Illustrated Sporting and Dramatic News*, the *Tatler*, and the *Stage* all reported in similar fashion. Side by side with reviews of *Dover Street to Dixie* were those of another new show, *Stop Flirting*, the West End London debut of Fred and Adele Astaire, described as "dancers of extraordinary agility in a novel style." The *New Statesman* praised the Astaires as dancers but expressed a strong preference for Florence's *Dixie* segment over their show.[37]

Cochran's gamble had paid off. Overnight, Florence Mills became the toast of London. As the congratulatory telegrams poured in, Cochran was pleased that he had once again delivered on his promise to present to London the best of the world's entertainers. Lew Leslie was pleased that he had another commercial success. Florence was pleased that she had earned, in a foreign land, honor and respect for her people. She was also more than a little relieved that the threatened opposition had not appeared. Congratulatory messages included one from one of Florence's most ardent opening-night fans, Irene Castle of the famous American ballroom dancing team Vernon and Irene Castle. "No one was as happy as I to witness your great success last night," Irene wrote to Florence next morning; "Your Tennessee number was beautiful. It made me want to cry and both my partner and I clapped our hands raw. I saw you first in *Shuffle Along* nearly two years ago and told Mr. Sissle then I was crazy about your work."[38]

It was clear that, once he tightened up the weaker parts of the *Dover Street* half, Cochran had a big success on his hands. The most pleasing evidence of the success of *Plantation Revue* came from his rival impresario, Albert De Courville. Impressed by the success of *Dover Street to Dixie*, De Courville started moves in early June to import *Shuffle Along* to England. Cochran, however, had already tied *Shuffle Along* in a tight contractual bind. Unfortunately, this meant English audiences never saw *Shuffle Along*. The closest they got to a taste of *Shuffle Along's* delights came when Florence added a reprise of the big hit from the show, "I'm Just Wild about Harry," to *Dover Street to Dixie*.

To demonstrate the enormity of Florence's London success, Lew Leslie took out a full-page advertisement back home in *Variety*. The caption, under her name, read "The Sensation of London." It included rave reviews from all the leading daily and weekly papers, fifteen of them in all, with the bottom caption declaring "Not One Adverse Criticism." The various descriptions of Florence, which emphasized her exotic appeal, included: "A lovely roguish, loose-limbed creature," "a sort of imp, who has reduced the grotesque in dancing and singing to a fine art," "a dusky electric spark," and "irresistibly roguish."[39]

The *Variety* ad triumphantly declared to American show business the commercial success Leslie had hoped for, worked for, and deserved. The black community didn't need to be told through *Variety*, however. Its own press, such as the *Amsterdam News*, the *Baltimore Afro-American*, and the *Chicago Defender*, had been gleefully spreading the good news already.

Meanwhile, in England, Florence and her troupe of singers and jazz musicians were achieving yet another kind of success: artistic and aesthetic. As the word began to spread about the show's exotic appeal, enthusiastic audiences flocked to *Dover Street to Dixie*. Prominent among them were members of the British royal family, including Edward, Prince of Wales. Known for his enthusiasm for all things American, especially jazz, the prince became one of Florence's keenest fans. He attended the show several times. In the secluded privacy of the royal box, safe from the prying eyes of the public, he would request encores from Florence and sing the words along with her.[40] One aristocrat saw the show more than thirty times and told Cochran that one week he took seats every night! There were other noteworthy fans whose lives were touched by Florence Mills at this time. One was the English actor John Gielgud. An eighteen-year-old drama student at the time, he attended theaters ravenously and kept all his programs, with handwritten comments preserving his opinions. Of *Dover Street to Dixie* he wrote: "The coloured people excellent in every way—Florence Mills particularly admirable."[41]

Even more impressed was the rising young English classical composer Constant Lambert. Florence's dancing and singing, and the music of the Plantation Orchestra, had a deeply moving effect on him. He was a precocious seventeen at the time, on a composition scholarship at the Royal College of Music. His friend Angus Morrison said later:

> Without a doubt this performance was one of the key experiences in his life, beginning not only his long preoccupation with jazz and the possibility of fusing and blending many of its rhythmic inventions and subtleties into the texture of more serious music, but also moving him in a far deeper way emotionally than any other music he had hitherto heard. I am convinced that the first time he saw the Plantation [Orchestra] was a moment of true inspiration—a moment he sought to recapture over and over again in his own music. The other strong impression made on him by the performance, exerting an influence more all-embracing and with even deeper emotional repercussions, was the incomparable personality of Florence Mills herself.[42]

With the serious appreciation of such people, a new kind of acclaim began to emerge beyond that normally given mere entertainment. For many of those who flocked to see the show, the performances entered the realm of artistry, an artistry rich in unfamiliar cultural elements. Those were the rich heritage of African-American culture presented through the jazz music of Will Vodery's Plantation Orchestra, the dancing of the chorus, and the personal genius of Florence Mills, who was steeped in that culture from her earliest years. In America in the 1920s, it was accepted that the black community could produce brilliant entertainers. That was a social niche they were permitted, even encouraged, to occupy. However, their talent still was seen as mere entertainment, not to be allowed the status and respect of the high arts. Geniuses like Roland Hayes, the powerful tenor, and Charles Gilpin, the great actor, were viewed as curiosities. They were largely constrained to perform material that defined them as "Negro" artists rather than artists without qualification. In London, however, these constraints did not apply. Respected critic St. John Ervine described Florence as "By far the most artistic person London has had the good fortune to see, something unequalled by any American playing here in the last decade."[43]

Another artist greatly impressed by Florence, and himself also a long way from home, was Indian painter and etcher Mukul Dey. He was an early associate of the great poet, novelist, and Nobel Prize–winner Rabindranath Tagore, with whom he shared a mission to revive neglected Indian art traditions. He was in London to study Western art, and his extraordinary achievement of reproducing the ancient artworks of the remote Ajanta caves had earned him a considerable stature in England. He made it a practice to create drypoint etchings of famous people he met. Fascinated by Florence, he asked her to sit for him, which she duly did. His etching of her was not publicly displayed until 1927, when the London *Sunday Times* enthused:

> As a rule, for obvious reasons, studio exhibitions have to be ignored, but in the case of Mr. Mukul Dey, the Indian artist, who is showing dry-points and drawings at 12, Relton-mews, Cheval-place Knightsbridge, the rule may be stretched. For one thing, Mr. Mukul Dey is the first Indian engraver to show here, and for another all Westerners are under an obligation to him for his copies of the Ajanta and Bagh frescoes, now in the British Museum—Among the dry-points and drawings there are some excellent portrait heads of interesting subjects, "Professor Albert Einstein" and "The Black Bird" (Miss Florence Mills) among them.[44]

Mukul Dey's drypoint etching of Florence is today a treasured possession of the Mukul Dey Archives, located at Santiniketan, West Bengal, India. Apart from Florence's personal impact, for many the Plantation Orchestra's music was their first opportunity to hear genuine jazz musicians. England had

had some exposure to black music before 1923. Will Marion Cook's Southern Syncopated Orchestra had performed there from 1919 to 1921, with Sydney Bechet and Edmund Thornton Jenkins among its talented membership. The term *jazz*, in England in 1923, was generally equated with a fairly anemic type of dance music or at best to Paul Whiteman's toned down "symphonic jazz." There was no sense of the power of real black jazz. Against this background, the Plantation Orchestra, even under Vodery's tight control as a theater orchestra, had enough true jazz content to be an eye-opener. Edith Wilson was a blues singer of some stature (in all senses of the word). Florence Mills, too, could perform in a wide variety of jazz styles, from blues, through hot numbers, to sentimental ballads. Finally there were the dancers, whose importance in jazz is too often ignored.

Along with the commercial and artistic success, Florence and her troupe found they were in demand socially in a way that would have been unthinkable in the racially obsessed United States. The London of 1923 was hardly comparable to 1920s and 1930s Paris, which welcomed black musicians and performers with open arms. Nevertheless, England was free of the stifling segregation of races that typified the United States. It was enjoying the era of "the Bright Young people," eager to try any new, daring experiences; cocktails, weekends on the Riviera, and American jazz music (whatever that might be).

Aristocratic and wealthy patrons who admired Florence's achievements were keen to entertain her in their fashionable homes. For Florence, it was a flashback to her early childhood, when the diplomatic set in Washington, D.C., had clamored for the services of Baby Florence in their salons. One such keen patron was Lady Nancy Cunard, heiress of the shipping family, a radical communist who espoused black causes. She would later scandalize society and her family by openly taking a black lover, jazz pianist and writer Henry Crowder. Nancy Cunard was noted for her lavish parties, and she invited Florence to one, a fancy dress occasion. She also invited Florence's friend, dancer Irene Castle.

Irene was aware that hostesses at those kinds of functions often invited celebrities as a ploy to give their guests free entertainment. Having learned earlier that her entrance was to be hailed with a blackout and a spotlight, Irene decided to foil Cunard's plans. She enlisted Florence's aid, sending her a telegram at the Pavilion: "May I borrow the costume you make your first appearance in as I wish to go impersonating you to Lady Cunard's party tonight. Can send for it at eleven o' clock and return it tomorrow evening. Telephone answer Embassy Club this evening. Will appreciate it very much, Irene Castle." Florence happily cooperated, the ploy worked, and a blacked-up Irene escaped recognition on arrival. The presence of two Florence Millses puzzled some guests.[45]

Another friend who called on Florence's goodwill at this time was a remarkable black South African, Sol Plaatje. From the later years of the nineteenth century right up to the 1930s, Plaatje was internationally active in promoting political rights for his countrymen. He spoke five or six languages and made frequent visits to England. He was in Canada and the United States during much of the period 1920–1922, speaking on platforms with both Marcus Garvey and W. E. B. DuBois. Plaatje had first met Florence when she was performing in *Shuffle Along* and formed a high opinion of her. On their meeting again in London, she was happy to introduce him to C. B. Cochran to seek support for Plaatje's venture, which was to print the Fellowship Hymn Book in the native languages of South Africans.[46] "I next met her," he said, "at Piccadilly Pavilion where she was starred in *Dover Street to Dixie*, a partly colored production, at around $400 per week. Her lucky husband was also in the cast. By permission of Mr. Cochran, the London theatre king, three members of the troupe sang gratuitously at my farewell concert on my last Sunday in London before I sailed for the Cape."[47] Among the attendance at Plaatje's farewell concert were some notable black English figures, including Evelyn Dove, a singer whose father had been a famous lawyer in Sierra Leone, and Gwendolen Coleridge-Taylor, daughter of the great black English classical composer.[48]

Florence participated in a more traditionally American social event on June 10, a baseball game played against the American Legion in which the Plantation players lost with the creditable score of 9 to 12. She was a keen baseball fan and admirer of the great Babe Ruth. "Even little Florence Mills was in uniform," said Johnny Dunn's report of the event to the *Chicago Defender*.[49] A photograph of Florence dressed in baseball gear for that occasion survives in the Schomburg Institute's collection. Apart from these events, Florence and her troupe also performed many charitable and special performances. There was a special matinee organized by the Countess of Athlone at the Prince of Wales Theatre on June 5 on behalf of the British Legion. There would, of course, have been many more had the ministry of labor not enforced a tight ban on extra engagements for the imported artists.

Dover Street to Dixie was Cochran's most successful show all that summer. In the heat of July it was taking in about $5,000 a week, and at the end of August it was still showing a profit at around $3,000 a week. Cochran, however, had overextended himself with his other ventures and was on the verge of bankruptcy. To stay afloat he needed to be able to bring in extra revenue by using Florence and the Plantation Orchestra in profitable cabaret and dance engagements, particularly during the coming winter. The ministry of labor, responding to pressure from local musicians, would extend their work permits only on condition that they undertook no such engagements.

Kid Thompson recalled, "There were so many people in England out of work, and the musicians were walking round with signs on their back, 'Get these darkies out of town,' so they could get the job before us." Cochran protested that by allowing Paul Whiteman's orchestra unlimited scope for such engagements, the ministry was being racist. In fairness to Whiteman himself, he actively lobbied on Cochran's behalf in the matter. Unsympathetically, the ministry merely responded that "Mr. Cochran is one of the first to feel the effect of the tightening up process."[50]

Bowing to the inevitable, Cochran closed the show. Soon afterwards he leased the Pavilion to Famous Pictures Corporation. *Dover Street to Dixie* had its last performance on September 1 and was replaced with a movie, *The Covered Wagon*, starring silent-screen heartthrob J. Warren Kerrigan. Ironically, film footage from *Dover Street to Dixie* has survived. It preserves Covan and Thompson's "Jailbirds" sequence and is catalogued in the British Pathe database with the following description: "Two black dancers dressed in striped outfits (convicts?) dance in front of a paddle steamer set. They do a bendy-legged tap dance. Lots of wild movements." Sadly, so far no footage that includes Florence's performance has been found.

To wind up *Dover Street to Dixie* and thank his successful black performers, Cochran hosted a special party for the whole company, with a few select white guests, at the Piccadilly Hotel. Under Vodery's baton the Plantation Orchestra performed what Cochran described as "extraordinary examples of most advanced orchestration." The evening stood out in the minds of the performers as one of their finest moments in England. It would be repaid enthusiastically when Cochran next visited the United States.

After the show closed, Florence and Kid decided to celebrate their financial and artistic success. Instead of going home directly, they traveled across the English Channel to Paris. Now that they had some money, they decided it was time for the honeymoon they had missed. With typical generosity they offered to take Willie Covan and his wife, also named Florence, with them. Florence Covan, also a talented dancer, had not been working in England, so they paid the Covans's fare across the Channel. Florence and Kid enjoyed the novelty of Paris and met some of the black entertainers who had already settled there, like Louis Mitchell and Buddy Gilmore. Wandering around the streets of Montmartre, they bought four saucy French watercolor cartoons for their planned new apartment back home.[51]

Perhaps fueled by reports of the Paris trip, a bizarre item appeared in *Variety* in late September. It said that Florence, billed as the Black [Eleonora]

Duse, was making a tour of European theaters and would soon perform on the Berlin stage, appearing in the biggest classical roles with casts of white actors.[52] Florence and Kid were by then back home in Harlem, and rumors were already circulating that she would star in a big show the following season. Florence had left the United States as Broadway's first major black female star. She had returned a full-fledged international superstar.

Notes

1. Seeley and Brox recording dates from Ross Laird, *Moanin' Low* (Westport, Conn.: Greenwood, 1996).

2. The exact timing of Robeson's *Plantation Revue* appearance is difficult to pin down. The *Shuffle Along* appearance was definitely in May–June 1922. The *Plantation* one is generally cited as sometime in 1923, but late 1922 has been suggested. The year 1923 seems to be established by the fact that the Tennessee song he mentions wasn't actually written till 1923. Pollard's account is in an undated, unidentified clipping in SCRAP, HAJC.

3. HAJC, undated, unidentified clipping.

4. Martin B. Duberman, *Paul Robeson* (London: Pan Books, 1991), 584.

5. Sheila Tully Boyle and Andrew Bunie, *Paul Robeson: The Years of Promise and Achievement* (Amherst: University of Massachusetts Press, 2001), 112.

6. Charles B. Cochran, *Cock-a-Doodle-Do* (London: J. M. Dent & Sons, 1941), 116.

7. Charles B. Cochran, *I Had Almost Forgotten* (London: Hutchinson, 1932), 219.

8. Charles Graves, *The Cochran Story* (London: W. H. Allen, n.d.)., 109.

9. For a detailed description of the controversy surrounding *Plantation Days*, see Howard Rye, "Visiting Firemen 13: The Plantation Revues," *Storyville 133* (Mar. 1998).

10. "Plantation Title Not Prevented in London," VAR, Mar. 22, 1923.

11. *Daily Graphic* (London), Mar. 6, 1923.

12. Hannen Swaffer, "The Scandal of Negro Revues," *Daily Graphic* (London), Mar. 5, 1923, 7.

13. VAR, Apr. 5, 1923, 3.

14. Bob Thomas, *Astaire, The Man, The Dancer* (Sydney: Collins, 1985), 45.

15. *Lynn Daily Evening Item*, Apr. 18, 1924, and Mark Tucker, "Ellington: The Early Years" (Urbana and Chicago: University of Illinois Press, 1991), 98.

16. ChDef, Feb. 24, and *Billboard* magazine, Mar. 3, 1923.

17. Salem Tutt Whitney, "Salem Sez," ChDef, Feb. 24, 1923, 6.

18. Willie Covan is one of the legendary names of jazz and tap dance. Starting out as a pick at six years, he went on to form his own team, the Four Covans, in 1917. In the heyday of Hollywood musicals he became MGM's chief tap choreographer and

tutor to the stars in a string of famous musicals. Many remember him as the man who taught Debbie Reynolds to tap for "Singing in the Rain."

19. AMST, Apr. 4, 1923, and ChDef, Apr. 7, 1923, 6.

20. VAR, Apr. 26, 1923.

21. Marcus Garvey, "Negro Problem in England," *Negro World*, Mar. 31, 1923, 1.

22. NYT, Passenger list, Apr. 28, 1923.

23. "Race Line Drawn on Ship," NYT, Apr. 29, 1923.

24. Howard Rye and Jeffrey Green, "Black Music Internationalism in England in the 1920s," *Black Music Research Journal* 15:1 (spring 1995).

25. A good brief account of the orphanage can be found in Jacqui Malone, *Steppin' on the Blues* (Urbana: University of Illinois Press, 1996), 136–137. A full account is available in John Chilton, *A Jazz Nursery: The Story of the Jenkins' Orphanage* (London: Bloomsbury Book Shop, 1980).

26. Jeffrey P. Green, *Edmund Thornton Jenkins* (Westport, Conn.: Greenwood, 1982), 126.

27. Coterie of Friends Souvenir Programme, May 13, 1923, SCRAP, HAJC.

28. "Wonderful London Yesterday," *Daily Graphic* (London), May 15, 1923, 5.

29. VAR, Apr. 26, 1923.

30. Undated, unidentified clipping, SCRAP, HAJC.

31. James Harding, *Cochran: A Biography* (London: Methuen, 1988), 101, and "Wonderful London Yesterday," *Daily Graphic* (London), June 2, 1923, 5.

32. C. B. Cochran, *Secrets of a Showman* (London: Heinemann, 1925), 414–415.

33. *Sketch* magazine, June 13, 1923, 544.

34. Cochran, *Cock-a-Doodle-Do*, 117.

35. *Sunday Pictorial*, June 3, 1923, 8.

36. *Times* (London), June 1, 1923.

37. "Dixie and the Astaires," *New Statesman*, August 11, 1923.

38. SCRAP, HAJC.

39. VAR, June 21, 1923, 39.

40. Willie Covan, from DJKT.

41. Mander and Mitchenson Theatre Collection. Also published in *John Gielgud's Notes from the Gods*, Ed. Richard Mangan (London: Nick Hern Books, 1994), 58.

42. Richard Shead, *Constant Lambert* (London: Simon Publications, 1973), 38–40.

43. Quoted in James Weldon Johnson, *Black Manhattan* (New York: Da Capo, 1991), 198.

44. Irene Castle telegram, June 15, 1923. SCRAP, HAJC, and VAR, "Irene Castle in Cork at Fancy Dress Ball," July 4, 1923, 2.

45. *Sunday Times* (London), May 20, 1923.

46. *The African World*, Aug. 25, 1923.

47. Sol J. Plaatje, *Kimberley Diamond Fields Advertiser*, Nov. 14, 1927. I am indebted to my friend Bearnard O'Riain in South Africa for tracking this down.

48. Brian Willan, *Sol Plaatje, South African Nationalist* (London: Heinemann, 1984), 290, and Jeffrey Green, "Conversations with Leslie Thompson," *Black*

Perspective in Music 12:1 (spring 1984). There is an apparent conflict between these sources, which give the farewell concert as being in October and Plaatje's account in the *Advertiser*, which has the *Dover Street to Dixie* performers at his farewell. Plaatje, writing in 1927, probably confused the two events, leaving it an open question who the other performers at the earlier concert were.

49. ChDef, July 21, 1923, and for reference to Babe Ruth see PhTr, Dec. 12, 1927.

50. *Star*, July 28, 1923, 11.

51. Many years later Kid gave the cartoons to his Australian friends Bobby and Gracie Le Brun, and they still hang proudly in Gracie's Newcastle home. I have assumed they were acquired on this trip rather than the longer 1926 one as they were planning their new home about this time, and the later trip would have involved carrying the pictures around for eighteen months including a year in England.

52. VAR, Sept. 27, 1923.

CHAPTER SIX

~

Dixie Dreams

The Star Returns

If Florence was popular at home before she went to England, her popularity knew no bounds after her triumphant return. To the theatergoing public, she was now an international superstar. To her own people she was a heroine who had brought credit to the race. Above all, it was her modest charm that endeared her to all. The theatrical correspondent for the *Amsterdam News* rhapsodized, "As we look back to the early days when little Florence was putting over her songs with such good effect at Mrs. Downs's little Lincoln Theatre, we recall with a feeling of satisfaction the cute little miss who always had a smile and a good word for those with whom she was brought into contact."[1]

She resumed her usual cabaret show at the Plantation. The signs of her new stardom were soon visible. Press advertisements announced she was to make a guest-star appearance in the *Greenwich Village Follies*. The *Follies* had started in Greenwich Village in 1919 as a rival to the *Ziegfeld Follies*. It was so successful that it soon moved uptown and by 1920 was on Broadway at the Winter Garden, conveniently the same building that housed Florence's Plantation as its roof garden theater. By 1923 it was one of Broadway's top attractions.

One of the stars of the *Greenwich Village Follies* of 1923 was future modern-dance great Martha Graham. She had made a name for herself with the famous classical Denishawn Company for several years. She found herself at loose ends when she was not included in the troupe for an Asian tour and joined the *Follies* out of financial need rather than enthusiasm. She ended up enjoying it, saying "I was considered an exotic personality onstage (at least in that it resembled Denishawn) and to my delight, each night one of my so-los would stop the show."[2] Martha Graham's showstopper was scene five, the Garden of Kama, an exotic theater piece based on Indian love lyrics, with scanty costumes. She recounts how, when they were performing it on the road in Boston, which had a strict moral code for shows, a policeman pointed to the accompanying showgirls and said, "Put something on them so they are respectable." When one of them pointed to Martha, equally scantily clad, he said, "No, she's all right, she's art."[3]

Florence's appearance at the prestigious Broadway show was greeted as a well-deserved honor. Not since Bert Williams in the *Ziegfeld Follies* had a black performer had a major featured role in one of the leading Broadway extrava-ganzas. However, not everyone was pleased. One of the regular cast bitterly re-sented the idea that a black woman should have higher billing. She rallied some supporters, and they threatened to walk out of the show. Martha Graham did not join the protest. The ringleader was the same Australian-born Daphne Pollard who had participated actively in the protests against imported artistes in London. Whatever basis her British-Australian origins might have given her for protesting against Americans in London, Pollard's protest against Florence in Florence's own country looked like straight racism.

Born in Australia in 1890, Pollard went to America for the first time at age eight, with her family's Pollard Lilliputian Opera Company. She played vaudeville and theater engagements with some success during 1914 and 1915 in a touring piece called *The Candy Shop*. She went to London in 1917 and continued performing there until 1921, establishing a reputation in lighter pieces. She returned to America in 1921 and played the Palace Theater in New York. A 1920 article describes her as "the smallest star on the stage to-day. With it she has an impishly pretty face with great blue eyes and a slightly tipped up nose. . . . She invests each effort with a wide variety of action, for besides her grotesqueries of countenance and 'physical jerks' she is a great dancer."[4] Pollard may have jealously viewed Florence Mills as a darker ver-sion of herself and resented the success of her darker alter ego.

Despite Pollard's intervention, Florence carried off the engagement with her usual style and aplomb, running for at least two weeks. The management averted the threatened walkout when it took out advertisements that gave Pollard headings the same size as those of Florence's original billing. Florence's appearance came in scene nine of the first half, titled "An Impressionistic Plantation." The *New York Times*, in its staid fashion, commented, "She sang half a dozen songs in her more or less familiar manner and was warmly received by a capacity house that ran to standees." Florence's loyal fans hailed her success with a flood of congratulatory telegrams, including messages from Maude Russell, dancers Grace and Eddy Rector, Will Vodery, and Irving Berlin, who addressed his to "The greatest of all colored performers."[5]

Martha Graham shared her second feature, scene fourteen, "A Spanish Fiesta," with a Spanish family group, the Cansinos, the same group that had followed the Keith Orpheum circuit as the Panama Trio toured the parallel Pantages circuit. The act consisted of parents Elisa and Eduardo and two daughters. Graham recalled that while she was making up to go onstage, their five- or six-year-old youngest daughter, Margerita, not part of the act, would sometimes crawl around under her chair. This little girl would later be known to the world as movie star Rita Hayworth. Perhaps the young Rita Hayworth also crawled around under Florence Mills's chair during her *Follies* engagement.

Following her celebrity appearance in the *Greenwich Village Follies*, Florence resumed her regular *Plantation Revue*. There were rumors of a new show in the offing. Meanwhile she received numerous offers to make celebrity appearances and to play benefits and special events. She featured on a special program on radio station WHN in celebration of her *Follies* appearance.[6] On November 11 she did a benefit performance for Hungarian children at the Manhattan Opera House. On November 25, the Dressing Room Club staged a "Midnite Franic" at the Lafayette Theatre with an all-star bill that included Thompson and Covan, and Florence with the Plantation Orchestra. The Dressing Room Club was founded around 1919 to promote the interests of black show business folk from all facets of the industry: performers, promoters, musicians, and composers alike. The committee of the club included many respected veterans of black theater, among them Jesse Shipp as stage manager and Florence's former Tennessee Ten associate H. Qualli Clark on the board of directors.

Sometime in November came an opportunity for the cast members of *Dover Street to Dixie* to repay a debt. The party that C. B. Cochran had given in their honor before the show closed in London had stayed in their memories as a very special event. Cochran was now back in New York seeking spectacles to present for the British Empire Exhibition of 1924, to be held at Wembley Stadium in London. In typical Cochran fashion, his plan was to restore his financial fortunes by filling Wembley Stadium with one of the most grandiose and unusual spectacles the British public had ever seen: a full American rodeo.[7] When they knew Cochran was back in New York, the performers were keen to show their appreciation of his hospitality. They laid on a special performance of *Plantation Revue* to which Cochran could invite as many friends as he liked. Among the guests he invited were Lady Diana Duff-Cooper, Alice Delysia, Pearl White (famous star of the silent movie series *The Perils of Pauline*), Gertrude Lawrence, Beatrice Lillie, and Morris Gest. Florence's performance in a new piece, parodying the "Wooden Soldiers" routine from *Chauve Souris*, struck Cochran as being "as great in its way as Pavlova's Swan Dance."[8] No doubt Morris Gest, as the one who introduced "Wooden Soldiers" to America, in *Chauve Souris*, was amused at this clever parody.

In early December, along with the *Plantation Revue* cast, Florence performed at a special dinner dance and cabaret at the Commodore Hotel for the premiere of Jackie Coogan's new film *Long Live the King*. Also on the bill were Fannie Brice and Martha Graham. Florence enjoyed being billed alongside some of the legendary names of American show business but would have taken more pleasure from an event that occurred later in the month. The crème de la crème of the black entertainment world staged a special luncheon in her honor. It was held, under the patronage of the Dressing Room Club, in the home of Oma Crosby, a veteran black vaudevillian with whom Bricktop had gained some of her earliest experience.

The purpose was to celebrate Florence's success and the credit it was bringing to black entertainment. The published program devoted two pages to her career. Many of the people present had known her throughout most of that career, even before her fame, as a friend and fellow artiste. On behalf of the board of directors, famous magician Black Carl made Florence an honorary member and presented her with a diamond-studded medal. He described it as "a token of the esteem with which her high place in theatricals is held by her fellow performers and her race." Responding with tears flowing down her cheeks, Florence, in her reply, talked of her love for her fellow artistes. She said, "If in any way I have done anything to lift the profession I am unconscious of it, and it was done only for love of my art, and for my people." Following the speeches, there was a silent toast to Florence's renowned predecessor, Aida Overton Walker.[9]

Reporting the event in the *Baltimore Afro-American*, J. A. Jackson noted: "She has the distinction of being the least 'up-stage' woman in the profession and has never been too busy to help any worthwhile benefit by donating a personal appearance, ofttimes with her whole show."[10] Proving the truth of his words, three days later Florence appeared at the Renaissance Casino in the *Inter-State Tattler's* "Benefit Sunday Evening." The *Tattler* also announced that she would "assist Santa Claus on Xmas morning." It was also reported that Florence and her *Plantation Revue* company were to be taken to prison on a Sunday afternoon, although not for any criminal activity. With Vodery's orchestra they presented *Plantation Revue* for the inmates of the notorious Sing Sing Prison.[11]

Throughout all this extracurricular activity, *Plantation Revue* continued to be highly successful in its Broadway location at the Winter Garden. In December, *Variety* featured a photo of Johnny Dunn, the Plantation Orchestra's well-known trumpeter, holding a coach-horn, a trumpet with a horn elongated by several feet. The paper noted he was offering to meet contestants for his claim to the title of world's Champion Original Trick Cornetist, applications to be sent to Lew Leslie. Finally, readers were invited to hear him play "Bambalina" in *Plantation Revue*, where it was featured as a specialty dance for Eddie Rector. This was obviously a piece of Leslie's slick promotion. Dancer Louis Simms, who was a member of the famous dance troupe the Copasetics, recalled being taken as a child performer to see Florence at a theater across the road from where he was playing. He remembered her and Johnny Dunn playing call and response to each other, she on the stage and Johnny with his long cornet in the pit.[12]

As 1924 dawned there was still no sign of Florence's predicted new show. On January 25 the rest of the cast gave her a surprise birthday party. Somewhere around this time, Kid Thompson fell out with Lew Leslie over his role in the show. "I didn't have no new material and he had nothing for me to do in particular."[13] He left the show to play as a single act on the Loew's circuit. "I could do a single, like Bill Robinson, Dotson, and all those fellows doing the same thing. I didn't go out to make a lot of publicity but I made good. I wasn't going to get too far away from Florence, but I was able to work all the time 'cause the Loew's Circuit has got thirty or forty houses around Yonkers, White Plains."

It was a purely professional separation, but the news soon spread that Kid Thompson was no longer in Florence Mills's show, which inevitably led to speculation of a more personal rift. Bizarrely, a large firm of lawyers approached Kid with a proposition that he sue a wealthy admirer of Florence for "alienation of affection." The man had sent her a present of an expensive vanity case from Cartier, with a letter describing it as a "token of esteem" and expressing appreciation of her performances.[14] The man's lawyer read more into Kid's professional separation from Florence than was warranted. Behind his client's back he cooked up a scheme with another lawyer to persuade Kid Thompson to sue for a large sum of money for "alienation of affection."

Kid recalled, "They had me to come to the office two different times. I went there one day and found out what they wanted. They told me what they wanted, and I said, 'Well I don't do it like that.' They said, 'You think it over, it'll be worth so much, so much.' A couple more days they called me back with that theme and I went back and put the same thing. I said, 'Florence's record is clear and I won't be dragging her through no courts or nothing like that.'"

Although he talks about doing a "single," Kid actually did a double act with Willie Covan at this time. For a while they were doing two engagements a day, split between New York and Philadelphia. They did two shows at the Palace (and later the Hippodrome) and would then catch the eight or nine o'clock train to Philadelphia and work two shows in a nightclub.

The early part of 1924 was a quiet period for Florence professionally, business as usual at the Plantation cabaret, with occasional special engagements. However, there were important events on the domestic front for her and Kid. Despite the rumors of rifts, they were idyllically happy. They had just bought themselves a new house, a five-story brownstone right in the middle of Harlem, at 220 West 133rd Street. They set about furnishing it in style, with carpets imported from China and a music box that played records without rewinding. "Quite the finest music box in Harlem," according to singer Jules Bledsoe.[15] Pride of place went to the beautiful Steinway Grand piano, a Model M five feet seven inches wide, in mahogany with a brown art lacquer finish. The Steinway Company delivered it on February 7.

February 1924 also saw Florence return in triumph to the Harlem stage for a two-week engagement at the Lafayette Theatre. Having come home an international star, she was guaranteed a hero's welcome. A strong set of vaudeville support acts accompanied the *Plantation Revue* component, including Covan and Thompson. The delighted inhabitants of Harlem gave her a rapturous welcome home, with lots of ovations, bouquets of flowers, and encores. There wasn't a Lafayette sharpshooter in sight. The *Amsterdam News* commented enthusiastically on Florence's tap dancing skills in the "Wooden Soldiers" number with renowned dancers Eddie Rector and Leonard Ruffin.[16]

The most telling review was that of the fastidious drama critic for the *Messenger*, Theophilus Lewis:

"Superb," "Incomparable" and "Gorgeous" keep insisting that they are the only adjectives suitable for use in a skit on the carnival of fun and song presented by Florence Mills in collaboration with Will Vodery and his orchestra. Not more than twice in my life, if ever, have I seen such delicately sensuous entertainment as *The Plantation Revue*. . . . The vital force of the revue proceeds from the personality of Miss Mills. . . . Here is jazz with the shrieks and blares refined out of it, so that it pulses on the ear in a blend of restrained harmony and elemental rhythm, with now and then a hint of melody. If you close yours eyes you can easily imagine that it is simply an audible expression of Miss Mills' fragile person.[17]

While Theophilus Lewis credited Florence Mills and Will Vodery with producing a more refined style of jazz at the Lafayette, the next day, Tuesday, February 12, another claimant to this achievement was mounting the podium at a different New York venue. On that afternoon Paul Whiteman gave a concert at the Aeolian Hall. The concert was a showpiece for Whiteman's symphonic jazz. It featured a mixture of straight jazz pieces in the Whiteman style, a selection of jazz-based or "jazzed" classics, and some new symphonic pieces. The symphonic half included "George Gershwin's intricate and musicianly *Rhapsody in Blue*, played by the brilliant young composer to orchestra accompaniment."[18] *Variety* concluded that Whiteman's performance proved that "jazz will never die. It is a part of modern American culture and an absolute necessity."

There is no doubt Whiteman's Aeolian Hall concert was a major landmark in American music and popular culture. However, it is safe to assume that jazz remained untamed despite either it or Florence's Lafayette venture. At least she and Will Vodery did not make grandiose claims in that direction. However, by now the black press had taken to referring to her as the "Queen of Jazz."

The relatively quiet professional period gave Florence time to enjoy her new home. Early in April she entertained a large group of friends in a belated birthday celebration, which was probably also a housewarming party. An elaborate meal was served, although probably not cooked by Florence herself, whose only claim to culinary skill was that she could boil water. She would have contributed, however, to the music and dancing that went on till the small hours.[19]

A week later she was a guest at a lavish occasion at the Café Savarin, where 500 people gathered to honor Dr. W. E. B. DuBois. DuBois, editor of the *Crisis* magazine and leading black social philosopher of the era, had just returned from official duties as special envoy of the United States at the inauguration of the president of Liberia. The gathering was a distinguished array representing the arts and commerce of both races. Jessie Fauset read a tribute from playwright Eugene O'Neill and Countee Cullen read an original poem.[20] For Countee Cullen the occasion was a big one. The invitation to read his poem was a mark of his emerging recognition. A romance was also blossoming that would soon lead to marriage between him and DuBois's daughter Yolande. However, it was his first meeting with Florence Mills that left him with one of his strongest impressions of the occasion. As it had so many others, her lack of affectation surprised him. James Weldon Johnson introduced him to Florence. "She extended us a cool and casual hand. . . . There was about her none of that raucous air that membership in the Methodist Church had taught us to expect of actresses. She was an agreeable disappointment and one that we wanted to undergo further."[21]

In May, Florence and Alberta Hunter were stars of a fashion show at Madison Square Garden highlighting the skills of black couturiers. *Billboard* reported, "Ten thousand people, and not anywhere nearly all Negroes, witnessed the show."[22] This was Florence and Alberta's first reunion since the Panama Club in 1917. In mid-June, Florence and her "Six Dixie Vamps" performed at a "Black Cat Day" dance at the New Star Casino for a black Masonic Shriners group.

In the lull in professional activity over these months, Florence had been working on a major new phase in her career. In mid-March, *Variety* reported that she was soon to go into rehearsal for a new show being written by Irving Berlin. A week later it announced she would open early in the summer in Chicago with a show to be called *Chocolate Drops* and would move later to Broadway with the Berlin-written show. The reference to Irving Berlin was probably a figment of Leslie's rich imagination. Berlin was one of the most in-demand songwriters of the time. The *Chocolate Drops* title wasn't accurate either, being the name for the female dancing chorus in the show. It was true, however, that Florence was working hard in rehearsal for a new show, intended not just for Broadway but also for the wider American public. Till then, fans had to venture to Broadway or Harlem to find out what all the fuss was about. Soon Florence would come to their doorsteps.

Dixie to Broadway

Although the early part of 1924 was quiet on the professional front, it is the happiest of times for Florence and Kid. She is at the top of her profession, idolized by her fellow African Americans for the international acclaim she has earned them. Everything is going well on the domestic and social front despite the false rumors of a rift. They are enjoying their new home in New York. Later it will be a secure base to return to between travels. It is also a home for Florence's adored mother Nellie. She lives on the ground floor with no worry about climbing stairs. Kid and Florence occupy the upstairs levels.

The home is rumored to stand on the site of the same tenement building the Winfrey family lived in during their early years in Harlem and were forced to vacate when the original building was torn down. It appeals to Florence to have the fine new building as her home. She and Kid were able to buy it outright from savings.

For two people who had spent most of their lives on the road, the home offers a haven of domestic bliss. They revel in the luxury of quiet domesticity. They have pet names for each other. Kid calls Florence "Mother" while she refers to him as "My boy, Kid." They bring Kid's father, in his sixties, to New York to see the house. He has never before been even as far as St. Louis. The experience of traveling on the Pullman train is daunting for him. Kid has paid for a sleeping berth, but he doesn't use it. He sits up all night. "Son, I'm going to tell you the truth. I was scared to go in with all those white folks in there."[23]

Kid and Florence know that this period of tranquil home life is only an interlude. The new show is beckoning and will soon send them back to a nomadic lifestyle. This time they are agreed there will be no separation of their careers.

The new show was called *Dixie to Broadway*. Florence was billed as "The World's Greatest Colored Entertainer: the Sensation of Two Continents." The show differed in one important way from her earlier ones. They had all been padded-out versions of the *Plantation Revue* format. The new show was a full-blown theatrical production, intended for presentation at major venues across the country.

Lew Leslie wasn't the only one keen to feature Florence in an elaborate presentation. Around the same time, Florenz Ziegfeld sought to tempt her away with one of show business's most glittering prizes, a starring role in his next *Ziegfeld Follies*. The offer was very attractive. It would put her on a par with the great Bert Williams as the first black woman claiming *Follies* stardom. More significantly, it would put her name alongside the greatest white stars: Fanny Brice, Nora Bayes, Eddie Cantor, Will Rogers. She would be featured out front, supported by a glittering parade of white chorus girls, breaking down one more barrier. However, she also realized it would mean separating herself from her fellow black performers. She would go on to major stardom, but she would have to do it alone. She would belong to Broadway and Times Square but no longer to Harlem and Lenox Avenue.

Lew Leslie knew the agony she confronted. Persuasively, he countered with the promise that he would feature her in an all–black revue that would be "as sumptuous and gorgeous in production and costume as *Ziegfeld's Follies*, *White's Scandals* or the *Greenwich Village Follies*."[24] The promise of employment for her fellow entertainers in the black community was the clincher. "I felt," Florence said, "that since [Bert Williams] established the colored performer in association with a well-known revue that I could best serve the Colored actor by accepting Mr. Leslie's offer."[25] Perhaps if Bert Williams had not already broken the *Follies* color bar, Florence would have seized that opportunity. The decision was a fateful one. Apart from the benefits for her race companions, it meant that from then on she would carry the full burden of each show on her tiny shoulders instead of being just one among a galaxy of highly paid stars. The responsibility and strain would be tremendous, but Florence never shirked responsibility.

Leslie's idea was that if the new show proved successful, it would be the forerunner of a permanent series of "All Colored Revues" in yearly editions, like the *Follies* and *Scandals*. Florence saw it as an opportunity to showcase black talent, saying, "The Leslie promotion appealed to me at once, not merely as an opportunity for personal advancement, but also as an institution that should be entirely characteristic of my race, and give my people an opportunity of demonstrating that their talents are equal to the most exacting demands of this popular form of entertainment, with the added quality of originality." In accepting Leslie's plans for the new show, Florence laid down one very firm condition—Kid Thompson would be back in the cast. She had been upset by the need to counter rumors of a split and even wilder rumors about her having affairs with other men. Possibly fueled by leaks about the phony legal case, these rumors had included an affair with a wealthy white man. To counter these stories she wanted Kid clearly visible by her side.[25]

The title of the new show was an obvious carryover from *Dover Street to Dixie*, although the songs were all new. As usual, Will Vodery's Plantation Orchestra provided the music. The composers were the familiar George Meyer, and Arthur Johnston who wrote his first hit in this show. Johnson was later famed for "Pennies from Heaven" and "Cocktails for Two." The lyricists were Roy Turk, from the original *Plantation Revue* team, and the prolific Grant Clarke ("Ragtime Cowboy Joe," "Second Hand Rose," and "Am I Blue"). Although the material was written by whites, the writers had significant links with the black entertainment tradition, especially Bert Williams. Librettist Walter DeLeon had written the last play Williams had starred in, *Under the Bamboo Tree*. Lyricist Clarke had contributed the words to Williams's 1911 *Ziegfeld Follies* hit, "Dat's Harmony."

Leslie lived up to his promise to provide lavish costumes. Florence had a variety of costumes, one rather brief. She joked, "The less clothes we show folk wear, the more they cost us." Her costumes ranged from elaborate, feathered, African-style garb with fancy headdress to overalls, gorgeous evening gowns, and full formal male attire. Costumes for the show cost $25,000 of an estimated $60,000 for the cost of the total production.[26] Leslie economized on the settings, relying on simple set pieces against a black velvet backdrop. One critic noted that the same fence, with flowery vines twining round it, served for three different locales as far removed from each other as Dixie and Russia.[27] The scenes were all played, in the jargon of vaudeville, in "one" (in front of the main curtain) or in "three" (using the full stage), thereby simplifying scene changes.

Over the life of *Dixie to Broadway*, the cast varied between thirty and thirty-six performers, although advertisements claimed there were over seventy in total. Many of the unnamed extras were young picks and chorus members. The cast included a dazzling array of talent. Shelton Brooks and Hamtree Harrington were now the leading comedians in the Bert Williams tradition. Apart from Florence, there were three excellent female singers in Cora Green, Lillian Brown, and Aida Ward. Aida was effectively Florence's stand-in for the next few years, although she never actually got the chance to star. Maude Russell, popularly known as the Slim Princess, and fresh from having been the first to dance the Charleston on stage, in *Liza* (1922), was a leading female dancer. Maude explained how Leslie lured her away from *Liza*. "[We] used to have a midnight show, Lew Leslie came to see the show and he saw me. He came back stage and asked me would I like to join Florence Mills's show. So I was dickering for money, you know, . . . and he agreed to give me $25 more than I was getting in *Liza*, so I left *Liza* and went with Florence Mills in *Plantation Revue*. That's how I got to join Miss Mills."[28]

There was almost a glut of outstanding male dancers, including U. S. Thompson, Willie Covan, Johnny Nit, Leonard Ruffin, Lew Keane, Byron Jones, Charlie "Cornbread" Walker, Danny Small, and Snow Fisher, all noted as significant figures in the Stearns's *Jazz Dance*. The female chorus line also included some notable names, including the beautiful Moses sisters, Ethel and Lucia, and Marion Tyler, who would one day become Mrs. Eubie Blake. Ethel Moses would later star in Oscar Micheaux's movies, billed in the fashion of the time as the "Harlem Harlow."

Dixie to Broadway, in two acts, maintained the revue format of lively, fast moving, very loosely linked sketches rather than the flimsy plot line that characterized *Shuffle Along* and its successors. As one critic put it: "No plot is allowed to clog the pace." There were originally twenty-eight scenes. By the time the show reached New York after a lengthy road tour, some less-successful items had been dropped or replaced, and the number of scenes in the mature version was down to twenty-four. The titles of many scenes reflected the "Dixie" theme, but as scholar Allen Woll points out, "Despite the [title] the show spent a great deal of the time north of the Mason-Dixon Line. The few obligatory southern songs seemed to fade in the context of the whole show, which had a northern and urban focus."[29]

The opening scene was a prologue titled "The Evolution of the Colored Race."[30] Critic and writer Alexander Woollcott detected in the prologue "a vestige of a plot" for the show. However, he expressed amazement that it somehow "managed to get Salome, Madame Butterfly, and Abraham Lincoln into the same theme."[31] An African American tradition of presenting educational pageants portraying the progress of the race from African origins, through slavery and emancipation, into modern times was well established. Adapting this idea into an entertainment setting allowed the writers to present a sequence of song types, from jungle dances to plantation and minstrel songs, and on to spirituals and jazz or blues. The late Mark Tucker, Duke Ellington expert supreme, believed that seeing this *Dixie to Broadway* segment may have influenced Duke Ellington when he developed ideas for his masterpiece *Black, Brown and Beige: A Tone Parallel to the History of the Negro in America.*[32]

Florence's first appearance, backed up by the full company, came in a new song, "Dixie Dreams." One of the specially written new songs, this was a languorous ballad featuring Florence as a lonely wanderer dressed in overalls, carrying a little bundle over her shoulder. "Dixie Dreams" perfectly encapsulated the wistful persona that Florence was so brilliant at portraying, and it quickly became a firm favorite with audiences.

Her second appearance, by contrast, came in the up-tempo "Jungle Nights in Dixieland." She emerged dramatically dressed in an elaborate feathered costume as a Zulu dancer, her red grass skirt contrasting with the Chocolate Drops, in flaring white wigs and short blue grass skirts. "It's jungle; or what I imagine a jungle might be like," said Florence. "I have never visited a jungle. It's an emotional dance."[33] Florence's third scene introduced one of her most successful songs, "Mandy, Make Up Your Mind." To the audience's surprise she appeared in male formal dress as the groom, with chorus girl Alma Smith as the tardy bride. All the company got into the act, either as bridesmaids, maids of honor or groomsmen. Florence's male attire was her tribute to Aida Overton Walker's famous "That's Why They Call Me Shine" routine. It also revived memories of performing with her sister Olivia years before, in the days of the Mills Sisters, when Olivia had played in male dress.

In the second half, the "Wooden Soldiers" piece, already used in *Plantation Revue*, was a showpiece for tap-dancing skills, especially for Florence. The Chocolate Drops, with Danny Small, portrayed the "Katinkas," or Russian dolls. Florence, accompanied by the male "Plantation Steppers," portrayed or parodied wooden soldiers. In the original, the beat of the wooden soldiers' feet had been realized through drum rolls. Now, with Florence and the male dancers, a rapid-fire tap dancing of human feet created a dramatic effect that delighted audiences. This was Florence demonstrating her mastery of tap, as taught to her years before by Bojangles in Chicago.

Late in the second half, the curtain descended and Florence was spotlighted, solo, for her big number, "I'm a Little Blackbird Looking for a Bluebird," the song destined to become her theme song for the rest of her life. It became the vehicle through which she sought to project her passionate plea for racial tolerance, set in the show that was to allow large numbers of middle-America theatergoers to see Florence Mills for the first time.

The Road to Broadway

Dixie to Broadway's route to Broadway had been almost as long as if it had traveled from Dixie itself. Before arriving at the Broadhurst Theatre on Forty-eighth Street, it made an extended tour of Atlantic City, Detroit, Chicago, Baltimore, and Boston. The jumping-off point, a sort of dress rehearsal, was at the Main Street Theatre in Asbury Park, New Jersey (almost New York), in mid-1924. This was virtually home ground for Florence. Her older sister, Olivia, had settled there to raise a family since retiring from show business. It provided a friendly setting for a tryout, as proven by Florence's congratulatory telegrams from many familiar names.

The first real test came when it opened for its second week at Nixon's Apollo Theatre in Atlantic City. *Variety's* out-of-town reviewer was there to check out what was in store for New York audiences. The review was mostly favorable while noting the need for "judicious doctoring" before the Chicago run. Enumerated on the positive side were Florence's personality, the brilliant dancing, and the attractive costumes. The negatives were some slow scenes and not enough humorous content. The music was compared unfavorably to *Shuffle Along* except for "Dixie Dreams."[34] Overall, Lew Leslie and his crew were reasonably happy with the verdict while working feverishly to address the adverse comments.

The Chicago opening occurred on Sunday evening, August 17, at the Garrick Theatre. For a week *Dixie to Broadway* competed head-to-head with the other leading black show, *Runnin' Wild*, playing to sell-out audiences at the Woods Theatre next door to the Garrick. To compete, *Dixie to Broadway's* top ticket price was held down to $2.00, compared with $2.50 for the opposition. Both benefited from the hardly coincidental presence in Chicago of the annual convention of the National Negro Business League, founded by Booker T. Washington in 1900. Its 400 delegates and their families helped to swell audiences for both shows. The price reduction for *Dixie to Broadway* was unnecessary as audience and critics responded enthusiastically. In a specially commissioned review for *Variety,* a noted black Chicago theater personality, George Bell, declared it "the best colored show ever presented." The wildest applause was for Florence and the male Plantation Steppers in "The Dance of the Wooden

Soldiers." After several encores, it ended in a cross-stage parade of the full group in response to audience demand.

Florence's solo performance of "I'm a Little Blackbird" stopped the show with several encores.[35] The impact of Florence's performance of this simple song is difficult to imagine today. Harlem Renaissance expert Bruce Kellner describes the song as banal.[36] Reading the words on the printed page does little to dispel this view. Nevertheless, in performance it had a remarkable impact, not only on general audiences, but also on hardened critics, intellectuals, and artists, black and white alike. The explanation lies in the extraordinary blend of pathos and humor Florence brought to it and the sincerity with which she sought to project its message.

Drama critic Theophilus Lewis was enraptured. "The melody is obvious and the lyric is ordinary. Nevertheless Miss Mills invested it with more fire and feeling than many a great actress is able to evoke from the poignant lines and tense situations of a masterpiece of drama."[37] Some years later, reviewing the history of black theater, Lewis declared: "My own most delightful moment in the Negro theatre, the peak pleasure of my experience there, was when I first heard Florence Mills's simple little song, "I'm a Little Blackbird." He went on to remark, "The song itself is quite commonplace in its sentiment, containing rather more propaganda than humor. But the way Miss Mills sings it, it becomes a passionate lyric flashing sparks of prismatic fire."[38]

Contemporary musicologist Marcello Piras is not prepared to dismiss the melody so lightly. "The song's general design and chord progression may sound trivial, but the structure of melody is highly unusual. It is based on a melodic pattern (a tone repeated five times, followed by a higher tone) which come a long way in music history, as an imitation of a bird song. This pattern is repeated FIFTEEN times in the song! And almost all of them are varied. I don't know of any other song with such a weird melodic contour."[39] This suggests that composer George Meyer drew on an extensive personal knowledge of classical music to invent an original melody with birdsong themes that would showcase Florence's noted birdlike tones.

Credit must go to the songwriters for tailoring the song brilliantly to Florence's personality, so much so that it has always been uniquely associated with her. It is rarely performed today by female singers. It crops up occasionally as a lively jazz piece, without vocal accompaniment. Although the professional songwriting team wrote the song for her, Florence certainly played a role in developing the theme, which was so close to her heart. In later years there was a tendency in the African American community to view the song with suspicion, as though somehow tainted with old stereotypes. Kellner links it with titles containing words like "bandana" and "brownskin." However, there is a huge irony in this attitude as the song was clearly seen and understood at the time to be a powerful protest against racial intolerance. It was actively promoted by Florence and endorsed by the black press as such. This effort is illustrated by these words in the *Baltimore Afro-American*:

It has been interesting to note the telling and subtle philosophy put across the footlights by some of our more successful actors whose talent enables them to grip the attention of large white audiences. Some time ago when Sissle and Blake came to Baltimore they put over a telling piece of racial lecturing in their presentation of "The Sons of Uncle Tom." No one who saw that effort could have mistaken its portent. Miss Florence Mills has gone Sissle and Blake one better in her Blue Bird song. Although touched here and there with comedy, she has taken the serious and reflective theme of Maurice Maeterlinck and used it as a vehicle to sing forth the higher and more modern ambitions of Negro youth. "I'm a little blackbird," she sings from her soul, "looking for a blue bird too." Even if one did not know the underlying theme of Maeterlinck's immortal "Bluebird," it would be hard to miss the forces that caused Miss Mills to write and sing this song. It is the spirit of youth struggling against oppression. This is another instance of use of talent to touch a more serious phase of racial contact, and Miss Mills has succeeded in doing it deftly and well."[40]

A factor that contributed to the later failure to appreciate the song's message is that its overtly antiracist references have been edited out in more recent performances. The words "just like all the white folks do" are nowadays typically rendered with the word "white" changed to "other" or "rich." Furthermore, the second verse, starting "Tho' I'm of a darker hue, I've a heart the same as you," is generally omitted completely, along with its overt reference to the Maeterlinck Bluebird theme. There is no doubt that Florence proudly presented her song as an anthem of racial tolerance and a plea for justice. At that time her intentions were widely understood and appreciated by her own people and by audiences generally.

While Florence was presenting her plea for racial tolerance and harmony, her own little theatrical community was not entirely harmonious. Hamtree Harrington, previously married to and later separated from Florence's sister Maude, was now in an amorous relationship with his current partner, ex–Panama Trio member Cora Green. Harrington, in a fit of jealousy over Green's suspected glances elsewhere, confronted her and "administered physical chastisement." The couple patched up their differences enough to enable them to continue their performances but not before word of their brawl had spread. To add to the excitement within the troupe, Maude Russell also got into a scrap with an importunate male, who allegedly needed fifteen stitches in his arm after Maude saw him off with a knife.[41]

On the bright side, during the last week at the Garrick, Florence received the good news that sister Maude had given birth to her first child, an eight-and-a-half-pound baby girl. Florence had helped Maude financially with the expenses involved.[42] Another birth at this time also helped lighten the stress caused by the strife within the troupe: a thoroughbred foal born on the farm of Sherman H. Dudley. Dudley had recently retired from managing his theater chain, on which Florence had so often performed, and had settled on his farm in Maryland to breed thoroughbreds as a hobby. In tribute to his show business associations, he decided to call two of his horses "Florence Mills" and "Harry Wills." (The latter was named for a popular black boxer of the time.) Florence went along as a guest of honor for the christening of her namesake. A bottle of champagne was poured over the horse, and Florence kissed it for good luck.[43]

Two more highly successful weeks in Chicago followed at the Great Northern Theatre before *Dixie to Broadway* moved on to Detroit, en route to Baltimore. Sad news came for Florence at this time: bankruptcy, at age fifty, of her English promoter and admirer, C. B. Cochran. The ambitious series of stage shows he had organized in 1923 had exhausted his funds, despite the financial success of *Dover Street to Dixie*. Cochran was very popular and trusted and most of his creditors would have been happy to wait, confident of his ability to trade out of his difficulties. Only one large creditor pressed, resulting in the bankruptcy. However, his role in Florence Mills's life was by no means over.[44]

The final week in Chicago also saw the cast of *Dixie to Broadway* reaching out to a wider audience via the increasingly popular medium of radio. The performers were featured on station WGN's *Midnight Scamper* from the Drake Hotel. The broadcast ran from 12:30 a.m. till 2:00 a.m. and featured the full cast. Florence joined with Billie Cain and Alma Smith on their specialty feature "Jazz Time Came from the South."

The Baltimore engagement of *Dixie to Broadway* opened at the Academy of Music theater on September 29. Reaction was favorable except for one white critic, who thought that black entertainers should stick to more traditional forms of black entertainment and not portray whites, Russians, and Chinese. The week's takings of $18,000 were a record for Baltimore. The show was held over for a second week, bringing in a healthy $13,000.

Interviewing Florence, the *Afro-American's* columnist found her "alluringly charming" and "mysteriously different."[45] He commented particularly on her friendly openness. Florence expressed her pleasure in the "evident appreciation shown by my people in the audience." She went on to comment that a new age had dawned for African American performers. "It is an age of evolution," she explained, "and now our turn has come. There was a lapse between the palmy days of Williams and Walker and today. There was an Indian craze, a Hawaiian year, and various other popular waves, and now they have turned to Negroes and here we are." Her sentiment was echoed in a popular Broadway joke of the time: "Lincoln freed the slaves for America and Lew Leslie freed them for Broadway."

The *Afro* reporter noted the obvious happiness of the marriage between Florence and Kid Thompson. He speculated that her lack of possession of a motorcar might be attributable to her well-known charitable character and her generosity to theatrical acquaintances in distress. Their interview closed on a note of sadness, the recent death of Florence's early partner, Kinky Caldwell Clarke. Kinky and her husband had been popular performers around the Baltimore region up to late 1921. An unexpected illness had carried her off sometime after that.

A happier occasion during the Baltimore run was Will Vodery's thirty-ninth birthday. Being a Baltimorean himself, with many friends in the area, Vodery spared no expense. He hired a hotel room to stage a party for his orchestra and the cast, plus about fifteen invited local citizens, about ninety in all. The Plantation Orchestra played for dancing into the small hours and was then joined by a band from Atlantic City for a serious jam session.[46] The Baltimore run finished on October 12, and the show rolled on to Boston at the Shuberts' Majestic Theatre.

Dixie to Broadway was so successful in Boston that additional Thursday midnight shows were added to satisfy the demand. The show grossed better than $20,000 for the first week. It finished in Boston with a Friday midnight performance on October 24, drawing a sellout house, with all seats sold in advance to a largely professional audience from the other theaters and show casts. As the Boston run finished its second week, Lew Leslie and his management team felt their show was now ready to face the demanding audiences of Broadway. Florence and Kid Thompson were looking forward to being back in their own home again in Harlem.

Notes

1. AMST, Oct. 10, 1923.
2. Martha Graham, *Blood Memory: An Autobiography* (London: Sceptre Books, 1993), 90–103.
3. Graham, 93.

4. *Keith's Theatre News*, Washington, D.C., ca. 1920–1921, Houdini Collection, Library of Congress Rare Books section. Pollard's later career saw her in Hollywood playing support roles in Laurel and Hardy comedies.

5. HAJC.

6. William Randle Jr., "Black Entertainers on Radio 1920–1930," *Black Perspective in Music* (spring 1977).

7. Charles Graves, *The Cochran Story* (London: W. H. Allen, n.d.), 113–115.

8. C. B. Cochran, *Secrets of a Showman* (London: Heinemann, 1925), 416–417.

9. "Captivating Actress Is Honored at Banquet by New Theatrical Club," PiCou, Dec. 29, 1923.

10. "Florence Mills Gets Diamond Medal," BAA, Jan. 4, 1924.

11. *Morning Telegraph*, Dec. 21, 1923.

12. The author was taken by Hyacinth Curtis to see Louis Simms at his apartment in Harlem in 1998 when he recounted his memory of seeing Florence Mills and proudly showed his Copasetics plaque.

13. HAJC Transcript of Kid Thompson interview.

14. HAJC Transcript of Kid Thompson interview.

15. Jules Bledsoe, "Harlem to Broadway—Florence Mills' Life," *New York Journal*, Nov. 5, 1927.

16. AMST, "About Things Theatrical," Feb. 20, 1924.

17. *Messenger*, March (Feb.?) 1924, 74.

18. VAR, Feb. 14, 1924.

19. "Florence Mills as Hostess," NYA, Apr. 12, 1924.

20. NYA, Apr. 19, 1924.

21. "The Dark Tower," *Opportunity*, Dec. 1927.

22. *Billboard* magazine, May 24, 1924.

23. HAJC: Transcript of Kid Thompson interview.

24. "Florence Mills Turned Down Offer to Appear in *Ziegfeld Follies*," ChDef, Aug. 23, 1924.

25. The man was not identified. It may have been the one who gave the gift that led to the proposed legal action. Richard Newman, in his Florence Mills article in Jessie Carney Smith, ed., *Notable Black American Women* (Detroit: Gale Research, 1992) mentions wealthy industrialist Otto H. Kahn, so he may have been the one.

26. Caption to photo "An African Princess," BAA, July 4, 1924, 1; also caption to photo "She Wears Anything," Sept. 26, 1924, 1; production estimate from "Dixie to Broadway," VAR, Nov. 5, 1924, 18–19.

27. D. Gillette, "The New Plays on Broadway," undated *Billboard* clipping, probably Nov. 8, 1924.

28. The sequence appears to be that Maude Russell was recruited initially by Lew Leslie as part of the replacement *Plantation Revue* while Florence was in England, and Maude then stayed on for the new show.

29. A. Woll, *Black Musical Theatre* (Baton Rouge: Louisiana State University Press, 1989), 110.

30. The description of the show given here reflects the version presented at the Broadhurst Theatre on Broadway in Oct.–Nov. 1924, which some view as Florence's first real Broadway theater performance. A detailed reconstruction can be found in Woll, *Black Musical Theatre*, 101–108.

31. Alexander Woollcott, "Rhapsody in Brown Presented," *New York Sun*, Oct. 30, 1924.

32. Mark Tucker, "The Genesis of *Black, Brown and Beige*," *Black Music Research Journal* 13:2 (fall 1993): 69–70.

33. "Florence Mills Interviewed between Dances," unidentified clipping, TC FLP.

34. Abel, "Out of Town Reviews," VAR, Aug. 6, 1924, 14.

35. Tony Langston, "*Dixie to Broadway* Is Rich in Talent," ChDef, Aug. 23, 1924, part 1, 6.

36. Bruce Kellner (ed.), *The Harlem Renaissance: A Historical Dictionary for the Era* (New York: Methuen, 1984), xix.

37. Theophilus Lewis, "Florence Mills—An Appreciation," *Inter-State Tattler*, Nov. 11, 1927.

38. Theophilus Lewis, "Magic Hours in the Theatre," PiCou, Mar. 5, 1927.

39. Marcello Piras, private correspondence with the author.

40. "Florence Mills Seeks Her Bluebird," BAA, Oct. 10, 1924. The writer errs in crediting Florence with authorship of the song, but she almost certainly contributed to the material developed for her. Maeterlinck's 1908 French play *L'Oiseau Bleu* (*The Blue Bird*) was the origin of the symbolic bluebird of happiness.

41. "Mills Show Principals Were in Lively Fracas," VAR, Sept. 10, 1924, 14.

42. Telegram in Florence Mills Collection, HAJC.

43. Undated, unidentified clipping, Florence Mills Collection, HAJC. The Dudley connection is mentioned in Tom Fletcher, *The Tom Fletcher Story: 100 Years of the Negro in Show Business* (New York: Burdge, 1954), 99. There is some guesswork involved here on timing. It is possible this event occurred in 1923, the year the horse was foaled, but there is no evidence that Florence had visited Chicago at any time that year. The horse shares the common horse birthday of January 1, so that offers no assistance. On the other hand, Florence's 1925 visit to Chicago seems too late for several reasons, and the horse was by then well launched on its racing career.

44. "C. B. Cochran Broke at Fifty," VAR, Sept. 24, 1924, 5.

45. "Marriage Is No Bar to Career: Florence Mills," BAA, Oct. 3, 1924.

46. BAA, Oct. 17, 1924.

~

CHAPTER SEVEN

The Great White Way

It's Getting Dark on Old Broadway

New York at last! *Dixie to Broadway* opened at the Broadhurst Theatre on Wednesday, October 29, 1924. For Florence and Kid the four-day break since the final Boston performance was filled with rehearsals and last minute polishing, followed by a nervous wait. Florence had been performing around Broadway for several years now, but the opening of *Dixie to Broadway* was her first full-scale mainstream theatrical production there. She and her show would face the same stern critics and high standards that confronted all theatrical presentations in that most demanding world of cynical and jaded entertainment appetites.

While *Dixie to Broadway*'s run was hailed as Florence's full-scale Broadway debut, it also signaled a major advance for all black entertainers. No black show had run on Broadway proper since the great days of Williams and Walker. Neither *Runnin' Wild* nor the more recent Sissle and Blake offering *Chocolate Dandies* had been able to get a real Broadway booking. Both had played the Colonial Theatre, around the same area as *Shuffle Along*. *Chocolate Dandies* could only get close to Broadway when *Runnin' Wild* left the Colonial Theatre. Florence and *Dixie to Broadway* were right on mainstream Broadway in the prime season.

The top price, $3.30, was a new high for a black show, proving the confidence of Leslie and his coproducers. Only the $5.00 cover charge at the Plantation on holiday nights exceeded it. The mainstream Broadway opposition facing the show included the usual *Ziegfeld* and *Greenwich Village Follies* and *Earl Carroll's Vanities*, the phenomenally long-running *Abie's Irish Rose*, and shows featuring Al Jolson, the Marx brothers, and Eddie Cantor. Nevertheless, *Billboard* reported that tickets were sold out four days before opening night and newspapermen were begging scalpers for seats.

The opening saw the usual parade of well-heeled first night glitterati, "the dress-suit and evening-clothes folks who make up the cream of Broadway."[1] Among them were many prominent black citizens. These included Billy King and Billy McClain (veteran entertainers); Mrs. Flournoy Miller; R. C. McPherson (Cecil Mack, the composer) and his wife, Dr. Gertrude Curtis; Mrs. Charles Gilpin; Mrs. Noble Sissle; and Will Marion Cook. Cecil Mack would see the number he cowrote specially for Aida Overton Walker in 1910, "That's Why They Call Me Shine," performed by Snow Fisher as part of the Williams and Walker tribute scene.

The reaction from the big names of the New York dailies' critical fraternity was overwhelmingly positive for Florence herself:[2]

- Alexander Woollcott (*Sun*): "Miss Mills . . . is a flashing and beautiful woman who lights up like a Christmas tree when she dances and is just as festive."
- Heywood Broun (*World*): "The method of Florence Mills is like that of no one else. . . . Now I have seen grace."
- Alan Dale (*American*): "Miss Mills is an amusing little personette. . . . There is no side to this hard working little star and she knows her business."
- Percy Hammond (*Herald Tribune*): "Miss Mills . . . dominated the sable revels. She looked like a nimble microbe and she was equally infectious."
- E. W. Osborne (*Evening World*): "A slender streak of genius. . . . She is the lithe embodiment of the song and the sorrow, the poetry and the pathos, and the rich comedy of her race."
- G. W. Gabriel (*Telegram and Mail*): "This sensational little personality, slim, jaunty, strung on fine and tremulous wires, continues to tease the public's sense of the beautiful and odd."
- Burns Mantle (*Daily News*): "Hers is the best of the numerous melodious voices and hers the personality that snaps the audience to attention whenever she appears. . . . She is a fascinating performer."
- *New York Times*: "There were times last night when emotional waves crossed and recrossed the footlights. . . . Miss Mills has style and nerve and a voice and personality."

The rest of the show also received positive critical reaction in the dailies. The consensus was that it lived up to the traditional lively vim and vigor associated with black entertainment. Reviewers gave the humor only a moderate rating, but there was high praise for the dancing, especially of Johnny Nit and the chorus lines. They singled out the "Wooden Soldiers" routine for special appreciation. Critical preferences for Florence's songs were shared equally among "Dixie Dreams," "Mandy, Make Up Your Mind," and "I'm a Little Blackbird." However, audiences reacted most demonstratively to the last.

Critics differed on the degree to which the show reflected "real" black entertainment, as opposed to imitation white. Alan Dale bewailed the growing tendency in black shows to "obliterate race peculiarities and to 'make up' white." In contrast, Heywood Broun commented, "There may be some objection that not very much which is pure African is to be seen in *Dixie to Broadway*, but for my part I have always felt that the nearness of Harlem to jungle mood or thought was slightly exaggerated." He felt that the performers' innate sense of rhythm did seem a racial characteristic. He added, "When I see a Negro child two or three years old come out and dance a little better than anybody at the New Amsterdam or the Winter Garden, I grow fearful that there must be certain reservations to the theory of white supremacy." This was obviously a reference to the young "picks" featured in the show. Remembering her own days as a pick, Florence was always happy to see them given a chance in her own shows.

A different critical slant cropped up later in the black press. The general and entertainment sections shared the first night critics' enthusiasm, largely repeating those reviews or summarizing them. The overall reaction was one of delight at the homage paid to a member of their race, but a different tone sounded in the more intellectually oriented journals, such as the *Messenger* and *Opportunity*. The *Messenger* was a black radical socialist journal founded and edited by A. Philip Randolph and Chandler Owen. It carried much original literary material of the Harlem Renaissance. *Opportunity* was the official journal of the National Urban League, an association that sought economic and social betterment for African Americans. It too was a forum for Renaissance literary figures and carried intellectual comment on black cultural and social issues.

In *Opportunity*, Roger Didier paid generous tribute to the show's good features but distinguished between the performers' exceptional talents and the quality of some of the material the white producers had given them. Of Florence, he said, "The diminutive, mercurial Miss Mills has more than her share of accomplishments—a soft, mellow voice capable of trailing off into incredible fineness; her body the essence of rhythm." However, these acknowledgments out of the way, he went on to criticize some features as tasteless.

> There is not only a repetition of the threadbare stereotypes of defunct minstrelsy but something which comes dangerously near to obscenity. The drop used throughout the show, gaudy and indecorous, pictures on one side a "comic strip" Negro stealing a chicken and on the other similar Negroes playing at dice. The over used razor crops up as the show goes on. . . . If there were no necessity for [these comments] "Dixie to Broadway" would doubtless be the greatest of so-called Negro shows."[3]

In what he described as a "tardy review" in the *Messenger* (it didn't appear till early 1925), Theophilus Lewis was even more scathing toward Lew Leslie. He absolved Florence from any blame:

> Florence Mills is incomparable. She is the most consummate artist I have ever seen on the musical stage. She has perfect control of both the technique of restraint and the technique of abandon. In the early scenes of *From Dixie to Broadway* she employs restraint. But when she sings her song "I'm a Little Blackbird," she lets herself out, and—My God! Man, I've never seen anything like it! Not only that, I never imagined such a tempestuous blend of humor and passion could be poured into the singing of a song. I never expect to see anything like it again, unless I become gifted with second sight and behold a Valkyr riding ahead of a thunderstorm. Or see Florence Mills singing another song.[4]

He devoted the rest of his article, apart from some praise for Shelton Brooks and Cora Green, to a tirade against Lew Leslie's lack of aesthetic sense. Having lampooned Leslie's taste in architecture and interior decoration, he went on to say, "It is really amazing how a man can take such material as Cora Green, Shelton Brooks, Florence Mills, Will Vodery's jazz orchestra, 247 yards of red silk, two dozen yaller gals, and a couple of junk automobiles and make a bad show of the ensemble. However, Mr. Leslie contrives to accomplish the feat."

Leslie would have argued that the stereotyped scenes in *Dixie to Broadway* were the stock-in-trade of most black shows of the time and that he was merely giving audiences what they wanted. Florence didn't express any public views on the issue, but she is on record as having complained that black critics were too generous and uncritical of black shows, so perhaps she would have sympathized with Didier's and Lewis's forthright expressions.[5] She was well read and not reluctant to express critical opinions of dramatic or literary material that reflected poorly on the character of black people. However, she had grown up with the conventions of the black entertainment world and viewed an old standby like the ghost scene, in which comedian Hamtree Harrington portrayed a blackface man paralyzed with fear before a haunted castle, as harmless fun.[6] Also, Leslie had delivered on his promise to provide employment for her fellow performers in a lavish show.

Lew Leslie didn't care too much what the black intelligentsia thought as long as the tills were making the right music, and they were. *Dixie to Broadway* ran for eight weeks and seventy-seven performances at the Broadhurst. Although this was a shorter run than either of the other leading black shows, *Runnin' Wild* or *Chocolate Dandies*, both of them had played a long way uptown, barely on true Broadway. *Dixie to Broadway* was also more profitable than *Chocolate Dandies*, which was very expensively staged. In today's era of megamusicals that last for years, eight weeks on Broadway may not sound like a lot, but for a black show on mainstream Broadway in 1924, it was a resounding success. The show could have stayed on Broadway for much longer, but touring offered better economic prospects.

Certainly the black press considered that *Dixie to Broadway* had achieved a breakthrough far outranking the other two shows. The *Washington Star* commented, "The impressive success of Florence Mills and her company shatters some deep-rooted theories heretofore existing relative to colored musical companies. 'No colored musical show can be a financial success on Broadway' has been a saying for years and regarded as incontrovertible." The news that *Dixie to Broadway* would have an open-ended engagement at a mainstream Broadway theater in the prime season had been "a piece of startling and unheard of news." It was described as the final realization of the dreams of the great, now mostly dead, figures of the Williams and Walker era.[7]

There were many similar articles in the black press celebrating the triumph of Florence Mills and *Dixie to Broadway* and relating them to past triumphs. Mrs. Downs, owner of the Lincoln Theatre, recalling Florence's early years for *Billboard*, noted, "The price of a dozen tickets to witness her work at the Broadhurst Theater now would have paid her weekly salary in those days." The NAACP considered it important enough that it put out a triumphant press release headed "Florence Mills Hailed as Genius."

With Florence's fame and high public profile from her success in *Dixie to Broadway*, the rumors about her private life surfaced again, including suggestions of affairs with white men. These related to the Plantation period when Kid Thompson went out on his own with Willy Covan. Although Kid had refused to be a party to legal stunts that might smear Florence's name, some of the gossip spread anyway. The *Baltimore Afro-American* staunchly denied the tales with a headline "Rumors Can't Hurt Florence." *Variety* backed this up with a report that Kid and Florence were a familiar sight together around Harlem cabarets and that it was to dispel such rumors that she had insisted Kid be in *Dixie to Broadway*.[8]

For a while Florence and Kid were back close to family and friends. She was a respected and admired figure on the social and dramatic scene. She was also a popular figure on Harlem streets, where the local kids knew she was an easy touch for ice creams or candies. She always enjoyed the company of kids. Less to her taste were the endless social functions for which she was constantly in demand. Her natural inclinations led her to steer away from these much of the time. Apart from theatrical benefits and major Harlem functions, she was not an enthusiastic socialite. She occasionally attended gatherings at the Harlem home of A'Lelia Walker or parties given by white theatrical admirers like drama critic Heywood Broun. She was not a regular at the literary soirées given by Carl Van Vechten, which so many black public figures attended. She and Kid still occasionally went to Harlem cabarets to socialize with their show business counterparts. In Kid's words, referring to big parties laid on by the show business moguls Ziegfeld and the Dillinghams, "Florence didn't want to go. She'd rather do justice to her work rather than go to some party and come in the next day all sleepy and couldn't do justice to her work."[9]

Florence much preferred to curl up with a book than go to social functions. Her reading tastes were wide, including the classic European novelists, but she also liked particularly to read works by black authors, including Walter White, Jessie Fauset, and Alexandre Dumas (*The Black Tulip*). Elsewhere she mentioned another great mixed-race European author, Pushkin. Her list also included *The Prince of Washington Square*, published in 1925. It has Harlem-based scenes with a mixture of white and black (rather stereotyped) characters. Little is known today of the author, Harry F. Liscomb, although libraries classify him as African American. Florence may have known him and wanted to encourage the young writer.

The New York residency also brought a former friend back into Florence and Kid's life, William Grant Still. They had become good friends when Still was in the pit orchestra of *Shuffle Along*. He stayed on after Florence had left *Shuffle Along* to go into her own show at the *Plantation*. The reunion would prove important for both of them, socially and professionally.

William Grant Still was born in Woodville, Mississippi, May 11, 1895, and raised in Little Rock, Arkansas. He was the acknowledged "Dean of Afro-American composers" by the end of his long life in December 1978.[10]

While pursuing his classical studies in the early years of the twentieth century, he had followed the route most readily open to talented African Americans, playing in dance bands and accompanying vaudeville acts. Early in his career he worked for W. C. Handy in Memphis, playing in Handy's Memphis Band and doing arrangements. In 1916 he made the first-ever band arrangements of "Memphis Blues" and "St. Louis Blues." When Handy and his publishing company moved to New York in 1919, Still joined the company.

In 1921 he joined Harry Pace's Black Swan Phonograph Corporation as music director, with Fletcher Henderson as the recording director. Around this time Still accepted a place in the *Shuffle Along* orchestra and started a lifelong friendship with Florence Mills and Kid Thompson. After the record-breaking New York run, he went on the road with *Shuffle Along* but subsequently returned to New York, where he rejoined Harry Pace's Black Swan Company, replacing Fletcher Henderson as recording director. In 1923 Still began several years of private study with avant-garde composer Edgar Varese. His symphonic poem *Darker America*, composed in 1924, was an early sign of his promise. He had already established a reputation as a jazz arranger and orchestrator, sometimes in collaboration with his friend Will Vodery. When a larger company took Black Swan over in 1924, he found himself unemployed again. To support himself while studying, he set up as a freelance arranger in New York.

This period was difficult for Still. His first marriage was falling apart, and there were four children to support. Will Vodery suggested he join *Dixie to Broadway*'s Plantation Orchestra as Vodery's musical assistant as well as taking a playing role. Still jumped at the offer, even though it would interfere with his classical studies, as it meant he gained a regular job and also the opportunity to renew his friendship with Florence and Kid Thompson.

Being back in New York at the head of a successful show gave Florence a high social profile. She was one of the featured artists at the annual NAACP benefit held at Happy Rhone's Club on November 17. The entertainment also included Alberta Hunter, Sissle and Blake, Bojangles Robinson, and Fletcher Henderson's Orchestra. Here society and stage mingled in a glittering event patronized by black New York's Top 400 as well as distinguished white guests like Mary White Ovington, Mr. and Mrs. Heywood Broun, and Mr. and Mrs. Carl Van Vechten. Black society leaders present included James Weldon Johnson, W. E. B. DuBois, Walter White, and their spouses. Also there was Langston Hughes, just back from Europe, who was flattered to find his reputation had spread and literary notables were lionizing him.[11]

Shortly after the NAACP function, Walter White, author and Assistant Secretary of the NAACP, entered Florence's world again. In a letter that was almost reverential in tone, he first complimented her on the quality of her show. He quoted his wife as saying it was the best show of its kind she had ever seen. He then went on to complain of two items. First was a double en-tendre song sung by Cora Green in the Harlem hotel bedroom scene, "A Nice Husband." Paying generous tribute to Cora's "lovely personality" and "beautiful dignity" when singing blues numbers, he declaimed the bedroom-scene song as sordid and vulgar. The second item addressed one of the back-drops. He described it as perpetuating the stereotype of the "proverbial chicken-stealing, dice-shooting, watermelon-eating, and razor-carrying Ne-gro." He concluded with a powerful tribute to Florence. He told her that a new dramatization of his novel "The Fire in the Flint" would appear on Broadway soon. He went on to say, "The fact that a presentation of such a play is possible is due in no small measure to the splendid pioneer work which you and other colored performers have done."[12]

What reply, if any, Florence made, or whether his plea produced changes, is unknown. It's likely she would have responded in some fashion to an ad-mirer as well known and influential as White. However, she would have had only limited influence on the production values for Leslie's settings. What-ever the case, the "Nice Husband" sketch continued to be part of the pro-duction in some form for the rest of its run. *Dixie to Broadway* continued at the Broadhurst right up to Christmas, including Christmas Day, to audiences typically 90 percent white. It regularly grossed $13,000 to $14,000 at the box office. As a result of the popularity of the show, Victor Recording Studios in-vited Florence for a test pressing of her two hit tunes, "I'm a Little Blackbird" and "Dixie Dreams." She went to the studio on Friday, December 12, and performed the two pieces with piano accompaniment. The Victor ledgers simply note, "Florence Mills, comedienne, with piano."[13] Alas, the old-style acoustic equipment could not capture the nuances of her soft, high voice. Edith Wilson told musician Frank Powers many years later, "Her tiny voice didn't register well on the primitive recording equipment and sounded nasal and tinny."[14] There is no trace of those test pressings today.

News of Florence's failed recording session traveled fast, and within five days her *Shuffle Along* friend Eva Taylor was in the Okeh studios. With hus-band Clarence Williams and his Blue Five, she recorded two *Dixie to Broad-way* numbers, "I'm a Little Blackbird" and "Mandy, Make Up Your Mind." Clarence Williams had been a leading figure of the jazz world since 1915, not only as a performer but more importantly as a composer, publisher, and en-trepreneur. In 1924 he was A&R (Artists and Repertoire) director for Okeh. His Blue Five included some of the top musicians of the day, including Louis Armstrong and Sydney Bechet.[15]

This session has gone down in history as one of the all-time classics of jazz, featured in many compilations. Armstrong and Bechet were in superb form and complemented each other wonderfully in their duets. Eva Taylor was in excellent voice. Bechet surprised all by turning up with a bizarre instrument, the sarrusophone, an odd combination of saxophone and brass. His playing on "Mandy, Make Up Your Mind" is the only known instance of a jazz record involving a sarrusophone. Although Eva's voice was very different from Florence's, this recording is one of the few clues available today to help us imagine what Florence Mills might have sounded like performing "Blackbird."[16]

About the time of these recording sessions, Shelton Brooks left *Dixie to Broadway*. He had failed to negotiate an acceptable increase in salary. His replacement, on Christmas night, was comedian Billy Mills (no relation to Florence), who had toured as early as 1910 with the noted black vaudeville team, the Whitman Sisters, whose careers spanned from the 1890s to the early 1940s. Mills filled Brooks's spot well and was an instantaneous hit, according to *Billboard*'s black columnist J. A. Jackson.

As the holiday season loomed, Florence found herself engaged in the usual year-end round of charitable and festive occasions. There had been a Thanksgiving fundraiser for the Charity Fund of the Eureka Temple, a black Masonic group. She distributed Christmas charity baskets at Madison Square Garden at the personal invitation of General Ballington Booth and his wife, Maud, founders of the Volunteers of America.[17] There was also a Black Cat dance for the Medina Temple, another black Masonic charitable group.

It was soon announced that after a brief holiday break, *Dixie to Broadway* would go on the road again. It was still grossing $12,000 to $13,000 weekly and could have continued on Broadway indefinitely. However, it was expected to make even more on tour. So ended the highly successful 1924, which saw Florence's talent open up mainstream Broadway to black entertainment for the first time since the long-past days of Williams and Walker. It also saw Florence, Kid, and Florence's mother enjoying their new home in Harlem.

Philadelphia, Here We Come

When fashionable America opened the February 1925 issue of one of its favorite magazines, *Vanity Fair*, it found something most unusual—a full-page portrait of a black woman! The banner caption read "Florence Mills Leads a Harlemquinade on Broadway." Underneath stood Florence, dressed in her "Dixie Dreams" overalls, carrying a hobo's bundle over her shoulder. World-famous photographer Edward Steichen had captured the characteristic pose.

The text exclaimed, "The exotic rhythm and accelerated pace, which have created a furor for the Negro revue, have reached a climax in *Dixie to Broadway.*" It was the first time any black person had been so featured in *Vanity Fair*, and it was an event not repeated until 1933, when Paul Robeson was featured for his role in the movie version of Eugene O'Neill's *The Emperor Jones*. Once again Florence had smashed the barriers of race. Thus the new year opened with a powerful endorsement of her new status.

The main destination for the new version of *Dixie to Broadway* was Philadelphia. The successful run in Boston had left the fans calling for more, so the troupe spent a week there first. By the time the *Vanity Fair* picture appeared, *Dixie to Broadway* had opened at the Philadelphia Lyric Theatre. On opening night, Philadelphia was swathed in driving, swirling snow. Inside the warm theater, the program was identical to that presented on Broadway except for changes necessitated by Billy Mills's replacing Shelton Brooks and the addition of Lillian (Lillyn) Brown, a classically trained soprano.

The reviews for *Dixie to Broadway* were as enthusiastic as in New York. Florence was "The apotheosis of pep; the Nth degree of personality," (*Ledger*) and the show received "wild applause" (*Tribune*). The "Dance of the Wooden Soldiers" and "I'm a Little Blackbird" were both noted as show stoppers. One reviewer wrote: "During the singing of her 'I'm a Little Blackbird Looking for a Bluebird' her listeners are stirred to an electric condition approaching frenzy and the little entertainer exhausts herself in encores." There was praise also for Johnny Nit's soft-shoe artistry and Lillian Brown's "Wagnerian opera voice." The follow-up advertisements promoted Florence as "The girl who drives you wild, the cyclonic colored riot."[18] *Dixie to Broadway* enjoyed a run of eleven weeks in Philadelphia, drawing high returns all the time. By the sixth week it had drawn over $100,000, a record for the Lyric. It was the Lyric's first show ever to have a midnight performance.

The usual extra, benefit performances also occurred. On February 22, Florence performed a guest spot in the inaugural charity performance put on by the local Theatre Treasurer's Club. Cast members from all the leading shows playing Philadelphia at the time gave their services free. The master of ceremonies was legendary American vaudeville and musical comedy star George M. Cohan, composer of "Give My Regards to Broadway." Other performers included Broadway star Joe Laurie Jr. and actor Raymond Hitchcock, star of the *Hitchy-Koo* revue series of a few years earlier. The mayor of Philadelphia, W. Freeland Kendrick, made the welcoming speech. In gratitude for their services, each performer received an attractive yellow satin ribbon with all their names and their shows printed on it.[19]

On the afternoon of that same day, Will Vodery, backed by his orchestra and some members of the cast of *Dixie to Broadway*, had presented a Sacred Concert at the Central Presbyterian Church to honor his recently deceased mother. He was a native of Philadelphia, and his mother had been a prominent worker for the local church. The event was so popular that disappointed crowds were still gathering long after the doors had closed at standing room only. The musical tribute included Handel's *Largo* as well as popular hymns.

One morning sometime in February, Kid Thompson went to the theater to collect his mail. The janitor said, "Did you know your partner's gone." "Who?" asked Kid. "Willie Covan came here and got his stuff, him and Leonard Ruffin, and went on about their business." Kid was amazed. There had not been any friction between him and his partner, and they were both getting a hefty $150 a week. The only explanation he could think of was that Willie was jealous of Johnny Nit's high profile in some of the dancing highlights. Willie Covan's replacement in the show was his brother Dewey Covan. Kid's new partner for his specialty feature was Charlie "Cornbread" Walker. Kid recalled, "I got Cornbread, we went out and had a rehearsal and went on just the same." By mid-February, Covan and Ruffin were playing the Keith circuit. One reporter described them as "specializing in the soldier drill and knee drop dances, which are features of Florence Mills' *Dixie to Broadway*."[20]

In March, Florence made another of the historic breakthroughs that characterized her ascent to fame. Philadelphia, the City of Brotherly Love, was not particularly noted for liberal policies on race relations, but Mayor Freeland Kendrick, although a Republican, was socially liberal. He invited Florence, Will Vodery, and the Plantation Orchestra to visit him and other city dignitaries at his reception room. The white press largely ignored this occasion, but it was the front-page story in the next issue of the black *Philadelphia Tribune*, which greeted the event with the headline "Mayor Meets Florence Mills Thereby Making History." There were two group photographs and headline phrases such as "Racial Triumph" and "Epoch Making."[21]

The mayor held individual meetings, first with Florence, then Will Vodery, in his private chambers. The mayor then joined the full group in the reception room. There the orchestra performed its opening overture and some extra pieces. At this point the entertainment was due to end. There had been no plan for Florence to perform. However, the mayor's generous gesture had touched her deeply. Rising spontaneously, she announced in her quiet-spoken manner that she would like to perform her feature number "I'm a Little Blackbird" as a personal tribute to the mayor. Enthusiastic applause brought her back for a repeated chorus.

This incident shows just how passionately Florence believed that her theme song was effective in putting across her message of racial tolerance. She explained later why she had felt impelled to perform her song in response to the mayor's gesture. "Sometimes when I begin the opening verse of that song my heart is full of tears. . . . In it I sense the struggle of a race for industrial placement [meaning social acceptance]." This time, however, she had felt very happy performing it. "I knew that in this visit to Philadelphia's mayor, the merit of my entire profession has been given notice. I think this act of Mr. Kendrick's does much to focus the public's attention to this fact; we weary stage children who do so much to cheer others are made very happy when we are taken as a legitimate part of the every day program carried on in the world." Typically, she interpreted the mayor's gesture as a tribute to her profession rather than to herself personally.

As if the Mayor's gesture was not sufficient to justify Philadelphia's claim to its soubriquet, a short while later actor Raymond Hitchcock staged a private banquet at a large city hotel for "stage celebrities now appearing here and in New York," reported the *Philadelphia Tribune*. The guest of honor, and "easily the center of attraction," was Florence Mills. In addition to the theatrical luminaries, many of the local social, business, and financial elites attended. The occasion was described as "one of the most elaborate ever ordered in this famous hostelry."[22]

By late March, a publicity handout for *Dixie to Broadway* announced, "Florence Mills, dynamic, brown skinned queen of all colored entertainers, will take her troupe of lightning dancers, harmony singers and merry funsters into their tenth week in Philadelphia on Monday evening at the Chestnut Street Opera House." They played two weeks at the new venue. Gloriously successful as the Philadelphia season had been, in early April it finally closed, doing strong business right up to the end. A triumphant week followed in Pittsburgh, where "I'm a Little Blackbird" was encored again and again. The promoters were keen to squeeze a little more out of the show's success, and rather than take it to more distant venues, they chose to return to Chicago.

Dixie to Broadway opened there on Easter Sunday night, this time at the Chicago Auditorium Theatre. The timing was inauspicious. The theater was not a good venue. The triumph of the previous visit could not be repeated. *Variety* reported poor houses for most Chicago theaters that week, and particularly bad ones for *Dixie to Broadway*,[23] which effectively sounded its death knell as a full-scale theatrical production. After a final week in Cincinnati, Florence headed back to her home base at the Plantation until the next step in her burgeoning career.

Plans for a new show started immediately. Buoyed by the remarkable success of *Dixie to Broadway*, Florence was eagerly looking forward to the fulfillment of Leslie's promise to feature her in an annual series. She declared:

> Our season in *Dixie to Broadway* has thoroughly demonstrated not only the popularity of an all-colored revue when produced on the same scale as the white musical extravaganzas of the present day, but also the feasibility—even the desirability—of making our organization a permanent institution of the American stage with a home theatre for our annual productions and limited tours following our New York engagement. And I am violating no confidence when I say this enterprise is well under way, with considerable work already accomplished on next season's revue.[24]

The new show didn't happen immediately. The *Dixie to Broadway* material continued to be the basis of Florence's performances for the present. There was no shortage of demand for her services in one form or another around New York. First came an engagement at the New York Hippodrome for the week starting May 27 as part of a "Bill of International Artists" assembled from the best of the acts that played over the Keith-Albee East Coast vaudeville circuit. The Hippodrome was the largest theater of its day, with a seating capacity of over 5,000. It was a leading vaudeville venue, second only to New York's Palace Theatre. Being in vaudeville again, this time as a featured act, brought back memories for Florence of her earlier days of struggle on the remote Pantages circuit. So successful was Florence's part of the show that it was held over for an extra week.[25]

Florence's segment was billed as a "Special engagement of the popular little star of *Dixie to Broadway* assisted by Will Vodery's Orchestra and the Eight Dusky Steppers." (One of the specialty acts sharing the bill was Texas Guinan, former western show sharpshooter and by then a well-known nightclub impresario, famed for her raucous style and her trademark greeting for audiences, "Hello, sucker!" Guinan's troupe of dancing girls, the Texas Strollers, included sixteen-year-old Ruby Keeler.[26] Ruby was destined to be a major star of Warner Brothers's musical movies and, along the way, to become Mrs. Al Jolson.) Among Florence's first-night telegrams was one from Paul Robeson: "I wish to be among those to wish you success in your new field. Regards to Edith and U. S."[27] Among the audience members who remembered Florence's performance years later was pianist and film star Oscar Levant, who would write, "[The incomparable Florence Mills] was the greatest Negro star I ever saw. She was thin and reedy and her voice was immeasurably poignant. She also danced wondrously."[28]

The time spent on the road with *Dixie to Broadway* had been demanding for William Grant Still. Although he enjoyed his friendship with Florence and Kid, he was struggling to maintain his studying and composing activities. He spent time alone at the theater out of working hours to get access to the pit piano and try out his musical ideas. At other times he would seek out black churches and revival meetings to absorb Negro music.[29] All the time he was working on a major new work, still under the influence of his teacher Edgar Varese.

The first public performance of Still's new work, *From the Land of Dreams*, occurred at a concert arranged by the International Composers' Guild in February 1925, while he was with *Dixie to Broadway* in Philadelphia. Still said he was "so nervous when it was being played that I scarcely heard it." The critics gave it a mixed reception. The negative comments made more impact on Still. He soon decided the modernist direction Varese had steered him in was not the right one for him, and he decided to change to an approach that would draw more on his black musical heritage.[30]

After *Dixie to Broadway* finished on the road, Still went back to working at the Plantation with Will Vodery. Not yet financially secure, Still was finding it necessary to play in the orchestra, even at one point reluctantly taking up the banjo. At some point, however, he inherited Vodery's mantle as musical director at the Plantation.[31] This gave him the stability to get back to his primary objective, classical composing.

Florence Mills was to play an important role in his first steps away from the Varese influence. After the International Composers' Guild concert, Still brought Florence to the Varese home to meet the composer and his wife. They were enchanted by Florence's "flowerlike loveliness" and became keen fans.[32] Shortly afterwards, Still approached Florence and asked her whether, if he wrote some jazz-flavored classical vocal pieces, she would perform them in concert. Florence was happy to do so even though the performance would be unpaid. She saw it not only as a chance to help her friend but also as an interesting challenge. Lew Leslie, mindful of the publicity opportunity, raised no objection.

The big social event in Harlem in early May was the farewell at the Bamville Club for the cast of the show *Chocolate Kiddies*, off to tour Europe and the Near East. Harlem show folk attended in large numbers. No such occasion could be complete now without Florence singing "I'm a Little Blackbird." The occasion gave her an opportunity to catch up with cast members Adelaide Hall and Lottie Gee, friends from *Shuffle Along* days. The show was also a triumph for the young Duke Ellington. He had produced four compositions on short notice for *Chocolate Kiddies*, and this event gave him important exposure as an emerging composer.[33] One of the pieces, "Jig Walk," was the hit of the show. There is no specific report of Ellington's presence at the farewell, but this is probably one of the many times he met the performer he would later immortalize in his composition "Black Beauty."

Florence's success at the Hippodrome was soon followed by something more impressive. The *Sunday Graphic* reported, with great fanfare, that she would head the bill at the Palace Theatre, New York:

> Florence Mills, the extraordinarily gifted colored girl who has given Broadway hit after hit to talk about, will be the headliner at the Palace Theatre tomorrow. Miss Mills will top a splendid program, will occupy the stellar suite of dressing rooms and be given all the courtesy for which the Palace management is famous among artists. To headline at the Palace is regarded in vaudeville as being the most enviable achievement possible in the two-a-day; it connotes supreme class. Florence Mills is the first artist of her race to be a Palace headliner, and it is an honor that she richly deserves.[34]

The material for the Palace engagement was similar to that for the Hippodrome except Johnny Dunn (cornetist) and Johnny Nit also performed. *Variety*'s reviewer, Jack Lait, praised the whole show enthusiastically, noting that Florence received plenty of curtain calls. He summed up, "It is too late now to more than repeat, for the record, that she is an artist, a personality, and in her way of handling an audience, a genius."[35] The black press was quick to latch on to this good-news story. Favorable reports and reviews from white papers were reprinted in the *Amsterdam News*, the *Chicago Defender*, and the *Baltimore Afro-American*. The Palace management was on the alert for any possible friction arising out of the anticipated large turnout of black patrons for the occasion. However, the week passed without incident. *Variety* reported, "The colored patrons purchased the 85¢ or less tickets, all upstairs."[36] The colored patrons included Josephine Baker and Mildred Hudgins, wife of comedian Johnny Hudgins. Years later Mildred told Jean Claude Baker, self-adopted son of Josephine Baker, of their pride not only at seeing one of their race headlining but also at being driven home to Harlem afterwards in Florence's chauffeured car as her friends.[37]

Also among those appreciating Florence's performance were her new fans, composer Edgar Varese and his wife, Louise. They came as guests of William Grant Still.[38] One who was not content to be just an audience member was Bill "Bojangles" Robinson. He insisted his act at the Riverside Theatre be on early so he could hurry to the Palace and make a guest appearance with Florence.[39] He understood just how historic the occasion was. Florence, in her inimitable fashion, had made another breakthrough and shattered another barrier. In a career that routinely overcame obstacles and set records, the significance of her Palace appearance is easy to underestimate today. Vaudeville is largely forgotten today, but in the 1920s it was the single most important source of public entertainment. Most of the great names of that era of American entertainment, Fanny Brice, George M. Cohan, Eddie Cantor, and Will Rogers, to name but a few, had come up through vaudeville, and above all they coveted the top spot at the Palace.

In the immediate aftermath of her Palace triumph, Florence took a brief break from performing. The Lincoln Theatre in Harlem took the opportunity to engage Vodery's orchestra along with part of the cast from Florence's show for a week. They featured Alma Smith as lead singer and Johnny Nit as lead dancer. An added attraction, reflecting his increasing popularity in Harlem, was Duke Ellington's band, then resident at the Club Kentucky.[40]

Apart from her brief break after the Palace, from May through October, Florence played continuously across the major Keith-Albee vaudeville houses in the New York region, including a return engagement at the Hippodrome. This was another of the special occasions when she and Bill Robinson performed together. "Combined for this engagement only," the playbill declared, listing Bill Robinson as "the Dark Cloud of Joy." Bojangles joined her onstage from the audience toward the end of her act and they performed several numbers as a duo, with him rounding off the performance with his tap Charleston.

Also on the bill of fare was Ray Huling and his Dancing Seal. While no picture has survived of Florence and Bojangles performing together, deep in the vaults of the Bettmann Archive is a picture of Florence teaching the dancing seal to Charleston. It may not have needed much tuition as, according to *Billboard*'s reviewer, amongst its many almost human talents, the seal could do "everything from tap dance to singing tenor."[41]

Florence and Bojangles's shared appearance was so popular that suggestions surfaced that they should team for a full-scale Broadway revue.[42] However, she was already working hard on preparations for her next show. They did get together briefly again, however, when Bojangles organized an elaborate benefit in late June for a popular black vaudeville veteran, Mae Kemp, who was widowed and in poor health. Mae Kemp was a sister of Florence's former mentor and loyal friend, Jesse Shipp. The benefit was staged at the Lafayette Theatre. Lengthy queues formed for "the sort of bill that only comes along once in a blue moon." The highlight of the evening came when the old *Shuffle Along* team of Miller and Lyles, Sissle and Blake, and Florence Mills were joined onstage by Bojangles for a special number that raised the roof.[43]

While these activities were keeping her busy, they also kept Florence close to home and friends rather than endlessly traveling. During her absence on the road and while she was playing the Keith-Albee houses, the Plantation had continued presenting its traditional revue-type entertainment without her. After *Dixie to Broadway* went on the road in mid-1924, the Salvins didn't want to close their successful cabaret venture, so they looked for a new attraction. Earl Dancer coaxed his reluctant partner Ethel Waters into applying. Ethel believed "Broadway and all downtown belonged to Florence Mills." At the audition, however, Ethel not only got the job but also a new song to introduce. "Dinah" proved a big success for her. "I won the wooden apple," she said, "the uphill job of following Florence Mills at the Plantation."[44] Nevertheless, it was a big success for Ethel—and also for a leftover from the just-closed *Chocolate Dandies*, Josephine Baker.

From the chorus, Josephine soon got a chance to be Ethel's stand-in when Ethel was ill. She had learned all of Ethel's numbers and was ready for such an opportunity. The payoff came when Caroline Reagan, an American-born Paris resident, had the idea of staging a black revue in Paris, to be called *La Revue Negre*. Her first preference was Florence, who was even advertised as a coming attraction at the Champs-Elysées Music-Hall but was unavailable. Ethel Waters, still wary of overseas performing, deliberately demanded an excessive amount. Josephine's performance had impressed Caroline Reagan, who offered her the lead in *La Revue Negre*. Josephine grabbed the opportunity, and the rest is history![45]

Florence returned to the Plantation in early November. In Ethel's words, she "came in on my smoke." More graciously, she added, "After all, it was her show and it had been built round her."[46] Ethel wasn't always so gracious toward competitors, but she had high respect for Florence. She knew they had both come up the hard way. When Florence opened again at the Plantation, one of the congratulatory telegrams was from Ethel Waters and Earl Dancer. Amid the various rumors of a new show for Florence, *Billboard* carried several reports that it was to be called *Anna from Savannah*, a misquoted reference to her old Aida Overton Walker "Hannah" number from *The Sons of Ham*, and would be written by Will Vodery, Alex Rogers, and George Gershwin.[47] In fact, capitalizing on the phenomenal success of her theme song "I'm a Little Blackbird," the opening name of Florence's new Plantation show was *Black Birds of 1925*, with music once again by George Meyer. The *Blackbirds* series initiated a new era in black entertainment and a major new chapter in Florence's career.

Notes

1. "Inside Stuff on Legit," VAR, Nov. 5, 1924, 15.
2. Summaries of these reviews appeared in "N.Y. Critics Hail Flossie Mills as a Genius," BAA, Nov. 8, 1924. Originals were in the relevant paper's issues for Oct. 30, 1924.

3. Roger Didier, "Dixie to Broadway," *Opportunity*, Nov. 1924, 345–346. The name Roger Didier was a pen name for noted journalist P. L. Prattis.

4. Theophilus Lewis, "Theatre," *Messenger*, early 1925, 18, 62.

5. George S. Schuyler, "Interviews with Actors," *Messenger*, Jan. 1925.

6. Shown by a comment re: Hamtree Harrington in "Looking across the Footlights," undated (1925), TC FLP.

7. "Racial Comedian's Dream Comes True," *Washington Star* article reprinted in ChDef, Dec. 13, 1924, 6.

8. BAA, Nov. 15, 1924, 6; "Inside Stuff on Legit," VAR, Nov. 5, 1924, 15.

9. HAJC: Transcript of Kid Thompson interview.

10. A useful summary of Still's life and career can be found in Bruce Kellner, ed., *The Harlem Renaissance: A Historical Dictionary* (New York: Methuen, 1987), 342. For a more detailed account, see Verna Arvey, *In One Lifetime* (Fayetteville: University of Arkansas Press, 1984).

11. PiCou, Nov. 22, 1924; Langston Hughes, *The Big Sea* (New York: Hill and Wang, 1963), 202; Arnold Rampersad, *The Life of Langston Hughes Volume 1: 1902–1941* (New York: Oxford University Press, 1986), 97.

12. Library of Congress, Manuscripts Division, NAACP Collection, Part 1 C.91, Reel 21.

13. Ross Laird, *Moanin' Low* (Westport, Conn.: Greenwood Press, 1996), 379.

14. The late Frank Powers, respected jazz musician, in personal e-mail message to the author.

15. For a summary of Clarence Williams's career, see Thomas L. Morgan and William Barlow, *From Cakewalks to Concert Halls: An Illustrated History of African American Popular Music from 1895 to 1930* (Washington, D.C.: Elliott & Clark Publishing, 1992), 121–123.

16. The two tracks are on many CD compilations including *The Complete 1923–1931 Clarence Williams Sessions: Volume 2—1923–1925* (Hot 'n' Sweet, AD065).

17. Telegram from Gen. and Mrs. B. Booth, Dec. 22, 1924, HAJC. They founded the Volunteers in 1896 after a dispute with his father, founder of the Salvation Army, over Americanization of the U.S. branch.

18. From Philadelphia paper's reviews of Jan. 20, 1925, or close thereto, held in the Free Philadelphia Library, including, among others, *The Public Ledger*, *Evening Ledger*, *Gazette*, *Bulletin*, *Inquirer*, *Record*, and "A Breaker of Records," undated, unidentified clipping in Gumby Scrapbook Collection, Columbia University.

19. The satin ribbon presented to Johnny Nit has survived and was generously donated to the Blockson Collection at Temple University in Philadelphia by the owner, Ms. Deborah Williams, in 2002.

20. PiCou, Feb. 14, 1925.

21. PhTr, Mar. 14, 1925. W. Freeland Kendrick was the mayor of Philadelphia from 1924 to 1928. He already had a reputation for philanthropy through his active role in the Shriners, a Masonic group. On his initiative the group established the first Shriners Hospital for children who couldn't afford medical treatment. Today there

are twenty-two Shriners hospitals open to all, regardless of race or creed. See www
.aladdinshrine.com/hospcc.htm (Nov. 30, 2003). He is also remembered today
through a rose named in his honor.

22. "Florence Mills Guest of Honor," PhTr, Mar. 28, 1925.

23. VAR, Apr. 22, 1925.

24. "Florence Mills to Have New Vehicle," BAA, May 2, 1925.

25. "Mills Act Is Holdover at Hip," BAA, May 9, 1925.

26. Hippodrome program, HAJC.

27. Telegram, Apr. 27, 1925, HAJC.

28. Oscar Levant, Memoirs of an Amnesiac (New York: Putnam, 1965), 67.

29. Arvey, In One Lifetime, 69.

30. Catherine Parsons Smith, William Grant Still: A Study in Contradictions (Berkeley: University of California Press, 2000), 222–223.

31. Parsons Smith, 220, 310.

32. Louise Varese, Varese: A looking Glass Diary, Volume I: 1883–1928 (New York: W. W. Norton, 1972), 243.

33. Duke Ellington, Music Is My Mistress (London: Quartet Books, 1977), 71, and Mark Tucker, Ellington: The Early Years (Urbana: University of Illinois Press, 1991), 120–139.

34. "Florence Mills Seen by Graphic Writer as Extraordinarily Gifted Girl," reprint from Sunday Graphic in AMST, June 24, 1925.

35. "Palace," VAR, June 24, 1925, 15.

36. VAR, July 1, 1925, 16.

37. Jean Claude Baker and Chris Chase, Josephine: The Josephine Baker Story (Holbrook, Mass.: Adams Publishing, 1993), 82–83.

38. Judith Anne Still, Michael J. Dabrishus, and Carolyn L. Quin, William Grant Still: A Bio-Bibliography (Westport, Conn.: Greenwood Press, 1996), 22.

39. Jim Haskins and N. R. Mitgang, Mr. Bojangles, The Biography of Bill Robinson (New York: William Morrow, 1988), 174.

40. VAR, July 8, 1925, 47.

41. Hippodrome Program, Oct. 26, 1925, and Billboard, Oct. 21, 1925. The picture of Florence and the seal can be located by searching www.corbis.com (Nov. 20, 2003) and doing an image search for "Florence Mills."

42. ChDef, Oct. 31, 1925, and Haskins and Mitgang, Mr. Bojangles: The Biography of Bill Robinson, 175.

43. AMST, July 8, 1925.

44. Ethel Waters with Charles Samuels, His Eye Is on the Sparrow (New York: Doubleday & Company, 1951), 183–184.

45. Johnny Hudgins letter to Kennard Williams, BAA, July 25, 1925; Baker and Chase, Josephine: The Josephine Baker Story, 92; and Phyllis Rose, Jazz Cleopatra (New York: Vintage Books, 1991), 63–64.

46. Waters, 185.

47. Billboard, Oct. 3 and 31, 1925.

CHAPTER EIGHT

~

A Blackbird Takes Wing

Black Birds and an Aeolian Concert

As 1925 draws to a close, Florence is at the peak of her profession. She has not only conquered Broadway and London but has successfully toured the major eastern U.S. cities and topped the bill in vaudeville's most prestigious venues. Although still the modest, reserved person she has always been, she has a newfound confidence in her capacity to be a role model and spokesperson for her race. With her increasing outspokenness off the stage, and her passionate promotion of the message of tolerance in her new theme song onstage, she is staking a claim to being more than just an entertainer. As 1926 approaches she is poised to take on surprising new challenges and to launch a series of shows that will set the pace for a generation of black entertainers.

Black Birds of 1925 opened at the Plantation on November 3, advertised as "the after dinner sensation in New York's smartest nightclub."[1] It was back to the cabaret floorshow setting for Florence, at least for a while. *Black Birds of 1925* is never mentioned in the history of the *Blackbirds* series. By the time it got to full theatrical presentation, it had become *Black Birds of 1926*.[2] Many of the songs and dances were carried over from *Dixie to Broadway*. There were some new songs, written once again by George Meyer. Most significant were the charming, plaintive "Silver Rose," "Smilin' Joe," and "Arabella's Wedding Day."

A few days before the opening, the announcement came that Florence was to make a concert appearance early in the new year at the Aeolian Hall.

She would perform in *Levee Land,* a modern suite for voice and chamber orchestra (twelve musicians) by William Grant Still. This was the set of songs Still had offered to write for her. They had both been working intensely on them for some time. For him the songs he planned to write for Florence were to be a tentative first step in a new direction. He wanted to move away from the modernist approach he had been taking under Edgar Varese's direction and turn instead to his black musical heritage. Drawing from the *Dixie to Broadway* theme representing "The Evolution of the Colored Race," the songs would portray black people in a traditional setting.[3]

Meanwhile, general audience reaction to *Black Birds* was very favorable. The *Baltimore Afro-American* critic was enthusiastic, quoting a wealthy patron's description of Florence as "A brownskin Texas Guinan" and praising the speed and skill of the dancing.[4] A critical note came from Sime Silverman, respected founder and editor of *Variety.* He criticized Leslie for providing banal material and admonished Florence for performing what he called a "cooch" dance, unsuited to her high talents and promise. "Cooch" was a term originally applied to pseudo-Egyptian or Turkish belly dancing popular in steamy burlesque shows but later applied loosely to any kind of sexually suggestive dancing performed in scanty clothing. Noting her forthcoming performance of Still's music at the Aeolian Hall as a sign of great potential, he urged her to adopt the high standards associated with the great black actress Abbie Mitchell if she aspired to great achievements.[5]

The *Amsterdam News* hailed the *Variety* article as vindication of earlier comments it had made on Leslie. It had quoted a complaint by Mary White Ovington, well-known white supporter of the NAACP, that black shows were failing to live up to the standards of Williams and Walker because they were relying on material written by whites. Picking up on this theme, the *News* urged Lew Leslie to draw on the skills of black composers of that era to provide material for Florence. The truth was Leslie had a benevolently stereotyped view of black capabilities beyond the performer's role. He is on record as expressing the view that white men "understand the colored man better than he does himself. Colored composers excel at spirituals but their other songs are just white songs with Negro words."[6] Nevertheless, he used Eubie Blake and Andy Razaf in some later shows.

If Lew Leslie read the criticisms leveled at him, it's doubtful he understood them. He had faith in his own ability to gauge what the public wanted and the necessary energy and enthusiasm to deliver it. In a world of hedgehogs and foxes, where the fox knows many things but the hedgehog knows one big thing, Leslie was a hedgehog. The one big idea of his life was his dream for the glorification of the black American "girl" in the same way that Ziegfeld was "glorifying the [white] American Girl." In Florence Mills he found his ideal and he pursued it doggedly, with total faith in his own judgment on matters of public taste.

What did Florence feel about the criticism? She had a fierce loyalty to her fellow black entertainers and understood the obstacles they faced in gaining recognition and employment. Leslie had made good on his promise to surround her with a show employing black performers and rivaling the style of the big white revues. She felt she had done as much as was in her power under the circumstances. Anyway, they both had other pressing matters on their minds.

Leslie had bigger plans for *Black Birds* than just the Plantation, or even Broadway. It was to be Florence's next big international venture. Florence's own mind was on much more immediate matters. Her Aeolian Hall performance was looming. Preparation for it was placing heavy demands on her time and energy because it came in addition to the normal grueling performance schedule at the Plantation: shows at 12:30 and 2:30 nightly. Having accepted the challenge of Still's material, she knew she would be under the spotlight of intense scrutiny from classical music experts. There would also be others keen to deride "uppity" blacks if it proved a fiasco. She must succeed, not just for her own sake but to prove that her people could rise to any challenge.

As 1925 ended, reports circulated that Florence was planning to build a theater to showcase black productions in Harlem. The story, which originated in the white press, was based on a rumor that she and Kid had made a large sum of money on a Florida land deal. The black press picked it up. The *Amsterdam News* treated it skeptically. The *Chicago Defender* ran with it, even claiming Florence herself had shown their reporter the plans for "a massive 4,000 seat theater."[7] The story doesn't seem to have been based on fact. Florence's earlier interview about the need for a permanent base, including "a home theatre" for her shows, may have encouraged it. She had also told journalist P. L. Prattis around this time that she would like to retire someday and run a vaudeville and movie house.[8]

The theater story also reflected a recurrent theme of Harlem society—the lack of a strong black legitimate theater to match the success of black entertainers. Individual performers like Charles Gilpin and Paul Robeson had succeeded in legit theater. Stock companies like the Lafayette Players, with Abbie Mitchell, Evelyn Preer, and Rose McLendon, were also achieving some success. Missing, however, were black playwrights and a theater to present their products. One exception was the young playwright Garland

Anderson. His play *Appearances* had achieved a three-week run on Broadway to favorable reviews but then folded for lack of financing. When famous white playwright David Belasco launched an appeal for funds to keep it going, Florence, Al Jolson, and James Weldon Johnson were among the donors.[9]

The story about the Florida real estate deal was only one of many circulating about Florence amassing fabulous wealth. *Variety* put her wealth into perspective in a year-end review of black show business. Florence was identified as the "highest-priced" black female performer. However, the unanimous conclusion of a group of experts was that the highest-earning female performer was undoubtedly "a woman who has never played in a white house in her life, Bessie Smith." She was a big earner because she was not under the control of a manager and his entourage, as Florence was with Lew Leslie.[10] In fairness to Leslie and his backers, they had to underwrite the heavy expenses of a lavish show, accepting the risks when returns were low. Bessie's overhead for her southern tent shows and TOBA appearances were minuscule by comparison.

While the rumors of wealth were exaggerated, Florence and Kid were earning handsomely. They were frugal in their own lifestyle although generous to family and friends as well as to charities. Both of them had grown up in poverty and knew what it was like to lack money. Interviewed about her views on money management during the Philadelphia season, Florence said she saved a large part of her money for a "rainy day." She commented:

> I have had so many friends that have earned enormous salaries for several years. I have seen them throw their money away right and left and when their popularity died down, and their salaries went down with their popularity until work was hard to obtain, they have had to call on charity to aid them. . . . I personally have salted away a great deal more than I have spent the past five years. My salary has been most substantial and I have not found it necessary to deprive myself of any of the luxuries of life but, should an accident befall me tomorrow and make it impossible for me to continue my work on the stage, I have enough salted away in good investments to take care of myself in a decent manner for the balance of my life.[11]

Florence's attitude had rubbed off on Kid. Although his early poverty had made him conscious of the value of money, he had been a gambler and was proud of his skill at it. He claimed to have won a diamond ring from jazz great Freddie Keppard. "I beat him out of a diamond ring; he tried to gamble, see, and I use to could gamble pretty good—cheat, you know." Then he said, "I used to gamble before I met Florence, but I cut it out."

Over the closing weeks of 1925 and the early weeks of 1926, William Grant Still and Florence worked intensely, preparing for her Aeolian performance. The pieces were complex and unlike anything she had previously performed. She did not read music, so Still played the pieces over and over with his one-fingered piano technique while she learned them by rote.[12] She had no opportunity to hear how they would sound in the orchestral setting that would accompany her in the live performance. In addition to the music, she had to memorize and perfect detailed dramatic instructions. The score gave precise details as to the position and attitude of the performer throughout. Examples include "Turn halfway, leaving side of face visible to audience, and view orchestra contemplatively" or "Remain facing audience. Smile approvingly and move body slightly in response to rhythm."[13]

For someone who was already a meticulously conscientious performer and a tireless rehearser, this was a stern challenge. She was conscious that her performance would reflect on her entire race, and she was determined not to disappoint. Her patience and willingness to accept instruction impressed Still deeply.[14] Nevertheless, perfecting her grasp of the unfamiliar music while maintaining her regular performance schedule was proving very stressful.

This period had another side. During a party in the Varese home, her host came across her on her own in a quiet corner of the house, away from the noisy groups. He was shocked to see she was crying. Fearing someone among the white guests might have insulted her, he asked, "Florence, what is the matter? Has anyone been rude to you?" Shaking her head, she reassured him in her small, soft voice, "It's because I've never been so happy. Everybody treats me like everybody and no one has even asked me to sing."[15] The incident also reflects Florence's highly strung state during this stressful period.

The four *Levee Land* songs, described as Still's first experiments in symphonic jazz, had contrasting styles.[16] The first, "Levee Song," is a lover's bluesy lament for her neglectful man, sung "very slow and very soft (as if heard from afar)." Number two, "Hey-Hey," is "moderately fast," the vocal consisting solely of the words "Hey-Hey" spoken three times, "as if surprised," "as if questioning," and "as if disgusted," each with precise instructions as to the singer's posture. "Croon," as the title suggests, is wordless, with the singer instructed to hum the vocal line "very slow." This humming would not have been hard for Florence as wordless vocalizing was one of her trademarks and helps to account for the frequent description of her voice as birdlike.

The last piece, "The Backslider," "moderately slow, with expression," is the most dramatic of the four. A tale of religion lost through "jazz," it might well raise a few frissons among a staid audience of "straight" classical fans and musicians. The following extract gives some sense of the flavor:

> Fo'kses, is you got religion?
> An' ef yo is,
> Do you wanna keep it?
> You ax me why?
> Well ah had religion onct
> But ah done los' it
> You ax me how?

(Here the singer casts a furtive glance at the orchestra and then says—sotto voce— to the audience)

> "Jazz"[17]

The concert took place on the evening of Sunday, January 24, 1926, under the banner of the International Composers' Guild. Edgar Varese and Carlos Salzedo had jointly founded the Guild a few years before to promote avant-garde music. Advance notices that a Broadway entertainer—and black at that—was to be featured at a concert of avant-garde classical music had created intense interest. As well as the usual notices in the New York Times and other suitable media, the Guild had issued a special one-page flyer with a portrait of Florence, announcing it as her "first concert appearance anywhere." The program described her segment as being "Songs with small Jazz Orchestra."[18]

The Aeolian Hall was packed for the event, many there "merely to witness Florence Mills in the role of a concert artist."[19] They included such notables as Arturo Toscanini, George Gershwin, Carl Van Vechten, James Weldon Johnson, Walter F. White, and Mrs. Otto H. Kahn, as well as the many distinguished musicians included on the program. Although Florence's presence was exciting the keenest interest, the evening included a selection of pieces by several composers. Levee Land was scheduled after the intermission. The program announced the Guild's "Second Concert of New Music," presented by Florence Mills (Concert Debut), Elsa Respighi (American Debut), Alfredo Casella, Ottorino Respighi, and a Chamber Orchestra composed of Germaine Tailleferre, Carlos Salzedo, and leading New York players conducted by Eugene Goossens. The first half consisted of new compositions by Goossens, Carl Ruggles—a relentless modernist—and Respighi, followed by four South American Indian folksongs sung by Mrs. Respighi.

Despite her years of experience as a performer, Florence was extremely nervous as she waited for her turn. Perhaps George Gershwin, who barely two years before had waited nervously in the same Aeolian Hall for Paul

Whiteman's introduction of his *Rhapsody in Blue*, felt a twinge of sympathy for her. To add to the tension, she and conductor Eugene Goossens had had limited time to rehearse the full orchestral version of the songs she had rehearsed only with the piano until now. Goossens, already an admirer of hers since her London visit in 1923, was delighted with her quick grasp of the material. He said, "All of these she rehearsed with me and a small orchestra in the record time of half an hour, a tribute to her superb musicianship."[20]

All her preparation paid off. The audience loved it. She performed several encores. Toscanini sat entranced and afterwards went backstage to congratulate her. The critics loved it as much as the audience, mainly because of Florence. Although mixed, or lukewarm, in their approval of Still's music, they praised Florence's performance:[21]

- Olin Downes (*New York Times*): The interest of the performance, the real interest and value such as it was, came from the performer. Miss Mills would never profess to be a finished singer along classical lines, but in her own way she was inimitable.
- *New York World*: Curious and elemental were these songs by this brilliant young Negro composer, plaintive in part, blue, crooning and sparkling with humor, and Miss Mills gave them a perfect interpretation. She sang them sensuously and lovingly, but she did more, she rolled her eyes here and she shrugged her shoulders there, and the audience squirmed excitedly and laughed like a good neighbor. It was a pretty jolly evening for a concert hall. Now, it's true although possibly a little rash to come right out and say that Florence Mills packed the house.
- *New York Evening Journal*: She had some extremely difficult things to sing—the sort that takes brains and vocal ability even to memorize— but she seemed just as much, or nearly as much, at her ease in them as though they had been honest-to-goodness jazz melodies. . . . The audience went wild over her. . . . We believe if she would give a programme of real Negro jazz songs and a handful of spirituals she would create a vogue that would outdo that of Roland Hayes and Paul Robeson put together.
- Abel (*Variety*): Miss Mills is herself. She is inimitable in her method of vocalization, and wisely enough, she is not phased by the venerable confines of Aeolian Hall. A temptation might be to strive for "finish" in her singing but she "Hey Hey'd!" in individual style and they loved it. . . . On top of all of which, Miss Mills hied herself [to] the Winter Garden building and came down to earth on two feet and gave them the usual "I'm a Little Blackbird Looking for a Bluebird."

The excited squirming of the audience mentioned by the *World* reviewer was in response to the jazz drama of "The Backslider." It may even have stimulated some ideas in George Gershwin's mind for his future *Porgy and Bess*, as it could well serve as an anthem for Bess. While several of the critics obviously felt that Florence injected a jazz flavor of her own into the proceedings, an examination of the score for *Levee Land* confirms she was faithfully following the composer's instructions.

The concert was an event that stayed in many people's memories for a long time. Still was asked in 1975 what he remembered as his first smash hit. He replied, "Well, I don't think there has ever been a real smash hit in the accepted sense of the term, but the thing I wrote for Florence Mills, the *Levee Land* suite, attracted lots of attention from the critics."[22] Respected critic Paul Rosenfeld, looking back on the history of the International Composers' Guild and its concerts, wrote, "Frequently the rewards were magnificent and memorable. Many of them, the single concert appearance of little Florence Mills, for example, enshrined their moments."[23]

Florence's success delighted Still, and he was philosophical about the mixed reactions to his music. After the reaction to *From the Land of Dreams* a year before, he had been questioning his Varese-influenced direction, and his later assessment of *Levee Land* was "a step nearer the idiom I was seeking yet it was still too extreme."[24] The *Musical Courier* reacted positively:

William Grant Still is a Negro musician with a first rate education. He did the orchestrations of several of the Broadway Dixie [sic] hits and knows his business. Last year he had a piece performed at an I.C.G. concert which was nothing more or less than a slavish imitation of the noises which Edgar Varese calls compositions. This year he had safely escaped from that baleful influence and gave the public four foolish jazz jokes—sung by Florence Mills in true and proper Broadway manner—and greatly enjoyed by the public. These works are so good, healthy, sane—such good musical fooling—that they place this Negro composer on a high plane in the super-jazz field just now in vogue.[25]

Still himself never arranged another performance of *Levee Land*.[26] When asked about it in later years, he would reply, "Where can we find another Florence Mills?"[27] The work vanished into obscurity until recently, when the William Grant Still Music Company restored it from old photostats. It was finally performed again in 1995 for the one hundredth anniversary celebration of Still's birth. The Northern Arizona University Wind Symphony Orchestra (Dr. Patricia J. Hoy conducting) performed, with Florence Mills's singing role taken by Celeste Headlee, granddaughter of William Grant Still.[28]

Still's later indifference to his own creation may help to explain why this significant event has been overlooked and not given the significance it deserves as an important event in the Harlem Renaissance. There is also the question of what motivated him to undertake such a curious venture in the first place. There may be a link between the two. The Aeolian concert took place at the peak of the Harlem Renaissance. This was the era of the "New Negro," who was expected to fulfill the high intellectual expectations of the cultural leaders of the Renaissance. The attitude of these leaders toward entertainers and jazz musicians was ambivalent. In Doctor Samuel Floyd's words, "In the early years of the Renaissance, there was a sharp line dividing intellectuals from 'show people.' As far as creative artists were concerned, literary writers, classical musicians, and actors in the legitimate theater were in the former category, while the latter category comprised jazz and pop musicians and other entertainers."[29]

Still moved comfortably between both camps. He knew the entertainment world intimately, having supported his musical development through his work there. As the rising genius of "serious" music, he was clearly also one of the intellectuals, well equipped to further Alain Locke's dream of a fusion between "the art music and the folk music."[30] Florence Mills, on the other hand, was one of the "other entertainers," the motley crew of dancers, singers, comedians, and special acts whose livelihood depended on the reactions of audiences, largely white and often with stereotyped expectations. Still understood the hopes and ideals of the entertainers. He had been one of them, lived with them, suffered their failures and lived their triumphs with them. He perhaps also understood that they were the real vanguard of black culture. At the same time, by 1926 he was an admired intellectual figure, recognized by the leaders of the Harlem Renaissance as one destined to excel in the field of classical music. He was in a position therefore to exert some influence.

When William Grant Still invited Florence Mills to sing his compositions in concert, he was displaying to the intellectual leaders of the Harlem Renaissance, in front of an international and multiracial audience of their peers, that his friends the entertainers also had style and talent. He was also paying back something in return for the support their world had given him over the early years of struggle. These motives may also explain his seeming indifference to *Levee Land* in later years. With the dramatic performance on that glittering night, it had served its purpose, a brilliant flare briefly illuminating the firmament of the Harlem Renaissance, bearing testimony to the dignity and talent of a generation of black entertainers, personified by Florence Mills.

Florence followed her triumphant concert appearance by heading off to deliver her regular performance at the Plantation. It was business as usual, but her achievements had been proudly witnessed in the black community. The NAACP released a press statement hailing the event as a milestone.[31] However, the effort had affected her severely, and less than two weeks after the concert, *Variety* reported, "Through constant hard work, Florence Mills now starring in the Plantation Cabaret, finds herself under the care of a specialist. While her condition isn't alarming, she has reached a point where a let up of her stage work is necessary before a collapse." It pointed out that Florence had worked eighty-seven of the previous ninety weeks.[32] The *Pittsburgh Courier* also reported that she had been ordered to rest. "The task of appearing in two different kinds and two different classes of vocal energy was naturally a little too strenuous."[33] Clearly Florence had pushed herself to the limit of her endurance, and the burden of carrying so much on her shoulders was taking a toll on her health.

There were no further reports of ill health, and any break Florence took must have been short as the Plantation continued business as normal. Anyway, even if she was off the stage for a while, she was not out of the public eye. In fact, the matter that kept her before the public eye was her absence from a different stage. Still recovering from the stress of the Aeolian Hall concert, she found herself at the center of a controversy not of her own making. In February 1926, at his Belasco Theatre on Broadway, David Belasco—the renowned "Bishop of Broadway," staged a melodramatic production, *Lulu Belle*, by Edward Sheldon and Charles McArthur. It was the instant scandalous success of the Broadway season. A huge production with a cast of 112, it was the story of a flamboyant black prostitute and sometime cabaret performer from Harlem. Lulu Belle was a latter-day Carmen who seduced decent men away from their families and discarded them until finally one of them strangled her. The settings included a crowded street scene in San Juan Hill (years later the setting for the movie *West Side Story*) and a black cabaret in Harlem.[34]

Renowned white actor Lenore Ulric played the part of Lulu Belle in blackface. Other white actors, some in blackface, played most of the other leading parts. The street and cabaret scenes required ninety-three black actors, twenty-one with speaking parts. The Lafayette Players' Evelyn Preer had a second-lead part as the wife of Lulu Belle's first victim. Careful staging ensured minimal contact between the white and black cast members. Lenore Ulric's "vamping" scenes were all with white cast members.[35]

While the play excited much controversy among the theatergoing public at large, the black community had its own debate. Some saw it as a good opportunity for black actors. Others felt it portrayed blacks in a degrading fashion. A specific issue of debate was the rumor that Lulu Belle's life was partly based on that of Florence Mills. Picking up on this theme, *Vanity Fair* published a full-page Edward Steichen portrait of Lenore Ulric as Lulu Belle, captioned "Lenore Ulric—Enacting a Dusky Heroine." The subheading read, "As a Florence Mills in 'Lulu Belle,' a new play depicting the rise of a gorgeous mulatto."

Furious about the implications of the story, Florence gave an interview to the *New York Graphic* to set the record straight from her point of view.

> Though I have not seen "Lulu Belle" yet, I have read the script of the play. It is not founded on the story of my life. That has nothing to do with my refusal of the part now played so splendidly by Lenore Ulric.
>
> What would my people think if I took the lead in a production which paints the Negro race in such a light? Why can't producers pick out more plays like "Appearances" by Garland Anderson, which show the nicer side of colored people?
>
> Even if I had accepted the role I couldn't think of it. I couldn't feel it. I wouldn't be true to my own self if I stooped to such a representation of my people.[36]

While making her opinions clear Florence had characteristically paid Lenore Ulric a gracious compliment. The only similarities between the character Lulu Belle and Florence Mills were that both had grown up in slum conditions and both were cabaret entertainers. In all other respects they were total opposites. Nevertheless, the rumor had taken hold. The *Amsterdam News* put the question directly to Lenore Ulric herself. She replied, "I have had the script for Lulu Belle in my trunk for six years. Mr. Sheldon and I planned it in Chicago. I visited the black and tan districts there for local color. The role seemed too utterly unsympathetic to attempt then." Her statement claiming a long-term lease on the part seems to conflict with Florence's claim to have been offered it. Nevertheless, Florence's assertion can be confirmed independently.

First, in May 1925, about the time the play would have been in development, Florence had received a letter on Belasco Theatre stationery, signed by Belasco's general stage director Burk Symour. It asked her, "Will you kindly inform me when it will be convenient for you to have a chat with Mr. Belasco in reference to some plans he has in mind for you." Florence's reply, dated May 8 on New York Hippodrome stationery, offered to meet Belasco any day the following week. She suggested Lew Leslie, to whom she was under contract, accompany her as her manager. The outcome of this exchange is unknown. However, given Florence's high profile at the time, Belasco could not have offered her anything less than a starring role.[37]

Further confirmation of Florence's assertion comes from Paul Robeson's biographer, Martin B. Duberman, who relates that Belasco had approached Robeson with a plan for the play to star him, Florence Mills, and Charles Gilpin. Robeson's wife, Essie, was keen to accept, but Paul disliked what he saw as stereotyping. He refused the offer although he stayed on good terms with the play's authors. One of them later apologized to him for some of the racial terms used in the play.[38] This account seems to confirm beyond any doubt Florence's claim she was offered the role and refused it. It's tantalizing today to contemplate the possibility of a major Broadway production in 1926 starring Paul Robeson, Charles Gilpin, and Florence Mills.

Lulu Belle was a highly successful production, gaining many plaudits for Lenore Ulric. A clue to the possible origin of the rumor connecting the play to Florence's life story appeared in an advertisement in the *New York Times* on February 25. It read, "Was *Lulu Belle* written from the life of Florence Mills, who appears nightly after the theatre at the Plantation, Broadway and 50th Street?" Whether Lew Leslie invented the rumor or was merely cashing in on it is unclear, but Romeo Dougherty, theatrical columnist of the *Amsterdam News*, pointed the finger directly at him as the originator.[39]

Farewell to Harlem

While the furor over *Lulu Belle* raged, Florence kept her regular schedule at the Plantation. Rival cabaret shows in New York at the time included the English *Charlot Revue* with Beatrice Lillie, Gertrude Lawrence, and Jack Buchanan and songs by Noel Coward; the rising Duke Ellington at the Kentucky Club; and *Texas Guinan's Revue* at her own nightclub. The latter still had Ruby Keeler, plus future movie star George Raft claiming to be the fastest Charleston dancer in town.[40] There were rival colored shows at the Cotton Club, Connie's Inn, and the Club Alabam.

The Club Alabam show had a stellar lineup that included Abbie Mitchell, Clarence Robinson, Fredi Washington, Elida Webb, Ethel Moses, and Hyacinth Curtis. Although *Blackbirds* and the Club Alabam show were competitors, they were now also part of a team. Rehearsals were going on furiously behind the scenes to blend them into an enlarged *Black Birds of 1926*. The fruits of this effort became visible late in March. Advertisements appeared in the New York press announcing a limited engagement of Florence Mills at the Alhambra Theatre in Harlem with a cast of seventy-five people in a "gorgeous new revue," Lew Leslie's *Black Birds of 1926*.[41] The Alhambra engagement was an out-of-town, or more accurately out-of-continent, tryout for Florence's next overseas venture. Charles B. Cochran had, as his friends confidently expected, successfully relaunched his career as a theatrical impresario. In his undying determination to give London the best of world theater, he had decided to bring Florence Mills back. This time she would star in her own full-scale show without any local distraction.

For the extended *Black Birds* production, Leslie recruited Clarence Robinson, Ethel Moses, and Hyacinth Curtis from the Club Alabam revue. Clarence Robinson was a talented singer and dancer who later found fame as the highly regarded choreographer of the Cotton Club shows as well as the original stage show of *Cabin in the Sky*. Ethel Moses and her sister Lucia had been in *Dixie to Broadway*. Hyacinth Curtis had originally joined the *Plantation Revue* in 1923, during Florence's absence in London. This was her first time performing with Florence. Her account of how she came to join the *Plantation Revue* casts an interesting light on Lew Leslie's work methods.

Curtis's career began when she went to a basketball game as an ordinary spectator with no show business affiliations. The intermission entertainment featured dancing girls from the Plantation. "I wanted to see these beautiful girls that I had seen come to the basketball game. I guess they were guests, because after the basketball games there was dancing and they usually had some stars or somebody, and the girls were so gorgeous I wanted to see their show." The show's wardrobe mistress was a friend of her sister's and sneaked Hyacinth in behind scenes to watch the show.

Lew Leslie and Maude Russell, passing by, saw her. Chucking her under the chin, Leslie said to Maude, "That's a pretty little girl." Asked by Leslie if she wanted to be a dancer, Hyacinth replied, "Well, I'd have to find out from home, my mother. I've never danced before." Turning to Maude, Leslie asked, "Could you do something with her?" "Give her to me," said Maude. Hyacinth recalls, "She taught me. She took all the patience in the world to teach me. I was clumsy as the dickens. She taught me, and that was how I got started." What had started was a career for Hyacinth that took her to Europe with Florence and later to thirteen years at the Cotton Club.

Merging the two companies into a cohesive show presented a major challenge. Lew Leslie was a laissez-faire choreographer, only occasionally contributing an original idea, such as the "Wooden Soldiers" parody, and usually relying heavily on the knowledge and skills of the dancers themselves to come up with new routines that pleased him. On the matter of rehearsing and polishing the material, however, he was a hard taskmaster.

Hyacinth Curtis recalled, "Rehearsals are very hard. We didn't have any union in those days. You might rehearse all afternoon and half of the night."

She also remembered Leslie as concerned for the welfare of his performers. "He was very good to his stars. He used to send me home in a cab at nights and make me lie down and rest and get big bottles of milk for me to drink in between, when I was resting, because I had never stayed up that late, worked those hours." Lena Horne painted a similar picture of Leslie as a tough taskmaster who was also warmly supportive: "He was the first man I ever worked for who did not act like a boss. He and his brother were old-fashioned Jewish people with that traditionally strong Jewish sense of family and they drew me into their life."[42]

Before the show could go on, the Alhambra had to be converted from a film house. The changes required forty hours of nonstop work, after which the cast drilled relentlessly to get ready for the curtain to go up. The chaos continued right up to the curtain call. A backstage observer noted, "Dressing rooms are scarce. Small booths have been rigged in the wings, like square tents, for the chief dancing girls. You see their shadows on these tent walls as they squirm into their costumes. "Hell!" comes an anguished voice. She has miscalculated with a pin. "Hey!" the electrician bawls, "Get me them thousand watt lamps."[43]

The opening on Easter Monday was a guaranteed success with the Harlem hometown audience, which included Paul and Essie Robeson. The professional critics reacted with their characteristic mixture of adulation and complaint. The often cynical George Jean Nathan wrote rapturously, "If in all the country, there is a woman white or black, who is the combined expert in pantomime, song and dance, and the magnetic vitality, that this Miss Mills is, I must have been attending a meeting of the Slate and Tile Roofers' Union when she exhibited herself." Proclaiming Florence the greatest female player on the stage, he declared, "What Jolson is among the men, she is among the women."[44] He praised her in particular for being a true and authentic representative of her race, with no concessions to white influence. Entertainer Marion Warner saw Black Birds as a little girl. She recalled that after Florence had done many encores of "I'm a Little Blackbird," Paul Whiteman stood up and begged her to sing it one more time.[45]

On the negative side, Theophilus Lewis, writing in the Messenger, was predictably contemptuous of Lew Leslie's theatrical taste, while being lavish in his praise for Florence. He wrote, "I regard Florence Mills as the best comedienne of our time. This side of idolatry . . . I admire her as much as any man." However, he went on to chide Florence for continuing to accept the material offered by Leslie, advising her that failure to present audiences with new, original material would compromise her long-term future. The Evening Telegraph, noting the success of the Harlem-based production, commented that the opposition black show, *Tan Town Topics* at the Lafayette Theatre, was also doing well. This production starred Florence's sister Maude and Adelaide Hall with Fats Waller's ten-piece orchestra in the pit.

The *Black Birds* company was scheduled to leave for France on the steamship *La France* on Saturday, May 15. The three-week run at the Alhambra was originally due to finish on April 25. The Alhambra was a small theater with high prices and a steady stream of downtown visitors. Florence became concerned at reports that many Harlemites and friends of hers were missing out. She asked Leslie to extend the run and increase the number of one-dollar seats. In a paid advert in the *Amsterdam News*, she invited all her friends and supporters to come. She promised autographed pictures of herself for the ladies at matinee performances. The show was extended again, for the week of May 3, "Positively the last week before leaving for Paris."[46]

Those final weeks at the Alhambra leading up to the departure were busy ones for Florence, socially as well as professionally. Coincidentally, the same edition of the *Amsterdam News* that featured a large photo of her under a caption "Sailing for Europe Soon" also featured two other noted women of the Harlem Renaissance. Sadly, it carried news of the tragic fatal crash of celebrated black aviator Bessie Coleman; more happily, it announced the marriage of A'Lelia Walker, heir to the Madame C. J. Walker hair-straightener fortune.[47]

Somewhere around this time Florence met again the equine namesake she had helped launch on its racing career in Chicago a few years before. The horse had gone on to achieve a sparkling record. Her victory in a prestigious Lexington, Kentucky, race, the Ashland Oaks, may have been the trigger for the celebration that brought them together at the Plantation. The bay mare's track record for all 1926 was stunning: eleven first, eight second, and three third places in thirty-four starts. Her prize money for that year totaled $15,770. The Ashland Oaks win was worth $3,359 and was significant enough to put the horse on the front cover of *Thoroughbred Record* with jockey Edward Legere. Legere rode four winners at the Lexington event and was a successful local jockey, although his best run in the Kentucky Derby was sixth place in 1925. Over a four-year racing career the mare won $42,374 (about half a million in today's dollars).[48]

The prize-winning mare named after Florence was guest of honor at a special Sunday night party at the Plantation to celebrate her racing success. A tongue-in-cheek report noted, "Prominent people from the racing world will see the horse occupy a ring table built into a stall, with a flowered feedbag full of Salvinized oats as his [sic] trophy. Miss Mills will sing fitting specialty numbers for the approval of *Florence Mills*, the horse, and whips will be given away as souvenirs."[49] The reference to "Salvinized oats" was a sly reference to the Plantation's ability to provide liquor to its clients despite Prohibition.

The final week's performance at the Alhambra, billed as the "Parisian edition," also saw the name of Johnny Hudgins, a dancing, miming clown, appear on the bill. Hudgins was one of Leslie's inspired choices. He had been performing since 1916 or earlier, billed as "the colored Charles Chaplin." His specialty was a silent mime act known as "Wah Wah." He once explained the origin of the curious name: "One night [in *Chocolate Dandies*] I got hoarse and the trumpet man [Louis Metcalf, later famous with Duke Ellington] was making these sounds and I just moved my mouth. The trumpet player caught the way I was moving my mouth and I cut out all the singing and went into pantomime with that trumpet of his. I named it 'Wah Wah.'"[50] The audience loved it, and so, as he put it, he "lucked onto the 'wah wah' thing." Langston Hughes and Milton Melzer included Johnny Hudgins under the "Dancers" heading in their "Golden Dozen" lists of the all-time-greatest black performers, although he probably belonged in a special "Mime" category of his own.[51]

Another Johnny in the show was dancer Johnny Nit. His contract for the tour was signed only on May 3. The delay may perhaps be explained by a curious addendum, signed by him and Lew Leslie at the same time, which bound the artist to accept a 20 percent pay cut for the first four weeks in Paris. This was a typical piece of Lew Leslie cost cutting, and other cast members may have had to sign similar waivers.[52] Leslie demonstrated his hard business side in other ways as well. Kid Thompson's sister, Minnie Jones, had been Florence's theater maid since Kid brought her to New York a few years before. Florence's contract required Leslie to pay for a maid, but he told Kid, "It is not absolutely necessary to take a maid to Europe. Help is cheaper over there. I'll get a maid when I get to London." He thus saved the transport costs each way, and Minnie missed her European trip.[53]

In the lead-up to the departure came a flurry of farewell events. Harlem show folk competed with each other to pay homage to Florence's success. One event, organized by Bojangles and his wife, Fannie, was held at the Exclusive Club, founded by the recently murdered Barron Wilkins. Dinner and refreshments were served as guests arrived from their shows at the Club Alabam, the Cotton Club, and Connie's Inn. Florence was presented with a gold and silver cup.[54] About a week later, another elaborate farewell party with Florence as guest of honor took place at Small's Paradise. Bojangles was there, as well as the Whitman Sisters. Dancers from the Cotton Club revue provided entertainment. Charlie Johnson's resident band included a very young Benny Carter in its reed section. When the master of ceremonies introduced Florence, the applause was so loud that she had to pantomime her thanks. She was presented with a steamer rug and a leather-cased notebook to use on her voyage. Bandleader Fletcher Henderson was presented with a leather folio of handkerchiefs in honor of having achieved a record Broadway run.[55]

Early in May, Lew Leslie received confirmation from the William Morris agency that the management of the Ambassador Theatre in Paris had deposited $25,000 with the American Express office in Paris. This sum guaranteed transport each way and two weeks' salary for the entire company. All was now in order, and on Saturday, May 15, forty members of the Black Birds company set sail for Paris on the liner France.[56]

Notes

1. Flyer for the Plantation, reproduced in Robert Baral, Revue: A Nostalgic Reprise of the Great Broadway Period (New York: Fleet, 1962), 15.

2. A brief comment is necessary on the nomenclature for the Black Birds/Blackbirds series of shows. When the series started, Lew Leslie clearly had in mind an annual revue like Ziegfeld's Follies of or George White's Scandals of, so he called it Black Birds of 1925, with "Black Birds" as two words. This style was maintained for the Alhambra presentation of Black Birds of 1926 and again in Paris. However, in London the show was presented in 1926 simply as "Lew Leslie's Black Birds" and in 1927 as "Lew Leslie's Black Birds, 2nd Edition." The British press varied widely as to whether they called the show "Black Birds" or "Blackbirds," and many people adopted the latter form in referring to it. By the time Blackbirds of 1928 came on the scene, Leslie had also adopted that usage and retained it for the rest of the series. I have followed the original form, Black Birds, except in quotations or where referring to the later versions, but I have also treated Black Birds of 1926 and Black Birds of 1927 as synonymous, respectively, with "Lew Leslie's Black Birds" and "Lew Leslie's Black Birds, 2nd Edition."

3. Carol J. Oja, "'New Music' and the 'New Negro': The Background of William Grant Still's Afro-American Symphony," Black Music Research Journal 12:2 (1992): 155–156.

4. "Florence Mills Is 'Brownskin Guinan,'" BAA, Nov. 14, 1925.

5. Sime Silverman, "Black Birds (With Florence Mills)," VAR, Nov. 18, 1925, 47.

6. Quoted in Allen Woll, Black Musical Theatre (Baton Rouge: Louisiana State University Press, 1989), 97, from an unidentified article in the Lew Leslie File, TC FLP.

7. "About Things Theatrical," AMST, Nov. 18, 1925, and "Florence Mills Is Planning Theater," ChDef, Dec. 19, 1925.

8. Notes from P. L. Prattis interview, Barnett Collection, Chicago Historical Society.

9. "Big Firm Offers Garland Anderson $20,000 If He Can Raise $10,000," AMST, Dec. 30, 1925.

10. "Colored Show Field," VAR, Dec. 30, 1925, 28.

11. Untitled document from TC FLP. This is one of a number of typed documents in the file, which appear to be copies of publicity handout material or journalists' transcripts. It is not always clear how faithfully they reflect Florence's own words, but in this case there seems to be no reason not to assume they do.

12. Verna Arvey, In One Lifetime (Fayetteville: University of Arkansas Press, 1984), 69.

13. William Grant Still, "Hey Hey," from score of Levee Land (Flagstaff, Ariz.: William Grant Still Music), n.d., 28.

14. Arvey, 69, and Judith Anne Still, Michael J. Dabrishus, and Carolyn L. Quin, William Grant Still: A Bio-Bibliography (Westport, Conn.: Greenwood Press, 1996), 22.

15. Louis Varese, Varese: A Looking Glass Diary (New York: W. W. Norton, 1972), 244.

16. For a valuable technical and stylistic analysis, see Oja, 155–159.

17. Still, Levee Land, 57–62.

18. Flyer and Program, HAJC.

19. Catherine Parsons Smith, William Grant Still: A Study in Contradictions (Berkeley: University of California Press, 2000), 223.

20. Eugene Goossens, Overture and Beginners (London: Methuen, 1951), 233.

21. Quotes respectively from: Olin Downes, NYT, 25; New York World; New York Evening Journal, all Jan. 25, 1926; and Abel, VAR, Jan. 27, 1926.

22. Eileen Southern, "Conversation with William Grant Still," Black Perspective in Music, No. 3 (1975).

23. Herbert A. Leibowitz, ed., Musical Impressions: Selections from Paul Rosenfeld's Criticism (London: George Allen & Unwin, 1970), 137.

24. Parsons Smith, 224.

25. Musical Courier, Jan. 28, 1926. The review was probably written by the editor H. O. Osgood, who wrote a book on jazz in 1926 in which he praised Florence.

26. Although Still himself was never again involved in a performance of Levee Land, he mentions in his personal notes (see Parsons Smith, 224) a radio performance in Germany by Juan Harrison, presumably the Juan Harrison who performed in Dixie to Broadway. An article in the BAA, Apr. 5, 1930, "Believe It or Not—This Boy Arranges Whiteman's Music," mentions performances in Germany (presumably the Juan Harrison one) and France.

27. Arvey, 69.

28. Northern Arizona University Wind Symphony, CD. Music of Afro-American Composers, available through William Grant Still Music, see above.

29. Samuel A. Floyd Jr., "Music in the Harlem Renaissance: An Overview," in Black Music in the Harlem Renaissance, ed. Samuel A. Floyd Jr. (Knoxville: University of Tennessee Press, 1993), 18.

30. Paul Burgett, "Vindication as a Thematic Principle in the Writings of Alain Locke on the Music of Black Americans," in *Black Music in the Harlem Renaissance*, ed. Samuel A. Floyd Jr. (Lenoxville: University of Tenneesee Press, 1993), 37.

31. NAACP Press Service, Press release, "Florence Mills Sings at New York Concert of Modern Music," Jan. 29, 1926.

32. "Florence Mills 87 Weeks of Work in 90—Must Rest," VAR, Feb. 10, 1926, 43.

33. PiCou, Feb. 20, 1926.

34. Full cast details from the Philadelphia opening can be found in VAR, Feb. 3, 1926, 23.

35. "White and Colored People Do Not Mix on Stage," VAR, Feb. 3, 1926, 23.

36. AMST, Feb. 17, 1926, quoting from *New York Graphic* of preceding week.

37. The two letters are in SCRAP, HAJC.

38. Martin B. Duberman, *Paul Robeson* (London: Pan Books, 1991), 83, 595, n. 38.

39. AMST, Mar. 3, 1926.

40. "Cabaret Bills," VAR, Jan. 20, 1926. Also Abel Green and Joe Laurie Jr., *Show Biz from Vaude to Video* (New York: Henry Holt, 1951), 217.

41. AMST, Mar. 31, 1926. Some confusion surrounds the length of the Alhambra run. Two sources (Woll, *Black Musical Theatre*, 124; Peterson, *A Century of Musicals in Black and White*, 36) cite a six-week run. This confusion probably originates from a Dudley Nichols report in the *Philadelphia Free Ledger*, Apr. 11, 1926. The original intention appears to have been that the show would run April 5–25 (three weeks), but this term was extended initially to May 2 and then to May 9 (five weeks). See "Florence Mills and Company Leave for Paris" and "Johnny Hudgins Added to the Florence Mills Show," AMST, Apr. 21 and 28, 1926.

42. Lena Horne and Richard Schickel, *Lena* (London: Andre Deutsch, 1966), 94.

43. Dudley Nichols, "Mills of the Gallery Gods," *Philadelphia Free Ledger*, Apr. 11, 1926.

44. "Colored Actress Given the Palm by George Jean Nathan, Yah," *Cleveland Herald*, Apr. 16, 1926, quoting *New York Telegram*, Apr. 11, 1926.

45. Jeff Kisseloff, *You Must Remember This* (New York: Schocken Books, 1989), 315.

46. "Florence Mills and Company Leave for Paris" and adjacent advertisement, AMST, Apr. 21, 1926.

47. AMST, May 5, 1926.

48. "Racing at Lexington" and "Results at Lexington," *The Thoroughbred Record*, Lexington, Kentucky, May 1, 1926, 525 and 529, respectively, and cover photograph. Also "Equine Line Product Information: Florence Mills," *The Jockey Club Information Systems Inc.* Current dollar conversion based on U.S. Consumer Price Index figures to 2000.

49. Undated, unidentified clipping in HAJC. This event was suggested to be about two years after the Chicago launch and had to be before Florence went overseas so is assumed to be around the time of the Ashland Oaks victory.

50. Based on notes from an interview in the Mura Dehn Manuscript Collection, Dance Collection, New York Public Library Performing Arts Library. For Louis Metcalf link see his entry in John Chilton, *Who's Who of Jazz*, 4th ed. (New York: Da Capo, 1985).

51. Langston Hughes and Milton Melzer, *Black Magic: A Pictorial History of the Negro in Performing Arts* (New York: Crown Publishers, 1968), 337. Sadly, in later years, his act fell victim to the distaste that overtook anything that smacked of the old blackface tradition. A reappraisal today would probably conclude he was not truly a blackface performer in the bad old sense but, rather, a traditional clown whose unique clown identity happened to be blackface in the same way that Marcel Marceau's Bip is a whiteface clown or Emmett Kelly's "Weary Willy" was a redface (or at least red nose) one. This point was made by the *Baltimore Afro-American* in a 1924 article that said, "Johnny does no 'Uncle Tom' stuff, and in this respect differs from a number of blackface comedians."

52. Legal contract and addendum between Johnny Nit and Lew Leslie. Original in the Blockson Collection, Temple University, Philadelphia.

53. HAJC. Transcript of Kid Thompson interview. Minnie Jones made it to Paris later, as wardrobe mistress with *Blackbirds of 1928*.

54. Undated, unidentified clipping in HAJC. While Wilkins was alive, the Exclusive Club catered mainly to a wealthy white clientele but probably changed after his death.

55. "Tyler Guest at Miss Mills Party," BAA, May 15, 1926.

56. "$25,000 Deposited for Mills Co. Protection," VAR, May 12, 1926, 2; and "Sailings," VAR, May 19, 1926.

CHAPTER NINE

~

Looking for a Bluebird in Europe

Les Oiseaux Noir

Unlike on the *Albania* in 1923, Florence was now famous enough for her name to feature in the *New York Times* list of dignitaries sailing on the *France*. Other notable passengers included U.S. tennis stars Vincent Richards and Howard Kinsey as well as Hollywood writer Anita Loos and her husband John Emerson. Loos's contact with Florence made a sufficient impression that the writer later mentioned Florence briefly in her famous novel *Gentlemen Prefer Blondes*.[1]

The voyage of the *France* was uneventful. There were no reports of racial slurs, as on the *Albania* three years earlier. Neither were there heavy seas of the kind that had flooded the costumes of the chorus girls of *Chocolate Kiddies* a year before.[2] The liner docked in calm conditions at Le Havre. A gaggle of French journalists and photographers were eagerly awaiting their first glimpse of Florence Mills. What was she like? Would she look black? Would she look white? Lew Leslie had organized a press conference on board, with Florence reclining on a wisteria-colored lounge. *Comoedia's* reporter came away with only one impression—"two immense eyes, two drops of coffee in the cream."

Bricktop had also been looking forward to seeing Florence. Her diary noted Florence's arrival, along with the Charleston lessons given that day to Cole Porter and the usual accounting of bottles of champagne consumed at her club.[3] At this time Bricktop did not own her own club and was still managing the tiny Grand Duc, where Langston Hughes had found employment a while before, for its proprietor, Gene Bullard. A sizable colony of African Americans lived in Paris now, eager to see and meet Florence, Kid, and their troupe. Most notable was Josephine Baker, recently successful in *La Revue Negre*. Others included Louis Mitchell, who had come to Paris originally with Vernon and Irene Castle and whose Jazz Kings had been spreading the jazz gospel in Paris for several years; Sam Wooding, who had recently left *Chocolate Kiddies* to form a new orchestra in Paris; and Buddy Gilmore, who had performed with Florence's old friend Kinky years before and was now attracting attention with his flamboyant drumming style.

The venue for *Black Birds* (*Les Oiseaux Noirs* in the local language) was one of the most elegant theaters in Paris, Les Ambassadeurs. It had existed in various forms since the mid-eighteenth century and stood at the entrance of the Champs-Elysées, near the Place de la Concorde. Famous stars linked with it included Yvette Guilbert, Mistinguett, and Maurice Chevalier.[4] Not everyone was pleased that this hallowed sanctum of the traditional French *chanson* was to feature noisy American music. The columnist for *L'Illustration* nostalgically bewailed its invasion by cacophonous jazz.[5] The theater-cum-nightclub had been made over in a decorative floral garden layout for the occasion. It had a pink theme including roses, wisterias, and hydrangeas, with fountains illuminated by colored lights. It could seat 1,000 patrons at champagne tables in a cabaret-like setting. The ceiling opened to the sky but could be closed completely if weather conditions required.[6]

The troupe had a week to rehearse and adapt to the new environment. The opening night was Friday, May 28. Florence was more than usually nervous because she had been working hard to learn her material in French. She mastered it well enough to convince many that she spoke French fluently. One report said, "She has had all her songs translated into French and has mastered them in that language; only the large percentage of English-speaking visitors among her audience prevents her from singing more than one song *a la Parisienne*." However, a piece of paper in her scrapbook also suggests she had an insurance policy. It consists of the words of "Blackbird" spelled out phonetically. For example: "Je suis un oiseau noir, Qui cherche au fond du ciel l'oiseau bleue" was rendered as "Je swee un waso nwar, Kee shairsh a fondu see el l'waso blu."[7]

Except that some material was in French, the show was much the same as that advertised as "the Parisian version" at the Alhambra in Harlem. One exception was that Florence sang the Plantation's 1925 hit, "Dinah." Presumably she felt that Paris was well away from Ethel Waters's turf or that it would have been her song anyway had she not been on the road when Ethel introduced it. The large cabaret setting did nothing to inhibit Florence's style on opening night. She was familiar with such settings from her Panama Café days and at Barron Wilkins's Café and the Plantation. On her first appearance, she emerged out of a birthday cake carried onstage by a "baker." A witness described the reaction. "Directly Florence Mills began to sing there fell an immediate hush. The buzz of conversation and all the noises of a big restaurant died away."[8] Her opening number was the wistful "Silver Rose"—"Rose d'Argent" in French.

There was a special late performance on the first night to allow theatrical people to attend. Prominent first nighters attending after their own shows included the Dolly Sisters (Casino de Paris), Mistinguett (Moulin Rouge), prominent music hall star Parisys (Concert Mayol), and veteran comedian Dranem. Also buzzing around excitedly was one of Florence's most enthusiastic French fans, Maurice Chevalier. Having already seen her in America, he was eagerly advising all he met to expect something special. He buttonholed the journalist for *La Rampe* on the way in. "You are going to see Florence Mills. She is a great artist. You have no idea what true black artistry is."[9]

Not one to miss the opportunity of a dramatic entrance, Josephine Baker arrived late, wearing a white ermine floor-length coat and a black velvet evening gown and escorted by eight white men in tails. After the show she went backstage to greet Florence, much to the chagrin of Johnny Hudgins, whose open door she swept past.[10] Florence had been an important role model for Josephine. Her soft, high voice was easier to imitate than the tones of the blues queens and vaudeville shouters of the era. Florence's presence on her turf might be seen as competition in some sense, but the opportunity to greet her idol as a star in her own right was too good for Josephine to miss. In any case, Josephine Baker already had a secure niche in Paris. She had recently abandoned her original launching pad, *La Revue Negre*, at the Champs-Elysées Music-Hall, in favor of a more profitable contract at the Folies Bergère, where she was already a resounding success and introduced her famous banana dance.

Black Birds was an immediate runaway success in Paris, not only for Florence but also notably for Johnny Hudgins. His silent pantomime had an appeal that quickly made him a sensation with the French. Edith Wilson, the Three Eddies, and the Plantation Orchestra also received enthusiastic tributes. *Le Figaro* critic Jacques Patin declared himself enraptured by Florence's singing of "Silver Rose," with its poignant nostalgia, and reduced to tears of laughter by Johnny Hudgins's miming to Johnny Dunn's cornet. *La Rampe's* critic confirmed Chevalier's preperformance prediction. From Florence's first appearance till her singing of "Blackbird" near the end, he declared himself enthralled by her multiple talents. Johnny Hudgins he considered also a great artist, who could "with a gesture, a movement, create humanity." Kid Thompson's dancing on his knees was "inexplicable." The opening night's takings allegedly exceeded F450,000—about US$(1926)18,000. A *Comoedia* columnist suggested sarcastically that the director of Les Ambassadeurs should instantly be appointed French minister of finance. Another report indicating that weekly takings throughout that summer never dropped below $35,000 suggests that an opening night of $18,000 might have been possible.

Inevitably there were comparisons between Florence and Josephine Baker. Mistinguett saw Josephine as "quicksilver on roller skates," while Florence was an "artist she held in high esteem."[11] Louis Leon-Martin, for *Paris-Midi*, thought Florence Mills was "like a Josephine Baker designed by some conservatory, which had conferred extra skills on her while decreasing some gifts." Which ones he had in mind he didn't specify. Another suggested, "Take a coconut with its fiber, its rind, its lumps, then take an ivory ball with all its paleness, its smoothness, its caress of the eyes. There, side by side, you have Josephine Baker and Florence Mills. One is a rat that wriggles, but with so much spirit. The other is a bird of the isles."[12]

A more highbrow comparison came from eminent French ballet critic André Levinson. In *Theatre Arts Monthly* he attacked the idea that black jazz dance was genuine art, while expressing his admiration for Josephine. He saw her as an expression of primitive animality, whereas in Florence's case "there is not the slightest trace of the wild thing in this rococo Creole." Detecting signs that black dance might be evolving toward something less primitive, he concluded, "The mad arabesques of the incomparable Josephine can give us an almost shocking insight into our own more sombre depths, but Florence Mills, for instance, is developing into an almost precious elegance. It is no longer the tigress who stands before us but the marquise, who has rubbed a little burnt cork on her cheeks, instead of her customary rouge, before dancing a Court Charleston."[13]

It was precisely Josephine's raw primitivism that ensured she would remain queen of Paris, however much Parisians took Florence to their hearts. Josephine touched some deep spring in the Gallic spirit, whereas Florence's refined elegance resonated more sympathetically in Leicester Square or Oxford Circus than in the Champs-Elysées or on Montmartre. When Lena Horne asked Lew Leslie why this was so, his answer was that Florence wasn't glamorous. Based on her own later experiences in both cities, Lena concluded that Josephine seemed to the French like a "fabulous child of nature" who reminded them of lions and tigers and the jungle, whereas Florence was like a waif they could cry over and pity.[14] The critics, when they weren't comparing Florence to Josephine Baker, fell back on the inevitable bird comparisons. These included "a pretty brown dove that coos and flutters," an island bird, a nightingale, and a chaffinch. Apart from her performing talents, the feature that obsessed them most was her big, luminous eyes. The earlier "grains of coffee" comment was matched by "two black olives in a bowl of milk."

While the Black Birds were playing their first week at Les Ambassadeurs, the Sorbonne was hosting an international feminist congress. It was France's first ever but the tenth such in support of women's suffrage since 1904. Some 2,000 delegates had come from all over the world, a surprising number from aristocratic backgrounds. Lady Nancy Astor represented England, the Marchioness of Aberdeen represented the International Council of Women, and Princess Gabrielle Radziwill from Lithuania the League of Nations. There's little doubt that many of the delegates found their way to see Florence at Les Ambassadeurs and Josephine at Folies Bergère, witnessing the triumph of two black women in the world's most sophisticated city.[15]

Even in cosmopolitan Paris, the troupe could not completely escape the reach of racial prejudice. During the intermission on one of the early nights, a black man and a white woman stepped onto the dance floor. A group of Americans objected, and the management asked the man to stop dancing. When he refused, the management ordered the local tango orchestra to stop playing. Sensing the drama of the moment, members of the Plantation Orchestra picked up the tune. The dancers resumed, at the request of the woman's white French husband. At this the American group caused a further disturbance. Police were called, and the impasse was resolved only when the husband explained to the police that the black dancer, professionally known as Frisco, was his guest and was dancing with his wife at his request. The troublemakers were asked to leave.[16]

Florence was soon being described as "the idol of Paris," with celebrities flocking to pay homage to her talent, including Douglas Fairbanks and Mary Pickford. She was immediately in demand for special appearances and charity events. The first of these was a Grand Night at Claridges, featuring a mannequin parade from all the leading Paris fashion houses. The entertainment was a lineup of seventeen well-known female stars, including Argentina, the Dolly Sisters, and Cecile Sorel. Two days later, on Saturday, there was a gala for the Friends of France at the Champs-Elysées; on Sunday, a charity event at the Polish Embassy; and the following Saturday, a journalist's charity event. The most publicly significant of the charitable activities involving Florence was undoubtedly the Grand Gala Benefit for Eugenie Buffet, held at the Theatre Sarah-Bernhardt on the afternoon of Tuesday, June 22.

Fallen on hard times by 1926, Eugenie Buffet was one of the great figures of the era known as La Belle Epoque. This was the name the French fondly gave to the period of peace, prosperity, and tranquility from the final decade of the nineteenth century until the start of the First World War. Buffet had been a singer in the tradition known as *chanson realist*, "realist songs." She was also remembered for her devotion to injured troops during the war. Today her memory is preserved mainly through a popular *Art Nouveau* poster by Louis Metivet, a contemporary of Toulouse-Lautrec. The poster is one of a series promoting her shows at Les Ambassadeurs in its incarnation as a *café chantant* and is available in many commercial poster catalogs.

The program for the benefit listed more than fifty acts, all from the leading Paris theaters, plus classical musicians, opera singers, ballet dancers, and sports stars. Proudly at the top was Florence, accompanied by the Three Eddies, comedy dancers fron *Black Birds*, just ahead of Maurice Chevalier. The top billing was a reflection of alphabetization—"Ambassadeurs" ahead of "Casino de Paris." Among the other prominent names featured on the list was the great clown Grock. Grock was a whiteface pantomimist who evoked laughter through his continual struggle with inanimate objects. Chairs collapsed beneath him, and when a stool was too far from a piano, he would shove the piano to the stool. Florence was truly appearing with some of the very biggest names in world theater. Eugenie Buffet herself appeared at the benefit.[17]

As well as theatrical events, Florence also performed at private social engagements. Some of these were professional, as when the Baron Rothschild paid her to entertain his guests at occasional dinner parties. To her pleasure, she was always treated as an honored guest at these times rather than as a hired entertainer. An eyewitness described one such occasion: "The Baron himself led in this slim, elegant creature, whose stage genius places her among the great artists of the world. Miss Mills stayed a while in the great salon of the hotel. But she would not stay to supper. A glass of champagne at the buffet and away she went home."[18]

Even when Florence went to purely social events, she was still expected to entertain. One such occasion was an elaborate party at the riverside cottage belonging to Parisys, female singing star of the Concert Mayol, who had also featured at the Eugenie Buffet benefit. The large attendance at Parisys's party included Michel George-Michel. He was a prominent art critic, novelist, and friend of many famous artists, including Picasso and Stravinsky. It was he who had compared Florence to an ivory ball against Josephine's coconut. From Florence's side of the Atlantic was Pearl White, famous for her title role in the silent cliff–hanger film serials *The Perils of Pauline*. She and Florence had met before when Pearl had been one of C. B. Cochran's special guests at the welcoming party given in his honor at the Plantation in late 1924.

Playing in over 200 movies between 1910 and 1924, Pearl suffered serious injuries from doing her own stunts. Having also amassed a lot of money, she had settled in luxury in Paris by 1926. Perhaps she and Florence discussed their early experiences as child stars. Pearl liked to tell of her early years playing Eva in *Uncle Tom's Cabin*, a story viewed with suspicion by those who knew her tendency to spin yarns.[19] Around 2 a.m. the floor was vacated for Florence, Kid, and an unnamed colleague to give the obligatory demonstration of the "Charleston." Others joined in and the night was declared one of the great Parisian parties.[20]

Events like the Parisys party were noisy, crowded occasions of the kind that had limited appeal for Florence. She preferred the frequent get-togethers with Bricktop. On June 6, Bricktop noted in her diary that she had dinner with Florence, Kid, Lloyd Mitchell (one of the *Black Birds* dancers), and Nora Holt Ray. Nora was a well-known singer, a music critic, and an intelligent, wealthy, glamorous, somewhat outrageous Harlem Renaissance personality.[21] She was the model for the infamous Lasca Sartoris in Carl Van Vechten's novel *Nigger Heaven*. Nora, a keen admirer of Florence, took pleasure in introducing her and other entertainment figures to her wider acquaintance in Harlem society. One such was notable civil rights activist William L. Patterson.[22]

The following day Bricktop entertained the Three Eddies and two members of the *Black Birds* chorus, Mae Fanning and May Fortune. On July 11, Bricktop again entertained "Florence and girls," presumably the full troupe this time.[23] A topic of conversation at one of these gatherings was Florence's recent letter from Earl Granstaff, who had been the trombone player with the Plantation Orchestra during the 1923 London engagement. In his letter he recounted his experiences at an Istanbul cabaret and his travels along the way. En route to Istanbul, he had spent some time entertaining in Budapest. There he had found a magazine, all in Hungarian, featuring Florence, with a photo, and had forwarded it to her in the United States, in care of *Variety*.[24]

Early July saw some changes in the arrangements for Florence and the *Black Birds*. The Paul Whiteman Orchestra had arrived in town. The original idea had been that the *Black Birds* would move on and make way for the self-styled "King of Jazz," but they were too popular. A compromise was worked out whereby the two would alternate performances, night by night, between the Ambassadeurs and the Champs-Elysées Music Hall nearby. Initially Whiteman's Orchestra played at the Champs-Elysées and shared the bill at Les Ambassadeurs with *Black Birds*, retitled *Dixie to Paris*. Whiteman's supporting troupe included Harland Dixon. He was one of the all-time-great white dancers, a veteran of the minstrel era and a master of all styles.[25] For a short while patrons of the Paris entertainment scene had the chance to see some of the best white and black dancing from the United States on the same program. This arrangement prevailed for the two weeks of Whiteman's stay. Apart from the inevitable "Rhapsody in Blue," Whiteman's repertoire included his symphonic-jazz-style orchestrations and some novelty items involving a bicycle pump and two wind instruments played by one musician. His brand of "symphonic jazz" appealed to many French who found the black jazz in Montmartre clubs too extreme.

In later years, in the *Chicago Defender*, three black opera singers who had visited Les Ambassadeurs suggested that Whiteman had snubbed Florence during their shared engagement. He indignantly denied the allegation in a lengthy response to the *Defender*.

> We observed professional courtesy towards each other at all times. That anything of an unpleasant nature occurred between us, at this or any other time, is a malicious lie, invented from the whole cloth. My engagement was for but two weeks. She regretted the close of this engagement, as did myself and my orchestra. We enjoyed being on the same program with so fine an artist, and Miss Mills as well as those about her knew this well.[26]

Paul Whiteman's record of support and friendship for black artists is well documented. It is unlikely the story, whatever its origin, reflected any genuine discourtesy on his part. There was one ironic feature of his disclaimer, however. Completing his *Defender* letter, he wrote: "As to my being jealous of Miss Mills it sounds ridiculous for a musician to take issue with a profession. The respective fields are distinctly opposite." It obviously never occurred to the "King of Jazz" that Florence Mills and the Plantation Orchestra might have had better jazz credentials than himself.

On July 16, Irving Aronson's Commanders, one of Whiteman's leading competitors, replaced him at Les Ambassadeurs. At the same time, *Black Birds* began to share the program at the Champs-Elysées with the Commanders and the still present Harland Dixon. So Florence was starring nightly in two of Paris's major theatrical venues. Busy as this kept her, she still had an opportunity on Bastille Day to indulge her passion for baseball when she officially opened a game at the Elizabeth Stadium.

Sometime around late July or early August, Florence and Kid had the pleasure of entertaining some welcome transatlantic friends. Bill "Bojangles" Robinson and his wife, Fannie, had undertaken a six-week trip to Europe, visiting London and Paris. The voyage was mainly for pleasure although he played an engagement at the Holborn Empire Theatre. In London, Bojangles had astounded the press with his prowess in running backwards. He defeated a professional sprinter over 100 yards from a 25-yard start. On the Paris leg of their visit, the couple joined Kid and Florence for several days, seeing the sights and visiting museums. Some years later, when Bojangles listed the highlights of his life for columnist Louis Sobol, he included, "Visiting Florence Mills at the Ambassadeurs in Paris, while she was making her first sensation."[27]

For two weeks, from July 30 to August 12, the Champs-Elysées program featuring *Black Birds* and the Aronson Commanders also included a ballet performance, *La Vengeance des Dieux*. The ballet had a very distinguished cast. The choreography was by Nicholas Legat, a teacher of Nijinsky. Prima ballerina Nadine Nicolaeva was Legat's wife. Legat was a major figure of pre-revolutionary Russian classical dance in the Maryinsky style and had been a soloist to the czar. With his wife, in later years, he formed the Russian Ballet Society, which still offers training in the Legat style, preserving the traditions of Russian classical ballet.[28] The male lead at the Champs-Elysées was Anatole Oboukhoff, later the husband of famed ballerina Vera Nemtchinova, and a teacher under Balanchine at the School of American Ballet. So once again patrons of *Black Birds* had the opportunity to see great dance in contrasting styles, this time jazz and classical ballet.

The press proclaimed the final night of this engagement as the last chance to see Florence Mills and the *Black Birds*. There was to be a brief break in Florence's Paris career while the *Black Birds* went to the beach. More precisely they went to the Belgian seaside resort town of Ostend. It was the high season for holidays, and Parisians were happy to desert the cities for the beach. *La Vie Parisienne* declared that the real sign that the year's Paris season had ended was not the usual sporting events, like the Monaco Grand Prix, but the departure of Florence Mills and Paul Whiteman. In her final performance, in an impulsive gesture of thanks, Florence tore off the 'Rose de France' she was wearing on her bosom and threw it to the wildly applauding audience.

Ostend was the playground of the aristocrats and the crowned heads of Europe. Its showpiece was the Kursaal, a huge theatrical venue described as "the great, soul-searching, musical stage of the world's finest artists." The year 1926, when the *Black Birds* performed there, fell in the era of the third Kursaal. The original timber Kursaal was built in 1852. The second Kursaal, a stone building with oriental cupolas and domes, was built in 1865. The third Kursaal was a major modification to the second, a transformation that created a vast art complex incorporating a casino, magnificent salons and concert halls, a Royal Box, shops, and a post office.[29] Florence and her troupe were to perform there for the next week or so, in a building overlooking one of Europe's most popular beaches. In their spare time they could lie on the beach. If the sea was gray, as it can be there even in summer, there was always the opportunity to wander the promenades, sampling the local cooked shellfish, cockles, and winkles from the many carts that lined them.

The impresario who promoted the show at Les Ambassadeurs, Edmond Sayag, also provided the entertainment at the Kursaal for the holidays. He had spared no expense to entertain the wealthy casino patrons. Promotional advertisements announced the presence of "the two most celebrated orchestras in the world, Paul Whiteman, and The Commanders." There would also be "a treat for the eyes, Pavlova and her ballet, Florence Mills and her troupe, The Dolly Sisters, Florence Walton, Cortez and Peggy, alternating for your delight."[30] Few would have predicted that a little girl from the tenements of Harlem would share equal billing with the great Pavlova in the playground of Europe's aristocracy! The season at Ostend was short—just one week—but highly successful. The reviewer for the *Echo D'Ostende* was impressed with "the instrumental balance, finish, humor, poetry and frenetic delivery of the Plantation Orchestra." Florence Mills "sings with that vaguely sentimental humor dear to Anglo-Saxons; she dances with exceptional agility and comic eccentricity." Another saw her as "feline, piquant, eccentric . . . a little sentimental and very wild, at the same time."[31]

Florence's return to Les Ambassadeurs from Belgium was "triumphal." *Comoedia* noted that the ladies in the returning audience were "baring arms reddened by the sun, tanned necks and resplendent pearls." The break had been used as an opportunity to revise the show significantly, with new dances and songs. One of the new dances was the "Charleston," old hat back in the United States but now sweeping Europe like a storm. The new songs included "Mandy, Make Up Your Mind," "Jazz Time Came from the South," revived from *Dixie to Broadway*, and George Meyer's new "Arabella's Wedding Day." Florence, "transformed with new material and costumes," still had her "nightingale voice and brilliant eyes, like two grains of coffee fitted with electric lamps"—again the French fascination with her flashing eyes.[32]

It was nevertheless truly a farewell week for *Black Birds* in Paris. The new material was in reality a tryout for the planned opening in London. *Variety* noted that C. B. Cochran had closed his long-running but trouble-plagued *Cochran's Revue* and was eager to get *Black Birds* into the vacant London Pavilion as soon as possible. The remaining days in Paris were pleasant socially for Florence. August 28 was Kid Thompson's thirty-eighth birthday.

Baby Florence displays her trophies.
Moorland-Spingarn Research Center,
Howard University

Panama Trio in Kashmir cosmetics advertisement. Chicago Historical Society; From brochure "Beauty Health Success, The Kashmir Way" Photographer: Gushiniere

THE PANAMA GIRLS   15

Photos by Gushiniere

Coral Greene   Florence Mills   Ada Smith

Chicago's favorite cabaret entertainers and members of one of the niftiest vaudeville acts on the stage.

What they think of Kashmir?

Coral—"Is Kashmir an experiment?"
Florence—"No, it's a certainty."
Ada—"Well I should say so."

Kashmir Preparations are for men too.

The Florence Mills Trio, 1920 (Freddy Johnson, Florence Mills, U. S. Thompson). Photographer: Alden, N. Y.

Dover Street to Dixie: Scene from Dover Street segment; The Beggars Opera parodied. By permission of the British Library. Source: 'The Sketch', London 27 June 1923.

Dover Street to Dixie: Florence Mills and the Dixie Vamps with Will Vodery & Plantation Orchestra. By permission of the British Library. Source: 'The Sketch', London 27 June 1923.

Florence Mills as a plantation boy in The Plantation Revue, 1923. By permission of the Mander and Mitchenson Theatre Collection, London.

Florence Mills portrait, 1923. Photographer: James VanDerZee. © Donna Mussenden VanDerZee

Florence dressed for the English climate. By permission of the British Library. Source: Eve magazine, London 1923.

Florence Mills in male attire (Aida Overton Walker style) for Mandy's wedding. Johnny Nit Collection, courtesy Evelyn Cynthia Williams & Debbi Williams

Florence Mills, Roger Matthews and Lottie Gee in "Gypsy Blues" from Shuffle Along. Photographer: Nasib Studio

Florence Mills as seen by Mexican artist Miguel Covarrubias. From THE PRINCE OF WALES AND OTHER FAMOUS AMERICANS by Miguel Covarrubias, copyright 1925 by Alfred Knopf Inc and renewed 1953 by Miguel Covarrubias. Used by permission of Alfred A. Knopf, a division of Random House, Inc.

"Florence Mills leads a Harlemquinade on Broadway." Photographer: Edward Steichen/
Vanity Fair, © 1925 Conde Nast Publications Inc.

Lew Leslie in his prime. Photographer unknown

Bricktop and Florence at Le Grand Duc, Paris 1926. Courtesy Jim Lyons.

Sheet music cover, English edition (1926) of "I'm a Little Blackbird." Publisher: Francis, Day and Hunter

Florence and Kid Thompson in London 1926. Photographer Claude Harris, London

Florence, Johnny Hudgins and Black Birds chorus rehearse on roof of Pavilion Theatre 1926. Photographer Keystone View Company, London

The Black Bird's Southern Trio: Clinton C. Rosemond, a young Mabel Mercer and John Payne. Johnny Nit Collection, courtesy Evelyn Cynthia Williams & Debbi Williams. Photographer: The Perfect Photo Reproduction Company, London.

Florence was a cartoonists' delight. Various artists, unknown

Florence in her "Indian Habits" routine from Dixie to Broadway. By permission of the British Library. Source: Illustrated Sporting & Dramatic News, London 1926.

Publicity photo for Florence's last London appearance, at the Strand Theatre, 1927.
Photographer: Lenare

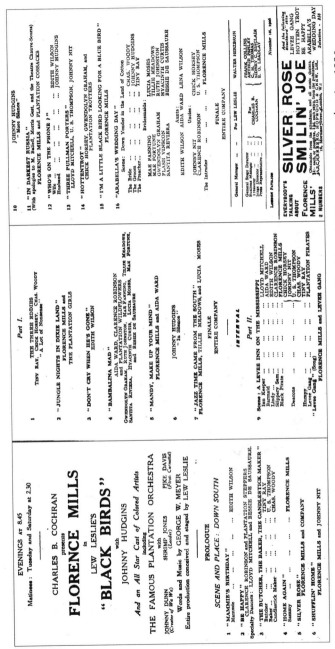

EVENINGS AT 8.45

Matinees : Tuesday and Saturday at 2.30

CHARLES B. COCHRAN

presents

FLORENCE MILLS

in

LEW LESLIE'S

"BLACK BIRDS"

with

JOHNNY HUDGINS

And an All Star Cast of Colored Artists

including

THE FAMOUS PLANTATION ORCHESTRA

with

JOHNNY DUNN   SHRIMP JONES   PIKE DAVIS
(Creator of Wa Wa)   (Leader)   (First Cornetist)

Words and Music by GEORGE W. MEYER

Entire production conceived and staged by LEW LESLIE

PROLOGUE

SCENE AND PLACE : DOWN SOUTH

1 "MAMMIE'S BIRTHDAY" ... ... EDITH WILSON
  Mammie

2 "BE HAPPY"
  CLARENCE ROBINSON and PLANTATION STEPPERS
  Specialty Dancers : LLOYD MITCHELL and BESSIE DE SAUSSURE.

3 "THE BUTCHER, THE BAKER, THE CANDLESTICK MAKER"
  Butcher ... ... TINY RAY
  Baker ... ... U.S. THOMPSON
  Candlestick Maker ... CHAS. WOODY

4 "HOME AGAIN" ... ... FLORENCE MILLS
  Sammy ...

5 "SILVER ROSE" ... FLORENCE MILLS and COMPANY

6 "SHUFFLIN' HOME"
  FLORENCE MILLS and JOHNNY NIT

Part I.

1 THE THREE EDDIES
  TINY RAY, "A Lot of Nonsense."

2 "JUNGLE NIGHTS IN DIXIE LAND"
  FLORENCE MILLS and
  THE PLANTATION GIRLS

3 "DON'T CRY WHEN HE'S GONE"
  EDITH WILSON

4 "BAMBALINA MAD"
  AIDA WARD, CLARENCE ROBINSON
  and PLANTATION WILDFLOWERS
  GWENDOLYN GRAHAM, RUTH JOHNSTON, MAE FANNING, TILLIE MEADOWS,
  SANTITA RIVIERA, HYACINTH CURTIS, LUCIA MOSES, MAE FORTUNE,
  and BESSIE DE SAUSSURE

5 "MANDY, MAKE UP YOUR MIND"
  FLORENCE MILLS and AIDA WARD

6 JOHNNY HUDGINS
  "In Silence."

7 "JAZZ TIME CAME FROM THE SOUTH"
  FLORENCE MILLS, TILLIE MEADOWS, and LUCIA MOSES

FINALE
ENTIRE COMPANY

INTERVAL

Part II.

9 Scene : A LEVEE INN ON THE MISSISSIPPI
  Inn Keeper ... ... LLOYD MITCHELL
  Barmaid ... ... AIDA WARD
  Lindy ... ... EDITH WILSON
  Slippery Sam ... CLARENCE ROBINSON
  Black Pirate ... FLORENCE MILLS
  Deacons ... { CHICK HORSEY / JOHNNY NIT / U.S. THOMPSON / CHAS. WOODY / TINY RAY
  Humpy ... ... PLANTATION PIRATES
  Levee Gang ...
  "Levee Gang" (Song)
  FLORENCE MILLS and LEVEE GANG

10 JOHNNY HUDGINS
  "More Silence."

11 "IN DARKEST RUSSIA."
  (With apologies to M. Balieff, Morris Gest, and the Theatre Chauve-Souris)
  FLORENCE MILLS and PLANTATION COSSACKS

12 "WHO'S ON THE PHONE ?"
  Wife ... ... EDITH WILSON
  Husband ... ... JOHNNY HUDGINS

13 "THREE PULLMAN PORTERS"
  LLOYD MITCHELL, U.S. THOMPSON, JOHNNY NIT

14 "HOTTENTROT" GWENDOLYN GRAHAM, and
  CHICK HORSEY PLANTATION TROTTERS

15 "I'M A LITTLE BLACK BIRD LOOKING FOR A BLUE BIRD"
  FLORENCE MILLS

16 "ARABELLA'S WEDDING DAY"
  Scene : Down Yonder in the Land of Cotton
  The Bride ... ... CHAS. WOODY
  The Groom ... ... JOHNNY HUDGINS
  The Preacher ... ... TINY RAY
  Bridesmaids : LUCIA MOSES
  MAE FANNING   TILLIE MEADOWS
  MAE FORTUNE   RUTH JOHNSTON
  GWENDOLYN GRAHAM   HYACINTH CURTIS
  FLASH VINSON   BESSIE DE SAUSSURE
  SANTITA RIVERA
  Aunts :
  EDITH WILSON   AIDA WARD   LENA WILSON
  Uncles :
  JOHNNY NIT   CHICK HORSEY
  CLARENCE ROBINSON   U.S. THOMPSON
  The Intruder ... ... FLORENCE MILLS

FINALE
ENTIRE COMPANY

General Manager ... ... WALTER HERZBRUN
  For LEW LESLIE

General Stage Director ...
Business Manager ...   FRANK COLLINS
Treasurer ...   ARTHUR DRISLEY
Stage Director ...   C.G.H. DE SINCLAIR   For CHARLES B. COUGHLAN
Press Representative ...   R.G. LINDSAY

London Pavilion   November 1st, 1926

Programme for Black Birds of 1926 at London Pavilion. Source: The Magazine Programme, November 1st, 1926

Florence painted in oils by Alexander Stuart-Hill. By permission of the Mander and Mitchenson Theatre Collection, London.

Florence as seen by Indian artist Mukul Dey. Dry-point etching; Artist: Mukul Dey, 1923. Courtesy Mukul Dey Archives, Santiniketan, West Bengal, India.

The funeral crowd, on street and in windows. Photographs and Prints Division, Schomburg Center for Research in Black Culture, The New York Public Library, Astor, Lenox and Tilden Foundations. Photographer: P. McDougall

Always keen to indulge him with gifts, Florence saw it also as a way of saying farewell to Paris, so she laid on a large birthday party for him at La Palermo restaurant in Montmartre with an elaborate four-course menu including lobster. Attending were the cast and various other guests, black and white, as well as several Paris socialites.[33]

Black guests from outside the cast included Josephine Baker, Nora Holt Ray, Spencer Williams (composer of "Basin Street Blues" and "Everybody Loves My Baby"), and Rosie Garland, wife of Will Garland, whose United Kingdom–based show had precipitated the racial controversy before Florence's 1923 visit to London. Everybody dressed up in style, Florence sedately in black and silver. The girls of the chorus wore frocks by fashionable Paris couturiers including Jean Patou. In the inevitable comparison with Josephine Baker, the press commented that Josephine danced always with white men, whereas Florence danced only with black men. "The Paris notabilities, who were her guests, did not perhaps understand why Florence Mills always sat among, as well as danced with, her own people."[34]

Another social event at this time helped Florence and Kid keep in touch with news back home. A group of prominent African Americans, including the promising young poet Countee Cullen, and his mentor, Alain Locke— the first black Rhodes scholar (1907)—made a summer visit to France.[35] One afternoon the group invited Florence and Kid to join them in climbing the tower of Notre Dame Cathedral for a close view of the gargoyles made famous in Victor Hugo's *The Hunchback of Notre Dame*. It was the second time Cullen had met Florence, the previous time being the DuBois dinner in 1924. Her serious outlook and keen intelligence made a big impression on him. "She knew things; her interest [reached] beyond her own concerns, she knew what her people were doing in other life expressions. And she was heartily troubled at the rocky way they went. All too slender for the bright, vivacious flame of her being, she was a great person, an artist of superior equipment."[36]

On September 3, Florence obtained a visa for entry to the United Kingdom. Her passport records her entry at Dover on September 7. She was granted a work permit for one month. The lone entry in Bricktop's diary for September 5 was "Florence Mills, 8 Macklinburg [sic] Sq, London."[37] So began the next major phase in Florence's career—although France did not give her up without a struggle. Having failed to negotiate an extension of the *Black Birds'* contract in Paris, Edmond Sayag took the extreme step of seizing all the costumes in a desperate bid to force Leslie to extend the troupe's stay. However, Leslie was already fully committed to C. B. Cochran in London, so the performers departed costumeless.[38]

A Blackbird Sang in Piccadilly Circus

The Mecklenburgh Square address Florence gave to Bricktop was in the Saint Pancras area of London, close to Bloomsbury. Bloomsbury is synonymous today with the famous literary set that flourished there in the 1920s. When Florence arrived there, it was a hive of bedsits and apartments popular with visitors to London. According to a contemporary guidebook, "Nearly every house displays the enticing notice 'boarding' or 'apartments,' and there are a large number of private hotels. The popularity of the district is accounted for by the fact that it is within easy reach of the City and West End and of the great railway stations; and partly by the attractiveness of the squares which are here more numerous than in any other part of the metropolis."[39]

Later Florence moved to Gower Street, not far from Bloomsbury but a bit closer to the theater. For at least some of their time in England, she and Kid Thompson lived at the home of European-based black entertainer Belle Davis and her husband, Scott Whaley. The English press noted that the couple shunned ostentation and "modestly went home on a bus each evening after the theater."[40] Anticipating a lengthy stay, cast members were keen to establish themselves in quarters that provided adequately for home cooking. Hyacinth Curtis recalled, "They tried to get small apartments, where they could cook, because the food was so lousy. We were there a long time, and we had become accustomed to the nice French restaurants. Everybody warned us about the English food, so everybody tried to get apartments where they could cook, and apartments were very easy to get in those days." Maybe it was easy for the girls, but Rudolph Dunbar, the Guianan-born clarinetist with the Plantation Orchestra and later a distinguished conductor in Europe, didn't find it so easy to get lodgings:

> The task of a colored man selecting a lodging room in the West End of London is not easy to accomplish. In several houses where there are "Rooms to Let" signs, if a black man should apply for a room, the landlady with discriminating nicety would say, "I am sorry but the room I had vacant has just been let." Others would say, "I am awfully sorry but I do not rent rooms to colored people." I have discovered that in order to be given consideration in renting a room the colored man must put on evening dress and be immaculate in his appearance. This only goes to show that a great majority of these people who keep lodging houses are wallowing in the unfathomable depths of ignorance.[41]

The well-educated Dunbar was also appalled to find that many ordinary English people assumed that, being black, he must be from Africa.

Cooking didn't appeal to Florence. We have already noted her remark "I can boil water. I wish I could cook. I never had to."[42] Nevertheless, she was very much at home in England despite the food and the climate. Just as Josephine Baker had found a spiritual niche in the flamboyant Parisian world, so Florence found herself in tune with the cool English reserve. One journalist who interviewed her wrote, "Miss Mills speaks English in a charming cultured voice and one of her minor ambitions is to cultivate the quiet English manner which she finds restful." Comparing the two cities, Florence said:

> I like Paris. They made me very happy in the most cosmopolitan pleasure city in the world. London is getting more and more like a pleasure city for the international crowd but it is still London, very English, not at all like Paris, which is not very French these days, with its American bars, cabarets, cocktails and American and English papers and periodicals everywhere. You can live in London without talking French but you can't survive in Paris unless you can talk American. But still I feel more at home here. There is a ring in the London crowd that you don't hear anywhere else—like the ring in the English sovereign.[43]

Black Birds opened at the London Pavilion, right on Piccadilly Circus. Florence knew it well already from *Dover Street to Dixie*. The timing was good. England was in a mood to be cheered up after the grim events of the recent general strike. The planned opening was postponed till the costumes could be recovered from France. Edmond Sayag, manager of Les Ambassadeurs, had claimed a contractual right to keep *Black Birds* in Paris for another ten weeks. Being thwarted, he denied that he was any longer bound to pay transport costs for the troupe. Only when Cochran made a quick flight to Paris to sort out the problem was the show able to open, two days late. In a sign the racial problems that beset the *Plantation Days* troupe in 1923 were not entirely gone, the resident orchestra at the London Pavilion raised objections to playing alongside musicians of color. To head off threatened labor action by the union, the management laid off the white musicians on a "No work–full pay" arrangement.[44]

There was one more flurry of trouble before the curtain went up. At the last moment, Edith Wilson discovered that Lew Leslie had cut one of her singing numbers, "Mammie," leaving her with one song and one skit. A furious Edith, already disgruntled at the disparity between her contracted pay and Florence's, held out on signing a contract. "[Florence] was getting a guarantee of $1,000 [a week]. Why, I wasn't getting anything like that." She demanded that Leslie give back her passport and let her return to America.[45]

The matter was resolved satisfactorily, and Edith's number was restored after the first night and was still on the playbill many months later. However, Spike Hughes recalled only one song by her, "Don't Cry When He's Gone," on opening night.[46] The incident may have been a ploy on Leslie's part to weaken Edith's bargaining position, in much the same way he would play Valaida Snow off against Ethel Waters some years later, in *Rhapsody in Black*.

The program for the show was based closely on the final version presented in Paris. The performance on opening night was a huge success. For the finale Cochran had revived a traditional practice of having each of the acts take an individual bow before the full company paraded for the final bow. When Florence's turn came, just ahead of the full ensemble, the audience would not let her go. She stood quietly, waiting for the tumult to die down, but it continued unabated. Eventually, she had to step forward and quietly say a few words of thanks. One reviewer noted, "She showed in the few words she spoke, as in everything she does, that she can do no wrong on the stage."[47] So enthusiastic was the response for the whole evening that even after the curtain calls were all completed and the cast had left the stage, a section of the audience stayed on to applaud the orchestra.

The critics in the dailies were also enthusiastic. The *Times*, noting in its stuffy fashion that "a coloured revue" had "been inevitable for some time," and complaining of the "orgy of jazz," nevertheless praised the energy and precision of the dancing, the humor of the Three Eddies, and the clever mimicry of Johnny Hudgins. It complimented Cochran for having found in Florence Mills a central figure with "personality, humour, agility and a voice worthy of better uses," concluding, "Life in Dixieland must be terribly exhausting."[48]

The *Daily Mail* was less staid in its approval, declaring the dancing had "to be seen to be believed." It singled out the Plantation Orchestra, the Pullman Porters scene, and Johnny Hudgins. Noting that Florence's rendition of "I'm a Little Blackbird" sent audience members "wild with delight," it declared her "impossible to compare with anyone else. She is original."[49] Even the old curmudgeon Hannen Swaffer couldn't summon up any bile. Declaring in *Variety* that his had been the most flattering *Black Birds* review, he went on: "I suppose the explanation is that I liked the show more than the others because I hadn't seen it before. I think if Mr. Cochran had not thrown me out, three years ago, I should have said then what I said this time, that Florence Mills is one of the supreme revue artists of her generation."[50]

Coming from the man who had penned such venomously racist words only three short years before, this was an extraordinary turnaround. Was Swaffer mellowing as he aged? A public declaration of his belief in spiritualism in 1924 might suggest it. There is ample evidence that the personality of Florence Mills won him over. Later events would show that his new tolerance was not just a passing phase. However, he could not yet entirely restrain his bilious side. He noted a theatrical associate's comment that "Florence Mills and her crowd are making jazz commit suicide. They do everything so confoundedly well that it's almost an insult for a white artist to try to do the same things." "Jazz committing suicide," he sneered; "I hope so." Also, just to show he was not yet the repentant racist he was threatening to become, his next column railed about black people in the more expensive seats of the theaters. When he asked some theater managers why they encouraged this practice, they told him, "They might be Indian Rajahs, for all we know."[51]

"Silver Rose" was the tune that made the biggest impression. One writer declared, "At every conceivable opportunity throughout [Black Birds] 'Silver Rose' is produced from somewhere. It may be hummed by the audience during the interval, shrieked out by the Wa-Wa, spanked on the piano or what not. You are ushered into your seat to the strain of 'Silver Rose,' ushered out of it to the same tune, and if you go on to a club afterwards—it may be the Embassy, Ciro's or the Café de Paris—it will follow you like a spectre."[52] George Meyer told The Melody Maker that his songs were written by either inspiration or perspiration, and that he had completed both "Silver Rose" and "Smilin' Joe" within an hour. "Silver Rose" is a particularly good example of a song tailored to the personality of the performing artist. As with "I'm a Little Blackbird," its words almost certainly had a significant contribution from Florence herself. It's a personal tribute from Florence to her much loved mother, who had worked for many years as a laundress. In the show Florence sang it to Edith Wilson as a "mammy" figure, and the line "I'm bringing happiness and sweet repose; No more backaches, washing clothes" was a clear reference to her mother.

The opening night's two shows netted Cochran almost £1,000, a highly satisfactory result. To celebrate the triumphal opening, he gave a party for all concerned at London's fashionable Kit Kat Club. The press noted that, rather than occupy center stage as the evening's celebrity, Florence preferred to eat a quiet supper among her own people. Although reporters attributed this preference to shyness at mixing with white people, the truth is that Florence simply preferred to mix with her own friends of whatever race. She preferred quiet conversation to raucous celebration. In Elisabeth Welch's words, "She was a shy person and didn't go to theatre parties. . . . There wasn't a sign of theatre about her, no sign at all. She wasn't flamboyant in dress, she wasn't flamboyant in character, she wasn't flamboyant in her humour."

Following the early reviews in the dailies, there was another wave in the weekly newspapers and the fashionable periodicals. The *Theatre World* declared Florence's "facile change from a sad exile to a 'vamp' warbling for a coloured sheik" an astounding tour de force.[53] It was soon obvious that *Black Birds* was not merely a popular success but was making a mark in artistic circles. It was also setting new trends in the fashion world. *Black Birds* made it fashionable to be black or to entertain black guests in the London of the mid-1920s. Sophisticated black entertainers like Leslie "Hutch" Hutchinson, the West Indian pianist, and Layton and Johnstone, the piano-vocal duo, had already established a niche for themselves in some fashionable quarters. With the arrival of *Black Birds*, hostesses fell over themselves to stage *Black Birds* parties. To have Florence Mills at your party was a guarantee of success. If you couldn't get Florence, then anyone from *Black Birds* would do.

A *Black Birds* mania possessed London for a while. Anything Florence did was liable to end up as the latest fashion fad. A golden anklet with lock and miniature key that she wore became a popular accessory. The *Ladies Companion* regaled its readers with the information that Florence called it "the golden key to happiness." There were Florence Mills dolls, and a woman shopping for a certain shade of creamy brown silk stockings simply asked for "the new Florence Mills shade."[54]

It had been Florence's big, luminous eyes that fascinated the French. For the English it was her slender legs that caught the imagination. Back in the *Shuffle Along* days, Aubrey Lyles had talked about her "legs like a canary." In England, Hyacinth Curtis recalled, they saw them as "like little sparrows. The English called them Chippendale legs." Another description referred to her as "All thin wrists and legs like toothpicks."[55] Florence was not flattered by this attention to her legs. According to Kid Thompson, "She was very sensitive about her legs; [she] used to get pads to build up her legs and make it look like her legs were big." Either the pretense didn't work or she soon abandoned it. With one interviewer she laughingly referred to her "canary legs," calling the anklet her "bird ring." "Every pedigree canary has an identification ring on its leg," she declared.[56]

The enthusiasm with which black people were being accepted and entertained in respectable circles as a result of *Black Birds* irritated the waspish novelist Evelyn Waugh. Author Anthony Powell recounted how Waugh, on issuing a minor invitation, would add, "It's not a party, there won't be a black man."[57] Nevertheless, the twenty-two-year-old Waugh was frequently in the *Black Birds* audience. His first such visit, in the company of prolific novelist Cecil Roberts, occurred during the second week. He noted in his diary, "All the artists were negroes and negresses."[58] Although the attention showered on black entertainers irritated him, Waugh lacked the confidence to disapprove openly of his friends' values.

A more admiring audience member during the opening week was John Gielgud, later a famous actor in a wide range of roles, from Shakespeare to Mortimer, and a knight of the realm. In 1923 the very young Gielgud had recorded his rapturous appreciation of Florence in his playbill for *Dover Street to Dixie*. This time it was a rather depressed Gielgud who went to the London Pavilion on the night of September 14. He had expected instead that he would be playing the lead in the opening of *The Constant Nymph* at the New Theatre that night. To his chagrin, Noel Coward was given the lead instead. Gielgud said, "On the first night, I could not bear to watch the play. I slipped off to see Florence Mills in *Blackbirds* at the London Pavilion, and only came back between the acts to the stage door of the New, where they told me the play was being enormously received." He did take over the lead in *The Constant Nymph* three weeks later when Coward became ill.[59]

A major factor in promoting the fashionable success of *Black Birds* and its cast was the enthusiastic patronage of members of the royal family. Once again Edward, Prince of Wales, was particularly noted for his frequent attendance in the royal box. Kid Thompson recalled that, as in 1923, "He sat right in the front row and sang songs with Florence," having eventually memorized all the tunes. Edith Wilson also recalled, "I used to do a number on stage, and he'd do it right along with me. He'd be in the box—they had curtains you could draw so you couldn't see from the side—and he'd be dancing right along with the show."[60] The prince was continuing a royal tradition of patronage of black music and entertainment that went back to his sixth birthday, in 1903. His special treat then was a private performance at Buckingham Palace of *In Dahomey* by the Williams and Walker Company. More recently, he had taken Charleston lessons from Bricktop, and he relied on stride piano player Luckey Roberts to ship him all the latest jazz and dance records from New York every month. Many believe it was he who gave Florence her English nickname "Little Twinks."

Edward's brothers, George, Duke of Kent, and Bertie, Duke of York (later George VI), were also frequent visitors to *Black Birds*. The Duke of York had, a few years before, married Lady Elizabeth Bowes-Lyon, known later as Queen Elizabeth the Queen Mother, who would live to celebrate her 101st birthday. Sometime around mid-November the Duke and Duchess of York were escorted to *Black Birds* by the Prince of Wales, already on his second visit in three weeks. The then Duchess of York remembered the experience for the rest of her long years. A letter to the author dated June 12, 1998, signed on the Queen Mother's behalf by one of her ladies-in-waiting, says,

"The Queen Mother does indeed retain vivid memories of Florence Mills and her delightful performances on the London stage. It is good to know her outstanding talent has been recorded in a biography." Other royalty who enjoyed *Black Birds* before the end of 1926 included the King of Spain and the Queen of Norway.

The enthusiasm of the young royals, especially the Prince of Wales, for *Black Birds* in particular and jazz in general was soon a subject of comment in the media. By the time the show finished its lengthy run, the prince had seen it between eleven and sixteen times or even more, depending on whose report you read. Swaffer, in *Variety*, complained about the royal family's lack of support for anything but syncopated music. Noting its rate of attendance at *Black Birds*, he huffed, "It will circulate slowly around the British Empire that the Heir to the Throne has a liking for coloured entertainments of a kind that would not be tolerated in South Africa or Australia."

In reality, Australians too were casting covetous eyes on Florence. Australian impresario Hugh D. McIntosh, who in 1908 established Sydney's Tivoli Theatre as the antipodean Palace of New York, had cohosted the superb party Cochran gave the cast of *Dover Street to Dixie* in 1923. In October 1926 a London-based talent scout for the Tivoli had cabled to Sydney,

[I] Think Florence Mills is one of the cleverest women on the stage. Coloured, sings, dances, acts and talks, and looks as good as it is possible for a dark woman to look. Wonderful troupe with her and her dancing is a revelation. Any one of her ballet could do a specialty dancing act. Troupe in its entirety would be beyond us for Australia as they get very good money, but I am on the look out to pull a couple of good dancing teams which would make a great act.[61]

The royals were the apex of England's class-conscious society, and the large aristocracy and upper middle class were always keen to follow their lead in matters of fashion and taste. The chance that the evening you went to the show might turn out to coincide with one of the prince's visits gave added spice to attendance at *Black Birds*. The society columnist for the *Lady* recounted how taking some French friends to the show almost backfired because they had already seen it in Paris. She noted with relief, "They had the opportunity of seeing the Prince of Wales in the audience, so, there again, the evening was a success."

This was also the era of the Bright Young People (BYP), wealthy young men and women about town who were eager to try the latest sensation—American cocktails, jazz, fast cars, holidays on the Riviera, and fancy dress balls, to name a few. The group included many of the literary and artistic figures of the era, the Sitwells (Edith, Osbert, and Sacheverell), Constant Lambert, Barbara Cartland, Cecil Beaton, and Oliver Messel. Oxford University was a major base for the BYP. They adopted the *Black Birds* with gusto, using the players as a theme for fancy dress parties, inviting them to functions, and seeking them out as dance partners. At one fancy dress party, where guests had to impersonate living personalities, several versions of Florence Mills showed up.[62] Party givers did well from hosting the entertainers. Edith Wilson told Daphne Duval Harrison of one party she attended. Florence and Ivan Harold Browning sang "Love Will Find a Way" from *Shuffle Along*, Edith Wilson and Aida Ward both did some of their songs from *Black Birds*, and finally Layton and Johnstone did some specialty numbers. Quite an evening's entertainment without going near a theater![63]

Not all party givers expected to get Florence's services free. Like his cousin in Paris, Baron Lionel Rothschild often paid her to entertain guests at his London townhouse or his country property in Buckinghamshire. As in Paris, she appreciated that the host always treated her with unfailing courtesy on these occasions. Some members of the Rothschild dynasty had a reputation for fast living, but Florence was fortunate to have contact with the more conventional representatives of this fabulously wealthy clan.

As well as the social lionizing, Florence and the *Black Birds* received more serious recognition as artists of significance. One of her most ardent fans was Arnold Haskell, ballet expert and author of many books on dance. In *Balletomania* he wrote, "The *Blackbirds* was one of the most important manifestations of theatrical art we have ever seen in London." He considered that Florence was "At all times a very great artist, with much to express about herself and her people, and with fine technical means at hand."[64] Another admirer from the world of classical dance was choreographer Frederick Ashton, who had known and worked with all the great dancers of the age. He described himself as so impressed with the tragic quality of Florence's dancing that he could still see her vividly in his mind's eye years later.[65] Ballet performers also worshiped at her shrine. "It is notable how much the show attracts other dancers. Anton Dolin has not missed a Tuesday matinee since the start and Massine, who saw it for the first time last week said 'After this all other dancing is futile. Never before have I seen creative artists able to achieve all they imagined.'"[66]

While the remarkable vitality of the dancing was a key element in the *Black Birds* appeal, for many the music was at least as important. Seeing Florence and the Plantation Orchestra in *Dover Street to Dixie* had deeply moved and influenced Constant Lambert. Interviewed in 1930 about his masterpiece *The Rio Grande*, an orchestral setting of a Sitwell poem, he said, "The idea for the music came from seeing Florence Mills in *Dover Street to Dixie* and from some of the music in *Blackbirds*."[67] He found Florence just as enthralling in *Black Birds* as she had been in *Dover Street to Dixie*, although he thought the Plantation Orchestra more sophisticated than in 1923. His friend Angus Morrison commented, "Florence Mills still retained an essential simplicity and childlike quality."[68]

The social admiration inevitably led to invitations to elaborate society functions. For Florence, attendance at such functions was a chore she accepted as part of her mission to win respect for her people. In the past, she had been more or less content to let her fame and achievements speak for themselves as advertisements for the abilities of her fellow African Americans. Only occasionally, as when she had the official meeting with the Mayor of Philadelphia, did she take an opportunity to state her views on race issues publicly. In England, however, she was noticeably more prepared to take a public stance.

The first evidence of this commitment was an article under her own by-line in the *Sunday Chronicle* entitled "The Soul of the Negro." In it she poured out her frustration at the obvious unfairness of racial prejudice. "It is the eternal burden of the coloured people—the penalisation for an accident of birth—to be made to feel out of focus with the rest of humanity. . . . How absurd it all is—how utterly unfair! There is not a coloured man or a coloured woman in existence who does not bitterly resent the sentiment that drives them beyond the pale."

In words reminiscent of Shylock's "If you prick us do we not bleed," she pleads for recognition of the essential humanity of her race. Drawing on the words of her theme song, "I'm a Little Blackbird," she reflects on "the tinge of melancholy which is always present in the Negro soul." Drawing hope from the progress achieved, despite the horrors of lynchings back home, she portrays the possibility of a better future. Finally, she reflects on her own life experience, concluding, "That I was able to win through at all was due to sheer determination to rise superior to prejudice."[69]

The next example of her new outspokenness came at an elaborate party in her honor staged at the Piccadilly Hotel in early November. Cochran was concerned that some members of the cast were becoming restive and homesick. To cheer them up, he staged a big festivity in their honor. Florence, "the star of stars," was the centerpiece. He invited many celebrities, including film star Tallulah Bankhead, singer-pianist Edythe Baker, and Viola Tree, actress daughter of the famous actor Herbert Beerbohm Tree. There was an elaborate special menu, with evocative southern titles like "Hors d'Oeuvre Kentucky, Supreme de Volaille Maryland, Salade Swanee River, and Soufflé Glace Florence Mills."[70]

Early in the evening it was suggested that Florence could sit with some of the distinguished white guests, as a sort of honorary white. Indignantly retorting, "I am coal Black and proud of it," she remained resolutely seated with her fellow cast members.[71] The event stirred her deep sense of anger and frustration at the pettiness of prejudice, and she fumed quietly throughout the evening. At the climax of the celebration, Cochran made a complimentary speech in her honor. When her turn came to reply, she launched into a soft-spoken but emotional response.

The details of what she said were similar to her *Sunday Pictorial* article. Her obvious sincerity had a deep effect on her audience. Cochran recalled, "She made a most moving appeal for an understanding with and the emancipation of the Blacks. The White people felt a lump in their throats and the coloured folk were hushed in respectful awe."[72] Another witness noted, "She began with the quiet words 'I am a member of the society for the advancement of my own race,' and continually referred, in a soft voice, full of pathos, to 'my people.'"[73] The society she referred to was the National Association for the Advancement of Colored People (NAACP). Florence had been a supporter of its work for some years and was actively promoting its cause in England.

The day after the Piccadilly party, Florence, along with a number of popular acts, including comedian Will Hay, was scheduled to make a broadcast on a variety program on the BBC. Whether she actually participated in the broadcast is not clear. There was much wrangling between Cochran and Leslie on the one hand and the BBC on the other over how many songs it would be reasonable to expect her to perform. "Florence Mills is not for sale like a pound of tea," Cochran trumpeted. He insisted that fifteen minutes was too long, and two songs was the most she could be expected to perform. The BBC initially balked at this number, but later reports suggest the broadcast took place.[74]

Besides their coyness with the BBC, Florence's managers also discouraged her around this time from accepting a proposal from a locally based company for some kind of film venture.[75] With her heavy commitments at the time, this decision was probably wise, but sadly it prevented later generations from enjoying a visual record of her performance. A venture Florence herself showed enthusiasm for was the possibility of playing Peter Pan in a forthcoming Christmas pantomime. "Peter Pan seems to me the greatest little figure that ever was," she said. "It's foolish to try and define him—as foolish as trying to define a sunset. He's just all of us who never want to grow up, and he's me. I wish I could play him once, just for fun." However, the part went to a white American actress named Dorothy Dickson, from Kansas City.[76]

Whether Florence did the BBC broadcast or not, there is no doubt that the Plantation Orchestra went to the recording studios around this time and cut four tracks from *Black Birds*, "Silver Rose," "Arabella's Wedding Day," "Smilin' Joe," and "For Baby and Me," without any vocal accompaniment.[77] Another recording session around that time repeated a pattern that was familiar from the United States. Once Florence popularized a song, there would usually be at least one other female vocalist to record it. In England, sometime soon after the opening of *Black Birds*, the popular London piano-vocal duo of Billy Mayerl and Gwen Farrar recorded "I'm a Little Blackbird" on the Vocalion label.[78]

As usual Florence's schedule had a significant number of charity and gala special events. A highly festive occasion was the annual Variety Ball, run as a charity fund-raiser by the British Variety Club on November 11 at Covent Garden Opera House. This was the big event of the year for show business folk who wanted to see and be seen. Most of the major stars attended or performed. The dance music featured the top hits of the various leading sheet music publishing houses, with support performances by stars from the relevant shows. Florence's showpiece was "Silver Rose." The attendance listed names like Jack Buchanan, Binnie Hale, Marie Kendall, and other great stars of British theater and variety, as well as Florence's fellow blacks, Layton and Johnstone. A more somber event came when the London Pavilion was given over to the "Not-Forgotten Association" for a special matinee performance in early December, at which a thousand disabled ex-servicemen attended from various hospitals.[79]

The Charleston was much in the picture for Florence at this time. A massive Charleston craze had been sweeping the country for months. Florence was regularly asked to demonstrate it at parties or to be a judge at Charleston competitions. Questioned by one journalist why she didn't feature it more in the show, she replied to her listener's amazement, "It is ridiculously easy, quite absurdly so"[80]—hardly a surprising response from one who had spent her entire life in the world of black dance. Nevertheless, the Charleston was looming in a large way for Florence. C. B. Cochran had decided to stage a Charleston Ball and Competition just before Christmas 1926. Since his recovery from bankruptcy, Cochran's fortunes had been rising. One of his greatest triumphs came when he was selected from 178 applicants for the post of manager of the Royal Albert Hall in 1926. The selection committee saw him as having the show business sense and business shrewdness to revive the Hall's flagging financial fortunes. Despite his credentials, the appointment was controversial.

The Albert Hall was a huge, magnificently appointed center for the promotion of the arts and sciences. It opened in 1871, dedicated to the memory of Queen Victoria's consort, Prince Albert. Its charter imposed strict, con-servative limits on the kinds of functions allowed within its hallowed precincts. By 1926 it was clear the expenses involved in its upkeep called for some relaxation of these rules, and a bill to ease them was introduced in Par-liament. Cochran's appointment as manager was, for the more conservative elements and their friends entrenched in the House of Lords, like a red rag to a bull. They claimed he would fill the Hall with circuses and prizefights, "One of those competitions in which a man earns a great many times the amount of a Cabinet Minister's salary for being knocked out in the space of a minute or two." They referred the Bill to a Select Committee. After hear-ings, which at times had a touch of high comedy, as the awfulness of Mr. Cochran was contrasted with the flawless character of everyone else associ-ated with the Hall, the committee found in his favor.[81]

Cochran badly needed a success to justify his appointment, but practical problems stood in his way. The Albert Hall had an infamous echo that made it unsuitable for some musical programs. Keen to stage an event that would fill the huge hall, he first considered a professional tennis competition fea-turing the great Suzanne Lenglen. When this brainstorm ran into problems, he came up with the idea of the Charleston Ball. The Ball was to run from 9 p.m. on Wednesday, December 15, until 5 a.m. the following day. It would feature a cabaret drawn from all the leading shows. Florence Mills, Johnny Hudgins, and the *Black Birds* would be the star attraction. There were com-petitions with generous prizes for professional and amateur dancers. Regional contests supplied the finalists from all over the country. The judges for the competitions included Fred Astaire, Jack Hylton, and Lew Leslie. At that time Fred and Adele Astaire were a big hit in the London version of *Lady Be Good*. George Gershwin had written "I'd Rather Charleston" specially for the show so as to cash in on the dance craze in England.

The Charleston Ball program alternated sessions of public dancing, cabaret entertainment, and the various dance competitions. The contests were classi-fied into ballroom Charleston (amateur), ballroom Charleston (professional), stage Charleston (amateur), and stage Charleston (professional). There was also a Charleston Troupe competition between the various cabaret dance troupes, including two sets of Britain's famous dancing Tiller Girls. There were four dance bands including the Plantation Orchestra; four cabarets plus the *Black Birds* (giving a "complete miniature revue"); various specialty acts, such as Nervo and Knox of the famous comedy troupe the Crazy Gang; and a grand finale bringing back the combined cabarets and dance troupes.

The occasion was a roaring success. Estimates placed the attendance var-iously at "over five thousand," and "almost ten thousand." The *Melody Maker* contented itself with merely saying, "All London must have been there." It described the *Black Birds* segment as "an event that will linger long in the minds of all present." One of those joining wholeheartedly in the revelry was Prince George, Duke of Kent. The *Daily Sketch* described the event as "one long triumph—eight hours of ceaseless gaiety, infectious music." Thousands of balloons were released at each interval. Four hundred of them carried coupons entitling the holder to copies of the Plantation Orchestra's recently released records. Describing the finale, the *Sketch* reporter wrote, "Johnny Hudgins was encored and encored until it seemed as if his marvellously unattached limbs must fall off. Then as a grand finale, Florence Mills appeared on the now glassy floor. Then thunder of applause as her slim body went through more amazing contortions than you could imagine in a nightmare."[82]

One of those present as a competitor in the stage Charleston (amateur) section was a young man named Louis Grad. Describing it years later, he said, "The atmosphere was electric. I had never seen so many great dancers assembled under one roof and the tension backstage was almost too much to bear." He won his section and a four-week engagement at the Piccadilly Hotel. The gig convinced him professional dancing was to be his life from then on. He became better known to the world later as Lord Lew Grade, one of England's leading show business entrepreneurs.[83]

An amusing side note to the Charleston Ball is the section of the program in which various authorities record their views on the origin of the Charleston dance. Florence offered a characteristically thoughtful opinion, based on history. "I have heard as many stories of the origin of the Charleston as I have heard cures for colds. I believe one relating to Pickaninnies dancing it on the Plantations outside Charleston, South Carolina in the late [eighteen] 'fifties, to the Negro tune called 'Take Your Foot Out of the Mud and Stick It in the Sand' to be the most authentic." Lew Leslie, on the other hand, forthrightly claimed the credit for himself. "It happened in my *Plantation Revue* six years ago when I hired a bow-legged coloured boy from Charleston, South Carolina. I found similar steps in his routine and developed the dance from these. . . . The song "Charleston" was introduced after the dance was seen at my *Plantation* and its rhythm taken from a specially arranged number written for me."

With the Charleston Ball, 1926 was drawing to a close for Florence and the *Black Birds*. Elated with the success of the event, Cochran staged a similar ball on Boxing Day, but it did not involve the *Black Birds*. By now the homesickness that had prompted him to stage his special party in November had taken a toll among the *Black Birds* cast. Hyacinth Curtis had returned to the United States before the Charleston Ball. She remarked years later, in her Harlem apartment, "I got homesick and wanted to see Momma and I came home. . . . It began to have the fog and all that sort of thing. It was very dreary; it was getting to be Christmas." Perhaps an equally pressing incentive for Hyacinth was that, by early November, Clarence Robinson had left the show to return to the United States. Romance had blossomed between him and Hyacinth in Paris and London, leading eventually to a lifelong marriage. Other members of the chorus were also intending to leave.

This was a pattern characteristic of long-running black shows in England and Europe. As original cast members dropped out for various reasons, imports from the United States, or often locally available black talent, would replace them. The replacements might be either African Americans based locally or locally born black people with American, African, or West Indian ancestry. In this case the main replacement was an English-based trio known as the Southern Trio. They comprised John C. Payne and Clinton C. Rosemond, both American born, and Mabel Mercer, the English-born daughter of an expatriate African American entertainer father and a Welsh-English white mother from a music-hall background.

The twenty-six-year-old Mabel Mercer had followed her parents into the entertainment world in her early teens. She sang with the Southern Syncopated Orchestra in 1920 and danced in Will Garland's *Coloured Society* show. In the early 1920s she joined the Southern Trio, which specialized in a cappella singing. Mabel also toured Europe and the Near East with *Chocolate Kiddies*. In later years she would become a figure of major importance in the American singing and cabaret worlds and an important influence on Frank Sinatra.[84]

Born in 1872, John C. Payne had come to England originally with the Southern Syncopated Orchestra. He had already had a substantial career in the United States, where he was noted for his ability to sing all parts from bass to soprano and specializing in falsetto. He was to play a significant role in Florence's world over the coming months. Through his friendship with a liberal-minded London aristocrat, Lady Cook, he had been able to acquire a home in Regent's Park Road, which became a focal point for expatriate African American entertainers. The other member of the trio, Clinton C. Rosemond, went on to a long career in black movies.[85]

Before Hyacinth Curtis left she had picked up on the gossip that was freely circulating among the girls in the cast about Florence's state of health. "She was tired, I used to hear the girls say she was so tired." The exhaustion that had temporarily laid her low after her Aeolian Hall concert was threatening again. There had been comment from early on about the number of scenes Florence was in. *Variety* had commented back in September, "There were some who felt Florence Mills was unduly prominent in the proceedings. She appears in practically every number."[86] She was also feeling the effect of the dreary London fog that Hyacinth mentioned. Although 1926 had been a year of great triumphs and achievement for her, Florence was now feeling drained and having difficulty maintaining the energy demanded by her performances. There was no doubt that she needed a break over the Christmas holidays while a new version of *Black Birds* was in preparation.

Notes

1. Anita Loos, *Gentlemen Prefer Blondes* (New York: Vintage Books, 1983), 31.

2. Garvin Bushell, as told to Mark Tucker, *Jazz from the Beginning* (New York: Da Capo Press, 1998), 54.

3. Bricktop's diaries, Rare Manuscripts and Books Division, Schomburg Institute.

4. Janet Flanner, *Paris Was Yesterday:1925–1939* (London: Angus and Robertson, 1973), 63–64, describes Les Ambassadeurs and its history.

5. *L'Illustration*, June 5, 1926, 586.

6. Advertisement, *Le Figaro*, May 26, 1926.

7. Cutting from *New York Herald*, Aug. 5, 1926, and folder "Professional lyrics," both in HAJC, Florence Mills Collection.

8. "Black Birds," *Theatre World*, Oct. 1926.

9. Georges Schmitt, *La Rampe*, June 15, 1926, 16.

10. Jean Claude Baker and Chris Chase, *Josephine: The Josephine Baker Story* (Holbrook, Mass.: Adams Publishing, 1993), 138–139.

11. Mistinguett, "Music Halls, Cirques & Cabarets," *Comoedia*, June 25, 1926.

12. Michel Georges-Michel, *Gens de Theatre Que J'ai Connu: 1900–1940* (New York: Brentano's, 1942), 230.

13. André Levinson, "The Negro Dance: Under European Eyes," *Theatre Arts Monthly*, Apr. 1927, 282.

14. Lena Horne and Richard Schickel, *Lena* (London: Andre Deutsch, 1966), 92–93.

15. Simone Rattel, "Le Congres Feministe," *Comoedia*, May 30, 1926.

16. "Americans Protest at Negro Dancing with White Woman," VAR, June 9, 1926.

17. The occasion went some way toward restoring Buffet's fortunes. She played the role of Napoleon's mother, Laetizia Bonaparte, in Abel Gance's classic silent film *Napoleon*, actually being filmed in Paris at the time of the benefit. In 1955, when Jean Renoir made *French Can-Can*, a somewhat fictionalized history of the Moulin Rouge, as his tribute to his painter father's loved Belle Epoque, he cast Edith Piaf in the role of Eugenie Buffet.

18. "The Shyness of Florence Mills," *Sketch* magazine, Sept. 22, 1926, 550.

19. Jean Prasteau, *La Merveilleuse Aventure du Casino De Paris* (Paris: Editions Denoel, 1975), 164.

20. J. Delini, "Une Nuit de Peche au Cottage Parisys," *Comoedia*, July 1, 1926.

21. See entry for Nora Holt in Bruce Kellner, ed. *The Harlem Renaissance: A Historical Dictionary for the Era* (New York: Methuen, 1984).

22. William L. Patterson, *The Man Who Cried Genocide: An Autobiography* (New York: International Publishers, 1991), 70.

23. Bricktop's diaries.

24. Earl Granstaff letter, June 3, 1926, HAJC.

25. Marshall and Jean Stearns, "Harland Dixon and Character Dancing," in *Jazz Dance* (London: MacMillan, 1968).

26. "Paul Whiteman Refutes Statement of Actresses," ChDef, Nov. 19, 1927.

27. Jim Haskins and N. R. Mitgang, *Mr. Bojangles, The Biography of Bill Robinson* (New York: William Morrow, 1988), 179; and "Your Broadway and Mine," *New York Graphic*, quoted in BAA, June 20, 1931.

28. John Gregory, *The Legat Saga* (Pennington, N.J.: Princeton Book, 1994).

29. Details from "Casino Kursaal Oostende" and other material kindly provided by Casino staff. The third Kursaal was destroyed in World War II and has since been replaced by the magnificent fourth Kursaal.

30. "Ostende Reine des Plages," *La Rampe*, May 15, 1926.

31. "Au Kursaal," *Echo D'Ostende*, Aug. 16(?), 1926, 1; Aug. 19, 1926.

32. "Plaintes de Jazz Dans Le Ciel Etoile des Champs Elysées," *Comoedia*, Aug. 26, 1926.

33. Signed copy of menu in SCRAP, HAJC.

34. *London Daily Sketch*, Sept. 6, 1926.

35. Tyler Stovall, *Paris Noir: African Americans in the City of Light* (Boston: Houghton Mifflin, 1996), 60. Michel Fabre and John A. Williams, *A Street Guide to African Americans in Paris* (Paris: Cercle d'Etudes Afro-Americaine, 1996), 86, has Cullen climbing the Eiffel Tower in August 1926, so I have taken this as the best indication of the likely timing.

36. Countee Cullen, "The Dark Tower," *Opportunity*, Dec. 1927. I have corrected an apparent typographical error, replacing "ached" with "reached" as seeming to more correctly reflect the original intent.

37. Bricktop's diaries, Sept. 5, 1926. Correct spelling is Mecklenburgh.

38. "Managerial Squeeze Delays 'Blackbirds,'" VAR, Sept. 15, 1926, 3.

39. *A Pictorial and Descriptive Guide to London and Its Environs*, 44th ed. (London: Ward, Lock, 1923), 144.

40. *London Daily News*, Nov. 2, 1927.

41. From the Folklore Project of the Federal Writers' Project (WPA) (Library of Congress). Dunbar was a graduate of the Damrosch Institute (now the Juilliard School) and famous in Europe years later as a symphony conductor and author of a standard text on playing the clarinet.

42. Notes from P. L. Prattis interview, Claude Barnett Collection, Chicago Historical Society.

43. Florence Mills, unidentified, undated clipping "Magic Moon That Brought Me Money," HAJC.

44. "Managerial Squeeze Delays 'Blackbirds,'" VAR, Sept. 15, 1926, 3.

45. Daphne Duval Harrison, *Black Pearls* (New Brunswick: Rutgers University Press, 1990), 186.

46. Spike Hughes, *Opening Bars* (London: Pilot Press, 1946), 306. I am indebted to Howard Rye's excellent research in "Visiting Firemen 9: The Blackbirds and Their Orchestras," *Storyville 112* (April–May 1984), 133, for drawing my attention to this passage.

47. "Old Fashioned Calls," *Sketch* magazine, Sept. 22, 1926, 550.

48. "Blackbirds: A Coloured Revue at the London Pavilion," *London Times*, Sept. 13, 1926.

49. "Coloured Show with Pep," *Daily Mail*, Sept. 13, 1926.

50. Hannen Swaffer, "London as It Looks: I Really Like the Mills Revue," VAR, Sept. 29, 1926, 3.

51. Hannen Swaffer, "Wonderful London Yesterday," *London Daily Graphic*, Sept. 20, 1926, 5.

52. Unknown magazine article, 123–125 (courtesy of Stephen Bourne Collection).

53. "Black Birds" review, *Theatre World*, Oct. 1926, 18.

54. BAA, Nov. 5, 1927, 1, and PiCou, July 16, 1927.

55. From Carolyn Hall, *The Twenties in Vogue* (London: Octopus Books, 1983), 83.

56. Undated, unidentified clipping, HAJC.

57. Andrew Motion, *The Lamberts* (London: Chatto & Windus, 1986), 154.

58. Michael Davie, ed., *The Diaries of Evelyn Waugh* (Middlesex: Penguin Books, 1979), 264.

59. John Gielgud, *Early Stages* (London: MacMillan, 1939), 119.

60. Charlotte Breese, *Hutch* (London: Bloomsbury, 1999), 49, quoting from *Tatler* (1926).

61. I am indebted to Ross Laird, discographer and music researcher, for this item from ScreenSound Australia.

62. Hall, *The Twenties in Vogue*, 32.

63. Harrison, *Black Pearls*, 187.

64. Arnold Haskell, *Balletomania* (London: Victor Gollancz, 1934), 287–293.

65. David Vaughan, *Frederick Ashton and His Ballets* (London: A & C Black, 1977), 78.

66. *London Daily Sketch*, Dec. 8, 1926.

67. Derek Patmore, "A Brilliant Young English Composer," *Everyman*, Oct. 16, 1930.

68. Motion, *The Lamberts*, 154.

69. Florence Mills, "The Soul of the Negro," *Sunday Chronicle*, Oct. 10, 1926.

70. Dinner Program in HAJC, Nov. 7, 1926.

71. Hannen Swaffer, "London as It Looks," *Variety*, Dec. 29, 1926.

72. Cochran, *I Had Almost Forgotten* (London: Hutchinson, 1932), 220.

73. Undated, unidentified clipping, HAJC.

74. "Resents London Radio Bid," NYT, Oct. 29(?), 1926, and "Latest Fashions in Radio," *Sunday Chronicle*, Oct. 31, 1926.

75. Letter from British Pacific Film Company, Dec. 2, 1926, HAJC.

76. "Why Not a Blackbird Peter Pan," *Sunday Chronicle*, Nov. 14, 1926, and "Florence Mills Would Be Peter Pan," NYT, ca. Dec. 19, 1926.

77. LP recording *Harlem Comes to London*, Swing Records "Historical Jazz" series SW 8444. The Plantation tracks are dated Dec. 1, 1926. The artists for the session are given as Johnny Dunn and Pike Davis (trumpets); Calvin Jones (trombone); Rudolph Dunbar, Nelson Kincaid, and Alonzo Williams (reeds); Shrimp Jones and George Smith (violins); George Rickson (piano); Maceo Jefferson (banjo); Bill Benford (tuba); and Jesse Baltimore (drums).

78. Ross Laird, *Moanin' Low* (Westport Conn.: Greenwood Press, 1996), 180.

79. *The Performer*, Nov. 17, 1926, and *London Times*, Nov. 16, 1926.

80. Undated, unidentified clipping in HAJC.

81. *Royal Albert Hall: Compendium*, 1974–1975, 104.

82. The description of the Charleston Ball draws on the following sources: "Official Programme: Charleston Ball and Competition"; Charles B. Cochran, *Cock-a-Doodle-Do* (London: J. M. Dent & Sons, 1941), 194–195; *London Daily Sketch*, Dec. 17, 1926, 5; *The Stage*, Dec. 23, 1926, 21; *The Melody Maker*, Jan. (?) 1927.

83. Lew Grade, *Still Dancing: My Story* (London: Collins, 1987), 38–39.

84. There are two biographies of Mabel Mercer: Margaret Cheney, *Midnight at Mabel's: The Mabel Mercer Story* (Washington, D.C.: New Voyage Publishing, 2000) and James Haskins, *Mabel Mercer: A Life* (New York: Athenaeum, 1987). Neither is very reliable on details of her early life. The information about the Southern Syncopated Orchestra can be found in Jeffrey Green, "Black Music Internationalism in England in the 1920s," *Black Music Research Journal* 15:1 (spring 1995).

85. For John Payne see "Looking Back on My Life" in Nancy Cunard, ed., *Negro: Anthology Made by Nancy Cunard, 1931–1933* (New York: Negro Universities Press, 1969), 331–335. For Clinton C. Rosemond's movie career, www.imdb.com/name/nm0741885/ (Dec. 9, 2003) shows 38 movies, mostly supporting roles.

86. "Managerial 'Squeeze' Delays Blackbirds," *Variety*, Sept. 26, 1926, 3.

~

CHAPTER TEN

Black Birds of 1927

The Christmas break gave Florence some rest and a chance to recover from the strain of constant performing. It was soon interrupted, however, by the inevitable rehearsal of new material. *Blackbirds of 1927*, officially known as *Lew Leslie's Black Birds*, 2nd Edition, opened on Saturday, January 15, 1927. Some of the content of the previous edition was repeated, but a large amount of new material was included. "Dixie Dreams," recycled from *Dixie to Broadway*, replaced "Silver Rose." Other changes in the first part included the replacement of Florence's "Jungle Night in Dixieland," "Mandy, Make Up Your Mind," and "Jazz Time Came from the South" with a new song, "Baby and Me," and a sketch involving Florence called "Come Take a Trip to Hades with Me."[1]

Her total number of scenes remained constant as she had now taken over the Aida Ward–Mabel Mercer "Bambalina Mad" role. Aida Ward had left the show by the time the 1927 edition opened. In "Come Take a Trip to Hades with Me," Florence appeared as a cute devil against a picturesque hell-fire background, with John Payne as Satan and various cast members in other devilish roles—Mabel Mercer was a "red-hot mama." In "Waika Kiki Blues" Florence, aided by her Hawaiian Blackbirds, dressed in ostrich feather costumes, simulated "the waves of the Pacific dancing on South Sea islands by means of expressive movements of her nut-brown arms."[2]

The critics reacted enthusiastically to the new edition of *Black Birds*. There was approval for the retention of popular items like Florence's tap-dancing in "The Wooden Soldiers," Johnny Hudgins's silent mimicry of a wobbly skater, the Three Eddies, Johnny Nit's dancing, and the risqué humorous sketch "On the Phone," by Edith Wilson and Johnny Hudgins. One critic even declared the success of *Black Birds* was "A proof of London's increasing artistic intelligence."[3] Of the new items, the greatest enthusiasm went to Edith Wilson dancing the "Black Bottom," the "rich, mellow voices" of the Southern Trio, and Florence singing "Baby and Me" and dancing her Hawaiian number. The *Daily Sketch* reviewer concluded, "But Florence Mills singing 'Baby and Me' remains with me as the most lasting memory of a very exciting evening." The general assessment, as usual, was that it was the incredible dancing vitality of the entire cast that gave the show its tremendous impact, but all were unanimous that it was the genius of Florence Mills that was the real heart of it.

- *Tatler*: And it is still Florence Mills who *is* the show. She is on in nearly every scene, but how could one get tired of watching that lively little face or those incredibly slim hands and ankles, and listening to that pure, clear voice.
- *Theatre World*: The "Blackbirds" still provide the most brilliant entertainment of its kind in Town . . . What can I say of Florence Mills, except to marvel once again at that lovely voice with its haunting cadences and flutelike quality, at that unbounded animation and energy and that wonderful sense of humour that transforms an ordinary jazz song like "I Ain't Got Nobody but You" into a masterpiece of quaint humour?
- *Sphere*: Miss Florence Mills stands out preeminently among these dusky harmonies; hers is a distinguished personality from the top of her sleek head to her slender wrists and ankles. Both in song and dance she remains inimitable.[4]

As usual the Prince of Wales was one of the first to attend the new edition, bringing Prince George and Lady Louis Mountbatten with him. Again the show's appeal for children was noted. Its engagement overlapped the school holiday period, and the *Daily News* observed that many parents were taking their children to *Black Birds* in preference to the traditional English Christmas pantomime.

As always, the fashion columnists were on hand. Florence's costumes attracted the approving attention of one: "Curiously fascinating, I assure you, is the contrast of dusky skin and shimmering white satin embroidered with diamante and a foam of white ostrich feathers over chiffon. Florence Mills wears this feather-skirted gown and has a white wig, too, while in another scene her gown shows the most fashionable contrast of colours and materials."[5]

The success of the new edition of *Black Birds* inevitably brought with it one of life's less endearing facets. Early in January the cast received income tax blanks for the recently ended financial year. Florence's own tax was paid promptly. Her accountants provided her with a receipt for $1,500 "in connection with remittances for the purposes of the Inland Revenue."[6] This amount, which would come to at least $15,000 in today's dollars, shows the scale of Florence's earnings. There is no doubt she and Kid Thompson between them were making a fortune by the standards of their poverty-stricken childhoods. They were also generally prudent in their handling of it. Kid told Helen Armstead Johnson, "Every week Florence got her contract in dollars and I got mine in pounds, and we was livin' off the pounds. I had a vault in London and put all the dollars in the vault."

Frugal though they were in their personal lifestyle, Florence did have one extravagance that didn't become public knowledge for a long time because she tried to keep it a secret. She had always been generous in performing for and donating to charities. In London in early 1927, she took this habit a step further. In Lew Leslie's words, she had taken to "going slumming." Leslie was referring to her practice, after the theater closed, of borrowing his car and chauffeur several nights a week or sometimes using a taxi.

Florence would say to Kid, "Let's bring a little happiness into the City of Despair," and off they would go on her personal mission from God.[7] She would direct the driver to go first to the East End, and along the way they would visit several hospitals, including the Metropolitan Hospital in the Dalston-Hackney area. At each stop the driver delivered gifts of flowers, fruit, or other delicacies, without the receptionists ever knowing the identity of the mysterious benefactor. This was Florence's way of usefully recycling the many tokens of appreciation that delighted theater patrons showered on her, as when Lord Lonsdale had once given every female member of the cast a bouquet of flowers and every male member a box of cigars.

When the hospital round was finished, Florence would direct the driver to head toward the Embankment on the river Thames. There London's down-and-outs, the debris of society, were to be found nightly, sleeping rough and relying on charitable agencies for food. En route, the car would stop at seedy roadside coffee stalls, and the driver would be directed to give money to any especially needy-looking patrons. At the Embankment, figures huddled on benches, trying to sleep through the wintry London weather, would be tapped on the shoulder and given money for a night's food and lodging.

Florence followed this routine anonymously for many months before her identity was finally revealed. On one occasion she invited a journalist she knew well and trusted, Reginald Simpson of the *Sunday Chronicle*, to go with her on her rounds—on the condition he didn't write about it. "I don't want you to publish anything," she said. "I don't like to make capital out of good work." His account, published after her death, described more or less the sequence above, except that she was traveling in a taxi and distributed the money herself. "Every now and then," he wrote, "she would stop the taxi and bring happiness to some derelict. I calculated that she must have given away nearly fifty pounds in this way." Another account reported, "Close to the last bench, almost under the shadow of Big Ben, Miss Mills saw the slim bent form of a young woman holding a child in her arms. To this girl the actress gave all that was left in her purse."[8]

Sometime in March the story of Florence's charitable actions leaked out in the theatrical columns, exciting some comments. *Encore* joked about what she might have said "when the homeless couple on the Embankment turned out to be a courting couple." When famous actor-director Sir Gerald Du Maurier publicly lambasted the theatrical profession for being stingy in its attitude toward charities, Florence was quoted as a shining refutation of his criticism.[9]

We can only guess at Florence's motives for these extraordinarily selfless activities. Not only was she giving away hard-earned money; she was giving her own time and personal effort after draining performances. Did she feel a need to give something back to the masses that had supported her? Did she have some intimations of her own mortality? Another possibility is that she felt some guilt at the amount of money she was earning. She knew the dollars were stacking up in the bank vault that Kid had rented. By the time they finally left England, they were able to cable home $35,000.

Kid described what happened when they went to the bank to do so. "Florence wasn't flashy. You never would think we had two dollars to rub together. Banker said, 'You know you can't cable under £500.' I said 'Well, that's all right.' . . . I went down to the vault and got the money. I had a little bag, little satchel and Florence was with me. My God, they was pressin' buttons round there and ordering, 'Bring in some tea, this is Florence Mills.'"[10]

It may also be that she intended to signify by her evenhanded charity toward those of a different background that her own people were not inevitably destined for a supplicant role. In any case, the immediate result of her charitable activities' becoming public was that she received a flood of letters detailing pathetic stories of hardship and suffering, including one from the aged widow of a famous comedian.

While Florence's midnight charitable ventures were stirring interest in England, she had not forgotten the folks back home. Early in February an announcement appeared in the *Amsterdam News*, signed by Florence Mills, Ivan Harold Browning of the Four Harmony Kings, and John Payne, announcing two scholarships in London for African American female singers, a soprano and a contralto, to study with Louis Drysdale, a West Indian voice teacher. The two girls were to live with Professor Drysdale and his wife at a very reasonable charge for full room and board. At the end of their training, a public recital would be arranged in London.[11]

Her people back home had not forgotten Florence either. It was nearly a year since they had seen her in America, but they followed her every move closely. In February and March, Theophilus Lewis, Lew Leslie's stern critic, wrote a comprehensive assessment of black theater that extended over three issues of the *Pittsburgh Courier*. He declared that, even including Bert Williams and Charles Gilpin, Florence Mills was "the greatest figure in the history of the Negro theater." Singling out her song and dance skit "Jungle Nights in Harlem" as epitomizing her genius, he wrote:

It is not just a song and dance when Miss Mills interprets it, but an exquisite little tapestry of humor and fantasy with a delicate gold thread of satire flashing through it; entertainment for a god. Here we have the key to her magic control of an audience; her ability to express the vulgar and commonplace in terms of delicacy and beauty. She senses some universal latent aspiration or some unfathomable bit of irony lying inarticulate in a million minds and with a single gesture or look, sets it free to soar heavenward. Then she instantly passes on to refine and embody some kindred emotion. The responsiveness of the audience to her slightest move or glance is really its reaction to the electric release of its own emotions. To us, who have been groping after happiness blindly, she reveals a momentary glimpse of its radiance. She is the bluebird of the Negro theater. Let us hope she is also its phoenix.[12]

While Lewis was singing her praises at home, Florence was once again giving expression to her views on race. Interviewing her for his regular celebrity portrait column in the magazine *Sketch*, popular British author and journalist Beverley Nichols asked if she had read Carl Van Vechten's recently published novel, *Nigger Heaven*. Van Vechten was a wealthy patron of the arts in New York with a keen interest in and admiration of black culture and music. He was a major figure of the Harlem Renaissance. Literary soirees held by him and his Russian-born wife, Fania Marinoff, brought promising black artists and writers together with the cultural elite of America. His novel was intended as a realistic, although sympathetic, portrayal of life in Harlem. The use of the offensive N-word in the title alienated many African Americans who had never read the book.

Florence, an avid reader, had of course read the book. In fact she had refused a large payment from a leading daily paper to review it.[13] She was one of a handful of notable Harlemites who featured in the novel under their real names. Florence would have recognized many of the fictional characters as based on people she knew personally. Lasca Sartoris was based on Nora Holt Ray, who had attended Kid Thompson's birthday party in Paris, and Randolph Pettijohn was based on Caspar Holstein, king of the Harlem numbers racket.[14] Florence told Beverley Nichols she did not like the book. "'They're so weak,' she said, "All the coloured people in that book crumple up when they are put to the test. They've no stamina—nothing. We're not like that," she said.

While many of Van Vechten's characters were less than admirable, Florence obviously had mainly in mind the self-pitying male protagonist Byron Kasson, whose weakness led to his destruction at the hands of the ruthless Lasca Sartoris. Nichols went on to describe Florence's fiery dismissal of the book:

Her dark eyes kindled, opened wide, showed a slumbering fire. "Do you know what all this does for us?"

"All what?"

"The—the attitude of the people who aren't coloured?"

I shook my head.

"It makes us fight—fight all the harder—till we come out on top. That's what it does."

"But I thought things were so much better, so much easier for all of you?"

"For some of us—yes. But down South . . . it's still terrible.—There isn't slavery any more—not real slavery—but there's something very like it."

She shut her eyes quickly. A line of black lashes over a delicate, coffee skin. Then she looked up again with that appealing smile of hers, and again, even through the smile I had a sense of "melancholy not quite forgotten."

"But it's all going to be better," she said. "It's all going to be much better. When you think of how things were sixty, forty—why, even twenty years ago, you can see the difference at once. It isn't only that we've got societies for our people down in the South. It isn't only that we can show them that we can make money as well as anybody else, that we're creative, that we're capable of doing great things in art . . . the whole spirit's altering."

And that was all she said about it, and all she said about herself. There was no bitterness, nor resentment, only pluck and a smile in the face of tremendous odds.[15]

Florence's interview with Beverley Nichols came just after she and Kid had spent a delightful weekend at the country home in Plymouth of John Payne's friend Lady Cook. Aida Ward, Edith Wilson, and C. C. Rosemond made up the rest of the party, which was Aida's farewell since she had left the show.[16] Florence had lived most of her life in large cities, seeing the countryside only on rail journeys. She told Nichols that her visit to the English countryside was a new experience for her. Away from the jangle and hubbub of Piccadilly Circus, she experienced a sense of peace she described in words of wonder.

> When it was night we went for a walk. There was a full moon—oh, the brightest moon you've ever seen. Brighter than that lamp outside. [Indicating a street lamp glimmering through the curtains.] Everything was very limpid and very still. I could feel the quietness of it all entering right into me. And I had an extraordinary instinct that I'd been there before—long ago—that it had all happened 'way back, in the distance. At night I couldn't sleep. I had to keep jumping out of bed and looking out on to the country and listening—to nothing—and looking up at the moon.[17]

Nichols was touched by her reaction and "glad to think that it was the quiet, kindly English countryside on which those intelligent eyes first rested."

There were not many such moments of tranquility for Florence. Along with the publicity for her charitable deeds and her public expression of her opinions on race, her normal schedule, both social and professional, still proceeded. At the end of January, she appeared at the London Hippodrome as part of a large cast in a concert supporting a group of Jewish charities. Her performance caused a minor sensation in Jewish circles. After she had sung several songs to enthusiastic encores, a member of the audience cried out for a song in Hebrew or Yiddish. A witness described what followed:

> The little dark-skinned lady on the stage paused for a moment, and in that moment her whole personality seemed to change. Then she sang us a lament, a monody of sorrow and suffering, a threnody of tears called "Eli, Eli." There were those present who did not follow the message of the chant in words and yet its meaning stirred the hearts of all and as we sang with her I saw many of the older people with tears streaming down their faces. Verily, here was a mystery. How had this little dark-skinned genius, Florence Mills, possessed herself of the secret key of song which could open the inner heart of Israel."[18]

The key to the mystery was, of course, Florence's Jewish manager Lew Leslie. His former wife, Belle Baker, had successfully featured the traditional hymn in vaudeville. He had taught it to Florence, who was fascinated by it, saying, "I am not a [Jew] but I feel the pain and the suffering and the sustaining hope as I sing it. How could I help feeling it? Such a theme has an appeal as wide as humanity." This was a reflection of the strong affinity Florence felt for the Jewish race, seeing them as kindred to her own people in their displaced status. Reminded on one occasion that much of her music was written by Jews, she replied, "I always say that the Negroes and the Jews are, in art, brother peoples. They are two of the three most ancient races in the world and they've retained their national characteristics through thousands of years. Both have a fund of natural simplicity and love of art to draw on."[19]

Florence was back at the London Hippodrome for a charity concert on Sunday, February 27, supported by the Plantation Orchestra. Also on the bill was England's favorite, the great Gracie Fields, known as "Our Gracie," who, similarly to Florence, had worked her way from poverty in the cotton mills of Lancashire to fame singing sentimental and comic ballads like "Sally [Pride of our alley]" and "The Biggest Aspidistra in the World." Also on the bill was G. H. Elliott, an American-born blackface performer known as the "Chocolate Coloured Coon." Whether he performed in blackface that time is unknown. The *Black Birds*, in their second edition, continued to be the social craze of London. A fancy dress ball held early in the year and attended by large numbers of the aristocracy had Lady Ashley and Mrs. Carter Campbell as two red devils from the Hades scene.[20]

Despite exasperation with his friends' fascination with black people, Evelyn Waugh noted in his diary in February, "We went later to the Blackbirds and called on Florence Mills and other niggers and negresses [*sic*] in their dressing-rooms." He intensely disliked what he saw as an obsession with people he viewed as his social inferiors. However, he lacked the confidence to challenge his friends' liberal views, except in the privacy of his diary. The entry recording his attendance at *Black Birds* was followed by a lengthy tirade over society's tolerance of Leslie "Hutch" Hutchinson's affair with an aristocrat's teenage daughter.[21] Yet Waugh felt impelled to return to see the show, as though fascinated by these strange people and Florence in particular. Many years later he would include Florence Mills and the Black Birds as minor characters in his masterpiece, *Brideshead Revisited*.[22]

The acerbic comments scattered through Waugh's diaries reflected the wider obsession with Florence and the craze for *Blackbirds* parties. It was impossible for someone like Waugh to ignore their prominence. Oliver Messel, a talented theatrical designer, gave one such party. Theatrical celebrities who attended and helped to make up an impromptu, nonstop cabaret included Beatrice Lillie and Alice De Lysia.[23] Messel's friend Derek Patmore described it:

The guests all came in oriental costume, some of them extremely beautiful, and Messel had decorated his large studio with white painted masks, Negroid sculptures, and lovely coloured draperies. As Oliver's parents were extremely wealthy, his parties were always lavish. Tall, handsome Negro dancers, dressed in white satin, danced with fair English girls—there was no colour prejudice in our world—and Florence Mills, with her brittle, birdlike grace, showed us how to dance the Charleston.

One of the guests was Robert Byron, famous later as an art critic, who turned up elaborately disguised as Queen Victoria.[24]

Waugh's dyspeptic view of the same party was much less rosy. "It was a crowded party with all the Blackbirds and all the Oxford Brian Howard set and [uninvited] stray and squalid stragglers. Cecil Roberts became insensible with drink, and curled in overcoat, vomited and pissed intermittently."[25] Oliver Messel himself commented, "[Parties of this kind] were organised with little money by the young generation themselves. It was the crazy resourcefulness of ideas, the oddness or incongruity of the setting which was aimed for."[26] Clearly the black performers were an exotic element adding a touch of spice, but as Anthony Blanche, Waugh's aesthete character in *Brideshead Revisited*, said, "They are not animals in a *zoo*, Mulcaster, to be *goggled* at. They are *artists*, my dear, very great artists, to be *revered*."[27] Waugh based the character of Anthony Blanche on the real-life figures of Brian Howard and Harold Acton, leaders of the Oxford set that inspired most of the more outrageous ventures of the Bright Young People (BYP). Both were fervent admirers of Florence.

While the attention was flattering and enjoyable for the black artists, there was a serious potential downside. Douglas Goldring, author of *The Nineteen Twenties*, attended many of these parties. He wrote, "the coloured artists [behaved] much better than their hosts." The problem was the prevalence of wealthy white female Don Juans intent on starting erotic liaisons with the male cast members. Goldring commented:

> The casts of these revues were made of talented and hard working Negro actors and actresses, most of whom were happily married and contented. I doubt very much if any of them had any particular desire to be taken up by London's Bright Young People. When, however, they found themselves invited after the show to what appeared to be the homes of London socialites they naturally accepted. . . . The Negro craze infected several women of what Victorians would call the "highest ranks of society," and some unpleasant scandals, due to the natural anger and jealousy of the wives, were only narrowly averted.[28]

Delilah Jackson recalled that performers who lived through the period had a name for these white society women who threw themselves at black men—"torpedoes"—a name reminiscent of the "grenades" familiar to Florence and Bricktop in their Panama Café days.[29] Such activities threatened a revival of the antagonism to black performers that had affected Will Garland's troupe a few years earlier. Sometime in February, Chick Horsey of the Three Eddies stabbed Johnny Hudgins for remonstrating with him over his relationship with a white woman. Fortunately the injuries were not serious. C. B. Cochran recalled, "We had a good deal of difficulty hushing up that little escapade, which had it been made public at the time, and in view of the antagonism which some people had towards coloured performers, would probably have put paid to one of my big shows."[30] News of the incident leaked across the Atlantic, and reports appeared in *Variety* and several black newspapers. Reports that Chick Horsey would be deported proved false, and he remained one of the Three Eddies in the show afterwards.

Florence herself did not escape attention as a result of some of these activities. Her prominence in London society and her attendance at fashionable occasions led once again to the inevitable rumors of affairs with prominent figures. The two unmarried princes were the most obvious targets. There has never, then or since, been any substantiation offered for such reports.[31] Elisabeth Welch put it in perspective when she told Stephen Bourne, "No, not at all. Florence wouldn't have an affair with anyone but Ulysses." The *Daily Sketch* was equally forthright; "Florence Mills is devoted to her coal black husband, Thompson, the dancer, notwithstanding all the many and mythical tales to the contrary."[32] Nevertheless, the rumors continued to circulate, and even some African Americans welcomed the idea that one of their own had ensnared royalty. One such was the popular spirituals singer and colorful personality Taylor Gordon. In his autobiography *Born to Be*, describing his arrival in London he wrote, "After getting our room and moving into it, I set out to find the charming actress, Florence Mills. She was playing at the Strand Theatre with her Blackbirds company at the time. The little lady was in her dressing-room. She had just returned from an affair with royalty."[33] With no evidence offered, Gordon was obviously living up to Harlem Renaissance expert David Levering Lewis's description of him as "always ready with a song or an outrageous remark about his own race."[34]

C. B. Cochran knew just how close the union was between Florence and Kid. "Kid was a simple fellow, and his wife, because of her reading, self-education, and a truly cosmopolitan grasp of modern intellectual and artistic movements, could make rings round him in the matter of culture. But their marriage was a great success, and the big fellow's adoration and admiration of his vivid wife were something worth seeing."[35] Florence's one extravagance in life was to give Kid expensive presents. On one occasion she gave him a $185 Tiffany watch that, to his regret, was stolen years later.[36]

Florence attended a different sort of party in early March, given by Turner Layton, an African American pianist and songwriter ("After You've Gone," "Way Down Yonder in New Orleans," "Dear Old Southland"). His collaboration in the partnership of Layton and Johnstone had made him a popular and respected figure on the English social scene. The party was at the studio of a rising young painter, Alexander Stuart-Hill, a member of the Royal Society of Portrait Painters. Layton gave the party to celebrate Stuart-Hill's completion of an oil painting of him, which had been accepted for display at the Royal Academy in April. The ubiquitous Evelyn Waugh was there to record the event in his diary, Sacheverell Sitwell having brought him. He described it as "all very refined—hot lobster, champagne cup and music." Florence, Johnny Hudgins, Alice Delysia, and, of course, Layton and Johnstone provided the music.[37] In the euphoria of the moment, Stuart-Hill suggested to Florence that he would also like to do a full portrait of her in oils, a proposal it pleased her to accept.

By April 1927, Black Birds had reached its 250th performance at the London Pavilion. Florence had performed in every one of them, never using an understudy, nor had she ever done so in her entire career. She never even had a formally appointed understudy. When a reporter in Philadelphia asked one of the male dancers who Florence's stand-in would be in case of accident, the reply was, "There would be a mob scene. Any girl here could do her stuff—maybe not so good, but she could do it." Aida Ward was probably the closest to an understudy that Florence ever had because her classically trained singing style enabled her to match Florence's wide voice range.

The content of the show had not changed much since the original second edition. A comedy team, Taylor and Williams, had been added to the first part. The rest of the cast was more or less unchanged except that Alma Smith, formerly in Dixie to Broadway, had joined. Author Rusty Frank describes her as "One of the best female tap dancers. Strong dancer with the power of a male dancer."[38] She took over the Hawaiian number, as well as helping out in others. One more significant change was that Will Vodery resumed his old role as leader of the Plantation Orchestra, having arrived on the Berengaria on March 18. Alma Smith's presence was intended to take some pressure off Florence. Even though her fatigued state had been obvious to many in the cast before the Christmas break, the new version still featured Florence as heavily as ever.

On top of Florence's other problems, she had now been performing through the depth of the English winter. Back in December, Hyacinth Curtis had noted the weather was beginning to be "very dreary." The foggy, dismal English cold was of a more bone-chilling variety than Florence had known back home, and it affected her severely. "Cold makes me miserable," she told the *Jewish Graphic*'s journalist. For someone performing intense physical activity, like her acrobatic dancing style, there was also the ever-present danger of injuring insufficiently warmed-up muscles. To another reporter she said, "Although I love your England, your climate does not love me. The dampness of the atmosphere affects my muscles and makes me feel stiff." To help her cope with the cold and damp, Lew Leslie had sunray lamps installed in her dressing room.[39]

The BYP's love affair with Florence and the *Black Birds* reached its peak around this time. The entire *Black Birds* troupe was invited to be the guests of the group of Oxford undergraduates who formed the backbone of the BYP. These included the Acton Brothers, Harold and William (Willie); Mark Ogilvie-Grant; and Robert Byron, who had appeared at Oliver Messel's party as Queen Victoria. Florence and her team traveled to Oxford on Sunday morning. After a quick lunch they toured the major colleges of the venerable university, including Christ Church, Magdalen, and Trinity colleges. An elaborate tea party given by Mark Ogilvie-Grant followed, and in the evening Willie Acton laid on a party in their honor. A large crowd of present and former Oxford notables attended. Many of them were people who would become famous as public figures in later years. After dinner there was dancing, and "many of the charming dusky guests, including Florence Mills, Edith Wilson and Alma Smith sang delightfully."[40] The experience appealed enough to some of the troupe that two, May Fortune and Ruth Johnson, were back in Oxford at another of Willie Acton's parties the following weekend.

Black Birds was still phenomenally successful at the Pavilion. According to *Variety* it had never taken less than $12,500 a week and had set house records for several nights. Nevertheless, after an eight-month run, as the winter drew to a close and with the summer season approaching, Cochran felt a need to find something new for his large theater. He announced that, after a short break, *Black Birds* would move to the Strand Theatre for a season before going on a provincial tour. It replaced Somerset Maugham's *The Constant Wife* at the Strand and was itself replaced at the Pavilion by Rodgers and Hart's *One Dam Thing after Another*, whose big hit was Jesse Matthews's performance of "My Heart Stood Still."

The plan for the switchover from the Pavilion was that the show would go to the Golders Green Hippodrome for a week, then everyone would take a break before resuming at the Strand Theatre on May 30. The last performance at the Pavilion was an emotional occasion for many. One of those present in the audience was Florence's adoring fan, composer Constant Lambert. It was also Johnny Hudgins's last performance with the show. His success in England had been so phenomenal that the *Baltimore Afro-American* reported Johnny Hudgins dolls on sale in England. He now planned a solo career on the continent, joining a large white revue at Les Ambassadeurs in Paris as the only black artist. The opening at the Strand was set for Monday, May 30. The Golders Green engagement finished on Saturday, May 21. The break, although a mere eight days, was more than welcome for Florence. The grueling pace of performing every night, plus matinees, charity performances, and special engagements, such as judging a costume parade at Fulham, was once again telling on her fragile health. However, her hopes for a peaceful few days' break were only partly realized.

At 10:22 p.m. Paris time on May 21, even as Florence and the *Black Birds* were giving their final performance at Golders Green, a small airplane circled the Eiffel Tower and touched down on the tarmac at Le Bourget airport, close to the city. From the plane, which had the words "Spirit of St. Louis" emblazoned on it, stepped Captain Charles A. Lindbergh. He had just completed the first nonstop transatlantic solo flight, between New York and Paris, an event that in its day had an impact comparable to the 1969 moon landing. The reaction to Lindbergh's achievement was extraordinary. Huge crowds thronged the streets of Paris to catch a glimpse of the world's newest hero. There was a series of civic receptions, parades, and functions in Paris in his honor. One of the most elaborate, a Grand Gala Reception by the Aero Club of France at the Théatre des Champs-Elysées, came on the evening of May 27. Proceeds from the event were to go to a charity for the families of French aviators who had lost their lives in pioneering exploits. Among the star-studded cast of entertainers were several current attractions from Les Ambassadeurs, including Irving Aaronson's Commanders and singer Helen Morgan, renowned French stage star Cecile Sorel, and American operatic diva Mary Garden. Also among them was the specially invited Florence Mills. She had traveled to Paris by sea on the Folkestone-Boulogne route for the occasion.[41]

That the French specially imported Florence for this reception is remarkable, given that Josephine Baker was already in Paris. Josephine had even interrupted her show at the Folies Bergère to announce Lindbergh's landing.[42] It may be that the French thought Florence's more refined image better suited to the occasion. At any rate, they considered it appropriate both black and white Americans should honor Lindbergh. It was also a remarkable tribute to

Florence's reputation and standing in Paris. While the *New York Herald Tribune* covered Mary Garden's performance at the Gala Reception in detail, Florence's presence went unnoticed by the press at large.[43] However, her presence is proven by her name on the official program and by her personal copy of the signed program, which became one of her treasured possessions and can be seen today at the Schomburg Institute. Although the occasion had interrupted her period of relaxation, it had also been a source of pride and pleasure. In later years Lindbergh's great flight would be commemorated in a new social dance, the Lindy Hop. Florence's presence as a jazz dancer at Lindbergh's official reception can be said to make her, in a symbolic sense, the original Lindy Hopper.

Florence returned to England, by sea again, immediately after the ceremony, reentering at Folkestone on May 28. She then extended her visa until August 20.[44] Back in London, the third edition of Lew Leslie's *Black Birds* opened at the Strand on May 30. Some doubt had hovered over the opening as the work permits for members of the cast were due to expire, but the Home Office granted an extension just in time. By then Edith Wilson had decided to follow Johnny Hudgins's lead and go to Paris. Their replacements were the old team of Cora Green and Hamtree Harrington, so Florence was joined once again by her former Panama Trio associate.

The content was substantially the same as at the Pavilion, but Florence's "Silver Rose" and "Mandy" replaced "Dixie Dreams" and "Baby and Me." Cora Green sang the song closely associated with Edith Wilson, "He May Be Your Man but He Comes to See Me Once in a While." Perhaps one of the most significant features of the new content was that, despite the pressures on her health, Florence had one scene more than before. She had taken over the "Comedy Black Bottom" routine previously done by Edith Wilson. Noticeable also was the extent to which the role of the members of the Southern Trio, particularly Mabel Mercer and John Payne, had expanded from their minor part in the first edition.

The third edition of *Black Birds* opened to a capacity crowd at the Strand. Although it continued to be popular with Londoners, it was not scheduled for a long run at the new venue. Nevertheless, it was proving more successful than Lew Leslie's concurrent venture. Emboldened by the unprecedented success of *Black Birds*, he had conceived the idea of a white version, predictably called *White Birds*. Backed by a wealthy sponsor and never one to think small, he looked for some big-name stars. The idea did not appeal to Noel Coward, but Maurice Chevalier accepted, with his soon-to-be wife, Yvonne Vallee. Anton Dolin, Ninette de Valois, and the duo who had recently recorded "I'm a Little Blackbird," Gwen Farrar and Billy Mayerl, joined them. One of the scenes was a parody of *Black Birds*, including three females in blackface as the Three Eddies. Mayerl said, "Our part in the show ended when the producer tried to separate Gwen and me; I had to appear half-dressed and Gwen, in an individual role, in brown cotton tights, had to give an imitation of Florence Mills. We both objected strongly."[45]

White Birds proved a total disaster for all concerned. Although praising Chevalier highly and Anton Dolin some, the critics damned it with phrases like "most idiotic," "nonsensical," "most witless efforts ever seen on the West End stage," and "irremediably bad." The backer, Everard Gates, rumored to have spent $250,000 on the show, wanted to sack Leslie, but several of the stars were under contract to him, so Gates had no choice but to buy him out. "Leslie will accept any lump sum that resembles money," *Variety* concluded. The show soon folded.[46] Relics of *White Birds* include a song written by Noel Coward, "What's Going to Happen to the Tots," and a Scott Joplin parody, "The Rout Trot," by Sir Arthur Bliss, occasionally heard in classical circles.

Although the strain of continuous performance was starting to tell heavily on Florence, the closing months in London had some pleasant social moments, among them weekend visits to Lady Cook's London home, Doughty House. This magnificent building had ample grounds commanding magnificent views of the Thames Valley, immortalized on canvas by painters such as Reynolds and Turner. Besides their philanthropic activities, Baronet and Lady Cook were collectors and patrons of the arts, having El Grecos and other old masters in their collection.

Lady Cook also embraced Florence's campaign for racial justice enthusiastically. She actively promoted the NAACP and the cause of black entertainers confronting prejudice in England. Florence greatly appreciated that Lady Cook arranged meetings between her English friends and the colored artists in her home as a way of promoting understanding between whites and blacks. These occasions were very different from the parties staged by the BYP in that they focused on genuine mutual understanding rather than fascination with what was perceived as exotic.

Another sign of Florence's popularity in upper-class English society was the invitation to her "and friends" to attend the wedding and reception, on June 2, of Honor Chedworth, daughter of Lord and Lady Kylsant, and Mr. Gavin Henderson. Lord Kylsant was the chief executive of the Royal Mail Shipping Line and had become a lord early in the 1920s for his achievements in building up the company. Gavin Henderson later inherited the title of second Lord Faringdon. The couple were members in good standing of the BYP. Romance novelist Barbara Cartland recalled that one of the notable stunts by the BYP was Gavin Henderson's setting fire to the Thames river at the famous Henley rowing regatta.[47] The marriage would not last long, being annulled in 1931. Gavin Henderson's socialist and pacifist sympathies led him later into an active career in labor politics and a key role in the British National Trust. Whether Florence and Kid attended the wedding or the reception is unknown. The lengthy list of guests published in the *Times* consisted mainly of titled nobility, and people with less than an "Honorable" attached to their name were unlikely to be noticed.

In June, Florence and Kid enjoyed a few days at the track, attending the famous Derby and Ascot race meetings. By then Florence was such a noted public figure that people would greet her in the street. Commenting on the friendliness of the English public toward her, Florence said, "At Ascot last week I walked through the paddock, just like the white people and nobody objected. At the Derby two weeks before, I had most wonderful receptions wherever I went." Hannen Swaffer's take on the same events was that "she was nearly mobbed in the paddock at Ascot, and cheered at the Derby."[48]

Around this time Florence's sister Maude recorded four blues-flavored songs with Fats Waller as her accompanist. Late in June, the fruits of Florence's sittings for the artist Alexander Stuart-Hill were unveiled to an appreciative public at the *Daily Express* Exhibition of Young Artists and attracted much popular notice. Under the title "The Queen of the Black Birds," it was featured as a full-page spread in *Sketch* magazine.[49] It is the only known oil painting of Florence done in her lifetime. She was delighted with the picture and flattered by the attention it gained at the gallery. Stuart-Hill presented her with an autographed copy, which she cherished. Characteristically, she was reluctant to go and see the original at the exhibition in case it might be construed as vanity. A special viewing was arranged for her. "She waited until the galleries were closed and everyone out, to tiptoe in, like a little kitten, and gaze at the portrait."[50]

A remarkable event occurred in the last few days before *Black Birds* closed in London. Florence gave an interview to her former critic, racist agitator Hannen Swaffer. There had been signs that Swaffer was mellowing and retreating from his earlier racist views. His long-standing rift with Cochran, dating back to Swaffer's abrupt ejection from *Dover Street to Dixie*, was resolved amicably. Morris Gest, the producer of *Chauve Souris*, whose "Wooden Soldiers" number Florence so successfully parodied in *Black Birds*, had persuaded them to reconcile when he happened to notice them both in the same restaurant.

In what was a virtual recantation of his earlier views, the cynical journalist wrote in almost adulatory terms about Florence, even allowing her to use his column as a pulpit for her views on the problems of race. He wrote, "For nine months now Florence Mills has been almost London's brightest star. If she were white she would be hailed as probably the greatest revue artist of her generation. . . . It must be a terrible thing to be a great artist and yet to bear always upon your skin the color of a subject race."[51]

The rest of the article was mainly a recital of Florence's views on the problems of race prejudice and the possibility of eliminating it. Commenting on the illogicality of prejudice, she pointed out, "In the South, colored mammies bring white babies up and actually feed them at their own breasts. Yet, when the same mammy has her own little black baby, the mother of the white baby does not allow her youngster to play with the Negro child. If a white person in a theatre is put next to a Negro, the white person objects. Yet the same white person will eat food cooked by a colored person and be waited on by another Negro."

There is no more dramatic evidence of the force of Florence Mills's personality than the remarkable role reversal it caused in Hannen Swaffer. That it was her doing there can be little doubt. More than twenty years later, he wrote, "It was Florence Mills, the grand-daughter of a slave, who more than anyone, won for [black performers] an equal status in this country," and, "She wasn't only a performer of world repute but an idealist and a valiant champion of liberty."[52] Swaffer's later actions and writings confirmed his genuine change of viewpoint, a remarkable demonstration that even the most bigoted racist can be won over by truth and sincerity.[53]

The run at the Strand ended on June 25, replaced by a troupe of Italian marionettes. *Black Birds'* next planned move was a provincial tour, but it was obvious Florence was becoming deeply weary of it all. Her health was beginning to worry her seriously. She was already thinking of returning to America and planning her next career step. She had responded to private overtures from Florenz Ziegfeld's agent at the Palace Theatre confirming that she would be available for the coming season. He had replied, "I have arranged with Mr. Ziegfeld for a show for you. I would appreciate [it] if you would keep this confidential as I would not like anyone to know about it until I speak to you."[54] It had been only four years since Florence had turned down Ziegfeld's earlier offer. Her interest now may have been a sign that she was weary of carrying a show almost entirely on her own name and talent. She had also more than fulfilled her original plan to create work for her fellow black artists in shows built round her. Those shows had launched both Johnny Hudgins and Edith Wilson on independent careers in Europe.

There were other hints of future plans. Leonard Harper was seeking to present her in a revue at Connie's Inn in Harlem. Reports in the *Baltimore*

Afro-American claimed that Paul Robeson had announced his intention to quit the stage in favor of films. His next venture was rumored to be a Cecil B. DeMille movie of DuBose Heyward's novel *Porgy*, with Florence Mills as his costar. One of these reports stated that Florence had severed connections with Lew Leslie, but the other said she had denied this. The fact that the Ziegfeld organization addressed its correspondence to "Miss Florence Mills, c/o C. B. Cochran" may support the idea of a split with Leslie.[55]

Florence's immediate problem was to honor her present obligations. She knew her health was running down, but the provincial tour was scheduled to run indefinitely. When Bricktop urged her to take a break for her health's sake, she had replied, "But, Brick, I can't put all these people out of work." By now she was waking up at night with severe stomach pains. Kid Thompson related how on one occasion she woke up in pain and suggested food might relieve it. "I'll get you something," he said. When she replied, "But it's the middle of the night," he said, "Don't worry, I'll find something."[56]

Florence was still performing as brilliantly as ever, but her own words told a story of pain and stress. "I love my work but my nerves have gone to pieces. I feel quite all right on the stage, but the minute I come off, I simply collapse."[57] It was now apparent her problems were more than just exhaustion and the cold English weather. She went for a full medical examination before the show was due to leave London. The somber advice was worse than she and Kid Thompson had feared. The pains she was experiencing were caused by a chronic inflammation that was a symptom of a more serious underlying cause, pelvic tuberculosis. Though pelvic tuberculosis is rare in the Western world today, it was common in the early part of the twentieth century, before the arrival of modern drugs, and is still a serious problem in many less developed countries today. It can be more or less dormant for ten to twenty years. When it finally shows, the symptoms typically include painful inflammation of the abdominal region.[58] The medical advice was that Florence needed an operation to deal with the symptoms and a cessation of work to give her a chance to recover from the illness.

Although Florence had known for some time that something was seriously wrong, the news was devastating. She and Kid agreed that she had to take a break and an operation was needed, but she preferred to wait till she was home and close to her family. They decided a restful holiday in the German spa town of Baden-Baden would help to build her strength for any future operation. First, however, she would see out the next few engagements of the show. In practice, this meant a grueling schedule of hops around the provincial centers of Glasgow (two weeks at the Alhambra), Manchester (two weeks at the

Palace), and Liverpool (two weeks at the Empire). The show gained high praise in all of these centers, and despite her ill health, Florence displayed the true trouper's dedication to the old rule that "the show must go on." Her performance was universally hailed as magnificent:

- *Glasgow Evening Times*: [I have] to pay tribute to the remarkable singing talents of Florence Mills. I hesitate to name her a genius, yet could any but a genius of some sort have given material such as hers a semblance of rightness and sincerity?
- *Manchester Guardian*: The great feature of the whole production is the dancing and Miss Florence Mills and the other coloured performers give us a merry and brilliant display in varied forms of the art. Miss Mills has a charming voice and the sweetness and evenness of its upper notes are very telling in her solos.
- *Liverpool Evening Express*: Florence Mills dominates the pot-pourri of song, dance, comedy and sketch, and to an impish gaiety she adds the attractions of a remarkably flexible and tuneful voice and nimbleness in the dance.[59]

The admiring fans were not to know of the pain and suffering masked by Florence's sparkling performances. The Liverpool engagement was the real end of the line for her in *Black Birds*. To mark her departure from the cast, she and Kid gave a farewell party for the entire troupe on the stage of the Empire Theatre. Mabel Mercer took over Florence's role in the show. One reviewer suggested that *Black Birds* without Florence was like "Hamlet without the Princess of Dark Men."[60] Florence accompanied the troupe to Bradford, Yorkshire, for their next engagement. The local *Bradford Observer* published her farewell message to the English public, again an impassioned plea for justice and fair play for her race. Later the NAACP made it the subject of a press release. She had said:

To return to my heart's one real and great ache, does personal popularity, enthusiasm and applause count for anything? I had hoped—and, in fact, I go on hoping, that for every friend I have made in this country, the colored people have also gained a friend. Britain is a Christian country. Surely Christianity knows no color.

Because the Great Creator made some of us different colors—be it black, brown or yellow—is it in the power of anyone honestly and sincerely Christian at heart to look down upon us as something inferior? Black sheep are certainly not to be found among people of one color only.

I now return to America, still hoping that my efforts have not been quite in vain. I shall return again, and may those friends I—and, I hope, my people—have gained not merely remain loyal and true but multiply many, many times.[61]

Florence and Kid returned to London, staying at the home of veteran black entertainer Belle Davis.[62] This ended Florence's magnificent sojourn in England as she and Kid prepared to make their way to the European continent, hoping to build up her health in readiness for an operation. They both knew she was facing the biggest challenge of her life, but first they would enjoy some well-earned relaxation.

Notes

1. The description of the show is based on copies of the Magazine Programme in the Bill Egan collection.
2. "Florence Mills Success," undated, unidentified clipping, TC FLP.
3. Hubert Griffith, *London Evening Standard*, quoted in AMST, Feb. 9, 1927.
4. *Tatler*, Jan. 19, 1927, 94; *London Daily Sketch*, quoted in AMST, Feb. 9, 1927; *Sphere*, Feb. 19, 1927, 312.
5. "Fashions from Stage & Stalls," *Illustrated Sporting and Dramatic News*, Jan. 22, 1927.
6. Letter in SCRAP, HAJC.
7. PhTr, Dec. 8, 1927.
8. "Stage Seers: True Charity," *Sunday Chronicle*, Nov. 6, 1927; undated, unidentified clipping in HAJC.
9. Undated, unidentified clipping in HAJC.
10. Notes from Kid Thompson interviews, HAJC.
11. AMST, Feb. 9, 1927. I have not been able to establish what came of the proposed scholarships.
12. Theophilus Lewis, "Magic Hours in the Theatre," PiCou, Feb. 26, Mar. 5, and Mar. 12, 1927.
13. Charles B. Cochran, *I Had Almost Forgotten* (London: Hutchinson, 1932), 222.
14. Carl Van Vechten, *Nigger Heaven* (New York: Grosset & Dunlap, 1926), 120, 162.
15. Beverley Nichols, *Sketch* magazine, Feb. 16, 1927, 304.
16. Ivan H. Browning, "Across the Pond," ChDef, Feb. 12, 1927.
17. Nichols, *Sketch*.
18. Miss Birdie Courtney, "Eli, Eli," *The Jewish Graphic*, Feb. 25, 1927, 19.
19. Undated, unidentified clipping, HAJC.
20. *Tatler*, Mar. 23, 1927, 509.

21. Michael Davie, ed., *The Diaries of Evelyn Waugh* (Middlesex: Penguin Books, 1979), 281–282.

22. Evelyn Waugh, *Brideshead Revisited* (Harmondsworth: Penguin Books, 1962), 231–236. Writing years later Waugh got the chronology wrong. He has *Blackbirds* in London during the Great Strike of 1926, when they were actually in Paris.

23. Charles Castle, *Oliver Messel: A Biography* (London: Thames and Hudson, 1968), 40.

24. Derek Patmore, *Private History* (London: Jonathan Cape, 1960), 65; *Cherwell*, Oxford, Mar. 12, 1927.

25. Davie, *The Diaries of Evelyn Waugh*, 282.

26. Castle, *Oliver Messel: A Biography*, 40.

27. Waugh, *Brideshead Revisited*, 233.

28. Douglas Goldring, *The Nineteen Twenties* (London: Nicholas and Watson, 1945), 227.

29. Delilah Jackson, private conversation with the author.

30. Cochran, *I Had Almost Forgotten*, 223.

31. Examples of such tales are in Alan Jenkins, *The Twenties* (London: Heinemann, 1974), 50; Sophia Watson, *Marina: The Story of a Princess* (London: Phoenix Giant, 1994), 88; Florence Mills article in *Notable Black American Women*, Jessie Carney Smith, ed. (Detroit: Gale Research, 1992), 755; and recent off-Broadway play *African Nights*, by Clint Jefferies.

32. *Daily Sketch*, May 28, 1926.

33. Taylor Gordon, *Born to Be* (Lincoln: University of Nebraska Press, 1995), 203. Gordon didn't arrive in London until June 1927. By then Florence was suffering exhaustion from overwork and would have been incapable of flirtatious liaisons even if she had the inclination.

34. David Levering Lewis, *When Harlem Was in Vogue* (New York: Oxford University Press, 1989), 212.

35. Cochran, *I Had Almost Forgotten*, 220.

36. HAJC, Kid Thompson interviews. The theft occurred in 1929 when Kid was in a show called *Woof Woof*.

37. Davie, *The Diaries of Evelyn Waugh*, 283.

38. Rusty Frank, *Tap! The Greatest Tap Dance Stars and Their Stories* (New York: Da Capo, 1990).

39. "Eli, Eli," *Jewish Graphic*, Feb. 25, 1927, 19, and *Liverpool Evening Express*, Aug. 3, 1927.

40. *The Cherwell*, May 14, 1937, 52.

41. Official program for "Gala Charles Lindbergh: Theatre de Champs-Elysées," May 27, 1927. HAJC. This is Florence's personal copy. Her passport [HAJC] notes her return via Folkestone.

42. Lynn Haney, *Naked at the Feast* (New York: Dodd Mead, 1981), 130.

43. "Lindbergh Off for Brussels at Noon Today," *New York Herald Tribune*, May 28, 1927, 1–3.

44. Florence Mills's passport, page 20. HAJC.

45. Peter Dickinson, *Marigold: The Music of Billy Mayerl* (Oxford: Oxford University Press, 1999), 96.

46. "Whitebirds Backer Wants to Air Lew Leslie," VAR, June 8, 1927. Reviews of *Whitebirds* in *London Daily Sketch* June 1, 1927; *London Times*, June 1, 1927; *Illustrated Sporting and Dramatic News*, June 11, 1927, 372.

47. Barbara Cartland, *We Danced All Night* (London: Arrow Books, 1973), 233.

48. Hannen Swaffer, "Two Women but One Public," *Bandwagon* 8:3 (Mar. 1949): 23.

49. "The Queen of the Black Birds," reproduction of Stuart-Hill painting, *Sketch* magazine, June 29, 1927, 639.

50. *New York Evening Graphic*, Nov. 7, 1927.

51. Hannen Swaffer interview in *London Daily Express*, ca. late June 1927, reprinted in AMST, Aug. 10, 1927.

52. Swaffer, *Bandwagon*, 21.

53. In 1933, when Swaffer wrote a lengthy adulatory article on Duke Ellington, he gave it the title "Soul of a Negro," the same title as the article Florence Mills had written six years earlier about the problems of race.

54. M. S. Bentham letter, June 14, 1927, HAJC.

55. "Robeson Quits Spoken Stage," and "Florence Mills and Paul Robeson May Play in 'Porgy,'" BAA, June 18, 1927.

56. Bricktop and Kid Thompson quotes related by Delilah Jackson in private conversation with the author.

57. "Bye Bye to a Blackbird," *Liverpool Evening Express*, Aug. 3, 1927.

58. Kid Thompson told Delilah Jackson and Helen Armstead Johnson that the doctors had diagnosed tuberculosis (TB) as Florence's underlying problem. TB was prevalent in Florence's world. Her father died of it, as did her sister Olivia many years later. For a description of pelvic TB, see Robert Jansen, *Overcoming Infertility* (New York: W. H. Freeman, 1997). The abdominal inflammation typically results from the TB's infecting the fallopian tubes.

59. Reviews from *Glasgow Evening Times*, July 5, 1927; *Manchester Guardian*, July 19, 1927; and *Liverpool Evening Express*, Aug. 2, 1927.

60. *Performer*, Sept. 28, 1927.

61. From *Bradford Observer*, reprinted in NAACP press release of Sept. 2, 1927 (Courtesy Gumby Scrapbooks, Columbia University, New York).

62. AMST, Aug. 10, 1927. Belle Davis and Florence probably met in Paris in 1926 because Davis spent time as a choreographer at the Casino de Paris in 1926–1927; See Rainer Lotz, *Black People: Entertainers of African Descent in Europe, and Germany* (Bonn: Birgit Lotz Verlag, 1997), 66, 87. Their paths probably crossed earlier also.

~

CHAPTER ELEVEN

Swing Low, Sweet Chariot

Even before *Black Birds* had finished, Florence had been telling friends like Ivan Harold Browning that she was going to a health resort for a rest cure. The departure on August 18 was necessary because her visa, extended on return from the Lindbergh gala, was due to expire on August 20. After crossing the English Channel, she and Kid traveled by rail and obtained visas to enter Germany at Karlsruhe on August 19. Their destination was the peaceful spa resort town, Baden-Baden, in the Black Forest region. The name means baths and comes from the magnificent spa baths dating back to Roman times and fueled by hot mineral springs . The town also boasts a luxurious casino and magnificent concert halls with historic links to Brahms and Liszt. It was a popular playground for the rich and famous in search of improved health. Today, having escaped the saturation bombing that destroyed most major German cities in World War II, it is still much as Florence and Kid found it in 1927.

Their arrival was noted in the gazette that recorded the names of new guests in all the major hotels, important news in a resort town. The list for the Holland Hotel for August 20–23 showed one "Thomson, Ullses [sic], artist, mit gattin [wife]."[1] Florence was once again Mrs. Thompson. The Holland Hotel, in Sophienpark, was right in the center of the town, beside the Leopoldplatz central square. It was close to the main thoroughfares and in easy walking distance of the major attractions and centers. With links going back to the early eighteenth century, it had been a first-class hotel from 1840 onward. By 1870 it had been converted to a palace "fit for dukes, princes and

Kaisers," with its own extensive grounds. While the town had even more exclusive hotels, the Holland Hotel is even today a fine and imposing installa-
tion. It has a reputation as one of Germany's finest seminar hotels.

Baden-Baden nestles in a relaxed setting, with the rolling Black Forest
hills visible nearby. It has a mild climate, and the forecast for September
1927 proclaimed a "fine and warm autumn month."[2] Visitors found plenty of
organized entertainment. Classical concerts were the most common fare during Florence's visit, with one lonely jazz band mentioned. Dances and mari-
onette plays took place in various public venues. There was also a performance on August 25 of Puccini's *Tosca* and on September 3, *Madame
Butterfly*. The energetic could enjoy "games of ability" and a visit to the international horse races. Besides all this, various "cures" and treatments were
on offer, reminding Kid Thompson of his early medicine show days.

Remote as Baden-Baden seemed from their homeland, Florence and Kid
could not entirely escape ripples spreading across the Atlantic. Just as they
were settling into their first few days of relaxation, the local paper carried a
banner headline "Sacco and Vanzetti Executed."[3] Sacco and Vanzetti, poor
Italian immigrants, a cobbler and a fishmonger, had links to the anarchist
cause in America. In 1921 they were convicted, in dubious circumstances, of
involvement in an armed holdup that resulted in two deaths. Their case became a major issue in liberal circles in America and around the world, and
their eventual execution in America in 1927 sent shock waves across Europe.
In 1977 the biased nature of their trial was at last formally recognized by
proclamation and their names cleared.[4] Their names crop up later in Florence and Kid's story. At the time, their fate was a chilling reminder of the
real world outside the cocoon of Baden-Baden.

Apart from the various organized events, one of the universally appreciated joys of Baden-Baden is to stroll in leisurely fashion along the Lichten-
taler Allee, one of the most beautiful tree-lined avenues in the world. It
winds through parkland alongside the bubbling Oos River. Here Florence
and Kid mingled with the visitors from the many hotels around. The guest
lists show these were mainly Germans with a generous sprinkling of other Eu-
ropeans and some Americans, probably all white. Even in cosmopolitan
Baden-Baden, the presence of a black couple would have aroused some interest in 1927.

Among those who may have cast a curious eye on the dark-skinned pair
were some guests of the luxurious Hotel Brenner, directly overlooking the
Oos River from its own private parkland. The list of arrivals there later in
Florence's stay included two names soon to be infamous in history, Joachim
von Ribbentrop and Ernst Rohm.[5] Ribbentrop would be Hitler's ambassador

to Britain during the prewar period and Germany's foreign minister throughout World War II, later hanged for war crimes. Rohm was one of Hitler's early associates, the leader of his Storm Troopers. Hitler had him murdered in the infamous 1934 Night of the Long Knives.[6] If they noticed the small black woman walking the avenues of Baden-Baden, it is doubtful they would have recognized her as the great Florence Mills although they would certainly have known her name. In 1932 Adolf Hitler, entertaining a young black American student from Heidelberg University, spoke knowledgeably about several African Americans, including Florence Mills.[7]

In 1927 the country was not yet the Nazi Germany von Ribbentrop and Rohm would help to create, and there were many congenial visitors happy to extend the hand of friendship to a respectable black couple. Kid Thompson recalled that during their time in Germany, he and Florence were entertained at the home of a baron. This gave them a chance to visit some of the beautiful vineyards in the surrounding countryside. Early in their stay at Baden-Baden, they also visited Basel, Switzerland, a mere ninety-minute train ride away. Letters to friends told that they were having a delightful time in Baden-Baden, resting and enjoying themselves. This included appreciating the delights of the ancient Roman baths. Their sojourn of almost three weeks in Baden-Baden finally finished on September 7. Their itinerary included Vienna and Berlin before Paris and home.[8]

Their purpose in going to Berlin was to visit Bricktop. She and Florence had always kept in regular contact. At the very time Florence was in Baden-Baden, Bricktop was also in Germany, on a venture to repeat her Paris success in Berlin. This was the era of the decadent, wide-open Berlin portrayed in the musical *Cabaret*. Bricktop thought it was a good time to launch a German version of her successful Paris nightclub. The idea was that she, in partnership with a local entrepreneur, would bring a black band to Berlin. However, some of the musicians let her down at the last minute, so the band she arrived with was not up to Berlin professional standards. Her new partners sued her for breach of contract and caused all her assets to be seized while she waited for a court hearing.

When Florence heard of Bricktop's plight, she instantly wired her some money and made plans to visit Berlin. Her own health came last when a close friend was in trouble. Traveling by rail Florence and Kid went first to Vienna, entering Austria via Salzburg. They spent a day or two sightseeing in Vienna, then made their way to Berlin through Czechoslovakia, coming back into Germany near Dresden. Their visit to Berlin was short, but Bricktop appreciated Florence's moral support in her time of trouble. Florence made light of her health problems, giving Bricktop no idea of how serious her condition was. With Florence's financial help, Bricktop eventually got back to Paris minus her jewelry.[9]

Having done a Samaritan deed for their friend, Kid and Florence headed to their next stop, Paris, by the Berlin–Paris express. They arrived in time for the celebrations of the extraordinary September 19 American Legion Convention. The American Legion is a powerful organization that looks after the interests of American service veterans. For the tenth anniversary of America's entry into the First World War and the arrival of the American Expeditionary Force on European soil, the Legion had come up with the radical idea of holding its annual convention in Paris. From late August onwards, an armada of ocean liners had carried thousands of ex-servicemen and in many cases their wives and families. They came from all over America to the city that symbolized European culture and decadence to small-town America. The huge organization had planned, down to the finest details, a program of commemorative activities and battlefield visits, culminating in a march through Paris on September 19. The French had initially responded enthusiastically to the potential tourist bonanza. They laid on massive logistical support with civic receptions by public officials and French veterans. They even declared a public holiday. However, Sacco and Vanzetti's execution on August 23 produced a revulsion that led to violent anti-American protests. There were widespread calls to cancel the celebrations, but to no avail.[10]

Kid Thompson, himself a veteran of war service in France, had ensured that he and Florence would be there for the big day. At the parade route, they found themselves an excellent spot in front of the grandstand. They shared it with Alberta Hunter and Nettie Compton, both veterans of Florence's time at the Panama Café. Memories flooded back of Chicago in the days of Jack Johnson and Tony Jackson. The gossip included Florence's news of Panama veteran Bricktop, still struggling with her legal problems in Berlin. Eagerly they watched the parade for veterans of the African American regiments. Alberta recalled, "The most thrilling thing in the whole world was a little brown-skinned fellow carrying the flag that led Kansas. He had the most beautiful smile and when the people saw him they cheered and threw up their hats."[11]

In the evening, they all went to a gala performance in Montmartre, presented in honor of the American Legion by the French minister of war. The master of ceremonies for the evening was the great French boxer Georges Carpentier. Of the twelve acts featured on the entertainment bill, three were African Americans and the rest mainly French. The African American acts were Johnny Hudgins (from the Moulin Rouge), Josephine Baker (from Folies Bergère), and Moiret and Fredi (from Club Alabam, New York). Fredi was Fredi Washington, Florence's old friend from *Shuffle Along* days. All three acts were close friends of Florence and Kid. Fredi was able to bring Florence up-to-date with the latest Harlem gossip.[12]

One more item they squeezed into their brief time back in Paris was a visit to the president of Liberia, also there on a visit. Before her departure from England, Florence was given a letter of introduction to President C. D. B. King from the Liberian Consulate in Liverpool. The president had seen Florence perform in *Shuffle Along* in 1921, when he was part of a delegation seeking to negotiate a foreign loan for Liberia. Kid Thompson told Delilah Jackson that at their meeting the president invited Florence to visit his country at some time. As the resettled African home of many freed American slaves, Liberia has always had special significance for African Americans.[13] Ironically, President King resigned in 1930 over allegations his administration had turned a blind eye to practices of slavery and forced labor. He is still commemorated by a Monrovia school named in his honor.

With the end of the American Legion activities, it was time for Kid and Florence to leave France and return to America on the liner *Ile de France*. They were returning with heavy hearts because they both knew Florence's health problems had not improved. The ship's passenger list had its quota of well-known names. The most famous was New York's mayor, Gentleman Jimmy Walker. *Billboard*'s list of famous names included Florence; two famous conductors, Walter Damrosch of the NBC Symphony Orchestra and Serge Koussevitsky of the Boston Symphony Orchestra; as well as operatic diva Anna Case, tenor Charles Hackett, and Irving Aronson's Commanders.[14]

The *Ile de France* was due to dock in New York on Tuesday, September 27. Following the tradition beloved of ship's entertainment officers, the night before landfall was the occasion of a gala concert, drawing on the many talents available among the passengers. The guest of honor, Mayor Walker, made a speech during the evening. The first part of the entertainment was a concert of classical music under Walter Damrosch's baton, with performances by Ruth Lorraine Close (principal harpist, Portland Symphony Orchestra), Anna Case (Metropolitan Opera), and Charles Hackett (tenor, Chicago Opera).

Following the classical performances, there was a mini cabaret in the Grand Salon. Irving Aronson and the Commanders provided the music. The acts included Dario and Irene from Les Ambassadeurs, Ramon and Rosita (dancers), and Rube Goldberg (famous cartoonist and designer of crazy machines). Also listed as "stars of the Blackbirds" were Florence Mills and U. S. Thompson. This was the first and only time Florence and Kid were billed as a double act. She had insisted on appearing even though, in Kid Thompson's words, "She was a very sick little girl then." She felt she had to show up because, as she told Kid, "Mrs. Walker has been so gracious to me on the way over." Florence sang "Mandy, Make Up Your Mind" as her featured number.[15]

Florence's imminent arrival on the Ile de France attracted keen interest back in New York. The theatrical press had followed her extraordinary successes in Europe, and the black press in particular had eagerly reported every story about her popularity and her efforts on behalf of her race. The black community hung on every word about her successes and her fame and popularity overseas. Heralding her imminent return, the Amsterdam News called on the members of the "colored" theatrical profession to be the first "to show the appreciation which we all feel for the wonderful manner in which she carried the story of an oppressed people." It referred to her as "a true ambassador returning after work well done."[16]

Not to be outdone, the New York Age hailed her as "a champion of the highest and best and noblest qualities of her race." "Her stand in defense of the colored performers in Europe," it declared, "will serve as a living testimony to the broadness of her heart and stamp her as a heroine, not only of the stage but the colored people generally." It went on to announce that the Colored Vaudeville Benevolent Association planned to meet her en masse, and it called for maximum support from the black community.[17]

The Ile de France docked at pier 57, at the foot of West Fifteenth Street. True to its word, the Colored Vaudeville Benevolent Association had organized a welcome for Florence that dwarfed the civic reception awaiting Mayor Walker. A cavalcade of about sixty gaily decorated automobiles plus taxis accompanied the huge throng. Taken off guard, Florence was mobbed by enthusiastic friends and well-wishers as Kid Thompson grappled with Customs and baggage handlers. First to greet her, inside the customs line, was her mother and family members. When she reached the pier, the crowd of theatrical friends swarmed round. Among the many were Eubie Blake, Miller and Lyles, Edith Wilson, Jesse Shipp, Evelyn Preer, Mrs. Bill Robinson, Edwin Small (Small's Paradise), Irvin C. Miller (Flournoy's brother and also a performer and producer), and Leroy Wilkins. Florence was plainly overcome, flitting around from friend to friend, shaking hands and being hugged.

In a brief session with the press, she merely spoke of her pleasure at the reception and her happiness at being home again. She declined to speculate on her plans, saying only that she planned a brief period of rest. The noisy cavalcade, with Kid and Florence in Irvin Miller's car, then headed uptown, along Broadway, across to Fifth Avenue, up into Harlem and Lenox Avenue, and finally to the family home on West 133rd Street. Florence Mills was back home in Harlem once again.[18]

The plan for Kid and Florence had been that she would arrive home rested and ready to confront the medical procedures necessary to get her back to full fitness and a resumption of her career. However, on arrival they discovered that her mother was not well and was worried about Florence's health. Florence therefore decided to play down any discussion of operations. She preferred to wait a while till her mother might be more relaxed. She slipped quietly back into daily Harlem life although, for someone with her high profile, anonymity was not possible. The shipside reception was only the first of several welcoming functions planned by her admirers.

They started with a formal banquet. Florence was the guest of honor at the Footlights Club, a black theatrical organization whose headquarters were just a few blocks from Kid and Florence's home. Many theatrical personalities attended, including illustrious and historical names of black theater, music, and society: Ford Dabney, Joe Jordan, pianist-composer Donald Heywood, W. C. Handy, Alain Locke, Evelyn Preer, singer-dancer Mae Barnes, Gertrude Saunders, and Miller and Lyles. Irvin C. Miller, the master of ceremonies, had organized a ten-course dinner. The evening was one of cheerful festivity and goodwill, with much speech making and joke telling. Accused of hiding under the table rather than speak, Mae Barnes said, "I talk with my feet but I must have music." Well into the evening, Aubrey Lyles's turn came. In a soft voice, he made a bitter speech that made it into the columns of the newly established *Time* magazine. The speech was not recorded in detail. The theme of it was a warning to Florence that she should not be seduced by the friendly overtures of Carl Van Vechten, who under the guise of promoting African American culture was actually seeking to bring it into disrepute. *Time* summed it up as a warning that Florence should "beware of Carl Van Vechten, lest she, pride of 'Race People,' lose race caste."[19]

The cause of Lyles's ire was criticism Van Vechten had made of black show promoters. In an article published in *Vanity Fair*, he had accused them of favoring light-skinned chorus girls over darker-skinned ones. He urged them to avoid the stereotyped humor beloved by white audiences and suggested that they should promote honest-to-God blues sung by Bessie Smith or Clara Smith rather than blues by Irving Berlin or Sissle and Blake.[20] It must have been galling for men like Miller and Lyles to hear such criticisms from a wealthy white socialite. They had done much to advance the cause of black show business and entertainers, but in their hearts they knew Van Vechten was at least partly right.

There was little need for Lyles to give Florence warnings of this kind. She had never been prominent in Van Vechten's social circle, and she had not liked his notorious book. However, he had never criticized her and was always respectfully admiring. Some years later, when sponsorship of a literary prize awarded by *Opportunity* magazine lapsed, Van Vechten filled the vacuum and renamed the prize "The Award in Memory of Florence Mills."[21]

While Aubrey Lyles's speech at the Footlights Club event stirred controversy in one direction, Florence was also peripherally involved in another raging controversy. Before the return of Mayor Jimmy Walker on the *Ile de France*, reports had circulated that he had been involved, while drunk, in racist incidents in an Italian nightclub. The accusation was that he objected to some black Brazilians' being allowed to dance with white women. Another report surfaced claiming similar events in Paris. In damage control mode, Mayor Walker vigorously denied the claims, and at a political meeting in Harlem, he pointed to his dancing and being photographed with Florence Mills on board the *Ile de France* as evidence of his good racial credentials. Nevertheless, the stories damaged his image in Harlem. The fallout came some weeks later, when Harlem elected black Republican Fred R. Moore, editor of the *New York Age*, as an alderman in place of Walker's white Democrat incumbent.[22]

Florence was in the limelight soon again as the guest star at the opening of a very fancy new Harlem nightclub, Club Ebony. It took place on the Wednesday following the Footlights Club event and was a glittering occasion. The new club was decorated in "a true jazz age atmosphere" by the outstanding painter of the Harlem Renaissance, Aaron Douglas. A reporter wrote, "The elite of Harlem and guests from Washington, Philadelphia, Atlantic City, Baltimore, New Jersey, downtown and Greenwich Village began arriving as early as eleven o'clock and kept the swank new club packed until five in the morning. Gorgeous gowns, furs, shawls, and jewels vied with the elegance of thick velvet carpets and silken damask upholstery while surrounding all were the startling blues, reds, yellows and blacks of Aaron Douglas's painted jungle and jazzboes."[23]

The attendance was a virtual roll call of Harlem Renaissance luminaries. Society and intellectual figures included W. E. B. DuBois, Madame A'Lelia Walker, and the recently maligned Carl Van Vechten. From the fine arts were Aaron Douglas, painter, and Lawrence Brown, accompanist for Roland Hayes and Paul Robeson. From the theater came Ethel Waters, Flournoy Miller, Earl Dancer, and Billie Cain, a regular in several of Florence's shows. The rest was a mixture of prominent socialites, journalists, and business people. The whole occasion was described as "By far the smartest affair of the budding season." Writers present included Jessie Fauset, Wallace Thurman, Eric Walrond, and Samson Raphaelson. Raphaelson was the Jewish author of the play *The Jazz Singer*, the film of which ushered in the era of talking movies. Raphaelson expressed his admiration for Florence with a card inscribed, "You are in the most thrilling things I ever saw."[24] He is probably also the original source of the playwright character who invites Lorelei Lee to a literary evening for Florence Mills in Harlem in Anita Loos's novel *Gentlemen Prefer Blondes*.[25]

Not to be outdone by the new club, Small's Paradise also laid on an elaborate welcome home for Florence, with two banquet tables set aside for her large, mainly show business party. Florence was described as "stunning, in a gown of heavy white satin trimmed with steel beads. In her ears she wore black pearls and a small string of pearls round her neck. Her slippers were silver of Parisian mode. Diamond bracelets completed the costume."[26] As the immediate excitement over her return died down, Florence was able to take a lower profile, but she and Kid were still visible at occasional functions around Harlem in mid-October. There were social visits to catch up with friends, including a visit to the office of the *Amsterdam News* to thank the editor for his coverage of her overseas adventures. She visited the Alhambra Theatre, scene of her last American triumph, sitting in a secluded corner in a box to avoid recognition. She had told the Alhambra's manager shortly after her return that she hoped to play there soon again. Mundane affairs such as registering to vote in a November 8 local election were also attended to, and she placed her legal affairs in the hands of a young African American attorney, Ralph Mizelle, who had been one of Kid Thompson's commanding officers in World War I.[27] Mizelle would soon marry an outstanding young graduate of Yale University School of Law, Jane Matilda Bolin, who would go on to be the first African American woman judge in the United States.

Florence didn't neglect plans for her future career either. Sometime during this few weeks, she, Kid Thompson, and Lew Leslie went to see Irving Berlin at the Music Box Theatre. There she did some kind of test recording, singing a Berlin song. "Irving Berlin himself," said Kid Thompson, "not no agents, not none of these record makers. Irving Berlin and Lew Leslie and me was the only three people there." This was probably a follow-up to the negotiations the Berlin Company had suggested while Florence was still in England.[28]

There were plans for a concert tour, including an appearance with the Boston Symphony Orchestra in Boston, before starting rehearsals for a new edition of *Black Birds*. There was also a report that Florence would be in the next production of the *Ziegfeld Follies*, possibly reflecting the correspondence with Ziegfeld's company while she was in England. The same report suggested plans also existed for a worldwide tour, including the Far East and Australia. Lew Leslie was already working on the next edition of *Black Birds*, again assuming Florence would be the star. He recruited trumpeter Demas Dean, just back from a South American tour, to fill a gap in the band. "I was elated at the thought of playing for Florence Mills," said Dean. "She was such a beautiful person."[29]

The public also had expectations and ambitions for her career directions. Reflecting on her next developments, the *Interstate-Tattler* commented:

> The masses love Miss Mills. More, they adore her. It is not too much to say that some of us even worship her, for it is only a step from the pedestal of a heroine to the immortality of a [goddess]. People always expect good gifts from a divinity. . . . It is Miss Mills' duty to give the people the one great gift within her power. The people want a national, or if you please, a race drama. . . . Miss Mills can do more than anyone else to satisfy the latent, unexpressed hunger for race drama.

Such was the admiration for Florence's versatility and talent that few doubted she had the ability to evolve in new directions, including straight drama if she chose. This theme of Florence's capacity to lift black show business to new levels had also been sounded by Ivan Harold Browning in his "Across the Pond" newsletter for the *Chicago Defender*. A feeling simmered that black entertainment was repeating stale formulae and was too controlled by white commercial interests. Carl Van Vechten's remarks had added fuel to this controversy. Browning wrote, "I have been and am still trying to get Miss Mills at the finish of this revue [*Black Birds*] to put on a real Race musical comedy. I firmly believe after she has done this here in London and then returned to America with her new European success she will do much in really bringing the Race show business back to the position it held four or five years ago. . . . Should Miss Mills do a Race musical comedy I feel it will be the greatest thing she has ever done for herself and her Race."[30]

Florence finally decided her surgery could no longer be postponed. She arranged to be admitted to the Hospital for Joint Diseases on Tuesday, October 25, then located at 124th Street and Madison Avenue. Having made the arrangements, she spent a quiet weekend preparing. On Sunday afternoon she went, unannounced and on her own, to the familiar old Lincoln Theatre, where Adelaide Hall was playing the matinee. Much to the surprise of young journalist Alvin White, she eased herself quietly into a seat in front of him.

> The audience hadn't noticed her, but onstage eagle-eye Adelaide had. Moreover, when she saw where Miss Mills was seated, Adelaide bowed deferentially in her direction, acknowledging THE presence. That audience got the mes-

sage. A raucous Lincoln Theatre welcome followed, and any oldtimer knows what that meant—those Lincoln audiences were notoriously vocal, quick to let you know how they felt. Graciously, Florence stood and bowed. She was home.[31]

It was three days later that Adelaide made her historic recording of "Creole Love Call" with Duke Ellington, using an innovative style of wordless vocalizing that may well have been influenced by Florence Mills.

On Monday, Florence was laughing and talking with friends. "They're going to operate on me tomorrow," she announced gaily. "I'll be back before you know it and then watch me. I've not begun to be what I was meant to be. I'm going to dance like the Mills's never danced before, and I'm going to sing as Florence never sang before. The first person that tells my mother where I'm going will die," she ended semiseriously and made a stabbing gesture with her hand. She laughed again and walked out, going to the hospital next morning.[32] Her mother was told she was going away for a rest. The public were told she was going in for a minor operation.

On Tuesday she went into the hospital, and a team led by Dr. Phillip Grossman operated on her as a private patient. It was obvious to the medical team from the outset that her condition was poor. The Amsterdam News reported, "Dr. Grossman was constantly in attention upon Miss Mills and she was surrounded by private nurses every moment of the day and night." Nevertheless her condition continued to worsen over the week following the operation, although Florence presented a cheerful appearance to her concerned friends and family. Lew Leslie visited her on the following Monday evening, and noting his worried state, she crooned the air to "Darktown Strutters Ball" to cheer him up.[33]

That Monday night her state declined sharply. In a final effort to save her, Kid Thompson gave blood for a transfusion, and the medical team operated again. Her condition did not improve. While Kid was sleeping at home, recovering from giving blood, the hospital phoned. As he slept through the ringing phone, a policeman was sent to raise him. Kid arrived just as, at four o'clock on the morning of Tuesday, November 1, Florence died. The voice that had delighted—and baffled—millions, from royalty to the tenements of Harlem, was silent.[34] The last song she ever sang was "Where the River Shannon Flows" to an Irish nurse who had been very attentive.[35] Her last recorded words, again to a sorrowing nurse, were, "I do not want to make people cry, even when I die. I want people to be happy always."[36] In the words of songwriter Porter Grainger, Florence Mills had "Gone to Join the Songbirds in Heaven."

Notes

1. Badeblatt und Amtliche Fremdenliste der Stadt Baden-Baden, Number 193, Monday, Aug. 22, 1927.

2. Badeblatt, Number 193. Notices of daily activities; also Badener Tagblatt, Aug. 30, 1927.

3. "Sacco Und Vanzetti Hingerichtet," Badener Tagblatt, Aug. 23, 1927.

4. "Sacco-Vanzetti Case," Microsoft® Encarta® 96 Encyclopedia.

5. Badeblatt, Aug. 26, 1927, Number 197.

6. On Rohm, see Dictionary of World History, ed. G. M. D. Howat (London: Thomas Nelson, 1973), 1299; on Ribbentrop, see Joachim von Ribbentrop, The Ribbentrop Memoirs (London: Weidenfeld and Nicolson, 1954) and John Weitz, Hitler's Diplomat (New York: Ticknor and Fields, 1992). The simultaneous presence of two prominent fascists at a luxury Baden-Baden hotel in 1927 may have been mere coincidence. Ribbentrop, although known to be a sympathizer, had not yet publicly associated himself with the Nazis in 1927. Rohm had fallen out with Hitler some years earlier and was still out of favor in 1927. Hitler did not recall him to lead the SA until 1930. Thus neither Ribbentrop nor Rohm was active in Nazi ranks in 1927, although they would certainly have known each other and moved in Nazi circles.

7. Roi Ottley, New World A-Coming: Inside Black America (Cleveland: World, 1943), 322–323.

8. Ivan Harold Browning, "Our European Letter," AMST, Sept. 7, 1927; Bob Slater, "Theatrical Jottings," NYA, 10, Sept. 21, 1927.

9. For an account of Bricktop's troubles, see Bricktop, with James Haskins, Bricktop (New York: Athenaeum, 1983), 134–136. Bricktop's memory of some of the details of Florence's visit were vague, as she thought Florence came by air from Hamburg, a port city in the extreme north of the country.

10. "The American Legion in Paris," New Statesman, Sept. 10, 1927. This is a comprehensive, if somewhat cynical, account of the background and organization of the American Legion Convention in Paris.

11. "Alberta Reports," AMST, Nov. 16, 1927.

12. Program, Gala Performance in Honor of the American Legion, Monday, Sept. 19, 1927, HAJC.

13. Letter of Introduction from Liberian Consulate, Liverpool, Aug. 10, 1927, HAJC. Also private conversation with Delilah Jackson re: Kid Thompson's account of invitation.

14. Billboard magazine, Oct. 8, 1927.

15. Program, Concert de Gala "Ile De France," Sept. 26, 1927, HAJC; R. Campbell, "Florence Mills Life Story," New York Evening Graphic, Nov. 9, 1927; Alvin White, "Let Me Tell You about My Love Affair with Florence Mills," Sepia, Nov. 1977, 59.

16. "At Home and Abroad," AMST, Sept. 7, 1927.

17. "Florence Mills to Reach New York Sept. 27," NYA, Sept. 24, 1927.

18. "Hundreds Throng Dock to Welcome Florence Mills," NYA, Oct. 1, 1927; and "Florence Mills Given Royal Welcome Home," *Inter-State Tattler*, Sept. 30, 1927.

19. "Florence Mills and Husband Guests of Footlights Club," *Inter-State Tattler*, Oct. 7, 1927; and "Florence Mills Warned," *Time*, Oct. 17, 1927, 13.

20. Carl Van Vechten, "Prescription for the Negro Theatre," *Vanity Fair*, Oct. 1925.

21. Victor A. Kramer and Robert A. Russ, eds., *Harlem Renaissance Re-Examined* (Troy, New York: Whitston, 1997), 140.

22. Various reports in NYA, Sept. 1, 1927; BAA, Oct. 1, 1927; NYA, Nov. 9, 1927; BAA, Nov. 12, 1927.

23. ChDef, Oct. 15, 1927. See also NYA, Oct. 8, 1927, and BAA, Oct. 15, 1927.

24. SCRAP, HAJC.

25. Anita Loos, *Gentlemen Prefer Blondes* (New York: Vintage Books, 1983), 31.

26. BAA, Eva Jessye column, Oct. 15, 1927.

27. Information gathered from following sources: "Florence at Small's," BAA, Oct. 15, 1927; AMST, Nov. 9, 1927; ChDef, Nov. 12, 1927; PiCou, Nov. 3, 1927; NYA, Nov. 16, 1927.

28. Delilah Jackson Kid Thompson interview tapes and HAJC: Interview transcript. Kid Thompson was very clear in both that he, Florence, and Leslie had met with Berlin with no one else present. He was less clear on what the song was, suggesting in one instance it was a Berlin song but elsewhere that it was "I'm a Little Blackbird." There might have been more than one song involved. The notes of Dr. Johnson's interview are not specific about timing and could be ambiguous on the possibility it was the 1924 Victor test session. However, with Delilah Jackson he was very clear that it was during Florence's final illness, after she had returned from England. If he was literally correct that no one else was present, i.e., no recording technicians, the meeting may have been an audition with Berlin rather than a recording session.

29. In *Storyville 49* and *72*, articles "Leon Abbey" and "Travellin' Man."

30. Ivan Harold Browning, "Across the Pond," ChDef, Feb. 12, 1927.

31. White, "Let Me Tell You," 56.

32. *New York Herald Tribune*, Nov. 2, 1927, HAJC.

33. AMST, Nov. 2, 1927, and *Washington Post*, Nov. 2, 1927.

34. "Blood Transfusion Failed to Save Florence Mills," BAA, Nov. 5, 1927.

35. Robert Campbell, "Florence Mills Life Story," *New York Evening Graphic*, Nov. 4, 1927. It's not surprising that Florence would know an Irish song like "River Shannon," not merely because of her early affinity for sentimental ballads, but because many jazz musicians had such tunes in their repertoire for practical reasons. The sleeve note to a Bunk Johnson record containing "River Shannon" notes: "During that lawless period, if a musician valued his health, it paid to have a few Irish tunes in his repertoire of good time music." Bunk Johnson (LP No. 64, American Music Records).

36. ChDef, Nov. 12, 1927, clipping in HAJC.

CHAPTER TWELVE

~

Bye Bye Blackbird

Harlem's Farewell

The news of Florence's death hit the people of Harlem and the wider black community like a thunderclap. They had believed she was in the hospital for minor surgery and would be out in a matter of days. Her death led to a spontaneous outpouring of grief unlike anything seen before. She was not only their unparalleled symbol of success and dignity before the world; she was also their beloved Flo, the modest, gentle, lovable friend who lived among them and entertained them.

Inevitably there were some rumors of foul play. One suggestion of poisoning was quickly disproved.[1] Later articles speculated that she would have survived if her condition had been treated more seriously or that she would have had better treatment from medical staff of her own race.[2] However, there is no doubt that she had the best medical treatment available and that her condition was extremely long before she sought treatment. The black press recognized this when reporting her death. They generally agreed that overwork was the real cause. The *Baltimore Afro-American* captioned her final shipboard photograph "Worked to Death," drawing attention to her "tired expression."[3]

The official cause of Florence's death was given in the press as "paralytic ileus." This is not very informative. Paralytic ileus is commonly a postoperative condition that can be an immediate cause of death but not the underlying cause. Appendicitis and peritonitis were the most commonly reported causes. The complications of the side effects of pelvic TB are similar in effect to a ruptured appendix. According to Delilah Jackson, the doctors told Kid Thompson at the time that, even if Florence had survived the initial surgery, the TB was so advanced there was little hope for her long-term survival. Neglect and overwork had long since taken her past any hope of recovery.[4]

There was inevitable finger-pointing in the aftermath of Florence's death. Lillyn Brown publicly accused Lew Leslie, saying "You worked her to death." He indignantly denied it, insisting, "I kept telling her to have that operation, but she said she didn't have time. She had too many people waiting for her."[5] Maude Russell still blamed Leslie seventy years later. "He helped kill her because he wouldn't let her go to the hospital. . . . When she should have been in the hospital, he had her working." Hyacinth Curtis recalled similar allegations against Kid Thompson in gossip between the female members of the cast. "I used to hear the girls say that he let her work too hard, her husband. Leslie adored her, he was very good to his stars." Kid Thompson had also defended himself against such charges, telling Delilah Jackson he had argued with Leslie over Florence's workload. "You've got my wife in seven scenes, that's too much." The truth was that none of them, including Florence herself, had realized what a fragile vessel she was. Her sense of responsibility as a role model prevented her from facing reality and getting essential treatment before it was too late.

The news of Florence's death spread rapidly around the world. In Paris, Alberta Hunter received a cable at 7:45 p.m. Paris time from Edith Wilson, saying, "Florence Mills passed away at 4:15 a.m."[6] Paul Robeson, having just made a triumphant debut in Paris, received almost simultaneously the news of Florence's death and the birth of his son, Paul Jr., born the day after Florence died. He wrote to his wife, Essie, "I weep every time I think of it. It really is heartbreaking."[7] In London C. B. Cochran's wife met him coming off a train to break the news, knowing how deeply it would affect him. The manager of the Moulin Rouge in Paris found Johnny Hudgins, between shows on Wednesday night, sitting in a quiet corner crying.[8] Alberta Hunter had phoned Johnny as soon as she received Edith Wilson's cable. Bill "Bojangles" Robinson was en route west when he received a cable and immediately passed it on to the *Chicago Defender*.

The person who had the melancholy duty of bringing the sad news to the family home was greeted by Florence's mother saying, "Don't tell me, I know, Florence is dead." Later reports stated that she had greeted Florence as she came off the ship with the words, "Baby, you've come home to die."[9] Telegrams and floral tributes began pouring into the family home from all over America and the world. They came from show people, both black and white, politicians and public figures, ordinary fans and family friends.[10]

White show business entrepreneurs represented included Florenz Ziegfeld, David Belasco, the Shubert Brothers, E. F. Albee, Charles B. Dillingham, Earl Carroll, Edmond Sayag of Les Ambassadeurs, and, of course, C. B. Cochran and Lew Leslie. White performers included Nora Bayes, Bonita, Al Jolson, Sophie Tucker, Texas Guinan, Fred and Adele Astaire, Marilyn Miller, Mae West, Paul Whiteman, Raymond Hitchcock, and Jack Benny. From the literary world there were Carl Van Vechten and Mrs. Alfred Knopf; from politics, Mayor Walker and Governor Al Smith; and from the aristocracy, Lady Cook, Baron Rothschild, and Viscount De Friese.

The black mourners constituted an unending who's-who list. From the distant past there were Sissieretta Jones (Black Patti) and Dora Dean (of Johnson and Dean), as well as Florence's former Washington, D.C., schoolteacher, Mrs. Hallie Queen. It would be tedious to list all the names represented by telegrams, flowers, or visits to the home and funeral parlor. Composers and writers included Will Vodery, Shelton Brooks, Noble Sissle, Irvin C. Miller, Aubrey Lyles, Flournoy Miller, Eubie Blake, Jesse Shipp, James Weldon Johnson, W. C. Handy, Luckey Roberts, Alex Rogers, and Chris Smith. A few of the vast number of performers included Ethel Waters, Earl Dancer, Evelyn Preer, Edward Thompson, Ivan Harold Browning, Mr. and Mrs. Leonard Harper, Bill Robinson, Billy King, Hamtree Harrington, Sherman H. Dudley, John Payne, and Buck and Bubbles. From sports and society, there were boxer Harry Wills, businessman John E. Nail, Mary McLeod Bethune, and A'Lelia Walker. There was a letter from the commanding officer of the 369th Regiment, the Harlem Hellfighters.

Earl Dancer coordinated the funeral arrangements on the family's behalf. Kid Thompson was too overcome with grief and exhaustion to cope with the practicalities. The funeral directors were the firm of H. Adolph Howell, at 2332 Seventh Avenue, the original "funeral church" (or what later would be called a funeral parlor). The John Joyce–Rodney Dade Funeral parlor still occupies the building today. Sunday, November 6, was the funeral date. It was still the practice then to have Sunday funerals. Florence's body was taken to the funeral parlor on the afternoon of the day of her death. The intent was that she would lie in state there for five days, until 1:30 on Sunday afternoon. There would then be a service at the Mother Zion African Methodist Episcopal Church, 151 West 136th Street. The burial was to take place at Woodlawn Cemetery.

Florence was laid out in a white satin dancing dress, with white stockings and silver slippers, resting on luxurious pillows. Her coffin, of handhammered copper, was said to be a replica of the one in which movie idol Rudolph Valentino had been buried just a year before. There were persistent reports the coffin had cost $10,000, but as we shall see later, this was not true. As floral tributes poured in, they were stacked in the funeral establishment near the coffin. This was the setting in which the distraught inhabitants of Harlem, and her other fans and admirers, had their last opportunity to see their idol, Florence Mills.

Stunned disbelief had been Harlem's initial reaction to Florence's death. She had gone in only for minor surgery. The reports coming out to all but her immediate circle had been reassuring. As the realization took hold throughout Tuesday, small groups of people stood around the streets in hushed discussion. Similar discussions were taking place downtown, around the show business district. It was little consolation that the world press was pouring out hundreds of column inches in praise of the much-loved genius. Harlemites had lost the one they thought of, above all, as one of themselves. They understood very well what the *New York Times* said in its editorial:

> The tributes paid to Florence Mills, as her body lies in state, are a hint of the service which she did to her race. Her fame in the international theatre is more than a sign of the advancement of negroes [sic]. She was one of the leaders whose accomplishment sets the whole racial movement a notch or two forward. No special plea or lenient judgement was suggested in her work. None was needed. When she danced and sang, no one said, "Wonderful for a negro." The quality of her performance, the very timbre of her voice, cut the ground from under the critic who might have liked to patronize. She presented no opening in the armor of her self-confidence for sentimentalizing. . . . Florence Mills "did her stuff" with an air of childlike enjoyment, knowing how good it was, certain of delighting her audience, performing always with a relish and assurance as far removed as possible from conceit. Other negro players now on Broadway and still others to come, will find that the slim dancer who blazed the way for them has set a high standard. . . . Not only actors but the negro novelists and poets should feel the air a little clearer and the road ahead plainer because of Florence Mills.

Once the funeral parlor doors were open, the crowds began to stream in, mainly blacks but many whites also. Of all classes, they came by day and night. The plan to close the funeral parlor at midnight on Wednesday proved too optimistic, and it stayed open till half past one in the morning. More than 10,000 people filed past during that day, including a delegation of 500 school children. They filed past in a steady procession that lasted eight hours. Forming a long queue on West 137th Street, they entered by the side door of the funeral parlor to walk through the little chapel and out the front door onto Seventh Avenue. A polite usher discreetly hastened those who tarried too long gazing into the casket. Solemn organ music played continuously in the background.

This pattern repeated over the remaining days. Despite dismal weather the crowds kept coming. By Thursday night an estimated 40,000 people had filed past. By then, relatives had replaced the white satin dancing dress, and Florence was now in her burial robes. These were an evening dress of silver metal cloth trimmed with rhinestones, a favorite of Kid Thompson's, with silver mesh hose and matching slippers. A jeweled clasp held the dress at the waist. There was a string of pearls around her neck and in her hands an ivory rosary.

One of those who came to see Florence was the noted black photographer James Van Der Zee, chronicler of all notable Harlem events. He photographed her in the casket, with the great lid open, and took a picture of the casket closed, surrounded by the floral arrangements. In each case he later applied his creative photographic editing techniques to add effects to the negative. With the open casket picture he created an effect of the sun's rays shining in on Florence through the mortuary window. An unfinished version of this photo has, instead, an older picture of Florence superimposed on the window at left, with another incomplete superimposition on the other side. He later abandoned this approach in favor of using the same pictures superimposed on opposite sides of the photo of the closed casket.[11]

By Saturday there was no letup in the crowds. People realized this was their final chance to see Florence Mills. The funeral parlor sign advertised "Remains of Miss Mills on view at one o'clock." In fact, they had to open two hours earlier by public demand. The doors didn't close finally until 2:00 a.m. Sunday, by which time the officials estimated 20,000 had filed past that day. Estimates of the total number over the five days ranged from 57,000 to over 100,000. Throughout the period members of the Colored Vaudeville Benevolent Association kept a constant guard of honor.

By Saturday, 200 huge floral pieces stood stacked from ceiling to floor in the funeral parlor. They included a large white cross from Florence's mother and family, a Bleeding Heart from Kid Thompson, Gates Ajar from boxer Harry Wills, and a red rose design from Florenz Ziegfeld. All Harlem believed an eight-by-four-foot Tower of Roses, from "a friend," was from the Prince of Wales. Getting this large collection to the service and the burial was a transport problem in itself.

As the day of the funeral approached, the police realized they were going to have a major crowd-control problem on their hands. The church in which the funeral service was to take place, the African Methodist Episcopal (AME) Church, popularly known as Mother Zion, is the oldest black church in America. It was founded about 1796, originally in Lower Manhattan. The present neo-Gothic church, built at an estimated cost of $450,000, opened in September 1925 to serve the growing black Harlem population. Including the gallery, it had a total seating capacity of about 2,100 people. Official invitations had gone out to at least a thousand, but many more were intent on being there. The real crowd-control problem, however, was the huge throng of people outside, who would have no chance of getting into the church.

The church service was due to start at one o'clock. The funeral parlor and the AME church were close to each other. The cortege would leave the mortuary between 12:00 and 12:30 and follow a winding route through Harlem, passing the Lafayette and Alhambra theaters, scenes of many of Florence's triumphs. The intent also was to ensure that the many thousands of ordinary Harlemites who would not be able to get into the church would have a chance to pay their final respects. Close to noon, twelve large automobiles arrived at the mortuary, accompanying the hearse, and collected the floral tributes. The male pallbearers who carried the coffin out were Will Vodery, Flournoy Miller, Aubrey Lyles, Dewey Weinglass (a leading dancer), Hamtree Harrington, George Rickson (Florence's pianist), James Marshall (former partner of Kid Thompson), and Leonard Harper.

Female honorary pallbearers were Ethel Waters, Cora Green, Gertrude Saunders, Aida Ward, Maude Russell, Edith Wilson and her sister Lena, and Evelyn Preer.[12] There was also a group of seventeen flower girls, all of whom had performed with Florence in one or more shows. They were Adelaide Hall, Hyacinth Curtis, Ethel Moses, Lucia Moses, Mae Fanning, Billie Cain, Bertha Weinglass, Lillian Powell, Evelyn Shepherd, Fanny Powell, Rose Singleton, Zelma Davis, Essie Worth, Vivian Harris, Pearl McCormack, Ruth Johnson, and Marion Tyler (in later years Mrs. Eubie Blake). The flower girls and honorary pallbearers were all dressed alike in grey crepe de chine costumes with grey silk stockings and black pumps. The honorary pallbearers also had close-fitting grey hats. They all lined up behind the hearse for the funeral procession, with the cars following. Kid Thompson, Mrs. Winfrey, and family members were in the first car.

Led by the one-hundred-piece Mitee Monarch Band of the Elks Lodge, the procession made its way slowly down Seventh Avenue to 125th Street. It then crossed to Lenox Avenue, Harlem's mighty central boulevard, before heading back up toward the AME church at West 137th. All along the route the streets were packed with people jammed into every vantage-point, observing in silence. "A sea of milling, shoving, pushing, jamming humanity thronged the entire block from Seventh Avenue to Lenox on 137th Street."[13]

Police and ambulances formed part of the cortege. On the way down Seventh Avenue, a cornet player from the band collapsed with a heart attack and died before the ambulance could reach him. When the procession reached 135th Street on the way back, the route to the church was blocked by an impenetrable crowd that resisted all police efforts to break through. The early police contingent of about a hundred had been soon increased to 150, or even 200, according to some reports. Reinforcements came from several outside areas. Eventually a diversion was made up 135th Street and the procession finally reached the church.

Meanwhile, at the church, a degree of pandemonium initially existed. The crowd had been gathering since 10:30 a.m. By one o'clock it was almost impossible to get within blocks of the church. From 10:30 a.m. onwards, the church was officially closed for the private funeral service. However, many of those who had attended the earlier regular morning service opted to stay inside. Even those who wished to leave found it difficult to do so, against the milling throng fighting to get in. Official invitees, already having had to fight their way through the dense crowd, found they could not gain access at the door. Eventually the polite but firm support of assistant pastors and thirty ushers finally cleared the main ground floor although the balcony and stairways remained packed solid.

With police backing, many invitees, including Al Jolson, were at last able to enter. An estimated 200 invitees never got in. Most witnesses agree that about 5,000 people had finally packed themselves into the 2,100-person church by the time the ceremony began. One description classified the attendance as "Those holding cards for the service; curious spectators, who refused to leave when the church's morning services were completed; those who wanted and tried to leave the church, but who were forced back by the impatient mob, and the uninvited, who forced a way into the church."[14]

When the funeral procession finally reached the church, the police found the only way to clear a passage for the hearse and the official party was to use their patrol cars as battering rams to compact the densely packed crowd. The cars carrying floral pieces went straight on, to await the final drive to the cemetery. It was two o'clock when the main entrance opened. As the hearse backed slowly up to the door, the band played hymns: "Blest Be the Tie That Binds," "Rock of Ages," "God Be with You Till We Meet Again," and "What a Friend We Have in Jesus." The watching crowd spontaneously joined in, singing as the coffin, covered in a blanket of roses surmounted by a sheaf of lilies of the valley, was carried to the altar by the pallbearers. The weeping flower girls covered it with their bouquets. Afterward the official party was ushered into place at the front of the church.

The elaborate service had been planned for days. Advance reports had said there was to be a choir of 600 voices and an orchestra of 200 instruments. A degree of hype may have been involved. The music was provided by the highly reputable Clef Club Orchestra, under its leader, violinist Allie Ross, and the twenty-member Carolina Choir, backed up by the fifty-strong regular Mother Zion choir. Although the Carolina Choir leader, Hall Johnson, was then little known, his Hall Johnson Choir would become famous in later years. He had been in the *Shuffle Along* pit band when Florence was in the show. Many press reports noted Hall Johnson's dramatic conducting. The funeral service was his first major public exposure in a long career.

The principal officiating clergyman was the pastor of the AME Church, Rev. James W. Brown. Master of ceremonies was the venerable Jesse Shipp. Twenty-eight members of the press filled two front rows on one side of the church. On the other side, the family and close friends and relatives filled three rows. Many notable figures, black and white, from all walks of life, the entertainment world predominating, sat in prominent positions. The rest of the attendance was just the mass of ordinary people eager to pay their last respects.

As the ceremony continued, the overcrowded building became stiflingly hot. The fragrant aroma of abundant flowers added to the stuffiness. Red Cross nurses and women of the church auxiliary circulated, giving aid to fainting or distressed congregation members from thermos flasks and spirits of ammonia. Within the church, as the coffin appeared on the way to the altar, the strains of Chopin's "Requiem" gave way to his "Funeral March." As the sounds of the March died away, Reverend Brown led the hymn "Come Ye Disconsolate," during which one of the choristers fainted and Cora Green broke down sobbing.

Outside the church the atmosphere was somber if less intense. The streets for blocks around were packed. Windows, fire escapes, and roofs were full. There were reports that people living opposite the church charged money for admission to good vantage points in their homes. At one point a small urchin fell twenty feet off a fire escape onto the crowd below. He broke an arm, and the woman he fell on suffered cuts and bruises. Fifty people fainted in the original police press to clear a way for the hearse. For these and many more, the nearby YMCA functioned as an emergency treatment center, while many others were taken to Harlem and Bellevue hospitals by ambulance.

The crowds, estimated at between 150,000 and 200,000, were the largest ever seen in Harlem. They stayed throughout the ceremony. In the words of one reporter,

Even after it had long been apparent that not another cubic foot of humanity could wedge its way into Mother Zion Church, the crowd stood its ground, its murmurings rising now to what seemed to those within a great wall of lamentation—or disappointment—pierced by an occasional shriek, now breaking into cheers and laughter. For more than two hours it played a weird symphonic accompaniment to the solemn Methodist service.[15]

Inside the church, the opening hymn was followed by a brief prayer. Pastor Brown then read a summary of Florence's life and her achievements. Hall Johnson's Choir, clad in white vestments, sang "Deep River," to much lamentation and some further fainting. The Pastor resumed with a eulogy, recalling Florence's dignity, charity, and helpfulness to others. He finished by suggesting there should be a memorial "to perpetuate her life and work" in promoting better race relations.

Jesse Shipp then read a selection from the hundreds of telegrams and messages of sympathy received by Florence's mother. A series of hymns and spirituals followed, sung by well-known members of the black community. A. A. Haston's rendition of "Flee as a Bird" was so moving that Florence's sister Maude collapsed and had to be led out. Jules Bledsoe sang "Lead, Kindly Light," urged on by responses from the gallery of "Sing it, brother," and "Oh yes, Lord." Jesse Zackery followed him with "Come Unto Me." At this point the dramatic tension heightened. Florence's former fellow performer, Juanita Stinette, rose to sing a song newly written as a tribute, entitled simply "Florence." She started off in a calm low voice. As the name Florence was repeated with each short stanza, her emotional pitch rose, and members of the audience began to stir. At the line "The hours you spent with us, Florence," she screamed and collapsed in a heap and was carried out, crying "Florence, Florence."

Clarence Tisdale completed the unfinished song, then went on to sing "Thou Wilt Keep Her in Perfect Peace," and Louetta Chapman sang "I Know That My Redeemer Liveth." The Hall Johnson Carolina Choir, to sobs and moans from the audience, finished with two hymns reputed to be favorites of Florence's, "Victory, O Lord" and "I'm a Pilgrim of Sorrow." The ceremony closed with some final prayers. It was shortly after four o'clock when the great entrance doors finally swung open again.

The final act begins. Once again the coffin is loaded into the hearse, covered with flowers. Outside, the crowd presses forward for a close view. Motorcycle police pry open a route for the procession on its way to the cemetery. The flower girls have to walk several blocks to reach their escort cars. The motorcycle escort leads off, riders dragging one foot on the ground to avoid collisions with the throng pressing for a glimpse of the coffin. At last they are on their way in the dimming November twilight. They head up Seventh Avenue, still through massed crowds, through the Bronx, and out toward Woodlawn Cemetery.

As the cortege leaves Harlem, an airplane swoops low over it and releases a shower of rose petals. The pilot is Hubert Fauntleroy Julian, "The Black Eagle," a flamboyant black aviator whose dramatic aeronautical feats have amused and captivated Harlem for several years. He was chartered by the Amsterdam News *for the occasion. The* News *had provided twenty-five wreaths for the purpose. Small's Paradise had provided fifteen, to be dropped in Harlem and over the grave.*[16]

At the entrance to Woodlawn, cars are parked by all except the immediate family. Mounted police replace the motorcycle escort, except for a lone motorcycle leading the hearse though the winding pathways, among great mausoleums dedicated to the rich and famous. The male pallbearers, the female honorary pallbearers, and the flower girls walk solemnly behind the hearse. Many hundreds, some reports say thousands, of mourners follow them. It is now past five o'clock, twilight, and the moon is rising as the party arrives at the grave. The site selected for Florence is on a grassy slope with overhanging trees. It is free of any overshadowing mausoleums or large monuments. Several hundred mourners, invitees who had failed to get into the church, have been awaiting the official party's arrival for hours.

The eight pallbearers struggle to get the heavy coffin up the slope. The gravediggers stand by in anticipation. Kid Thompson supports a veiled Nellie Winfrey. At the final moment, as the coffin is about to be lowered, she cries out, "For God's sake, please let me see my baby." The great lid of the coffin is lifted and Florence's mother looks at her through the heavy glass covering one last time. She breaks down crying and lamenting, to be joined by Ethel Waters, Cora Green, Gertrude Saunders, and Bertha Weinglass. Olivia and Maude try to comfort their mother.

As the coffin is placed in the grave, Hubert Julian's airplane once again dips low and releases its cargo of rose petals, showering the gathered mourners. Amid great lamentation from all around, the coffin is lowered into the grave, still covered with its blanket of roses and lilies of the valley, Lew Leslie's final tribute to Florence. When the last shovel of earth is laid, the great mounds of flowers are piled on top of the grave. The mourners shuffle sadly away as the moon comes up and a cold wind shakes the trees.

Returning from his flight, Hubert Julian told of seeing thousands of black birds flying past the plane as he released his floral cargo.[17] This was soon transformed in the press to reports that the blackbirds had been released *from* the plane, creating an enduring legend about Florence Mills. The story has grown over the years, like many urban legends. In some versions it is bluebirds that were released. Julian's original report is believable. The red-winged blackbird is common in eastern regions of the United States and forms large flocks. The region between Harlem and Woodlawn would have provided plenty of habitat for them in 1927. Although the story of blackbirds released from a plane has been popular over the years, the facts suggest that the blackbirds paid their own voluntary tribute without being caged.

Perhaps the last word on the events surrounding Florence Mills's funeral should go to Ernest K. Lindley, reporter for the *New York World*: "Florence Mills played to her last 'house' yesterday. It was the greatest show Harlem ever has had, or is likely to have again until another blackbird dances and sings her way from the tenements to such far-flung popularity."[18]

Memories of Florence: The Aftermath

On Monday, November 7, Harlem resumed daily life without its "queen of happiness." Immediately after the funeral, Florence's mother collapsed. For several hours during the night, reporters clustered around the family home, anticipating a scoop, but she disappointed them.[19] Reports of the funeral filled many columns for a while, but soon the press began to focus on the rumors of a huge estate left behind by Florence. There had been persistent stories that she had made a vast fortune from investments in Florida real estate.

Florence left no will. Her sole beneficiaries were her mother and husband. There was widespread disbelief when Ralph Mizelle, the family attorney, filed papers putting her entire estate at a value of $33,146 in personal property. This sum did not include the family home, which was in Kid Thompson's name. Several papers speculated about undisclosed real estate. No one ever produced evidence of any. The $33,146 is consistent with the amount Florence and Kid had cabled home from England. Previous earnings went to clear any debt on the house. Many years later Kid Thompson told Delilah Jackson, "I gave Florence's mother $8,000 of Florence's money, all the money Florence had in the bank."

Nevertheless, there was a tone of skepticism in several press reports,[20] probably due to earlier exaggerated accounts of Florence's earnings. As noted earlier, her shows made big money, but there were many claimants to share the pie. She and Kid did well from it but not on the scale many had imagined. Among the charges against the estate was the cost of the funeral, cited as $5,827.50, which clearly showed the reports of $10,000 for the coffin were exaggerations. Kid Thompson also denied rumors that Mother Zion Church had charged the family $1,000 for use of the premises. In fact a fairly nominal sum of $100 was paid.[21]

Speculation and innuendo about Florence's personal fortune faded away. The new topic of interest was how to honor and perpetuate her memory. Even before her funeral, calls were raised for some form of memorial. The topic had been raised again from the pulpit at her funeral service. Early reports had stated that a statue depicting her in a lively dancing pose would be erected over her grave. Noted Italian sculptor Antonio Salemme, a friend of the Robesons, was to undertake the commission. He had measured Florence for the purpose during her period of lying in state. Many years later Salemme told noted African American book collector Charles Blockson, curator of the Blockson Collection at Temple University, of making a death mask of Florence. The invitation came shortly after he had done so for Sacco and Vanzetti, who had been executed while Florence and Kid Thompson were in Baden-Baden.[22] However, Salemme never did make the statue. The gravesite is still marked by a simple but dignified stone cross.

A different idea replaced the plan for a statue. A Florence Mills Memorial Fund Committee was established. The elected officers of the committee were Jesse Shipp (president), Jimmie Marshall (vice president), Irene H. Jordan (recording secretary), W. C. Handy (financial secretary), and Henry Parker (treasurer). Kid Thompson and Lew Leslie were advisory members. A working committee of seven, Irvin C. Miller (chairman), Charles S. Gilpin, Clarence Robinson, Charlie Davis, Bob Slater, Troy Morse, and Paul Bass, organized a series of midnight shows to raise money for the memorial. It illustrates the seriousness of the commitment that all involved were people of high standing in the black community except for Leslie, the sole white member.[23]

The committee's original plan was to follow through on the statue idea, but discussing it in Florence's home shortly after her death, they decided on a different idea. "As the manifest interests of her life revealed themselves— her ambitions for lifting the profession to a loftier plane, her unheralded generosities to fellow artists, and to those in adverse circumstances—it was felt that the more fitting answer to her life in a memorial would be a building and organization designed to carry on her purpose."[24]

Based on an idea Florence had herself entertained while alive, they adopted a plan to create the Florence Mills Memorial Home for Negro Performers. They commissioned noted Canadian-born architect Louis Eugene Jallade to design a substantial building, to be funded by raising $400,000. It would contain "Adequate provision for the comfort and recreation of its members" and be "a center of activity where appeals of distress will be heard, substantial aid extended to the needy, wholesome recreation offered and advice of maturer members of the theatrical profession afforded those who need such assistance." The brochure issued by the committee showed the architect's drawing of a substantial six-story building.[25]

The fund-raising efforts got off to a strong start. A Monster Midnight Memorial Benefit was announced for December 3, just a month after Florence's death. It was to take place simultaneously at the three Harlem theaters, the Lincoln, the Lafayette, and the Alhambra. The list of volunteers announced as "positively appearing" included over sixty leading acts, both black and white. Famous white names on the list included Eddie Cantor, Fannie Brice, Irving Berlin, Fred and Adele Astaire, Cliff Edwards, Jack Benny, Ruby Keeler, Belle Baker, and Marie Cahill. The souvenir program carried adverts from a huge range of Harlem businesses and black performers. All the leading Harlem cabarets, including the Cotton Club, Connie's Inn, Small's Paradise, and the Nest, offered acts. Possible jazz orchestras included Fletcher Henderson, Fess Williams, Duke Ellington, and Aronson's Commanders.[26]

As with many show business ventures, the reality didn't live up to the hype. Some of the big white names—Brice, Cantor, Berlin—telegraphed support but regretted they wouldn't be able to appear. There was a sour taste when the show at the Lincoln was canceled at the last minute due to poor ticket sales, leaving some supporters in the lurch. Nevertheless, at the other two theaters, a glittering array of stars played to packed houses until 3:00 a.m. The shows raised somewhere between $4,000 and $5,000. The committee declared the event a great success despite press criticism over the Lincoln fiasco. Further benefit performances occurred in other major centers around the country. Chicago, Philadelphia, and Pittsburgh were first off the mark. The project gathered further momentum when Lady Cook cabled from England to express her desire to coordinate the committee's ventures on the other side of the Atlantic. She already had plans for benefits in London, Paris, Liverpool, and Glasgow.[27]

The Philadelphia benefit was on January 5 at the Gibson Theatre. Its performers included Ann Pennington, Charles Gilpin, Belle Baker, Jack Norworth, and Ethel Waters. It raised $1,300 after expenses.[28] Bojangles Robinson staged a benefit in Los Angeles on January 16. In February it was the turn of Washington, D.C., with a show at the Howard Theatre and a special, hour-long radio broadcast featuring Chappelle and Stinette, Tom Fletcher, Abbie Mitchell, and Eva Taylor and Clarence Williams.[29] At this point the Memorial Committee was progressing satisfactorily. Although still a long way from the target of $400,000, they had made a good start.

The first sign of dissension arose when Lady Cook announced the funds raised from her series of benefits in England would go to the NAACP. In a letter to Romeo Dougherty of the *Amsterdam News*, she described plans to stage a matinee benefit, with C. B. Cochran, at the London Pavilion. She stated that money raised for her "Florence Mills Fund" would go to the NAACP. In explanation she wrote: "Florence Mills was herself a member of this society, and always when speaking publicly in London she would refer to the good it was doing for her race. Its work is therefore known of in London, and presumably would be supported here. Florence Mills's private friends here also knew of her interest in the work of the NAACP as being the concrete expression of her own desire for the recognition of the advancement of her own people."

There was critical reaction to Lady Cook's initiative in the New York black press. The NAACP made no formal response. On its behalf James Weldon Johnson issued a statement saying they had not sought Lady Cook's action but it was welcome. Being solely based in England, it was not in conflict with the memorial efforts in the United States. The benefit in London went ahead with James B. Lowe, star of the recent film *Uncle Tom's Cabin*, eulogized Florence. He mentioned an incident of her having forestalled a suicide through her charity. This was a reference to a letter written to U. S. Thompson describing how a down-and-out, planning suicide on the London embankment, had gone on to redeem his life after receiving one of Florence's charitable gifts.[30]

In March the Memorial Association published for wide distribution around the country a brochure on its objectives and plans. Noting the occasion, the *Amsterdam News* posed the question, "Will everyone pull together and work for the common good of all his brothers." By this time Lew Leslie had resigned his association with the committee. The remaining members preserved white representation by co-opting Frank Schiffman, then manager of the Lafayette Theatre and later famous as manager of the Apollo. His Harlem base may have equipped Schiffman better for the job than Leslie.

The next sign of problems arose when a scheduled Washington, D.C., benefit, with Bojangles to star, was canceled due to a union ban on the Howard Theatre.[31] This brought to a head a more serious rift between Bojangles and the committee. He had already staged a benefit in Chicago that raised about $4,500. From the outset, however, he argued that a tangible marble or granite monument to Florence was the more fitting objective. He now refused to hand over any more money unless it was used for such a purpose. A bitter and extended legal battle between Bojangles and the Association resulted.[32]

Despite these setbacks the Association soldiered on. By mid-1929 Jesse Shipp had resigned. Irvin C. Miller, brother of Flournoy Miller and a promoter of many black shows, became president. Through Miller's initiative a house previously owned by him at 115 West 113th Street was acquired on favorable terms. It was fitted out as the new headquarters of the Florence Mills Theatrical Association. A large sign right across the front of the building proudly proclaimed the fact. With the opening of the home, the Association also now declared November 3 as the official date of an annual Florence Mills Memorial Day.[33]

However, the Association was fighting an uphill battle. The *Afro* correspondent declared the benefit run at the Casino theater in December 1929 a failure, saved only by Luckey Roberts's having recruited many acts. The committee firmly denied this and quoted Florence's mother as having enjoyed the occasion. There had been a respectable turnout of acts, including veteran white comedian Joe Frisco. He had performed with the Panama Trio at the Panama Café years before. Nevertheless, the story was a sad contrast with the account on the same page of a huge turnout for an NAACP all-star concert the following day.[34] By November 1930 the *Baltimore Afro-American* bewailed the poor attendance at the third Florence Mills Memorial Day service at Woodlawn Cemetery. It declared, "Only a handful attend third memorial." This appeared under a banner headline asking, "Has Fickle Broadway Forgotten the Original 'Blackbird'?" The accompanying article pointed out that Lew Leslie's latest edition of *Blackbirds* had dispensed with the Florence Mills commemorative item, "Memories of 1927," a prominent feature of the previous version.[35]

In early 1931 Bojangles finally won his legal argument with the Association. The judge accepted his claim he had been acting on his own initiative, not as an employee or agent of the Association, when he raised the money in Chicago. The money was still in a special account awaiting resolution of the issue. Bojangles claimed he had previously raised more than $9,000 for the Association. When they didn't use it for a monument, he had decided to keep the rest for that purpose himself. He declared that he hoped "to see a statue of Miss Mills in the form of a drinking fountain erected in the small park above Rockefeller City at 151st Street and Riverside Drive. If he is not successful in this he will turn over half of the money to Miss Mills's mother and give the remaining half to the city to be used for charity."[36]

Bojangles's project never came to fruition. Florence's mother died the day after the court verdict was handed down. Kid Thompson, performing in Shanghai, had to cable permission for the family grave to be opened for her interment. What happened to the money is unknown, but Bojangles presumably gave it to charity as promised. No one ever questioned Bill Robinson's charitable credentials or his devotion to Florence Mills. He helped organize her mother's funeral and was a pallbearer.

By early 1931 the Depression was biting hard across most of America but particularly in Harlem. The *Afro* reported, "Never before in the history of New York have so many actors been out of work as at the present time. The Florence Mills Theatrical Association has been turned literally into a soup kitchen and flop house for unemployed actors. For a while as many as sixty were fed daily at the establishment and a large number given lodging."[37] Finally the dream of the Association was realized, and Florence's monument was fulfilling its intended purpose. There were even dances organized by a social club there on Sunday evenings. Alas, it was not to continue for long. The Depression bit more deeply, and funds dried up. More and more donors and supporters struggled to look after themselves. By 1932 the home had closed its doors, and the memory of Florence Mills was slowly fading into oblivion.[38]

No other tangible monument ever was raised to her in Harlem or elsewhere, although an apartment building on Edgecombe Street was named after her.[39] Nevertheless, her memory still burned bright in the minds of many. One young man who was beginning to make a name in music would give her a lasting monument of sorts. Her great admirer, Duke Ellington, would immortalize her as his "Black Beauty" in one of his finest compositions, also known as "A Portrait of Florence Mills." The music would keep her memory alive for future generations to rediscover. Perhaps even yet a worthy monument will be raised. Or perhaps that monument is the superstar status achieved since by so many black entertainers for whom she paved the way.

Notes

1. Alvin White, "Let Me Tell You about My Love Affair with Florence Mills," *Sepia*, Nov. 1977, 61.

2. Editorial, *Messenger*, Dec. 1927 or Jan. 1928, 13, and "Flo Mills and Tiger Flowers Did Not Have to Die, Is Physician's Opinion," BAA, Feb. 21, 1931.

3. BAA, Nov. 5, 1927.

4. Delilah Jackson in private discussion with the author. The Order for Interment authorizing Florence's burial at Woodlawn gives the underlying cause of death as a condition known as pyosalpinx. This condition is consistent with pelvic TB as the underlying cause. Pyosalpinx is a typical result of the inflammation of the fallopian tubes caused by the terminal stages of pelvic TB and often leads to a rupturing effect similar to that of peritonitis. The onset of this condition would have caused the pains Florence experienced as the disease took hold.

5. Loften Mitchell, *Black Drama* (New York: Hawthorn Books, 1967), 79. Mitchell incorporated this dialogue into his Florence Mills–based play *Ballad of a Blackbird*.

6. Alberta Hunter diary, entry Nov. 1, 1927. Schomburg Institute.

7. Martin B. Duberman, *Paul Robeson* (London: Pan Books, 1991), 584.

8. "Pauvre Johnny!" *Comoedia*, Nov. 5, 1927, 5.

9. "Sudden Death of Star Causes International Mourning," *Washington Tribune*, Nov. 4, 1927.

10. The account of the lead-up to the funeral and the funeral itself is collated from several hundred articles spread over many newspapers and other sources from Nov. 1 to Nov. 16, 1927. The journals involved include, in no special order: *Amsterdam News, New York Age, New York Times, New York Herald Tribune, New York Evening Graphic, New York World, New York Journal and Evening Journal, Washington Post, Washington Star, Washington Times, Washington Tribune, Washington Daily News, Chicago Defender, Chicago Whip, Boston Chronicle, Boston Evening Transcript, Pittsburgh Courier, Philadelphia Tribune, Baltimore Afro-American, Los Angeles Times, London Daily Express, London Times, Sunday Chronicle, Paris Comoedia, Variety, Inter-State Tattler, Crisis*, and *Opportunity*. Minor details differ from one account to another, so this composite account may vary slightly from any particular version. Except where direct quotes are used, it would be pointless to attempt to cite specific sources for each element of the account because much of the material overlaps. However, two articles worth noting as containing useful summaries are W. A. McDonald's prizewinning article from the *Boston Evening Transcript*, Nov. 7, 1927, and White, *Sepia*, Nov. 1977.

11. For the mortuary portrait of the open casket and its unfinished version, see Deborah Willis-Braithwaite, *VanDerZee: Photographer 1886–1983* (New York: Harry N. Abrams and Smithsonian Institution, 1993), 17; a copy of the closed casket picture was long lost but was recently found by the author and is now restored to the VanDerZee Collection.

12. There appears to be general agreement that there were eight honorary pallbearers, probably the eight listed, but some variation occurs in the names, with Lottie Gee and Elisabeth Welch mentioned. However, a correction published in the AMST of Nov. 16 confirms the list given here.

13. BAA, Nov. 12, 1927, 1.

14. Thelma E. Berlack, "The Jazz Queen Is Dead, Long Live Her Memory," AMST, Nov. 9, 1927.

15. *World*, Nov. 7, 1927, clipping in HAJC.

16. "*Amsterdam News* Strews Grave with Roses," AMST, Nov. 9, 1927.

17. AMST, Nov. 9, 1927, as above. This also refers to blackbirds flying over the church earlier.

18. "S.R.O. in Harlem at Last Exit of Florence Mills," *New York World*, Nov. 7, 1927.

19. PhTr, Nov. 10, 1927.

20. "Florence Mills's Estate," NYT, Nov. 12, 1927; "Florence Mills Estate valued at $33,146.88," AMST, Nov. 16, 1927; "Flo Mills Estate May Total $75,000," BAA, Nov. 19, 1927, and "Real Value of Florence Mills' Estate Is Not Revealed in Report," NYA, Nov. 19, 1927.

21. "$1,000 Not Charged by Dr. Brown," AMST, Nov. 16, 1927.

22. PhTr, Nov. 10, 1927, and Charles Blockson, curator, the Blockson Collection, Temple University, Philadelphia, private conversation with Bill Egan, May 2000.

23. "Jesse Shipp Heads Flo Mills' Memorial," Inter-State Tattler, Nov. 11(?), 1927.

24. Brochure published by the Florence Mills Memorial Fund, in Schomburg Institute.

25. Memorial Fund Brochure.

26. "Florence Mills Testimonial," AMST, Nov. 23, 1927; advertisement in AMST, Nov. 30, 1927, and Souvenir Program, HAJC, Schomburg Institute.

27. "Benefit Shows Here a Success," AMST, Dec. 7, 1927; "Nobody Blundered, Says Jesse Shipp," AMST, Dec. 14, 1927; "Enthusiasm for Mills Benefits," AMST, Dec. 21(?), 1927.

28. Advertisement, PhTr, Dec. 29, 1927, and "$4,064 in Flo Mills' Memorial Fund," BAA, Jan. 21, 1928.

29. "Mills Fund Notes," AMST, Feb. 8, 1928.

30. "Letter from the Honorable Lady Cook, a British Peeress," AMST, Feb. 1, 1928; "Londoners to Have 'Flo' Mills Benefit," BAA, Feb. 11, 1928; "Lowe Praised Florence Mills in London Benefit," AMST, Mar. 14, 1928.

31. "Mills Fund Show Stopped," AMST, May 16, 1928.

32. "Flo Mills Memorial Cause of Suit," BAA, Aug. 31, 1929.

33. "Hundreds Visit the Mills Home," undated, unidentified clipping (possibly ChDef, around Aug. 14, 1929); "Actors Asked to Observe Flo' Mills Memorial Day," BAA, Oct. 26, 1929.

34. "Crowd Disappointed at Flo Mills Benefit," BAA, Dec. 21, 1929, and "Flo Mills Group Says Benefit Paid," BAA, Jan. 4, 1930.

35. BAA, Nov. 15, 1930.

36. "Bojangles Wins Flo Mills Suit," BAA, Jan. 31, 1931. The name Rockefeller City was a reference to the up-market Dunbar Apartments, financed by John D. Rockefeller Jr.

37. "Harlem Boasts Most Cosmopolitan Soup Kitchen," BAA, Mar. 21, 1931.

38. The original building occupied by the Florence Mills Theatrical Association still stands today pretty much unchanged and was occupied in 2002 by the New Testament Baptist Church.

39. This building still stands today, with the name "Florence Mills" in concrete over the entrance.

~

CHAPTER THIRTEEN

Florence Mills: A Reappraisal

The Singer

Florence Mills had one of the most remarkable voices of the twentieth century. There is an obvious paradox in such a claim for a singer whose voice we cannot hear today. The onus is on the claimant to provide supporting evidence. Such evidence exists in plenty in the words of her contemporaries. From the earliest age Florence was recognized as having a sweet and unusual voice, most effective in sentimental ballads. At three years old she was earning money for her family, singing Irish songs like "Little Grey Home in the West" and "Mother Machree" to the prostitutes for whom her mother provided laundry services.

Long before she became known in her own right, Florence's voice was attracting comment from reviewers of the shows in which she appeared anonymously. In an enthusiastic review of Nora Bayes's show in 1917, Lester Walton wrote, "There is also a little girl who sings in the first scene of Part I, who must even remind Miss Bayes that she is not the only warbler at large." Similarly in 1919, in Victoria, British Columbia, "The youngest of the trio possesses a clear, sweet voice," and in Vancouver, "A solo by one of the trio was well received, the singer possessing a rich, sweet voice." A review of *Folly Town* in 1920 noted: "One little girl displays a soprano that many an opera singer might envy. 'Nellie Gray,' 'Down on the Swanee River,' 'Hear Dem Bells' and other typically Southern songs were sung by the little bird-like soprano." Similarly a Tennessee Ten review noted, "One slender Topsy, a mulatta [sic] girl, captivated the house with her rendition of 'Suanee [sic] River,' sung in bird-like soprano." These comments of "bird-like" were the earliest attempts to classify the special characteristics that listeners detected in Florence's voice.

By 1920, the sweet, ballad style had been augmented with close harmony jazz rhythms perfected with the Panama Trio. She also drew on the heritage of the spirituals her mother sang and the black music she heard in church. Florence was well schooled in the traditions of black vaudeville, including music from the Williams and Walker and the Cole and Johnson shows. To these can be added exposure to ragtime and stride music through contact with Tony Jackson, Luckey Roberts, and, later, Eubie Blake. The characteristics of her voice that attracted attention were the high, soft, clear sweetness and her ability to use it to achieve special instrumental effects that baffled and delighted most listeners. Efforts to describe it led people into remarkable flights of verbal invention.[1]

- The method of Florence Mills is like that of no one else. She does not precisely sing, but she makes strange high noises which seem to fit in somehow with a rapidfire sort of sculpture. Sometimes the intent is the creation of the grotesque and then it fades into lines of amazing beauty. Now I have seen grace. —*Heywood Broun*
- The notes she warbles are real woodnotes, and you would say that her voice is untrained. Untrained because of its astonishing facility. This singer has taken her high C and come down again while more ponderous prima donnas are still debating the ascent. —*James Agate*
- And yet, after all, did she really sing? The upper range of her voice was full of bubbling, bell-like, bird-like tones. And there, perhaps, is the definitive word . . . "Bird-like." It was rather a magical thing Florence Mills used to do with that small voice in her favorite song, "I'm a Little Blackbird, Looking for a Bluebird"; and she did it with such exquisite poignancy as always to raise a lump in your throat. —*James Weldon Johnson*
- In her small throat she hides all kind of funny little sounds that flutter out and escape like sparrows from an inexhaustible nest. —*Dudley Nicholls*
- The first thing I remember about her is her voice. "Silver" is a hackneyed word to use about voices, but hers is distinctly silvery. . . . She sings gravely—one might almost say sedately—high silver notes like beams of light, floating into the dark auditorium. —*Beverley Nichols*

Some of the most telling comments came from professional music critics or other singers:[2]

- Larger, stronger, mellower voices have sounded off this platform and off the world's other stages. This one is tiny and delicate. But it has an infinitely relaxed, impersonal bird-like quality: One knows there has been no other voice exquisite exactly like it. A pure instrument, this sensuous, but not a human voice at all. —*Paul Rosenfeld, American classical music authority*

- Let me sing of Florence Mills, whose voice beguiles as it were an enraptured bird, whatsoever its plumage or lineage; beguiles, and saddens too, for the tones of it are all delicately edged. Her coloratura is as wide in range, as flexible in movement, as clean and sure in flight and descent as that of any ascetic prima donna. —*Basil Maine, classical music critic, bewailing the poor diction of English singers, and holding up John McCormack and Florence Mills as examples of excellence*

- The interest of the performance [*Levee Land*], the real interest and value such as it was, came from the performer. Miss Mills would never profess to be a finished singer along classical lines, but in her own way she was inimitable, and this was the way the composer would have desired. She more than did him justice. She would have made a flatter piece of music amusing, by her diction, by not trying to sing like a white woman, by the various inflections and qualities of her voice, with its odd see-sawing from what was guttural and according to our standards badly placed to the half reedy, half fluty character of the upper register. —*Olin Downes, conservative classical critic for the* New York Times

Some of her fellow performers and singers have tried to describe Florence's voice:

- *Maude Russell:* She had a little bird voice, she had the cutest little voice, I've never heard anybody with a voice like hers, it was shrill and so high, so high and she could sing a song and put it over so beautifully.

- *Elisabeth Welch:* She talked very quietly and sang her songs very quietly. Very hushed. Even if she was playing with a big chorus or something." And again, "It was girlish. It wasn't a big voice, but it was on a pitch. It was more like a young boy's voice. It wasn't throaty or nasal, it was placed right but it was youthful, it was boyish youthful and that was all part of her personality.

- *Alberta Hunter:* Florence Mills became as big a star as Bessie but she was the opposite. She was a hummingbird and dainty and lovely. Her little voice was as sweet as Bessie's was rough, and it was like a cello.[3]

  Describing King Oliver's trumpet playing, Alberta said, "He could play it as soft and sweet as the voice of Florence Mills."[4]
- *Gertrude Saunders* (Florence's predecessor in *Shuffle Along*, replying in 1968 to jazz researcher Frank Driggs, who asked her what kind of voice Florence had): "I think you'd call it a 'lyric soprano.' She had a very sweet voice—her delivery—and she had feeling. She sang a song with a soul. I was a trickster."[5]

The high regard in which so many critics, musicians, and experts held Florence Mills's voice was due to its foundation of musicianship. Although not formally trained, she had an innate musical sense that allowed her to use her voice as an instrument. It was this ability that led to the many comparisons with birds (hummingbird, dove, nightingale, blackbird) and musical instruments (cello, bells, violin, oboe, flute, saxophone). One proof of this musicianly skill was the speed with which she mastered her collaboration with conductor Eugene Goossens and his orchestra for the *Levee Land* performance. He described it as "a tribute to her superb musicianship."[6]

It isn't difficult to see why a voice with these unique characteristics, high and soft, could not register effectively on the acoustic equipment of the 1920s. In Edith Wilson's words, it "sounded nasal and tinny" in the studio environment.[7] Electric recording technology arrived just too late for Florence to benefit or for the world to have a chance to appreciate one of the century's most remarkable voices.

The Dancer

Florence Mills's high esteem as a singer is not surprising. Her equal esteem as a dancer is more surprising because she always performed alongside such an extraordinary collection of other outstanding dancers, male and female. However, even in such talented company she stood out because her dancing, like her singing, was an integral part of the expression of her unique personality and artistic genius. The absence of any moving images of her performance makes it difficult today to form a picture of her style. Apart from singing her praises in a general way, the literature of jazz and tap dance has little to say on technical matters. The recent revival of interest in tap dancing has led many people to take an interest in Florence as a tap dancer, but that was only one facet of her skill.

Those few alive to comment for this book who had seen her or performed with her give conflicting pictures of how big a factor tap dancing was. Hyacinth Curtis didn't recall tap playing a part at all in Florence's repertoire. Maude Russell ("She could dance and she could tap dance") and Adelaide Hall ("She could sing and tap very well") both remembered her as a tap dancer.[8] Perhaps the clearest perspective came from Leonard Reed, coinventor of the "Shim Sham Shimmy." He had seen Florence perform in 1925, when he went to see *Dixie to Broadway*. He still recalled her impact in 1987. "It was just a name on the marquee to me. But after I saw her, I forgot about whoever I came for." In response to my question about her tap skills, he replied: "She could tap, she could do a routine, but she wasn't a specialist tap dancer like Alice Whitman."[9] Reed had worked with the Whitman Sisters. Alice Whitman is universally recognized as the all-time greatest female tapper. For Florence, tap was just one more of a wide array of skills to draw on. However, there is no doubt that she was a master of it, as reviews of her performance of "The March of the Wooden Soldiers" routine showed.

It isn't surprising that Florence had excellent tap skills, given her early mastery of buck-and-wing dancing, which was one of the keystones of many later developments in tap. She herself said, "I never dance like a girl. I prefer to dance like a man. That's why I learned buck-and-wing dancing. I enjoy most dancing with the men in the 'Wooden Soldiers' number."[10] Another factor in her tap skills was the lessons she took from Bill "Bojangles" Robinson in Chicago around 1916. In 1931 he listed among the highlights of his life "teaching the young and unknown Florence Mills dance steps on the roof of 3028 S. State St., Chicago [Gertie Jordan's boarding house]."[11]

In addition to Bojangles's influence, Florence had an important mentor in husband Kid Thompson, who was one of the most outstanding exponents of many facets of tap dancing, such as the acrobatic, eccentric, and legomania styles. There were elements of all of these in Florence's dancing. The Stearnses describe eccentric dancing as "a catchall for dancers who have their own non-standard movements and sell themselves on their individual style."[12]

This was certainly true of Florence. She said:

It all depends on the audience. I never know what I'm doing. . . . I just go crazy when the music starts and I like to give the audience all it craves. I make up the dances to the songs beforehand, but then something happens, like one of the orchestra talking to me, and I answer back and watch the audience without appearing to do so. It's great fun. Something different at every performance. It keeps me fresh. Once in New York I fell down, literally. Did the split.

The audience thought I was hurt. I heard some sympathetic expressions. So I got up and started to limp comically. It got a burst of applause. Then I winked and that got another hand. So the producer ran back stage and asked me to keep it in. I did for several nights but other things happened and I forgot.[13]

That is a description of eccentric dancing; when C. B. Cochran wrote of the Charleston Ball that "as a grand finale, Florence Mills appeared on the now glassy floor. Then thunder of applause as her slim body went through more amazing contortions than you could imagine in a nightmare," he was describing acrobatic dancing.[14] Florence also performed the "Shake Dance" in *Dixie to Broadway* and *Black Birds*, earning the ire of *Variety* for doing a cooch dance. Hyacinth Curtis insisted that Florence's version was more tasteful than the term implied; "It wasn't a grind, not like they're doing now."[15] Charlie "Cornbread" Walker, who replaced Willie Covan in *Dixie to Broadway*, told Delilah Jackson that Florence could do a wide range of tap steps, "Triple Wing," "Falling off a Log," "Over the Top," "Through the Trenches," and many more.[16]

However, Florence combined all of these elements into what Peg Leg Bates described as "interpretive dancing."[17] In the words of Gertrude Saunders, Florence's predecessor in *Shuffle Along*, "A dancer . . . should be able to give her audience a message and her dancing should mean something definite. It must either tell them a story or reflect some emotion, happiness, jealousy, anger."[18] Florence was, above all else, a storyteller in dancing. Renowned ballet critic Arnold Haskell said of her, "Florence Mills had certain qualities that placed her apart. . . . The most noticeable is economy of gesture, the telling of a story in the essential tunes only, like a sketch by a great master. . . . I would put the late Florence Mills, as a dancer, on a par with any of the admittedly great artists of the dance. She had much to express and the power and means technically to express it.[19]

Florence's storytelling talent in dance could be directed equally to pathos or humor, to the grotesque or the beautiful. However, in James Weldon Johnson's words, "She had the good taste that never allowed her to be coarse. She could be *risquée*, she could be seductive; but it was impossible for her to be vulgar."[20] Above all, it was the element of surprise in everything she did that most fascinated her audience:[21]

- This sensational little personality, slim, jaunty, strung on fine and tremulous wires continues to tease the public's sense of the beautiful and the odd. There is an impudent fragility about her, a grace of grotesqueness, a humor of wrists, ankles, pitching hips and perky shoulders that are not to be resisted. —*G. W. Gabriel*

- She can charm you with all that is birdlike or squirrel-like in her. Or she can move you to instant laughter with the comical spirit that is always ready to break out of its so-small container. Or she can move something deep down in you with her genius for grotesquerie. The struttings and monkeyshines, the absurd awryness of things that she does, unexpectedly, as if they had just come into a whimsical, gay mind. —*Dudley Nicholls*
- She has a genius for grotesque. She becomes all mouth in a moment. She makes faces, her hands become crazy pointers. Her body struts and stalks and makes gollywoggles. She flings herself into hilarious postures, and all as spontaneously as a blackbird flirting his feathers while he whistles at the sun. —*Anon.*

Arnold Haskell wasn't the only ballet expert to express a high regard for Florence. André Levinson, noted French critic, saw her as a leader in the development of a more refined and subtle form of black dance.[22] When Buddy Bradley compared ballerina Alicia Markova to Florence Mills, choreographer Frederick Ashton reassured Markova, "You couldn't wish for a greater compliment."[23] Her legacy is acknowledged today in the form of the Flo-Bert Awards, named after her and Bert Williams, which annually honor outstanding contributors in tap dance.[24]

The Jazz Artist

"The Jazz Queen Is Dead," "Death Claims 'Queen of Jazz,'" "Throng Mourns Jazz Queen," "The Queen of Jazz in Her Wildest Dance": These were just some of the headlines and captions that greeted Florence Mills's death in the New York press in 1927.[25] The titles "Jazz Queen" and "Harlem Jazz Queen" were routinely bestowed on her in her lifetime. Today it is difficult to turn up any reference to her in learned works on jazz except perhaps as a footnote listing popular singers of the 1920s or documenting the subject of Duke Ellington's "Black Beauty." What does it matter, one might ask. Surely her reputation as a performer is secure enough without needing to be in the Jazz Hall of Fame as well? It certainly is, but the history of jazz is poorer for not claiming her as one of its own. Why, if she was so significant in the 1920s, is she overlooked now? Several factors may help to explain why.

First, the absence of recordings has undoubtedly made it hard for later generations to form a view of her contribution and significance. However, that same lack did not stop jazz historians from building legends around Buddy Bolden or writing extensively on the Creole Band. We do not have any recordings of Tony Jackson, but his fame in ragtime lore is secure.

Learned works immortalize great operatic performers and dramatic actors whose genius we can never experience.

Another possible reason is that the emphasis on Florence as a dancer and stage performer overshadowed her role in the world of jazz. Jazz fans, fed on a diet of recordings and concert hall performances, have largely forgotten that their music had its origins in the wider context of black music and culture, including the world of the entertainers.[26]

A third factor is that some jazz writers have lessened her status in an unwarranted fashion. Chief among them is English classical musician turned jazz fan Patrick "Spike" Hughes. Jazz fans owe a debt to Hughes for being one of the first intelligent critics of jazz. When most people writing about jazz in England considered Paul Whiteman the epitome of the genre, Hughes was writing perceptively about the true greats such as Louis Armstrong. However, he was a dogmatic young man in the 1920s. While Hughes rightly despised the taste for watered-down "symphonic" jazz, he went to the other extreme in wanting only what he saw as "hot" music. Even his idol, Duke Ellington, wasn't immune from Hughes's criticism for not always playing "hot." Ellington nicknamed him "The Hot Dictator" because of his narrow views.[27]

Hughes found the sophisticated style of Florence Mills too refined by comparison with his favorite, Bessie Smith. In similar fashion, he didn't like the smooth, virtuoso sound of Ellington trombonist Lawrence Brown.[28] However, in his autobiography, *Opening Bars*, he was not content merely to express his preference. He went on to say:

> I am prepared to admit my judgment was completely wrong and that if I heard Florence Mills today I would think quite differently about her. On the other hand, recalling the people who raved about her at the time and reflecting since on these same people's tastes in Negro music and dancing I have a hunch that I was right; for the people I have in mind were those who considered the Cotton Club to be "genuine" Harlem—as if any place were "genuine" Harlem that did not admit coloured guests. Many years after Florence Mills had died, Paul Robeson confirmed my original suspicion. He had admired her greatly, of course, but in his view the greatest of all genuinely Negro artists was Bessie Smith.[29]

This was gross misrepresentation on several counts. First, to associate Florence Mills, who in her years of stardom never performed in segregated venues, with the Cotton Club's policies, was completely unjust. To compound this with the suggestion that she was admired only by people ignorant of true black music and dancing was an insult to her fervent and knowledgeable admirers among her own people, many of whom are quoted here on the subject.

Worse than this was the fraudulent use of Paul Robeson's words as a put-down of one of his most admired compatriots. Hughes is here paraphrasing, in 1946, his own 1933 interview with Robeson. The original interview text went, "[Robeson] considers that even including Florence Mills, the greatest Negro artist he has ever heard is [Bessie Smith]."[30] By any sensible interpretation this pays a high tribute to Florence Mills, second only for Robeson to his greatest of all, Bessie. Yet in 1946 Hughes reinterprets Robeson's words to confirm Hughes's "suspicion" that Florence was not "genuine Harlem" or a "genuinely Negro artist." Unfortunately, Hughes's words have been quoted uncritically in several sources, with unknown damage to Florence's reputation.[31]

On the subject of Hughes's preference for Bessie's "hot" style over Florence's sweeter delivery, Duke Ellington said it all. "It don't matter if it's sweet or hot, just give that rhythm every thing you've got. It don't mean a thing if it ain't got that swing." No one who saw her ever questioned that Florence Mills, in jazz terminology, had "swing."

Another respected jazz and dance writer who was less than fair to Florence is Roger Pryor Dodge. Writing on Bubber Miley in 1958, he said, "For the Negro, a good beginning in music is a mother who sings at her chores; but later the desire to sell himself in show business leads to all kinds of professional expediencies. These may prove very harmful. The quick jump from blues singer to nightingale, like Florence Mills and the hundreds of lesser Florences, the off-color songs burlesquing Negro traits (interesting in their way, but not conducive to great jazz) . . . are all ruinous to art."[32]

Dodge's writings started in 1929, and he wrote this in 1958, so it isn't clear to what extent he was writing from personal knowledge of Florence as a performer. What he wrote is a travesty in two respects. First, anyone with knowledge of her career would have known there was never a "jump from blues singer to nightingale." Florence was always a nightingale, with ballads her specialty, although her versatility allowed her to handle blues capably. Journalist William Pickens even described her as "the best interpreter of the 'Blues' I have ever heard."[33]

The second travesty is the implication that Florence performed "off-color" songs, burlesquing her own people. Nothing could be further from the truth. She was renowned as a clean performer, and none of her material ever denigrated her people. It is true that like many great jazz artists, notably Billie Holiday and Fats Waller, she was given much banal material to perform. Like them, through her genius she turned the dross into gold. Dodge, like Hughes, in these words epitomizes the attitude of several early white devotees of jazz in espousing a purism that accepts only raw, earthy, primitive music as being "genuinely Negro." They failed to recognize the intertwined complexity of all the facets of African American culture, including popular entertainment, and hence the full complexity of the world of jazz.

So much for the detractors! What then is the evidence for Florence's jazz credentials? This question can be approached from several angles. First, by way of circumstantial evidence, are her associations—"you can know me by the company I keep." Apart from her early connections with jazz dance, through cakewalk and buck-and-wing dancing, by her midteens in Harlem she was performing alongside stride piano players like James P. Johnson, Willie "The Lion" Smith, and Luckey Roberts. Her years in black vaudeville also had important jazz connections. As William Howland Kenney has said, "American jazz, in its early search for a home, passed through the world of Afro-American vaudeville and musical theater. As a result, the development of jazz was influenced by show business and the particular constraints then imposed upon popular, black theater music."[34]

At the Panama Café in 1916, Florence was associating with the world of Chicago jazz and ragtime, including Tony Jackson, Glover Compton, Alberta Hunter, Mattie Hite, Mezz Mezzrow, and many others. The Panama Trio's singing between 1916 and 1919 was always described as jazz. They performed with Jelly Roll Morton in Los Angeles. With the Tennessee Ten, Florence was fronting a jazz band through whose ranks passed many notable names and which had important associations with the Creole Band.

Her rise to fame in *Shuffle Along* saw her performing with Eubie Blake and the *Shuffle Along* orchestra. By the time she was starring in her own shows, she was fronting the Plantation Orchestra, which caused Spike Hughes to say, "I was hearing for the first time [jazz] played with all its characteristic colourfulness and variety."[35] Thus her associations place her firmly in the jazz world.

The next approach is to look at the opinions of her knowledgeable peers. Did they consider Florence a jazz artist? Let them speak for themselves:[36]

- Jazz has a virtuoso technique all its own: its best performers, singers and players, lift it far above the level of mere "trick" or mechanical effects. Abbie Mitchell, Ethel Waters and Florence Mills; the Blues singers, Clara, Mamie and Bessie Smith; Eubie Blake, the pianist; Buddy Gilmore, the drummer, and "Bill" Robinson, the pantomimic dancer— to mention merely an illustrative few—are inimitable artists, with an inventive, improvising skill that defies imitation. —*J. A. Rogers*
- The musicians who did so much to give form and substance to early jazz have gone down in history and are the idols of the true aficionados.

Some great names of the past are instrumentalists like "King" Oliver, Jelly Roll Morton, "Kid" Ory, and singers Ethel Waters, Mamie Smith, Bessie Smith and the great Florence Mills. —*William Grant Still*

- For the first time I was hearing true jazz . . . and seeing true jazz—Florence Mills, Johnny [Hudgins], prince of clowns and the Three Eddies, masterly study in black and white. —*Arnold Haskell*
- Jazz singers, too, have not been without influence on the development of this music. Louis Armstrong, Cab Calloway and his hi-de-hi-de-o, Ray Nance and Joe Carroll, Dizzy Gillespie's oo-pap-da, and Florence Mills, Adelaide Hall, Alberta Hunter, Baby Cox, Billie Holiday, Babs Gonzalez and Ella Fitzgerald have all been outstanding jazz vocalists. —*Langston Hughes*
- One great negro jazz singer went with the death of Bert Williams. The outstanding singers of his race since then, men like Roland Hayes and Paul Robeson, seem to prefer more serious music. The jazz crown belongs to a member of the opposite sex—Florence Mills. Who will forget the sensation she made when she graduated from Harlem cabarets and came down town to steal the show in *Shufflin' Along*? —*Henry O. Osgood*
- *Maude Russell* (on *Shuffle Along*): Lottie Gee was more like the prima donna and Florence Mills was more like the jazz singer. *Bill Egan:* So would you describe Florence as a jazz singer? *Maude Russell:* Florence Mills was an all-round singer; she could sing a sweet song would make you cry, and then she could sing a jazz song and jazz it.

These quotations are all from people who were knowledgeable about jazz, lived through its evolution, and saw Florence Mills perform many times. Their testimony reflects the reality, however much the passage of time has obscured it today.

The final test is to look at available specific information about Florence Mills's style as a jazz performer. It is generally accepted that many features of jazz as we know it today had their origins in African music and dance survivals within the United States' African diaspora. These features include:

- Improvisation
- Tonal features and effects unfamiliar in the European tradition—including so-called blue notes and smears
- Sophisticated syncopation
- Call-and-response motifs

All of these are clearly identifiable as important characteristics of Florence Mills's performance style. Consider first improvisation, which caused Whitney Balliett to label jazz "the sound of surprise." Time and again, reviewers referred to the element of surprise in everything Florence did. In her own description of how her dances changed in response to random stimuli during performance, she said,

> I never know what I'm doing. . . . I just go crazy when the music starts and I like to give the audience all it craves. I make up the dances to the songs beforehand, but then something happens, like one of the orchestra talking to me, and I answer back and watch the audience without appearing to do so. It's great fun. Something different at every performance.

Again, in words redolent of the spirit of a jazz jam session,

> I'm the despair of stage managers who want a player to act in a groove. No groove for me. The stage isn't large enough for me at times. But it is during the midnight performances that I "let out" the most. We all do. Not that we overstep the conventions, you understand. But it's just the feeling that it's after hours, I suppose. And we whoop it up.[37]

Elsewhere she says, "Our show is essentially the same every night, yet it is different every night. This reserve force of happiness is always breaking out in unexpected places. And consequently our work does not seem like work, but is more like having a good time."[38]

C. B. Cochran had noted this attitude to their work by the musicians and performers.

> The devotion of these coloured folk to their calling is to my mind one of the secrets of their theatrical success. They simply live for their work. The musicians of Will Vodery's band, not content with the rehearsals in the orchestra pit, sat on the stairs or in the band-room all day practicing on their instruments. In the same way, the performers are more than happy if they can be allowed to rehearse their dances and acts the greater part of the time they are not actually busy with the public performances.[39]

What Cochran was witnessing was that life was a continuous jam session for the musicians and performers.

Just a few of the many comments on the role of spontaneous creation in Florence's performance include:[40]

- Her artistry is instinctive; her power of improvisation—she never sings two verses alike, and frequently interpolates embellishments that would make many a prima donna green with envy—belongs to genius, and that she has in her very eyelids. —*Herbert Hughes*

- She had in extraordinary measure the quality that distinguishes the Negro behind the footlights—the quality of seeming to enjoy it for its own sake, of making it up on the spot rather than of playing a canned act. —*Anon.*
- The supreme greatness of Florence Mills not only amused and entertained her audiences, but also lifted them on the aerial flight of her imagination. —*W. H. Ferris*

What characterized Florence Mills as a jazz artist most was the way in which she used her voice as an instrument. For all singers, the voice is their instrument, but she, more perhaps than any other, was noted for the way her voice resembled musical instruments. An important factor in this was her extensive use of wordless vocalizing. She was renowned for her ability to create odd effects with a special throat technique. This was a kind of yodeling that people struggled to describe. They used phrases like "In her small throat she hides all kind of funny little sounds," "amazing throat noises and screeches," "unexpected bell-like little noises and bubbling sounds," and "heart-taking bubbles of sound thronging out of her throat like champagne from a bottle."

Some contemporary descriptions of her jazz-inflected tonal qualities included the following:[41]

- Florence Mills's voice is the most sensitive and flexible I know; she plays with half tones and quarter tones like a violin. —*Daily Sketch*
- From the molten notes she goes into jazz slides and minors that somehow make music. —*Anon.*
- The Negro . . . saw that the saxophone could imitate the voice, and in the person of Miss Florence Mills saw that the voice could equally imitate the saxophone. —*Gilbert Seldes in "The 7 Lively Arts"*
- She had the gift for harmonies that baffle formal notation. —*Anon.*
- Her voice continues to be sometimes sweet and sometimes further from the pitch than Dixie is from Broadway. —*G. W. Gabriel*

It can safely be assumed that a performer of Florence's fame was a master of syncopation and rhythm, but lest there be any doubt, some testimonials are relevant:[42]

- Take the song "You've Got to See Sweetie Every Night," [the] melodic invention is weak, and the harmony reminiscent of that of the four hundred and third hymn of the "Ancient and Modern" book; but [Florence

Mills] invested it with an intense interest from beginning to end, and entirely by rhythmical means. —*Basil Maine*
- There is, to me, a hidden rhythm in the art of all coloured people—a super-syncopation behind their melodies. . . . And especially do I feel this with Florence Mills. —*Beverley Nichols*
- A veritable creature of syncopation, never completely still, but possessed of a wild, communicable spirit of dance. —*Anon.*

The final characteristic element of jazz identified above was the use of "call-and-response" motifs. Most people would recognize this element in the interaction between preacher and congregation in gospel music, but it is traceable as a key element in all black music. In Florence's case it was most obviously typified by the extraordinary rapport she created with audiences, as when one critic wrote, "There were times last night when emotional waves crossed and recrossed the footlights."[43] Her performance of "I'm Craving for That Kind of Love," in *Shuffle Along*, when in Eubie Blake's words she had the audience "screaming and hollering," is also an example.[44] In a more specific sense, it was exemplified in the interaction between her and Johnny Dunn when she would answer from the stage while he played to her with his four-foot-long coach trumpet from the orchestra pit.

All these pieces of contemporary evidence point clearly to the conclusion that Florence Mills was a jazz performer of major importance. She possessed a high level of natural musical ability, sometimes expressed in a unique nonverbal vocalizing approach. She demonstrated remarkable capacities for improvisation in her singing and dancing. Her observed performances exhibited all of the characteristics that have come to be associated with jazz at its best. It is time the world of jazz claimed her as one of its own again.

The Performer

Singer, dancer, actor, comedienne, mime: Florence Mills was all of these, but the whole was greater than the sum of the parts. Above all it was her versatility that impressed her contemporaries. In the words of Alvin White, "She could do it all"; the Nicholas Brothers said, "She could do everything"; and Willie Covan, "Florence Mills was an all-round performer."[45] Allied to this huge talent was an extraordinary rapport with her audience:

She can sweep an audience off its feet without the least apparent effort. Her talent is inborn and it combines the qualities of a clever comedienne, a gifted singer, a rhythmic dancer and a tantalizing mimic.[46]

Her control over an audience was so superb that at times it seemed almost supernatural. She not only had the ability to inspire tumultuous outbursts of applause. She also had that greater ability which compels an audience to sit in raptured silence.[47]

Like many great performers, Florence was a shy introvert offstage, but on-stage she reveled in the interplay with her audience and drew inspiration from it. "I love to watch the faces of the audience while I work. When I'm singing and dancing to the tune of "Jungle Town has Moved to Dixieland" . . . it seems as though they are all going to rise at any moment and join in. . . . When I sing 'I'm a Little Blackbird Looking for a Bluebird,' they all seem so sympathetic, as though they wanted to go out and catch one for me."[48]

Referring to an enthusiastic audience, she said, "This is a wonderful audi-ence, appreciative and understanding. Naturally, I like such an audience, and yet I like a stolid one too. When I am faced with a stolid audience, I know that I must make them my friends, and [I] am on my mettle."[49] And they did respond:

Hardly a performance passes that several in the audience do not rise in their seats as though impelled by some unknown power to take a part in the mad revelry, and numerous are the times when applause unrestrained breaks in upon dance and song numbers before their completion. The personality of Flo-rence Mills is perhaps responsible for much of this flattering reaction on the part of the spectator. . . . Her listeners are stirred to an electric condition ap-proaching frenzy.[50]

There were several facets of Florence's performing style that evoked regu-lar comment. One of the most noteworthy was her ability to transport her au-dience from a spirit of wild abandon one moment to a restrained pathos the next. She was, in Theophilus Lewis's words, "the supreme mistress of both abandon and restraint," and she could combine them, so that her wildest moments still had a core of melancholy. The following observations describe this unique ability.

- There are notes in her voice that come from far away and long ago with an infinite pathos and are an undercurrent to her gayety and comedy.[51]
- Infinite joyousness, sweeping back the tide of years and inducing a care-free mood of springtime, was, perhaps, her greatest gift; but with it, as a kind of undertone which now and again emerged, was an infinite pathos. Her fragility in itself was a suggestion of it, and her childlike abandon to the mood of the minute added to it.[52]

- With the same effortless ease of Charlie Chaplin revealing an unexpected vein of pathos in some perfectly ordinary event, Florence Mills brought tears to one's eyes purely by the quality of her voice and the sincerity of her acting.[53]

This ability to send conflicting signals caused one observer to comment, "On the stage I find her extraordinarily disturbing. She has the force of a wild animal and the intolerable pathos of a wild animal disciplined and restrained."[54] In the words of another, "When she was in the heart of one of her jungle numbers she was beside herself—more than a little mad. . . . Wailing her wah-wah songs, she was transported and utterly unsafe. In short, she belonged to the little legion of the truly great in the field of public entertainment."[55]

Another characteristic that endeared Florence to her admirers was her childlike air of unspoiled innocence, which evoked words like *imp, sprite, pixie, elf,* and *hoyden.* It had an asexual character that led many to see her as like an adolescent boy:

- She was like a child with that lovely, smiling face. Her personality [was] clean, happy, young and without any evil at all. . . . She was just a quiet, gentle, person and her boyish, youthful, young thing came out on the stage. —*Elisabeth Welch*
- She is a fascinating creature to look at with the skinny legs and body of some athletic boys of thirteen or fourteen, black smoothed bobbed hair and a large, very large, Negro mouth. . . . Perhaps her chief charm is that she is neither man nor woman nor boy nor girl but adolescent. Even in her song "You Got to See Sweety" she is more like a child playing at lovers than any possible White or Negro fiancée. One feels quite sure she would not care twopence how long her lover stayed away. —*New Statesman*

It was this childlike and androgynous quality in her performance that allowed Florence to perform some of the raunchier numbers, such as "I'm Craving for That Kind of Love," and "I've Got What It Takes," without appearing vulgar. Kimball and Bolcom commented, "Florence Mills was hardly the earthy creature 'I'm Craving for That Kind of Love' had been written for, but she gave to the part, by all accounts, an ingenuousness that added greatly to the ensemble."[56] She delivered such potentially risqué numbers with a sly, saucy humor that mischievously undermined the overt intent of the song so that it became in effect a private joke between her and her audience.

Above all, what allowed Florence to play on the emotions of an audience, and brought together her multifaceted talents in an alchemy that caused hardened critics repeatedly to use the word "genius," was her outstanding ability as a mime. Mime, or mimicry, is defined as the art of conveying meaning "solely by gesture, movement, and expression."[57] Florence's capacity to use this as an integral part of her performance was noticed as far back as the Panama Trio days. She had thoroughly perfected it by the time of her stardom, and it was the basis of much of the comedic strain in her performance:

- She is a born comedienne, and as only a born comedienne can, she is able, by the flash of an eye, or pucker of the lips, to carry the situation from the broadest fun to something that closely resembles a sob.[58]
- Her gestures were poetry, the seemingly unconscious movements of her body were music. With the simplest gesture or expression she could convey a thought or enkindle a feeling it would require volumes to interpret.[59]

To support this skill in mimicry, Florence drew on a repertoire of special little tricks and techniques of her own. One such was a way of smacking the palm of her hand with her fist that was described as "electric."[60] In Kid Thompson's words, "She could flaunt, you know, a lot of things, and make her eyes look so good." Maude Russell tried to explain her impact:

She used to dilate her nose; she used to do her nose like this [demonstrates, dilating nostrils]. She could do her nose like that and people would just scream. She was cute, and she had a lot of other little tricks that made her very lovable. She had a little round face. Her face was round, her little nose flat; she could take this nose and dilate and do 'em like that, and she had beautiful great big eyes. She could roll those eyes. She was just about the cutest thing you would ever lay your eyes on.

Florence's style was totally natural. In C. B. Cochran's words, "There was not a false note in any part of her performance." This does not mean it was effortless. She was too consummate a professional for that. It was very much "the art that conceals art." In her own words, "All my life I have worked and practiced hard. The little glance or movement that looks so easy on the stage often takes hours of rehearsal to get it just right."[61] On her ability to portray characters with an "unusual fidelity," one columnist noted, "From the moment Miss Mills is handed a lyric to study she endeavors to sink her personality so completely into it that she becomes for the time being the character [she] is portraying."[62]

And finally, Florence's status as a performer may be best assessed by some of those who knew best.

- *Duke Ellington:* When he gave his first Carnegie Hall Concert in 1943, he sought to honor the truly great figures of black performance by presenting musical portraits of them. His three selections were Bert Williams, Bill "Bojangles" Robinson, and Florence Mills.
- *Langston Hughes:* In *Black Magic: A Pictorial History of the African American in the Performing Arts,* Hughes (with Milton Melzer) named "Golden Dozens" in nine categories of entertainment. However, the introduction to the lists identified a select few "all-time greats" about whom "there can be little argument." These were Ira Aldridge, Buddy Bolden, Black Patti, Ernest Hogan, Bert Williams, and Florence Mills.
- *James Weldon Johnson:* "As a pantomimist and a singing and dancing comedienne she had no superior in any place or any race."[63]
- *C. B. Cochran:* "Florence Mills was one of the greatest artists that ever walked on to a stage. But for her colour she would have been internationally accepted as one of the half-dozen leading theatrical personalities of this century."[64] And on her death he said: "With a full consciousness of a glib misuse of the word genius, I deliberately apply it to Florence Mills. I have introduced to London no artist more characteristic, more interesting, more fascinating."[65]
- *Paul Robeson:* In 1924, expressing his optimism for the bright future of black theater, he singled Florence Mills out as "in a class by herself."[66] Many years later, in 1952, speaking about the fundamental role of black performers in creating modern popular music, he listed the great black singers and dancers who had inspired the world of pop music. The only names that appeared on both lists were Bert Williams and Florence Mills.[67]

The Person

The key to understanding Florence Mills's success as an entertainer and performer lies above all in her character and personality, which were very much a reflection of her African American heritage. Although she was photogenic, and her pictures capture the elfin appeal that commentators noted, contemporary accounts are unanimous that she was not a classic beauty:[68]

- "She sure was no raving beauty. Cute, yes." —*Alvin White*
- "She wasn't what you'd call a beauty." —*Elisabeth Welch*

- "She wasn't even pretty but she only had to walk out on the stage and everyone stopped breathing." —*Eubie Blake*
- "She had no more aphrodisiacal appeal than an angleworm, being one of the unloveliest creatures imaginable. She was thin to the point of emaciation—her arms and legs were like brown macaroni, and her little face with its snapping, fiery eyes, was positively simian. But when she sang! Everything was forgotten." —*Washington Daily News*

Although Florence lacked the glamour the world associates with great classic beauty, people instinctively saw her as beautiful because of the inner character she radiated. In Willie Covan's words, "Her character was beautiful, she was beautiful to go round with, she had a personality, liked everybody in the world, she loved the world and she was reaching out to people, she was smiling and laughing with everybody."[69]

For Elisabeth Welch also, it was Florence's character that made people feel an affinity with her. "Florence had a smallish head and a joyful smile. She wasn't a noisy person at all. She was very gentle and had a nice, kind face. People adored her without even knowing her. . . . Everybody loved her, especially when she sang. She was like a child with that lovely, smiling face." Elisabeth also believed that people saw this natural goodness reflected in Florence's stage presence. "That was her strength on the stage as well. It came over. This joyousness and the songs she sang. She didn't belong in show business really. She was so sweet, and loved by everybody."

The goodness and purity people divined in the performance was equally reflected in Florence's daily life and dealings with the people around her, in a dozen ways. It was reflected also in the lack of scandal in her life. She was never associated with alcohol, drugs, or high living in any way. Despite the occasional unfounded rumors of affairs with famous figures, her marriage to Kid Thompson was idyllically happy. C. B. Cochran noted, "[Their] marriage was a great success, and the big fellow's adoration and admiration of his vivid wife were something worth seeing."[70] Maude Russell, who outlived five husbands herself, was more blunt. "Listen, you know about Florence; Florence was such an angelic person, there's very little to write about her. There was never any scandal attached to her, and she was married and she stuck real close to her husband, and she didn't do anything but go to work, and work and go home, work and go home."

A characteristic that often surprised those meeting Florence for the first time was her unfailing courtesy to all. A star of her stature and fame was expected to show some temperament or swagger, but Florence was free of such attributes. C. B. Cochran recalled, "Her modesty indeed was almost embarrassing.

Whenever anyone went into her dressing room she would jump up to greet her visitors, and she was always the last to sit down—a touch of courtesy that never failed to impress me."[71]

This attitude was equally true for everyone she met, journalists, stagehands, public, or children. Reporters noted it: "Florence Mills [is] another than the flashing and kaleidoscopic person of the footlights in the shelter of her dressing-room. Modest and subdued, she almost shrinks from praise."[72] "Florence Mills in temperament remained the same after she reached fame as she had been before—she was the same sweet little soul. She was, of course, proud of her achievements but it never affected her to the extent of forgetting those in her profession less fortunate than she."[73]

She lived simply, never owning an automobile. When not touring on the road, she was a familiar figure in Harlem, approachable by all the children in the neighborhood, who knew they could rely on her to provide ice cream or candy. Actress Edna Mae Harris, who lived on 132nd Street, told Delilah Jackson that she would see Florence walking along her street to work whenever her shows were playing in Harlem.

As well as courtesy and modesty, generosity was one of Florence's most noteworthy traits. Young Michael Anglo used to play around the theaters where his father was a professional outfitter to theatre folks in the 1920s. He enjoyed meeting the many black entertainers, but fifty years later, "I remember Florence Mills, best of all, with her big soft eyes, her soft voice and gentle manners. She once tipped me a pound note and on another occasion gave me a very large jigsaw puzzle."[74]

Florence's covert charitable actions in London have been described already, but they were only part of a wider pattern. Kid Thompson related how, after her death, working-class people from the neighborhood turned up at the house to tell of her charitable acts, which he had never known about. "To her," he said, "it was a sacred privilege to help a weak brother or sister, and she never told. If the person returned the money all well, and if not, she never complained."[75]

Florence extended the same courtesies to her professional peers. "She never feared competition and was never jealous. She believed in surrounding herself with the best of talent and in giving her associates their just share of applause."[76] In return, she was accorded an extremely high level of respect across the industry. C. B. Cochran observed the results of this. "She held Harlem . . . in the hollow of her hand. She was the queen of coloured America. I have never seen anything in the theatre to compare with the loyalty and veneration which she excited among colleagues in a show. 'Why, sho Ah'll woik all night ef Miss Mills say so,' or, 'Would Miss Mills lak' et?' or,

'Miss Mills say so den dat goes,' were typical remarks that one heard all the time when *Dover Street to Dixie* or *Blackbirds* was in rehearsal or running."[77]

Yet another factor that took people by surprise when they met with Florence was her cool intelligence. They invariably expected this childish figure of infectious gaiety and laughter to be a carefree, sunny piece of fluffy femininity. Instead they encountered a serious, well-read, well-spoken woman, knowledgeable on contemporary social issues and actively concerned for her fellow human beings. It surprised the reporter who interviewed her for *Home Notes*, a women's magazine of the day, to discover that "Florence is quite a serious minded girl and can speak eloquently of the aspirations of her race. She is also highly cultured and takes a great interest in music that is far removed from the jazz stuff which is the essential feature of her public performances."[78] This was a reference to her enthusiasm, noted by Hannen Swaffer, for the music of black English composer Samuel Coleridge-Taylor. Although Coleridge-Taylor had died in 1912, his music was hugely popular in England, especially "Hiawatha's Wedding Feast," a setting of verses from Longfellow's poem. Florence probably had several opportunities to hear it performed during her time in England.

Swaffer also noted her interest in books by Pushkin and Dumas, both of whom had African blood.[79] Elsewhere she indicated her keen interest in black novelists, citing Jessie Redmon Fauset and Walter White as examples, and contemporary black drama, with Evelyn Preer and Clarence Muse as some of her favorites.[80] C. B. Cochran had ample opportunity to notice Florence's intellectual capacity and was impressed by it. "Kid was a simple fellow and his wife, because of her reading, self-education, and a truly cosmopolitan grasp of modern intellectual and cultural movements, could make rings round him in the matter of culture."[81]

A lovable personality, a generous nature, and a keen intelligence are not of themselves enough to ensure artistic and popular success, even when allied to an exceptional talent. The remaining characteristic fundamental to Florence's success was her sense of responsibility, commitment, and loyalty. She was absolutely loyal to family, friends, fellow performers, the people of her race, and ultimately, as proven by her charitable activities in London, to any member of the human race who needed her help.

In the early stages her sense of responsibility and commitment was directed toward her professional duties, always giving her utmost in performance and being totally reliable. Once fame arrived, after *Shuffle Along*, she saw the opportunity to use her new status to benefit her fellow black performers. Lew Leslie shrewdly used this to persuade her to stay with him rather than take up Ziegfeld's historic offer to make her the first black woman to star in the *Follies*. The London engagement in *Dover Street to Dixie* opened her eyes to the possibility that she had the power to go even further and achieve something for her entire race.

After London, and the subsequent triumphant guest role in *Greenwich Village Follies*, she began to see herself as an ambassador for her people, with a mission to undermine the folly of racism by showing its illogicality. In the words of Theophilus Lewis, "She always regarded herself as our envoy to the world, and she was probably the best one we ever had. The world must be shown not only that we can produce genius but that we also possess dependability, stamina and courage. Florence Mills showed it."[82]

The first overt sign of her new consciousness came with the inclusion of "I'm a Little Blackbird" in the new show *Dixie to Broadway*. Florence not only promoted its message onstage but also used it on public occasions, such as her meeting with the Mayor of Philadelphia, to spread her gospel. Finally, in England, she went beyond her role as a performer and became a public spokesperson for her people and for the NAACP, talking to news columnists, writing columns herself, and using any available forum for her views.

Her approach was always diplomatic and nonconfrontational, believing in the power of persuasion and good example. She firmly believed the goodwill created by the pleasure she and her associates gave to the public would result in a change in people's attitudes. She took pleasure in the belief that this was so, telling Hannen Swaffer, just before she left England, "I want to help the colored people. I realize that in my line of work, I am doing much to help them. The stage is the quickest way to get to the people. My own success makes people think better of other colored folks. . . . I feel our visit here has done a lot of good. No one has complained about us. Some people have been to see our show, not only two or three times, but twenty or thirty times. This must surely have helped."[83]

The *Pittsburgh Courier* shared these views.

Florence Mills was more than an actress. She and the entire Negro race felt that she was an ambassador of good will from the blacks to the whites; a potent factor in softening the harshness of race feeling; a living example of the potentialities of the Negro of ability when given a chance to make good. She possessed brains, confidence, industry and tact—the very foundation of success in any field of endeavor.[84]

In the end Florence's sense of commitment and duty contributed to her early death. Her personal interest and well-being must not take precedence over the employment of others, her obligation to the public, her determination to earn credit for her race, and finally her mother's ill health. At the end, aware that she was dying, her concern was still only to comfort those around her. Perhaps, at last, death came as a relief and solace, lifting a heavy burden that she had carried for too long. For her people, the grief expressed at the funeral was a reflection of the knowledge that they had lost one who truly had been their greatest ambassador.

Her Legacy

Is it still possible, seventy-five years after the death of Florence Mills, to identify her legacy in any of the fields she graced so memorably in her short life? There's no doubt that at the time of her death, it was widely assumed her memory was indelible and her legacy undeniable. Not only did the national press in the United States and most of Europe report her death as a major news story, but many United States and overseas newspapers judged it worthy of editorial comment. Some examples of their sentiments:

- "Her fame in the international theatre is more than a sign of the advancement of Negroes. She was one of the leaders whose accomplishment sets the whole racial movement a notch or two forward." —*New York Times*
- "Hereafter the world will never speak of Carmencita and Pavlova without calling Florence Mills to mind." —*Washington Tribune*
- "The inspiration of her career will never be lost to her race. More than any other person in the field of the arts she typified the spirit and personality of the Negro." —*Chicago Defender*
- "She proved that merit triumphs as it should. Color cannot conquer courage!" —*New York Evening Journal*
- "No history of the past decade will ever be adequate without liberal mention of Florence Mills." —*Pittsburgh Courier*
- "There was something in Florence Mills which made her unforgettable, and the queer little break in her voice, and her soft, lisping accent, will haunt us poignantly now that we know we shall never hear them again." —*London Daily Telegraph*

The *Telegraph* was right; those who had seen Florence would never forget her. But generations pass, and soon the small handful left today who actually saw her will be gone. Eventually the only test of her legacy, as with any other such, is to ask, How is the world different today because of her. Where are the signs of her passing, either visible or found only by patiently drawing back the veils of time? We can look in several places.

In the field of performance, it is more as a singer than as a dancer that her main impact can be found. Although she was a remarkable dancer, her era was filled with so many phenomenally gifted black dancers, men and women, that she can mainly be seen as one of the many carrying on the tradition rather than as a stylistic innovator in her own right. Nevertheless some important contributions are identifiable.

In jazz dance her major contribution was the opportunities her shows created for so many of the other talented dancers of the period. They included, among the men, Willie Covan, Eddie Rector, Johnny Nit, Clarence Robinson, and Charlie "Cornbread" Walker. Among the women were Maude Russell, Alma Smith, and Hyacinth Curtis, who went on to a long career at the Cotton Club.

In the wider field of modern dance, the exposure of London and Paris to authentic black dance by Florence and her two shows had a significant impact on the rising generation of progressive exponents of modern dance. Arnold Haskell saw a specific influence on the younger English dancers, especially Penelope Spencer, whom he admired greatly. "[Florence Mills] had a powerful influence on Penelope Spencer in the most formative period of her art. . . . Her influence on the younger dancers has been enormous." It was Florence's ability to convey emotion and tell a story in her dance, combining jazz and pantomime, that impressed Haskell and the French André Levinson as well as progressive composers and choreographers like Constant Lambert, William Walton, and Frederick Ashton. The impression made by Florence and the *Blackbirds* also created the opportunity for Buddy Bradley to make a long-term career as a choreographer and dance teacher in England.

While there were no recordings through which Florence could influence later generations of singers, there is no doubt she has an important place in the history of popular and jazz singing. She was no blues shouter. In Alvin White's words, "She couldn't belt out a song but she could sure put one over." Her primary genre was ballads, vaudeville songs, and show tunes. The late Doc Cheatham, a great admirer of hers, described her to me as singing "mostly show tunes" but "with a jazz spirit." It struck me then that this could be equally truly said of the great jazz singers like Billie Holiday, Ella Fitzgerald, and Sarah Vaughan.

Drawing a comparison with the superb Abbey Lincoln, Will Friedwald, in his book *Jazz Singing*, bracketed Florence, not with the Bessie Smith tradition, but in "the other stream of black chanteuses," with Ethel Waters and Elisabeth Welch.[85] He could have added Mabel Mercer, Adelaide Hall, and perhaps Eva Taylor. She was a major influence for all of these ladies. They had either actually performed with her or known her performance style well.

In 1976 the then 81-year-old Eva Taylor told a Swedish interviewer that Florence Mills was her favorite artist and had been a strong influence on her singing. Although Ethel Waters and Florence were quite different in personality, which showed in their performance, Ethel's initial reaction to the lineup at the Plantation was that their singing styles were too similar for her to follow Florence.

Ivie Anderson, later to join Duke Ellington, was performing in a Florence Mills vein in the late 1920s, even including "I'm a Little Blackbird" in her repertoire. Mabel Mercer, Adelaide Hall, and later Valaida Snow and Lena Horne, all inherited Florence's mantle in the Lew Leslie *Blackbirds* series. Both Adelaide and Lena Horne were directly pressured by Lew Leslie to sound like Florence Mills, a task both resisted as unreasonable.[86] Another who consciously sought to emulate her was Josephine Baker. A biographer wrote, "It was to good effect that Josephine had studied Florence Mills and Yvonne Printemps, imitating their light, bright voices."[87] Ironically, Florence's sister Maude, who was recorded, is remembered as a capable blues singer, although hardly a shouter in the full Bessie Smith–Ma Rainey tradition.

Based on her nonverbal, instrumental singing, a strong case can be made for Florence's role as a technical innovator in jazz singing. Nonverbal jazz singing is usually linked to the scat tradition, which is often deemed to have started with Louis Armstrong's 1925 "Heebie Jeebie Blues." Ella Fitzgerald also excelled in it. Scat singing typically involves the use of nonsense syllables. It doesn't necessarily involve mimicking a particular instrumental sound but simply releases the singer from the tyranny of words.

The *Grove Dictionary of Jazz* says, "Many kinds of wordless vocalizing are exploited by jazz singers, from expressive growls and screeches to gentle humming."[88] Florence engaged in precisely this style of vocalizing, and was compared to various instruments, several years before Armstrong's scat innovations became popular. The following description by Beverley Nichols of one such demonstration is instructive:

> Do you remember the part where she sings "Too-ty-tooty-too"? It sounds ridiculous, but I cannot think of any other way of describing it. It occurs in a number called "Baby and Me," where, as a sort of coloured Vesta Tilley, she prances across the stage with two "babies" on either side. During the chorus to this song she sings an obbligato, high and clear, to the words "Tooty-too-too." It is like one of those flute obbligati in which Donizetti delighted in the florid period of "Lucia." You cannot forget it if you have heard it, because it is a childishly spontaneous form of art which is different from anything one has heard before.[89]

Asked to explain this technique, Florence told Nichols that she had developed it years before in a show down South, probably while teamed with Kinky Caldwell in 1915. She explained she was drawing on the memory of the way her mother used to croon wordlessly to her as a child. Crooning, screeching, yodeling: Many such terms were used to describe Florence's non-verbal singing. The closest equivalent in recorded jazz would be the wordless singing in some Duke Ellington records, originated by Adelaide Hall in 1927 and later practiced by Kay Davis. Adelaide never admitted any such influence by Florence and probably didn't consciously have it. However, she had been familiar with Florence's singing and performing since 1921, so there was ample time for the idea to have germinated by 1927. William Grant Still explicitly used Florence's ability in this direction in the specially written Aeolian Hall songs, one of them the wordless piece called "Croon."

It is easier to identify Florence's impact on the wider world of black entertainment. Apart from the immediate work opportunities she created for her supporting casts, she ushered in remarkable changes that opened new doors for later generations of black divas in stage and screen. Before her time the typical pattern of black shows on Broadway, from Williams and Walker through to Miller and Lyles, had been built around two male (blackface) leads, with female stars relegated to subsidiary roles. The shows typically had a loose plotline based on the antics of the male leads.

The shows that Leslie built around Florence dispensed with this format and adopted the revue style, with a versatile female lead. As Alvin White said, "Florence knocked most of this folderol into a cocked hat. She was a leading lady, wide-eyed ingenue, dancing soubrette. She could do it all." James Weldon Johnson summed it up:

> On October 29, 1924, exactly one year after the opening of *Runnin' Wild*, Florence Mills came to the Broadhurst Theatre in *Dixie to Broadway*, and New York had its first Negro revue. For the Florence Mills show broke away entirely from the established traditions of Negro musical comedy. Indeed, it had to, because she was the star. . . . On the night of the production of *Dixie to Broadway* New York not only found itself with a novelty in the form of a Negro revue, but also discovered that it had a new artist of positive genius in the person of Florence Mills.[90]

The idea of a black female star on Broadway was revolutionary at the time, and despite some stereotyping in the surrounding material, Florence's own performance was free of any blackface elements. Elisabeth Welch, having lived through it all, understood how important Florence's breakthrough had been. "It was the blackface entertainers who pushed open the doors, and then it was the 'natural' faces like the Florence Mills's that allowed the ordinary colored person on to the stage, and they [white audiences] accepted us as coloreds."

The other important development was Florence's breakthrough into the international arena. Apart from In Dahomey in 1903, black entertainment had been a minor curiosity in Europe until 1923. Dover Street to Dixie proved that a show starring black people could be a mainstream draw in a top-line theater in Europe. Black Birds of 1926 added confirming evidence and cemented a tradition that opened doors for a generation of black entertainers.

Finally, to what extent did Florence achieve her most cherished goal, to improve the state of her people? Perhaps the clearest evidence of this was the more than 150,000 people who thronged the streets of Harlem for her funeral. They were in no doubt that she had achieved remarkable advances for them. Her shining example had lifted their morale and inspired them, not only in Harlem but in every African American community in the United States.

As well as lifting the morale of her people, she had undoubtedly also won much goodwill in the hearts and minds of thinking white Americans. She had been the living proof that stereotypes were meaningless. And whatever she may or may not have achieved in America, there could be no doubt of her achievements in Europe, especially England. The words of a reformed racist illustrate this perfectly. "[Another vital influence in the artistic life of Britain] was the advent of Negro performers of all types, who are now successes in London, almost as a matter of course. It was Florence Mills, the grand-daughter of a slave, who more than anyone, won for them an equal status in this country." —Hannen Swaffer, 1949[91]

However unrecognized it may have been in recent years, there can be no doubt that Florence Mills's legacy is still a significant factor in the world today.

Florence in Her Own Words

Florence Mills spoke and wrote articulately, and even eloquently, on matters she cared about. She also answered questions from journalists patiently and thoughtfully. Her words have been freely quoted in the main text, but some further examples will illustrate her thinking and outlook on many topics.

On the revue as her preferred medium:

I prefer the revue type of musical entertainment to the operetta and musical play. It is the ideal tonic for the well-known tired business man and for the seldom spoken of tired business woman. There are no suffering ingenues and jilted lovers, no kings to call out the army or execute at daybreak, no hardened parents disciplining their children—nothing to recall the many trials of a busy day. The songs and dances, beautiful girls and scenery, and the comical bits of nonsense that make up the revue, seem to me best fitted to entertain, and to supply the mental relaxation that all of us occasionally require. . . . Of course, we have our bit of romance. I think every play should have that, and I think that our Mandy is as sweet a bride as ever strutted the path that leads to the altar.[92]

On her musical heritage:

I belong to a race that sings and dances as it breathes. I don't care where I am, so long as I can sing and dance. The wide world is my stage and I am my audience. If I didn't feel like that I wouldn't be an artist. The things you do best for other people are the things you would do just as well for yourself.

Our singing and our music are part of our history and tradition. We put a "folk-spirit" into everything we do. We have no great symphonies. But in our songs palm trees grow and the sun shines through them. The jungle grows dark and grows light. It is our laughter and our tears; it is our home and our exile. It's getting up in the morning and going to bed at night. When I sing and dance on the stage of the theatre I am often a million miles away. Maybe I'm down south, maybe farther away than that. When I work the hardest I often see folks sleeping in the sun and places lazy with heat, where it's quiet and still.[93]

On the Charleston:

Asked on one occasion why she did not feature "The Charleston" more in her show, Florence replied, to her interviewer's amazement, that it was because it was so easy to do. "It is ridiculously easy, quite absurdly so."[94] The watered-down version of the dance practiced in England also amused her.

I smile to myself when I see you do so sedately, with such good taste, the Charleston in your ballrooms. It is the dance of my people, of our piccaninnies, the happiest dance in all the world. They were Charlestoning in Kentucky before the Civil War. Do you know how the Charleston came to New York? It came on the feet of the coloured piccaninnies.

The piccaninnies used to play around the plantations of the South. Today they play around the subways of New York. Years ago you could see them dancing the "Take Your Foot Out of the Mud and Stick It in the Sand" step outside the subways of 42nd and 50th Streets. Their grandfathers did it to the "[Rubato] Pulse" rhythm long ago, when they came, as slaves, from the plantations.

The pix's would do it for money. They'd stop. Throw them a quarter and they'd Charleston till Doomsday. So it got to the clubs, dance restaurants, and cabarets. I like to see it, especially the nice new quiet way you do it, because it reminds me that there is somewhere a common tie linking all the races which make up mankind.[95]

On living the simple life:
Asked why she didn't patronize fashionable London hotels, Florence replied, simply, "I'm the wrong color."

I deplore the fact that we are lionized in London, but I don't see how you can help it. I prefer to keep with my own people. I live simply in Gower Street with other coloured folk, and try to keep quiet. I never go out unless I am compelled. I never go to fashionable restaurants, like some of the girls do when Lew Leslie's back is turned. I want to help my people, that is all.[96]

On Park Avenue versus Harlem:
Along with the rumors of Florence's great wealth came a story that she had bought an expensive Park Avenue apartment to flaunt her color among rich white people.

I did not live in Park Avenue. I have no idea how the rumor spread. I have heard it said I lived there for spite. I should find it a rather expensive way of being spiteful, spending $8,000 or even $10,000 a year on an apartment merely to spite somebody.

Besides, I love being with my own people. I feel at home amongst them. We do not seek white people's society, and we are a very happy family, although a large one.

In America we have our own restaurants and cabarets and theatres, and your people come to see our shows. The white people say, "Let's go slumming," they seek us out.[97]

On wishing on the moon:

When the moon is new, just a slim sliver of cool silver, like a slim slice of melon with sugar on it, you English people go quietly, shyly, out, and look at him, and revolve three times, curtsey, turn the money in your pockets, and wish a wish. It is a bit of magic that all your lives you never grow out of—a bit of enchanted childhood from which you hate to part.

And the very young among you sometimes murmur silently in your private minds, or maybe whisper to mammies or nannies: "I wish I could go to the moon. What is the moon like? What are the people of the moon like?" But when you grow up you laugh and know that you will never go to the moon or know what the moon folk are like. And it was like that with me when, as a pic-caninny, I heard of London and dreamed of going there one day.

I too, in my schooldays, peeped over my left shoulder at the new moon, the money moon we call it, and made a wish. Mine was that I should see my name shining on the signs of a big theatre as brightly as the glorious money moon. I prayed hard and worked hard that my wish should come true.[98]

On her natural style:

I have never learned to dance or sing. Whatever talents I have were born in me. It is perfectly natural for me to sing and dance. If I hear a song I sing it in my own way, a way which is not perhaps what the composer intended.

But I must make one correction. Before I first came to London, three years ago, I took a few singing lessons because I wanted my voice to be at its best for London. Now that I'm in London again, I am going to take some lessons here, in order to protect my voice and keep it in good condition.[99]

On spirituals:

We of the younger generation think them very old-fashioned. We all learned them at our mother's knees. All of my friends sing them. They were the hymns of our people. But I'm afraid the next generation of colored people will not sing them. As folk songs they are gradually dying out.[100]

On race prejudice:

My greatest ambition is to see the white people ignore the colored question. This depends entirely on ourselves. For ten years now the colored question has not been so acute. White people realize that the colored people are educated and more progressive. Conditions are better.

Yet even today, there are many colored boys in America who, after being trained as lawyers and doctors, have to become train attendants because they are black and there is no place for them. Yet it is ridiculous to think that we are different from white people, because we are educated and brought up to think the same way as you. After all, it is white authors whose books we read and it is a white culture that surrounds us.

Yet if we voice our opinion we are downed. Sometimes I have started to ar-gue and then heard: "What right have you to talk. You are black."[101]

Expressing optimism that change and equality were inevitable:

After all, what can we expect in just over sixty years, and it is only that since we became free men and women. But I do feel it an injustice that our colored men who fought in the war should not have been allowed when they returned to America to wear the uniform they so proudly donned.[102]

Asked if the color bar in America was still as strict:

No, it isn't but in America I keep mostly to my own people. You see we live our own life there, and find our own amusements, in our own theatres and so on. We have, as you know, some fine actors, Paul Robeson who acted in London recently, Gilpin, and others.[103]

On the success of *Dixie to Broadway*:

It has always been my contention that art should draw no color line. It has been the most gratifying experience in my life to find that I am right. To have been instrumental in establishing a precedent for an annual colored musical comedy on Broadway more than recompenses me for having given up a "Follies" contract.[104]

Notes

1. Quotations respectively from the *World*, Oct. 30, 1924; James Agate, *Immoment Toys* (London: Jonathan Cape, 1945), 153; James Weldon Johnson, *Black Manhattan* (New York: Da Capo, 1991), 199–200; AMST, Feb. 9, 1927; Dudley Nicholls, "Mills of the Gallery Gods," *New York News*, Apr. 11, 1926; and Beverley Nichols, *Sketch* magazine, Feb. 16, 1927.

2. Quotations respectively from Louise Varese, *Varese: A Looking Glass Diary Volume I: 1883–1928* (New York: W. W. Norton, 1972), 243; "Bad English Vocalism," NYT, May 15, 1927; "Music," NYT, Jan. 25, 1926; and Whitney Balliet, *American Singers* (New York: Oxford University Press, 1988), 27.

3. Alberta Hunter in Whitney Balliet, *American Singers: 27 Portraits in Song* (New York: Oxford University Press, 1988), 27.

4. Frank C. Taylor, with Gerald Cook, *Alberta Hunter* (New York: McGraw Hill, 1987), 35.

5. I am indebted to Chuck Haddix and Kelly McEniry of the UMKC Marr Sound Archives, for finding this quotation for me in the Frank Driggs Jazz Oral History Collection.

6. Eugene Goossens, *Overture and Beginners* (London: Methuen, 1951), 233.

7. The late Frank Powers, jazz musician, in private e-mail message to the author.

8. Adelaide Hall interview, Stephen Bourne Collection.

9. Leonard Reed phone conversation with the author, May 2000 and David Hinckley, "The Golden Age—he was there," *New York Daily News*, Apr. 13, 2004.

10. "Florence Mills Interviewed between Dances," in TC FLP.

11. "Your Broadway and Mine," *New York Graphic*, quoted in BAA, June 20, 1931.

12. Marshall and Jean Stearns, *Jazz Dance* (London: MacMillan, 1968), 232.

13. "How She Dances," *Philadelphia Public Ledger*, Jan. 25, 1925.

14. Charles B. Cochran, *Cock-a-Doodle-Do* (London: J. M. Dent & Sons, 1941), 195.

15. Stearns, *Jazz Dance*, 235; "Cabaret Reviews," VAR, Nov. 18, 1925; H. Curtis interview.

16. Delilah Jackson, Private conversation with the author.

17. In 1996 the author discussed by telephone with Clayton "Peg Leg" Bates his views of Florence Mills's type of dancing and how it related to tap dancing. Peg Leg Bates became famous in *Blackbirds of 1928* for his remarkable skill as a one-legged tap dancer.

18. "Gerty Interviewed," ChDef, July 9, 1921.

19. Arnold Haskell, *Penelope Spencer and Other Studies* (London: British-Continental Press, 1930), 19, 25.

20. James Weldon Johnson, *Black Manhattan* (New York: Da Capo, 1991), 199.

21. Quotations from, respectively, "Dixie to Broadway," *New York Telegram and Evening Mail*, Oct. 30, 1924; "Mills of the Gallery Gods," *Philadelphia Free Ledger*, Apr. 11, 1926; unidentified clipping, Apr. 6, 1926 (*Morning World?*); "Florence Mills Life Story," PhTr, Dec. 22, 1927.

22. André Levinson, "The Negro Dance under European Eyes," *Theatre Arts Monthly*, Apr. 1927.

23. David Vaughan, *Frederick Ashton and His Ballets* (London: A & C Black, 1977), 78.

24. For information on Flo-Bert Awards see www.nytap.org/ (accessed Dec. 12, 2003).

25. AMST and *Graphic*, Nov. 2; *New York Evening Graphic*, Nov. 3; and *New York Journal*, Nov. 5, 1927, respectively.

26. See Samuel A. Floyd Jr. *The Power of Black Music* (New York: Oxford University Press, 1995).

27. Mark Tucker, *The Duke Ellington Reader* (New York: Oxford University Press, 1993), 67, and Mark Tucker, "Duke Ellington and Europe. . . . In the 1930s," www.jazzportugal.net/cgi-bin/wnp_db_dynamic_record.pl?dn=db_escritos_e_entrevistas&sn=escritos&rn=20 (accessed Dec. 1, 2003).

28. James Lincoln Collier, *Duke Ellington* (London: Pan Books, 1989), 130.

29. Spike Hughes, *Opening Bars* (London: Pilot Press, 1946), 305–306.

30. Spike Hughes, "Close-Up 6: Paul," *Daily Herald*, May 4, 1933.

31. Two such books are Chris Goddard, *Jazz Away from Home* (New York: Paddington Press, 1979), 92; and Paul Oliver, ed., *Black Music in Britain* (Milton Keynes: Open University Press), 52.

32. Roger Pryor Dodge, *Hot Jazz and Jazz Dance* (New York: Oxford University Press, 1995), 248.

33. W. Pickens, "Florence Mills, Democracy and Stage," PhTr, Nov. 10, 1927.

34. William Howland Kenney III, "The Influence of Black Vaudeville on Early Jazz," *Black Perspective in Music* 14:3 (fall 1986): 233.

35. Hughes, *Opening Bars*, 307.

36. Quotations from, respectively, J. A. Rogers in Alain Locke, ed., *The New Negro* (New York: Touchstone, 1997), 220–221; William Grant Still, *The William Grant Still Reader* (Durham, N.C.: Duke University Press, 1992), 213; Arnold Haskell, "Further Studies in Ballet: Negro Dancing"; *Dancing Times*, date unknown, 455; Langston Hughes, *Famous Negro Music Makers* (New York: Dodd Mead, 1955), 167; Henry O. Osgood, *So This Is Jazz* (Boston: Little, Brown, and Company, 1926), 44; and Maude Russell interview, Bill Egan Collection.

37. "How She Dances."

38. "Florence Mills Again Gives Interview to a Leading European Publication," AMST, Aug. 3, 1927.

39. Charles. B. Cochran, *I Had Almost Forgotten* (London: Hutchinson, 1932), 223.

40. Quotations from, respectively, "Leaves from an American Diary," *Daily Telegraph* (1921?); *New York World*, Nov. 3, 1927; and PiCou, Dec. 3, 1927.

41. Quotations from, respectively, AMST, Feb. 9, 1927; unidentified (*Morning World?*) Apr. 6, 1926; Gilbert Seldes, *The 7 Lively Arts* (New York: Sagamore Press. 1957), 101; *New York World*, Nov. 3, 1927; *New York Telegram and Evening Mail*, Oct. 30, 1924.

42. Basil Maine, *Receive It So* (London: Noel Douglas, 1926), 45–46; Beverley Nichols, *Sketch* magazine, Feb. 16, 1927; and unknown, undated clipping, TC FLP.

43. NYT, quoted in BAA, Nov. 8, 1924.

44. Eubie Blake "and his girls," record notes to *Eubie Blake Song Hits*, (EBM-9, E. Blake Music, 1976).

45. Alvin White, "Let Me Tell You about My Love Affair with Florence Mills," *Sepia*, Nov. 1977; Nicholas Brothers, discussion with author, 1996; Willie Covan, from Delilah Jackson–Kid Thompson interviews.

46. "The New Plays on Broadway," *Billboard* magazine, Oct. 29, 1924.

47. Theophilus Lewis, "Florence Mills—An Appreciation," *Inter-State Tattler*, Nov. 11, 1927.

48. "Looking across the Footlights," clipping (*Philadelphia Free Ledger*, Jan. 1925?), TC FLP.

49. AMST, Aug. 3, 1927.

50. "Stirs Emotional Reaction in People," unidentified clipping in TC FLP (Jan. 1925?).

51. "Florence Mills—Artiste," unidentified clipping in TC FLP.

52. *London Daily Telegraph*, Nov. 3, 1927.

53. From Richard Shead, *Constant Lambert: His Life, His Music and his Friends* (London: Simon Publications, 1973), 39–40.

54. Undated, unidentified clipping, HAJC.

55. Leonard Hall, "Show Shopping," *Washington Daily News*, Nov. 3, 1927.

56. Kimball and Bolcom, *Reminiscing with Sissle & Blake* (New York: The Viking Press, 1973), 118.

57. "Mime," Microsoft® Encarta® 96 Encyclopedia, © 1993–1995 Microsoft Corporation.

58. Unidentified clipping in TC FLP.

59. Theophilus Lewis, "Florence Mills—An Appreciation," *Inter-State Tattler*, Nov. 11, 1927, 2.

60. Editorial, AMST, Nov. 9, 1927.

61. Undated, unidentified clipping, SCRAP, HAJC.

62. "How She Plays Parts," undated clipping in TC FLP (*Philadelphia Ledger*, Jan. 1925?).

63. James Weldon Johnson, *Black Manhattan* (New York: Da Capo, 1991), 199.

64. Charles B. Cochran, *I Had Almost Forgotten* (London: Hutchinson, 1932), 219.

65. C. B. Cochran, quoted in AMST, Nov. 9, 1927.

66. Paul Robeson, "An Actor's Wanderings and Hopes," in Philip S. Foner, ed., *Paul Robeson Speaks: Writings, Speeches, Interviews 1918–1974* (London: Quartet Books, 1974), 69.

67. Paul Robeson, "The Negro Artist Looks Ahead," in Foner, 299.

68. Quotations from, respectively, White, *Sepia*; Welch, Bourne Collection; Rudi Blesh, *Combo USA* (Philadelphia: Chilton Book Company, 1971), 209; and Leonard Hall, "Show Shopping," *Washington Daily News*, Nov. 3, 1927.

69. Willie Covan from Delilah Jackson Kid Thompson tapes.

70. Cochran, *I Had Almost Forgotten*, 220.

71. Cochran, *I Had Almost Forgotten*, 221.

72. "Florence Mills as She Appears," Clipping (1925), TC FLP.

73. Dave Peyton, ChDef, Nov. 5, 1927.

74. Michael Anglo, *Nostalgia: Spotlight on the Twenties* (London: Jupiter Books, 1976), 8.

75. Robert Campbell, "Florence Mills' Life Story," *Evening Graphic*, Nov. 4, 1927.

76. Verna Arvey, *In One Lifetime* (Fayetteville: University of Arkansas Press, 1984), 68.

77. Cochran, *I Had Almost Forgotten*, 220.

78. Undated clipping in HAJC.

79. Hannen Swaffer, Florence Mills interview, *London Daily Express*, reprinted in AMST, Aug. 10, 1927.

80. Notes from P. L. Prattis interview in Claude Barnett Collection, Chicago Historical Society.

81. Cochran, *I Had Almost Forgotten*, 220.

82. Theophilus Lewis, "Florence Mills—An Appreciation," *Inter-State Tattler*, Nov. 11, 1927, 2.

83. Swaffer, Florence Mills interview.

84. Editorial, PiCou, Nov. 12, 1927.

85. Will Friedwald, *Jazz Singing* (New York: Charles Scribner's Sons), 387–388.

86. Bo Scherman, LP notes from *The Legendary Eva Taylor with Maggie's Blue Five*, Kenneth Records KS 2042.

87. Jean Claude Baker and Chris Chase, *Josephine: The Josephine Baker Story* (Holbrook, Mass.: Adams Publishing, 1993), 171.

88. Barry D. Kernfeld, ed., *The New Grove Dictionary of Jazz* (Ann Arbor, Mich.: MacMillan Reference Ltd., 1988).

89. Beverley Nichols, *Sketch* magazine, Feb. 16, 1927, 304.

90. James Weldon Johnson, *Black Manhattan* (New York: Da Capo, 1991), 196–197.

91. Hannen Swaffer, "Two Women but One Public," *Bandwagon* 8:3 (Mar. 1949): 21.

92. From "Looking across the Footlights," undated clipping, TC FLP.

93. From "Florence Mills as she appears," undated clipping, TC FLP.

94. Undated, unidentified clipping in HAJC.

95. "Magic Moon that Brought Me Money," undated clipping (1926), HAJC. I have corrected "Ribato" with "Rubato," a dance or music term denoting "flexibility of tempo to assist in achieving expressiveness."

96. Swaffer, "Two Women but One Public," 21.

97. Swaffer, Florence Mills interview.

98. Florence Mills, "Magic Moon that Brought Me Money."

99. Clipping, undated (1926?), unidentified (London *Star*?), HAJC.

100. Clipping, undated (1926?), unidentified (London *Star*?), HAJC.

101. Swaffer, Florence Mills interview.

102. Unidentified clipping (1926?) in HAJC.

103. AMST, Aug. 3, 1927.

104. "Florence Mills—Artiste," undated (May 1925?) clipping, TC FLP.

Black Beauty

Florence Mills and Duke Ellington

The single factor that has done most to keep Florence Mills's name in the public eye since her untimely death is her musical portrait composed by Duke Ellington in 1928, originally named "Black Beauty." For his first Carnegie Hall Concert (1943), he also titled it "Portrait of Florence Mills." Over the years, as Ellington's fame and stature grew, "Black Beauty" always remained in the orchestra's repertoire. With each recording, and reissues of recordings, sleeve-notes diligently report it as Duke's tribute to a singer and dancer who, by the later years, was forgotten and obscure.

"Black Beauty" inspired this book and the years of research that have gone into it. A remarkably beautiful and creatively original piece of music, it will stand forever as Duke's heartfelt tribute to one of the great heroes of his race and as one of his greatest compositions. It has indissolubly linked the names of Duke Ellington and Florence Mills for as long as Ellington's achievements will be honored. However, the story of the connections between Florence Mills, Duke Ellington, and "Black Beauty" is not as simple as appears on the surface. It's worth exploring before examining the music itself.

Apart from their shared racial heritage, a significant item of commonality between Duke Ellington and Florence Mills was that they were both originally Washingtonians. Duke was always proud of his D.C. background. He believed that Washingtonians had extra style. This showed in the pride he took in always presenting a smart image. He described it in his autobiographical work

Music Is My Mistress. "Rex Stewart [Ellington trumpeter] came out of the same Washington school system that I did, and his intellectual ambitions were typical of the Washingtonians of that time, when people believed that if you were going to be something, you ought to learn something and know something. . . . Rex Stewart had been taught the responsibility of commanding respect for his race and to this end he maintained an offstage image very deliberately."[1]

Duke's confidence and poise came from his comfortable middle-class upbringing. Florence came from a poor background, but Washington gave her a special confidence also. Being the darling of the diplomatic set as a child performer gave her a poise that reflected in the refined image she too always presented.

There was only three years' difference in their ages, but Florence was already an established performer of many years' experience by the time Duke followed her to New York. He was twenty-four when he moved there in 1923. By then Florence had already achieved stardom in *Shuffle Along* and had her own show on Broadway. When the starry-eyed Duke considered going to New York, Harlem was the pulsating Mecca that drew him. In *Music Is My Mistress* he said, "We were awed by the never-ending roll of great talents there." When he listed those talents, the first on his roll call of over fifty names was Florence Mills.[2] Many years after Florence's death, while Duke was in the hospital recovering from a hernia operation, he wrote:

> The skyline from [my windows] is an inspiring sight. I have spent three weeks in bed here, not too ill to be thrilled daily by a view of these skyscrapers, and with plenty of time for ample meditation.
>
> It is natural, perhaps, that I should think of many subjects, some serious, some fanciful. I spent some time comparing the marvelous sky-line to our race, likening the Chrysler Tower, the Empire State Building and other lofty structures to the lives of Bert Williams, Florence Mills and other immortals of the entertainment field.
>
> I mused over the qualities which these stars possessed that enabled them to tower as far above their fellow artists as do these buildings above the skyline.
>
> And it seemed to me, from where I was lying, that in addition to their great talent, the qualities which have made really great stars are those of simplicity, sincerity, and a rigid adherence to the traditions of our own people.[3]

This statement bears eloquent testimony to his esteem for Florence. Further evidence comes from his first Carnegie Hall concert in 1943. It included his Portraits of the three people he considered the all-time greatest African American performers. They were Florence Mills, Bert Williams, and Bill "Bojangles" Robinson.

Yet despite all this evidence of Duke's knowledge of Florence's achievements, a degree of mystery surrounds their relationship. There is no documented record of a personal meeting between them. There is no doubt such meetings did occur. Both were based in Harlem between 1923 and 1927 albeit with lengthy absences in Florence's case. In several instances he was part of the replacement for her during those absences. All the performers living in Harlem in those days congregated at the same after-hours clubs. Duke and Florence had mutual friends. When Florence came to New York in 1921, Bricktop got her a job at Barron Wilkins's club. When Duke came in 1923, it was Bricktop who got him a job at Wilkins's. During 1923 Duke was living in the apartment of Leonard Harper and Osceola Blanks, friends and fellow-performers of Florence.[4] Duke played occasional dates at the Plantation in 1923, when Florence was away in England.[5] His orchestra supported the Plantation Orchestra at the Lincoln Theatre in July 1925 when Florence took a break and the rest of the Plantation Revue cast played there for a week.[6] His orchestra also replaced her briefly at the Plantation when she went to England again in 1926. They probably met when Florence performed at the 1925 farewell for the *Chocolate Kiddies* troupe before their departure for Europe. Ellington had written music for that show.

Despite the absence of an identified meeting, there can be no doubt that Duke Ellington and Florence Mills crossed paths in Harlem. There can be little doubt also that he saw her perform, probably many times. Mark Tucker thought that seeing the "Evolution of the Colored Race" scene in *Dixie to Broadway* may have influenced Ellington's major extended composition *Black, Brown and Beige*.[7]

Ellington's "Black Beauty"

After Florence's untimely death in 1927, a flood of commemorative material, poems, songs and sheet music appeared. Eva Taylor and Clarence Williams, Andy Razaf, Fats Waller, and several of Florence's show business associates made recordings. Duke Ellington provided piano accompaniment on two such tracks by Marguerite Lee, but they were never released. Ellington must surely have felt he could do better in the tribute line. In early 1928, fund-raising for a Florence Mills memorial was at its height. The Ellington Orchestra participated in some of the events.

In March the orchestra went to the recording studios and cut two takes of "Black Beauty."[8] The musicians returned for another version, the author's personal favorite, on March 26. In October Duke recorded a solo piano version, which is an excellent example of stride piano in the style of his mentors James

P. Johnson and Willie "The Lion" Smith. In the hundreds of radio broadcasts by Ellington from 1927 to 1930, "Black Beauty" was one of the most played pieces.[9] Over the many years since its first presentation, "Black Beauty" has been acknowledged as one of Ellington's finest early compositions. Much has been written about it. One of the first and most significant examples was the review by R. D. Darrell, a classical music expert. He was one of the earliest to appreciate Ellington's importance as a contemporary composer.

Reviewing the recently released "Black Beauty" and "Take It Easy" in the *Phonograph Monthly Review* of September 1928, he wrote: "Both rank with his finest efforts. The curiously twisted and wry trumpet passages, the amazing piano solo in 'Black Beauty,' the splendid melodic urge that animates even the most eccentric measures, are all characteristic of his unique genius for the expression of an overwhelming nostalgia and bitterness in a new idiom, and one entirely his own." In 1932, when Darrell wrote a lengthy and perceptive essay on Ellington, he gave it the title "Black Beauty."[10]

Since then many have written about "Black Beauty." A few examples include:[11]

- "Clearly one of Ellington's 1920s gems . . . a complete and extraordinarily shapely piece of music." —*Dan Morgenstern*
- "One of Ellington's most beautiful compositions." —*Gunther Schuller*
- "Black Beauty ranks as one of the orchestra's most resplendent compositions." —*John Edward Hasse*
- "The most enchantingly beautiful melody ever conceived in the stride idiom." —*Gary Giddens*

Many have also identified "Black Beauty" as an important step in Ellington's development as a composer and a pianist. James Lincoln Collier thought it showed his ability to step outside the conventional mold of popular songwriting. "In 'Black Beauty' we have an early example of Ellington's tendency to write consecutive, rather than repetitive, melody."[12] For Riccardo Scivales, "*Swampy River* and *Black Beauty* somehow start two basic facets of Ellington's mature style, that is his harmonic enterprise and that remarkable trend towards terseness, which will later be one of the most significant and influential aspects of his piano artistry."[13] French jazz expert Hugues Panassie saw "Black Beauty" as an example of Duke's "gift for conceiving charming and melancholy melodies which in no way resemble the usual jazz melodies."[14] Martin Williams thought it showed how Ellington's piano playing matched his orchestral style. "The style is orchestral; it imitates the band. If we compare, say, the 1928 piano version of 'Black Beauty' with his orchestration, we can hear him virtually assigning the piece, finger by finger, off the keyboard to his horns and reeds."[15]

So "Black Beauty" rated well from its first appearance. The Ellington orchestra played and recorded it often from the late 1920s through the 1930s and into the early 1940s. It wasn't till the famous 1943 Carnegie Hall concert, however, that it was first publicly associated with Florence Mills's name. Over many years it became generally accepted that he wrote it specifically for her in 1928. Among those confidently asserting this were Duke's son Mercer Ellington and close friend Stanley Dance. Some noted cultural significance in the fact that as early as 1928 Duke was using the words "Black" and "Beauty" to honor a black woman.[16]

However, they were all writing with hindsight after the 1943 Carnegie Hall concert at which Duke's "Portrait of Florence Mills" was formally unveiled. After much diligent searching, aided by many knowledgeable experts, I can say with confidence that there is no example of an earlier published linkage. Writing in *Downbeat* magazine in 1943, before the Carnegie Hall concert, Helen Oakley Dance explained that Ellington planned three musical portraits as part of the program. They would include the already known portraits of Bert Williams and Bill Robinson. There would also be a new one for Florence Mills, featuring Johnny Hodges.[17] At the concert, the piece presented as "Portrait of Florence Mills" proved to be the familiar "Black Beauty." Mark Tucker believed that pressure to finish the ambitious extended suite *Black, Brown and Beige* in time for the concert prevented Ellington from completing the new Hodges piece. So he fell back on the ready-to-hand "Black Beauty."

While the facts here are not in dispute, they raise some intriguing questions. The most obvious is whether Duke Ellington had Florence Mills explicitly in mind when he originally wrote "Black Beauty" in 1928. In private correspondence, the late and much-lamented Mark Tucker posed the case for the negative. "My hunch would be that Ellington wrote a dance piece for the Cotton Club, then perhaps titled it with an allusion to Mills." This is plausible, and a conclusive case one way or another is probably impossible to prove now. Nevertheless, there are some strong arguments that Duke Ellington did have Florence Mills in mind when he originally wrote "Black Beauty." One can approach the topic from two angles. The first deals with external facts surrounding the composition. The second looks at internal features of the music.

For the first, there are some strong circumstantial pointers to a link. Accepting that Duke ran out of time to produce a new portrait for the Carnegie Hall concert, why then did he select "Black Beauty" as the fallback? There must have been something special about it that made it the right choice. It is unlikely he would have let himself run out of time for the planned Florence Mills portrait if he didn't know he had to hand, in "Black Beauty," a piece that already encapsulated the person he was portraying. Several things suggest this might be so.

"Black Beauty" made its first appearance in early 1928. The March recording date probably followed an earlier introduction at the Cotton Club. This was precisely the time when grief-stricken Harlemites, including Ellington, were engaging in memorial and fund-raising events for a Florence Mills monument. Duke himself took part in one of the early commemorative recordings (the unissued Marguerite Lee tracks).[18] It would have been natural for him to respond musically to a significant event like Florence Mills's death. Her other composer-admirer, Constant Lambert, did so with his beautiful "Elegiac Blues." We know that Ellington wrote his first extended composition, "Reminiscing in Tempo," in response to his mother's death.

One might ask why he didn't just call the piece "Portrait of Florence Mills" at the time. However, Ellington didn't adopt the idea of using the word "portrait" in his titles until 1939, with his tribute to Willie "The Lion" Smith. By then he had established a status for himself that gave him the authority to play the role of a musical poet laureate for his people. In early 1928 he was still an emerging figure, yet to gain widespread recognition.

Another tantalizing possible link is the use of "Black Beauty" as one of the musical themes in the short film featuring Ellington, *Black and Tan Fantasy* (1929). The film concerns (coincidentally?) the story of the tragically early death of a beautiful young dancer. Freddi Washington, a personal friend of Florence's, played the part of the dancer. Freddi had rented Florence's apartment from U. S. Thompson after Florence's death and was probably living there when the film was made.[19] If Florence Mills had inspired "Black Beauty," Ellington would have considered it a particularly suitable choice for inclusion in a movie about a beautiful young dying dancer.

On the second level, the music itself also yields evidence. "Black Beauty" has a two-part structure that beautifully parallels the dual themes of the vivacious dancer and a wistful lament for her tragic early death. Since the music came so soon after Florence's death, a connection is easy to imagine. Several commentators have noted the existence of these contrasting themes.

Describing "Black Beauty" as "one of the loveliest tunes Ellington ever wrote," Gary Giddens adds: "But what makes it doubly fascinating is the fact that he uses what had been considered a very brash, raucous, dancing kind of rhythm to support it."[20]

In a detailed analysis of its musical structure, James Lincoln Collier wrote:

> The piece consists of two strains, the first one an ordinary thirty-two bar AABA form, the second a simpler sixteen-bar form employing a very common set of chord changes, most familiar as "Sweet Georgia Brown." The second strain, in A flat, is bouncy; the first, in B-flat, is much more pensive and is undergirded by harmonies which were quite sophisticated for the time.[21]

Musicologist Marcello Piras examined "Black Beauty" in depth. In a speculative essay on male/female figures in Ellington's writing,[22] he suggested the A strain to be a portrait of Florence Mills. His research then developed and expanded into a new essay (in preparation), in which a much more complex and layered symbology is unearthed. Now, Piras thinks that "Black Beauty" is a detailed description of a Florence Mills theatrical act, larded with hints in the melody and the orchestration. The muted trumpet is identified with her singing, while the rhythmic variation of the A strain, for piano, banjo, double bass, and drums, evokes a tap-dancing duo routine. These and other references pointing to her may sound cryptic to present-day listeners but would have been quite clear and recognizable for a contemporary audience who knew her shows and repertoire.

None of this evidence offers conclusive proof that the 1928 "Black Beauty" was originally an explicit portrait of Florence Mills. Taken altogether, however, it provides persuasive circumstantial evidence for that claim. There is one final subjective, unscientific but powerful proof. The first time I heard "Black Beauty," I knew it was a depiction of a living, breathing person. At that time I had never heard of Florence Mills, but now, after ten years of studying her life and career, I know that "Black Beauty" is Florence Mills!

For those still not convinced, there can be no question that, one way or another, "Black Beauty" is Duke Ellington's "Portrait of Florence Mills" and will forever so remain. The twenty or so recorded versions we have by Ellington himself can never now be increased, but the piece continues to attract newer generations of musicians by its beauty and the complex challenge it presents. It will live on as an enduring tribute to its subject.

Notes

1. Duke Ellington, *Music Is My Mistress* (London: Quartet Books, 1977), 124–125.

2. Ellington, *Music Is My Mistress*, 36.

3. Mark Tucker, *The Duke Ellington Reader* (New York: Oxford University Press), 1993, 131.

4. Mark Tucker, *Ellington: The Early Years* (Urbana: University of Illinois Press, 1991), 22; and *The Duke Ellington Reader*, 90, 291.

5. Tucker, *Ellington: The Early Years*, 98.

6. *Variety*, July 8, 1925.

7. Mark Tucker, "The Genesis of *Black, Brown and Beige*" in *Black Music Research Journal* 13:2 (fall 93): 69–70.

8. The original recording, in two takes, was by Duke Ellington's Washingtonians on Brunswick E27093 and 4. It was also titled "Firewater." A suggestion that it originated from a Bubber Miley theme seems to have come from a note in a Rutgers vertical file by jazz historian George Hoefer. This theory seems unlikely as Duke's occasional "borrowings" from his musicians usually resulted in the men being featured on the piece or receiving partial composer credits. Arthur Whetsel was the original featured trumpeter for "Black Beauty." In private correspondence with the author, the late Mark Tucker expressed skepticism about a Miley contribution, noting that Hoefer provided no substantiation.

9. William Randle Jr., "Black Entertainers on Radio," in *The Black Perspective in Music* (spring 1977).

10. Both items by Darrell are reprinted in Tucker, *The Duke Ellington Reader*, 33, 57.

11. For sources of these quotations, see Dan Morgenstern, sleeve notes to CD Bluebird ND96952, *Duke Ellington and His Orchestra: Early Ellington (1927–1934)*; Gunther Schuller, *Early Jazz* (New York: Oxford University Press, 1968), 336; John Edward Hasse, *Beyond Category: The Life and Genius of Duke Ellington* (New York: Da Capo, 1995), 141; and Gary Giddens, *Visions of Jazz: The First Century* (Oxford: Oxford University Press, 1998, 110).

12. James Lincoln Collier, *Duke Ellington: The Life and Times of the Restless Genius of Jazz* (London: Pan Books, 1989), 119.

13. Riccardo Scivales, "Ellington's Piano: A Long Way," in *Ellington: Beyond Categories of XX Century*, ed. Stefano Zenni (International Conference held in Prato, Italy, Teatro Metastasio, February 22, 1999; organized by Stefano Zenni), report unpublished.

14. Hugues Panassie, *The Real Jazz* (New York: Smith and Durell, 1942), 180.

15. Martin Williams, *Jazz Changes* (New York: Oxford University Press, 1992), 265.

16. Mercer Ellington, *Duke Ellington in Person* (Boston: Houghton Mifflin, 1978), 42, and Stanley Dance, Eulogy at Duke Ellington's funeral, quoted in Tucker, *The Ellington Reader*, 381.

17. Helen M. Oakley (Dance), "Ellington to Offer 'Tone Parallel,'" *Downbeat*, Jan. 15, 1943, reprinted in Tucker, *The Ellington Reader*, 155.

18. Tucker, *Ellington: The Early Years*, 216, 306, based on research by Ellington expert Steven Lasker.

19. Hyacinth Curtis told me of spending time in the apartment as Fredi's guest when Fredi rented it after Florence's death.

20. From a transcript of an interview with Gary Giddins (a.k.a. Giddens) published on the website for the Ken Burns documentary film *Jazz*. See www.pbs.org/jazz/about/pdfs/Giddens.pdf (accessed Dec. 1, 2003).

21. Collier, 118–119.

22. Marcello Piras, "Character/Environment, Male/Female in Ellington's Writing," in *Ellington: Beyond Categories of XX Century*, ed. Stefano Zenni (International Conference held in Prato, Italy, Teatro Metastasio, February 22, 1999; organized by Stefano Zenni), report unpublished.

APPENDIX 2

~

Other Commemorative Items

Poetry

In the immediate aftermath of Florence's death came a flood of commemorative items. The *Amsterdam News* noted, "Never before has the literary department of the *Amsterdam News* had contributed to it, in so short a space of time, so many poems." It quoted briefly from eleven of them, generally heartfelt tributes from ordinary citizens of Harlem with no great literary pretensions. One however, titled "You Live On in Memory," was penned by lyricist Jo Trent, who had collaborated with Duke Ellington on *Chocolate Kiddies* a few years before.[1]

The flood of poetic tributes was mirrored in other black papers, the *Defender*, the *Philadelphia Tribune*, the *Baltimore Afro-American*, and others. Strangely, one of the best didn't surface till 1931, and then in a most unlikely medium. It appeared in the only issue ever of a proposed quarterly literary magazine called *American Autopsy*. The white editor of the magazine, Harold Hersey, is best remembered today as the king of "gangster pulp" publishers and was probably the author of the poem.[2] Titled "Florence Mills Blues," it was written in a style somewhat reminiscent of Langston Hughes:

> A high yaller baby on the golden stairs,
> She'll take Lord Jesus unawares,
> Jesus, Jesus unawares,
> A Blackbird singin' the latest airs,
> The St. Louis Blues on the golden stairs.

Over the years occasional other poetic tributes appeared, but the best has been a recent one, by African American poet and literature professor Colleen McElroy, titled "A Charleston for Florence Mills."[3]

Music

Along with the early outburst of poetry, there was also a rush to publish and record commemorative songs for Florence.[4] One of the first to succeed was Eva Taylor, along with her husband Clarence Williams. The *Defender's* report that the music was written, published, and recorded within twenty-four hours of Florence's death was a mite exaggerated but not too far off the mark. The recording session was completed at the Okeh studio on November 4, and the record was widely available quite shortly thereafter. The session recorded two songs. The first was "May We Meet Again Florence Mills," written "In memory of our beloved Florence Mills" by Clarence Williams and Eva Taylor. The second, composed by Porter Grainger, was "She's Gone to Join the Songbirds in Heaven." Eva was accompanied on both by Clarence on piano, and by a cello.

Also on November 4, Andy Razaf, as "Croonin' Andy Razaf," recorded for the Columbia label two songs written by him and "dedicated to the late Florence Mills." They were "Empty Arms" and "All the World's Lonely (For a Little Blackbird)." Only the second of these was a direct tribute to Florence. The first was a general lament for a lost loved one.

On November 8 the Vocalion Company recorded three numbers. Walter Richardson, a veteran of black shows as far back as Ernest Hogan and Williams and Walker, recorded "Gone but Not Forgotten," composed by Mandy Lee and Bob King.[5] Marguerite Lee recorded "You Will Always Live in Our Memory," the same Jo Trent number previously mentioned, as well as Porter Grainger's "She's Gone to Join the Songbirds." Marguerite Lee had been a performer in black vaudeville, and her path would have crossed Florence's at times. She was later married to Ellington trumpet player Arthur Whetsel. Although Vocalion advertised the pending release of the Lee tracks, they were apparently never issued. Nevertheless, the session is notable for the fact that the accompaniment for the recordings was provided by the Duke Ellington Trio, comprising Ellington himself on piano with violin and cello. Participating in a session recording lugubrious tributes to Florence may have helped inspire Ellington's "Black Beauty."[6]

It wasn't until November 14 that the Victor studios weighed in with their tribute, but this time five titles were recorded. The first of these was by Juanita Stinette Chappelle, singing her own song, which she had so dramatically failed to complete at the funeral service, simply titled "Florence." Carroll C. Tate (tenor) recorded two songs with violin and piano accompaniment, the previously mentioned "Gone but Not Forgotten" and "You Live On in Memory," the Jo Trent song mentioned earlier. Violinist Bert Howell sang "Bye Bye, Florence," written by Mike Jackson. Probably the most noteworthy facet of the Victor session was that all five tracks had the accompaniment of Fats Waller, mostly on his beloved church organ, which the company had accidentally acquired with the disused church building that was their headquarters. More significantly, one of the pieces recorded was Fats's own personal tribute on solo organ, "Memories of Florence Mills." Unfortunately, both takes of Fats's personal tribute to Florence, probably the only intrinsically interesting part of the session, were destroyed without being issued.

The last entrant in the commemorative stakes was the American Record Corporation (ARC). On November 17 three tracks were recorded by a singer called Gladys Thompson, the aforementioned "May We Meet Again, Florence Mills," "She's Gone to Join the Songbirds," and "Gone but Not Forgotten." Gladys Thompson was an occasional performer in black shows between 1917 and 1928 and may have been related to Edward Thompson, actor and husband of Evelyn Preer.[7]

The Eva Taylor tracks appear to have been the most popular. They were strongly promoted through the black press, one ad quoting the chorus:

> She had a smile for everybody,
> A hand for anyone that's down,
> Tho' her skin is brown,
> She'll be winging round
> With the song birds in Heaven.[8]

Copies of this record (78 rpm) were still widely available in secondhand record shops in the 1940s and can still be found today.[9]

Although the tribute songs were all rather maudlin laments, their evident sincerity gives them a certain sentimental charm in retrospect today. The fact that some noted jazz names were involved has meant that several of them have been included, much to the astonishment of unsuspecting jazz critics, in the encyclopedic CD reissues that abound nowadays.[10] The *Penguin Guide to Jazz on CD* remarks that some of them are "Very strange stuff."[11] One of Fats Waller's biographers comments:

A [measure] of Mills's stature can be deduced from Waller's understated accompaniments for two of the vocalists in the two takes from this session that survive. Although these songs are of an excessively sentimental and religious nature, and although they are sung in an exaggerated manner, Waller's playing contains not a hint of satire. . . . [It is difficult] to believe that sentimentality of this magnitude would have passed without some cheeky comment from him unless he were entirely sincere in expressing it.[12]

Not all the tribute songs written then or later appear to have been recorded. One titled "Goodbye, Flo, Goodbye" was from the pen of Chris Smith ("Ballin' the Jack" and "He's a Cousin of Mine,"). It was issued in sheet music form, but I am not aware of any record.[13] In 1940 another song was added to the list, this time with music composed by W. C. Handy and Joe Jordan and words by Olive Lewis Handy. It was called "Remembered (Impressions of Florence Mills)" and was one of a number of such pieces included in a book called Unsung Americans Sung, edited by W. C. Handy. The sheet music was also published by Handy, but I am not aware of any recording having been made.[14]

By far the most significant Florence Mills musical commemorative event to occur in 1927, and one of lasting importance, came from her adoring fan English composer Constant Lambert. He gave very eloquent expression to his grief at her early death in an exquisitely haunting gem, the Elegiac Blues. Presented in the three-minute blues–popular song format, the genre in which she herself had excelled, it is his first piece written in a jazz idiom, albeit a classically flavored one. In restrained minor chords, it builds slowly to a delicate climax of loss and grief, then fades gently away into a despairing silence. Although short in form, it has been widely acknowledged as a minor masterpiece. Originally written for the piano, it was later scored for orchestra. Recordings in both forms are available on CD today.[15]

While Elegiac Blues is Lambert's direct personal expression of homage to Florence, most of his major works bear some trace of her influence and that of the Plantation Orchestra. In 1928 his most famous work, Rio Grande, was released. About it he said, "The idea for the music came from seeing Florence Mills in From Dover Street to Dixie and from some of the music in Blackbirds."[16]

Although Florence was already beginning to fade from the wider public's memory in 1928, some additional musical commemorations appeared that year. Blackbirds of 1928, Lew Leslie's next in the series, which would have starred Florence, had a segment called "Memories of 1927." In it Aida Ward impersonated Florence while Adelaide Hall sang a song titled "Here Comes My Blackbird," in tribute to Florence. The song does not appear to have been recorded at the time and does not feature in the "original cast recording."

"Original cast" was somewhat of a misnomer. The recording was not made till four years after the show opened, and the session included only two original cast members, Adelaide Hall and Bill Robinson, along with numerous other people, including Ethel Waters, Duke Ellington, Cab Calloway, and the Mills Brothers. In spite of its neglect at the time, the Dorothy Fields–Jimmy McHugh song has established a niche for itself in later recordings by traditional jazz bands such as that of England's Chris Barber.

The first-ever review of Duke Ellington's time at the Cotton Club, in a revue with music by Fields and McHugh that predates *Blackbirds of 1928*, suggests that Aida Ward may have been singing a tribute song then. "Aida Ward, who reminds one of a Florence Mills in her song delivery, is a charming song saleswoman and the particular luminary of the proceedings. Miss Ward seems to be the nearest approach to the sainted blackbird-looking-for-a-bluebird. Her own "Broken Hearted Black Bird" will become a standard for Miss Ward like other ditties did for Miss Mills."[17] If this was a new song, it appears to have vanished without trace. Aida, like Florence, was never recorded. Another possibility, given the involvement of the same songwriting team, is that it was an earlier version of the song that surfaced later as "Here Comes My Blackbird" in the *Memories of 1927* segment of *Blackbirds of 1928*.

Having identified the musical items that were dedicated to Florence Mills, it is probably appropriate to say something briefly about some well-known songs that are sometimes mistakenly associated with her. Many people believed that the beautiful tune from *Blackbirds of 1930* by Eubie Blake and Andy Razaf, "Memories of You," was written for Florence. Dramatist Loften Mitchell even used the words "A Rosary of Tears" from the song as the title of an article about Florence.[18] Asked explicitly about this matter, Eubie Blake said, "No, Florence Mills wasn't in that show." He explained that the song was written for Minto Cato and tailored to her ability to sing a high C. In later years Eubie, always the ladies' man, appears to have been in the habit of telling many lady friends, including young girls, that he wrote it for them.[19]

It was not unknown, of course, for a song to be written for a performer and privately dedicated to a loved one, as happened with Irving Berlin's "Blue Skies," written for performer Belle Baker but privately dedicated to Berlin's daughter Mary Ellin.[20] Furthermore, the two men who wrote "Memories of You" knew Florence Mills well and wrote it for the show she had pioneered and over which her memory always hung. It would not be surprising, therefore, if she were at least a partial inspiration for the song. Neither was it surprising that audiences would make a connection between her and the tune, especially because its predecessor show in 1928–1929 included the segment called "Memories of 1927," dedicated to Florence. So, while "Memories of You" was not written "for" Florence Mills, it might well have been written "about" her.

The Guinness Jazz Companion hints at the possibility that Florence might have been the inspiration for Duke Ellington's "Sophisticated Lady," but no basis exists for this speculation. The inspiration for the tune is uncertain, but John Edward Hasse suggests it was a composite tribute to three high school teachers Ellington admired.[21] Finally, in view of confusion on the part of not only Noel Coward but, above all, C. B. Cochran, it is worth noting that Florence's special song was not "Bye Bye Blackbird" but "I'm a Little Blackbird." Both Coward and Cochran shared this confusion when writing from memory many years after the events they were describing.[22] I have had the experience of asking an elderly lady in Harlem if she had heard of Florence Mills and being treated to a few bars of "Bye Bye Blackbird" in response, so the confusion is perhaps understandable.

Miscellaneous Other

Although the Florence Mills Commemorative Association produced no lasting tangible result, and Bojangles's memorial drinking fountain was never built, and Antonio Salemme's statue wasn't created, there were occasional memorials to Florence over the years. Many years after her death a fine apartment building on Edgecombe Avenue in Harlem was named after her. The name "Florence Mills" can still be seen over the entrance. Her name can also still be faintly discerned on the gable end of what was, during the 1930s, the thriving Florence Mills Theatre at 3511 South Central Avenue in Los Angeles, near the junction with Martin Luther King Boulevard. The Los Angeles Florence Mills Theatre was a prominent nightclub during the 1930s and 1940s. It was one of eight theaters along Central Avenue that served the local community in those years, when Central Avenue was a swinging scene. It now stands vacant, after several transformations, including a period as a video store.[23]

Unfortunately, the building at 220 West 135th Street in Harlem that has been designated a historic building under the name "The Florence Mills House" is not the home Florence and her mother lived in. This was 220 West 133rd Street, so the street names have obviously been confused, probably caused by a wrongly captioned newspaper photograph at the time of her death. It is also now too late to designate the correct building with similar status as it was demolished and replaced by a retirement home some years ago.[24]

Apart from buildings, Florence was remembered in a variety of other ways. In the 1930s, when Amy Ashwood Garvey, ex-wife of Marcus Garvey, went to London and became involved in African diaspora politics, she cofounded with her friend Sam Manning, noted calypsonian, a Florence Mills nightclub, which became a focal point for black intellectuals in London for some years.[25] A not very successful 1937 all-black gangster movie, "Dark Manhattan," was dedicated to her.[26] Quite recently she was honored by the government of Grenada in a set of stamps that also included Billie Holiday and Bessie Smith.

Florence was a persistent figure in race memory as the years went by. Whenever African Americans gathered to celebrate their heritage, her name was likely to crop up. A 1952 commemoration of the life of Carter G. Woodson, African American historian, presented twenty-four figures from the African American Hall of Fame, starting with the Queen of Sheba and progressing to Ralph Bunche. Florence was among them, along with Booker T. Washington, Mary McLeod Bethune, and Frederick Douglass.[27] Duke Ellington's My People celebrated a similar group in 1963, including the soon-to-be-assassinated Martin Luther King.[28] When veterans of black entertainment gathered in 1979 to celebrate their history in a magnificent show called Black Broadway, a segment called "Tribute to Florence Mills" featured her old colleagues Edith Wilson and Elisabeth Welch performing, respectively, "I'm a Little Blackbird" and "Silver Rose."[29]

A Florence Mills Award was given to Clara Ward for the Ward Singers in January 1954.[30] I don't know whether this was a one-time event, but the concept of an award in Florence's name was to find more significant realization in 1989 with the institution, by Delilah Jackson, of the annual Flo-Bert Awards.

A Harlem-born artist of note who has commemorated Florence in one of her magnificent story-quilts is Faith Ringgold. The quilt, "The Bitter Nest Part 2: Harlem Renaissance Party, 1988," is on view at the National Museum of American Art, Washington, D.C. It is reproduced in her book of memoirs, "We Flew over the Bridge," and can also be seen on the Internet.[31]

The most recent event contributing to preserving Florence's memory was Dr. Helen Armstead Johnson's presentation of her lifetime collection of materials related to African American entertainment to the Schomburg Institute. The collection includes valuable personal material related to Florence Mills and entrusted to Dr. Johnson by Florence's husband, U. S. Thompson. The collection has recently been the subject of a magnificent exhibition staged by the Schomburg Institute, and the material in it is now available for scholarly research.

Perhaps this book will awaken new interest in the idea of a permanent memorial to its subject.

Notes

1. AMST, "Poets Profuse with Miss Mills Poems," Nov. 9, 1927, 4.

2. *American Autopsy*, Jan. 1932, published by Headquarters Publishing (Harold Hersey); available at www.pulpgen.com/pulp/biglist/data/data010.html (accessed Dec. 1, 2003). I am indebted for the suggestion of Hersey's authorship to pulp expert and republisher John P. Gunnison.

3. Colleen J. McElroy, *Travelling Music* (Ashland, Ore.: Story Line Press, 1998), 70.

4. For general information on the commemorative songs I am indebted to Tom Lord, *Clarence Williams* (Chigwell: Storyville, 1976) (especially page 421), and Ross Laird, *Moanin' Low* (Westport, Conn.: Greenwood Press, 1996).

5. According to Laird, in *Moanin' Low* (324–325), two different Mandy Lees recorded in the 1920s, so one of them is probably the cocomposer here. One of the Mandy Lees had recorded Florence's "Aggravatin' Papa" in 1923.

6. Mark Tucker, *Ellington: The Early Years* (Urbana: University of Illinois Press, 1991), 216, 306, based on research by Steven Lasker. Laird (325) quotes issue numbers without comment on release.

7. The fact that Laird (541) cites issue numbers for three different labels suggests these tracks were issued.

8. PiCou, Nov. 26, 1927.

9. Lord, 221.

10. The Eva Taylor tracks can be found on *Eva Taylor in Chronological Order*, Document Records DOCD-5409; the Victor tracks, with Fats Waller accompaniment, are on *The Chronological Fats Waller*, Classics 689.

11. Richard Cook and Brian Morton, *Penguin Guide to Jazz on CD*, 3rd ed. (London: Penguin Books, 1996), 1319.

12. Paul S. Machlin, *Stride: The Music of Fats Waller* (Boston: Twayne Music Series, 1985), 70.

13. Copy of sheet music held in the Rare Books and Manuscripts Division, Schomburg Institute.

14. W. C. Handy, ed., *Unsung Americans Sung* (New York: Handy Brothers Music Company, 1940), 115. A copy of the sheet music is held in the Rare Books and Manuscripts Division, Schomburg Institute.

15. Piano versions are available on Anthony Goldstone, *Holst-Lambert*, Chandos, Chan 9382, and Richard Rodney Bennett, *British Piano Music of the '20s and '30s*, EMI Classics, CDM 5 65596 2. The orchestral version is on Royal Ballet Sinfonia and Barry Wordsworth, *British Light Music: Discoveries 3*, CD WHL 2128.

16. Derek Patmore, "A Brilliant Young English Composer," *Everyman*, Oct. 16, 1930.

17. Abel Green, *Variety*, Dec. 7, 1927, quoted in Tucker, *The Ellington Reader*, 31–32.

18. "Florence Mills Rosary of Tears," *Amsterdam News*, July 3, 1965, 24. Mitchell seems to have got this view from actor George Wiltshire—see Loften Mitchell, *Black Drama* (New York: Hawthorn Books, 1967), 77–78.

19. Eubie Blake interviews from the Hatch-Billops Collection in the Sound and Recordings Division, Schomburg Institute. I am indebted to Terry Waldo and Marsha Rose Joyner for anecdotes illustrating Eubie's penchant for telling various female friends he dedicated the song to them.

20. Mary Ellin Barrett, *Irving Berlin: A Daughter's Memoir*, 54–55.

21. Peter Clayton and Peter Gammond, *The Guinness Jazz Companion* (London: Guinness Books, 1989), 33; John Edward Hasse, *Beyond Category: The Life and Genius of Duke Ellington* (New York: Da Capo, 1995), 189.

22. Noel Coward, *Autobiography* (London: Methuen, 1986), 100; Charles B. Cochran, *I Had Almost Forgotten*, 221.

23. See website: www.usc.edu/dept/LAS/history/historylab/Vernon_Central/ BLOCKS/BLK_08/BLK_08_CENTRAL_3511.html (accessed Dec. 1, 2003).

24. This building was wrongly identified, probably sometime in the 1970s, by the National Park Service in its National Register of Historic Places. I have provided the Register, at its request, with documentary evidence to prove the error. They have acknowledged the incorrect listing but advised that there is no legal basis for delisting a building which has not had its physical integrity compromised.

25. See website: www.basauk.com/aa_garvey.htm (accessed Dec. 1, 2003).

26. Daniel J. Leab, *From Sambo to Superspade* (Boston: Houghton Mifflin, 1976), 176–177.

27. Leigh Whipper, *These Were They*, presented by Carter G. Woodson Junior Negro History Group, Feb. 9, 1952. From Leigh Whipper papers, Moorland Spingarn Collection, Howard University.

28. Hasse, *Beyond Category*, 350.

29. *Black Broadway* was presented at the Avery Fisher Hall on June 24, 1979, by George Wein as part of the Newport Jazz Festival and subsequently at a number of other venues. It would make a superb CD.

30. *Sepia Record*, Jan. 1954, 19.

31. Faith Ringgold, *We Flew over the Bridge: The Memoirs of Faith Ringgold* (Boston: Bullfinch Press, 1995), 112, and www.faithringgold.com/ringgold/d41.htm (accessed Dec. 17, 2003).

Bibliography

In addition to the books listed below, many useful articles were found in the following series:

The Black Perspective in Music, 1973–1990, published by Dr. Eileen Southern.
Black Music Research Journal, 1980–present, published by the Center for Black Music Research (CBMR), Columbia University, Chicago.
Storyville Magazine, 1965–1995, published by Laurie Wright, Chigwell, Essex, England.
Opportunity: A Journal of Negro Life, 1923–1949, published by the National Urban League.
Messenger, 1917–1928, published by A. Philip Randolph and Chandler Owen.

Agate, James. *Immoment Toys*. London: Jonathan Cape, 1945.
Anglo, Michael. *Nostalgia: Spotlight on the Twenties*. London: Jupiter Books, 1976.
Arvey, Verna. *In One Lifetime*. Fayetteville: University of Arkansas Press, 1984.
Baker, Jean Claude, and Chris Chase. *Josephine: The Josephine Baker Story*. Holbrook, Mass.: Adams Publishing, 1993.
Balliet, Whitney. *American Singers: 27 Portraits in Song*. New York: Oxford University Press, 1988.
Baral, Robert. *Revue: A Nostalgic Reprise of the Great Broadway Period*. New York: Fleet Publishing Corporation, 1962.
Blesh, Rudi. *Combo USA*. Philadelphia: Chilton Book Company, 1971.
Blesh, Rudi, and Harriet Janis. *They All Played Ragtime*. New York: Oak Publications, 1966.
Bordman, Gerald. *American Musical Comedy*. New York: Oxford University Press, 1982.

———. *American Musical Theatre: A Chronicle.* New York: Oxford University Press, 1978.

Bourne, Stephen. *Black in the British Frame.* London: Cassell, 1998.

Boyle, Sheila Tully, and Andrew Bunie. *Paul Robeson: The Years of Promise and Achievement.* Amherst: University of Massachusetts Press, 2001.

Bradford, Perry. *Born with the Blues.* New York: Oak Publications, 1965.

Breese, Charlotte. *Hutch.* London: Bloomsbury Book Shop, 1999.

Bricktop. *Bricktop.* With James Haskins. New York: Athenaeum, 1983.

Bushell, Garvin. *Jazz from the Beginning.* As told to Mark Tucker. New York: Da Capo, 1998.

Carney Smith, Jessie, ed. *Notable Black American Women.* Detroit: Gale Research Inc., 1992.

Cartland, Barbara. *We Danced All Night.* London: Arrow Books, 1973.

Castle, Charles. *Oliver Messel: A Biography.* London: Thames and Hudson, 1968.

Cheney, Margaret. *Midnight at Mabel's: The Mabel Mercer Story.* Washington, D.C.: New Voyage Publishing, 2000.

Chilton, John. *A Jazz Nursery: The Story of the Jenkins' Orphanage.* London: Bloomsbury Book Shop, 1980.

———. *Who's Who of Jazz,* 4th ed. New York: Da Capo, 1985.

Cochran, Charles B. *Cock-a-Doodle-Do.* London: J. M. Dent & Sons, 1941.

———. *I Had Almost Forgotten.* London: Hutchinson, 1932.

———. *Secrets of a Showman.* London: Heinemann, 1925.

Collier, James Lincoln. *Duke Ellington: The Life and Times of the Restless Genius of Jazz.* London: Pan Books, 1989.

Cook, Richard, and Brian Morton. *Penguin Guide to Jazz on CD,* 3rd ed. London: Penguin Books, 1996.

Cunard, Nancy, ed. *Negro: Anthology Made by Nancy Cunard, 1931–1933.* 1934. Reprint, New York: Negro Universities Press, 1969.

Davie, Michael, ed. *The Diaries of Evelyn Waugh.* Middlesex: Penguin Books, 1979.

Davis, John P., ed. *The American Negro Reference Book.* New Jersey: Prentice Hall, 1966.

Dickinson, Peter. *Marigold: The Music of Billy Mayerl.* Oxford: Oxford University Press, 1999.

Dodge, Roger Pryor. *Hot Jazz and Jazz Dance.* New York: Oxford University Press, 1995.

Duberman, Martin B. *Paul Robeson.* London: Pan Books, 1991.

Ellington, Duke. *Music Is My Mistress.* London: Quartet Books, 1977.

Ellington, Mercer. *Duke Ellington in Person.* Boston: Houghton Mifflin, 1978.

Fabre, Michel, and John A. Williams. *A Street Guide to African Americans in Paris.* Paris: Cercle d'Etudes Afro-Americaine, 1996.

Fisher, Leslie H., and Benjamin Quarles. *The Negro American: A Documentary History.* Illinois: Scott Foresman, 1967.

Flanner, Janet. *Paris Was Yesterday: 1925–1939.* London: Angus and Robertson, 1973.

Fletcher, Tom. *The Tom Fletcher Story: 100 Years of the Negro in Show Business*. New York: Burdge, 1954.

Floyd, Samuel A., Jr. *The Power of Black Music*. New York: Oxford University Press, 1995.

———, ed. *Black Music in the Harlem Renaissance*. Knoxville: University of Tennessee Press, 1993.

Foner, Philip S., ed. *Paul Robeson Speaks: Writings, Speeches, Interviews 1918–1974*. London: Quartet Books, 1974.

Frank, Rusty. *Tap! The Greatest Tap Dance Stars and Their Stories*. New York: Da Capo, 1990.

Friedwald, Will. *Jazz Singing*. New York: Charles Scribner's Sons, 1990.

Georges-Michel, Michel. *Gens de Theatre Que J'ai Connu: 1900–1940*. New York: Brentano's, 1942.

Giddens, Gary. *Visions of Jazz: The First Century*. Oxford: Oxford University Press, 1998.

Gielgud, John. *Early Stages*. London: MacMillan, 1939.

Gluckstein, Sir Louis, ed. *Royal Albert Hall: Compendium, 1974–1975*. London: Albert Hall, 1975.

Goddard, Chris. *Jazz Away from Home*. New York: Paddington Press, 1979.

Goldring, Douglas. *The Nineteen Twenties*. London: Nicholas and Watson, 1945.

Goossens, Eugene. *Overture and Beginners*. London: Methuen, 1951.

Gordon, Taylor. *Born to Be*. Lincoln: University of Nebraska Press, 1995.

Grade, Lew. *Still Dancing: My Story*. London: Collins, 1987.

Graham, Martha. *Blood Memory: An Autobiography*. London: Sceptre Books, 1993.

Graves, Charles. *The Cochran Story*. London: W. H. Allen, n.d.

Green, Abel, and Joe Laurie Jr. *Show Biz from Vaude to Video*. New York: Henry Holt, 1951.

Green, Jeffrey P. *Edmund Thornton Jenkins*. Westport, Conn.: Greenwood Press, 1982.

Gregory, John. *The Legat Saga*. Pennington, N.J.: Princeton Book Company, 1994.

Hall, Carolyn. *The Twenties in Vogue*. London: Octopus Books, 1983.

Handy, W. C., ed. *Unsung Americans Sung*. New York: Handy Brothers Music Company, 1940.

Haney, Lynn. *Naked at the Feast*. New York: Dodd Mead, 1981.

Harding, James. *Cochran, a Biography*. London: Methuen, 1988.

Harris, Rex. *Jazz*. London: Penguin Books, 1952.

Haskell, Arnold. *Balletomania*. London: Victor Gollancz, 1934.

———. *Penelope Spencer and Other Studies*. London: British-Continental Press, 1930.

Haskins, James. *Mabel Mercer: A Life*. New York: Athenaeum, 1987.

Haskins, Jim, and N. R. Mitgang. *Mr. Bojangles, the Biography of Bill Robinson*. New York: William Morrow, 1988.

Hasse, John Edward. *Beyond Category: The Life and Genius of Duke Ellington*. New York: Da Capo, 1995.

———. *Ragtime: Its History, Composers and Music*. New York: Schirmer Books, 1985.

Horne, Lena, and Richard Schickel. *Lena*. London: Andre Deutsch, 1966.

Howat, G. M. D, ed. *Dictionary of World History*. London: Thomas Nelson, 1973.

Hughes, Langston. *Famous Negro Music Makers*. New York: Dodd Mead, 1955.

———. *The Big Sea*. New York: Hill and Wang, 1968.

Hughes, Langston, and Milton Melzer. *Black Magic: A Pictorial History of the Negro in Performing Arts*. New York: Crown Publishers, 1968.

Hughes, Spike. *Opening Bars*. London: Pilot Press, 1946.

Jasen, David. *Tin Pan Alley*. New York: Omnibus Press, 1988.

Jenkins, Alan. *The Twenties*, London: Heinemann, 1974.

Johnson, James Weldon. *Black Manhattan*. New York: Da Capo, 1991.

Kellner, Bruce, ed. *The Harlem Renaissance: A Historical Dictionary for the Era*. New York: Methuen, 1984.

Kernfeld, Barry, ed. *The New Grove Dictionary of Jazz*. New York: MacMillan Reference Ltd., 1988.

Kimball, Robert, and William Bolcom. *Reminiscing with Sissle & Blake*. New York: Viking Press, 1973.

Kisseloff, Jeff. *You Must Remember This*. New York: Schocken Books, 1989.

Kramer, Victor A., and Robert A. Russ, eds. *Harlem Renaissance Re-Examined*. New York: Whitston Publishing Company, 1997.

Krasner, David. *A Beautiful Pageant: African American Theatre, Drama and Performance in the Harlem Renaissance*. New York: Palgrave MacMillan, 2002.

Lahr, John. *Notes on a Cowardly Lion*. New York: Alfred A. Knopf, 1969.

Laird, Ross. *Moanin' Low*. Westport, Conn.: Greenwood Press, 1996.

Levant, Oscar. *Memoirs of an Amnesiac*. New York: Putnam, 1965.

Lewis, David Levering. *When Harlem Was in Vogue*. New York: Oxford University Press, 1989.

Liscomb, Harry F. *The Prince of Washington Square*. New York: Frederick A. Stokes, 1925.

Locke, Alain, ed. *The New Negro*. New York: Touchstone, 1997.

Lomax, Alan. *Mister Jelly Roll*. London: Pan Books, 1959.

Loos, Anita. *Gentlemen Prefer Blondes*. New York: Vintage Books, 1983.

Lord, Tom. *Clarence Williams*. Chigwell: Storyville, 1976.

Lotz, Rainer. *Black People: Entertainers of African Descent in Europe, and Germany*. Bonn: Birgit Lotz Verlag, 1997.

Machlin, Paul S. *Stride: The Music of Fats Waller*. Boston: Twayne Publishers, 1985.

Maine, Basil. *Receive It So*. London: Noel Douglas, 1926.

Malone, Jacqui. *Steppin' on the Blues*. Urbana: University of Illinois Press, 1996.

Mangan, Richard, ed. *John Gielgud's Notes from the Gods*. London: Nick Hern Books, 1994.

Marks, Carole. *Farewell, We're Good and Gone*. Bloomington and Indianapolis: Indiana University Press, 1989.

McElroy, Colleen J. *Travelling Music*. Ashland, Ore.: Story Line Press, 1998.

Mezzrow, Milton "Mezz," and Bernard Wolfe. *Really the Blues*. London: Corgi Books, 1961.

Mitchell, Loften. *Black Drama*. New York: Hawthorn Books, 1967.

Morgan, Thomas L., and William Barlow. *From Cakewalks to Concert Halls: An Illustrated History of African American Popular Music from 1895 to 1930*. Washington, D.C.: Elliott & Clark Publishing, 1992.

Motion, Andrew. *The Lamberts*. London: Chatto & Windus, 1986.

Nichols, Beverley. "Florence Mills or a Lonely Blackbird." Chap. XLIV in *Are They the Same at Home?* London: Jonathan Cape, 1927.

Oliver, Paul, ed. *Black Music in Britain*. Milton Keynes: Open University Press, 1990.

Osgood, Henry O. *So This Is Jazz*. Boston: Little, Brown, 1926.

Ottley, Roi. *New World A-Coming: Inside Black America*. Cleveland: World Publishing Company, 1943.

Panassie, Hugues. *The Real Jazz*. New York: Smith and Durell, 1942.

Pastras, Phil. *Dead Man Blues: Jelly Roll Morton Way Out West*. Berkeley: University of California Press, and Columbia College, Chicago: Center for Black Music Research, 2001.

Patmore, Derek. *Private History*. London: Jonathan Cape, 1960.

Patterson, William L. *The Man Who Cried Genocide: An Autobiography*. New York: International Publishers, 1991.

Peterson, Bernard L., Jr. *A Century of Musicals in Black and White*. Westport, Conn.: Greenwood Press, 1993.

———. *Profiles of African American Stage Performers and Theatre People, 1816–1960*. Westport, Conn.: Greenwood Press, 2001.

———. *The African American Theatre Directory, 1816–1960*. Westport, Conn.: Greenwood Press, 1997.

Prasteau, Jean. *La Merveilleuse Aventure du Casino de Paris*. Paris: Editions Denoel, 1975.

Rampersad, Arnold. *The Life of Langston Hughes Volume 1: 1902–1941*. New York: Oxford University Press, 1986.

Ribbentrop, Joachim von. *The Ribbentrop Memoirs*. London: Weidenfeld and Nicholson, 1954.

Riis, Thomas L. *Just before Jazz: Black Musical Theater in New York, 1890 to 1915*, Washington: Smithsonian Institution Press, 1989.

Ringgold, Faith. *We Flew over the Bridge: The Memoirs of Faith Ringgold*. Boston: Bullfinch Press, 1995.

Rose, Al. *Eubie Blake*. New York: Schirmer Books, 1979.

Rose, Phyllis. *Jazz Cleopatra*. New York: Vintage Books, 1991.

Rosenfeld, Paul, and Herbert A. Leibowitz, eds. *Musical Impressions: Selections from Paul Rosenfeld's Criticism*. London: George Allen & Unwin, 1970.

Sampson, Henry T. *Blacks in Black and White: A Source Book on Black Films*. Metuchen, N.J.: Scarecrow Press, 1977.

———. *Blacks in Blackface: A Source Book on Early Black Musical Shows.* Metuchen, N.J.: Scarecrow Press, 1980.

———. *The Ghost Walks.* Metuchen, N.J.: Scarecrow Press, 1988.

Schuller, Gunther. *Early Jazz.* New York: Oxford University Press, 1968.

Seldes, Gilbert. *The 7 Lively Arts.* New York: Sagamore Press, 1957.

Shapiro, Nat, and Nat Hentoff. *Hear Me Talkin' to Ya.* New York: Dover Publications, 1955.

Shead, Richard. *Constant Lambert: His Life, His Music and His Friends.* London: Simon Publications, 1973.

Slide, Anthony. *The Encyclopaedia of Vaudeville.* Westport, Conn.: Greenwood Press, 1994.

Smith, Catherine Parsons. *William Grant Still: A Study in Contradictions.* Berkeley: University of California Press, 2000.

Smith, Willie "The Lion." *Music on My Mind.* New York: Da Capo, 1978.

Sobel, Bernard. *A Pictorial History of Vaudeville.* New York: Citadel Press, 1961.

Southern, Eileen. *The Music of Black Americans: A History.* 3rd ed. New York: W. W. Norton, 1997.

Stearns, Marshall, and Jean Stearns. *Jazz Dance.* New York: Macmillan, 1970.

Still, Judith Anne, Michael J. Dabrishus, and Carolyn L. Quin. *William Grant Still: A Bio-Bibliography.* Westport, Conn.: Greenwood Press, 1996.

Still, William Grant, and Jon Michael Spencer, eds. *The William Grant Still Reader.* Durham, N.C.: Duke University Press, 1992.

Stovall, Tyler. *Paris Noir: African Americans in the City of Light.* Boston: Houghton Mifflin, 1996.

Taylor, Frank C. *Alberta Hunter.* With Gerald Cook. New York: McGraw Hill, 1987.

Thomas, Bob. *Astaire, The Man, The Dancer.* Sydney: Collins, 1985.

Tucker, Mark. *Ellington: The Early Years.* Urbana: University of Illinois Press, 1991.

———. *The Duke Ellington Reader.* New York: Oxford University Press, 1993.

Tucker, Sophie. *Some of These Days.* New York: Garden City Publishing Co., 1946.

Ulanov, Barry. *A History of Jazz in America.* New York: Viking Press, 1952.

Van Vechten, Carl. *Nigger Heaven.* New York: Grosset & Dunlap, 1926.

Varese, Louise. *Varese: A Looking Glass Diary Volume I: 1883–1928.* New York: W. W. Norton, 1972.

Vaughan, David. *Frederick Ashton and His Ballets.* London: A. & C. Black, 1977.

Vincent, Ted. *Keep Cool: The Black Activists Who Built the Jazz Age.* London: Pluto Press, 1995.

Waters, Ethel. *His Eye Is on the Sparrow.* With Charles Samuels. New York: Doubleday, 1951.

Watson, Sophia. *Marina, the Story of a Princess.* London: Phoenix Giant, 1994.

Waugh, Evelyn. *Brideshead Revisited.* Harmondsworth, Middlesex: Penguin Books, 1962.

Weitz, John. *Hitler's Diplomat.* New York: Ticknor and Fields, 1992.

Willan, Brian. *Sol Plaatje, South African Nationalist.* London: Heinemann, 1984.

Williams, Martin. *Jazz Changes*. New York: Oxford University Press, 1992.

Willis-Braithwaite, Deborah. *VanDerZee: Photographer 1886–1983*. New York: Harry N. Abrams Inc. and Smithsonian Institution, 1993.

Woll, Allen. *Black Musical Theatre*. Baton Rouge: Louisiana State University Press, 1989.

Zenni, Stefano, ed. *Ellington: Beyond Categories of XX Century* (International Conference held in Prato, Italy, Teatro Metastasio, February 22, 1999; organized by Stefano Zenni), report unpublished.

Index

~

About the Author

Bill Egan was born in 1937 and spent his early years in Ireland, where he developed a love of jazz before spending most of his life in Australia as an information technology professional. After retirement from a senior executive position with the Australian government, he completed a university course in professional writing, and went on to spend ten years researching and writing the life of Florence Mills.